BULLFROGS, BINGO, AND THE LITTLE HOUSE ON THE PRAIRIE

HOW INNOVATORS OF THE GREAT DEPRESSION MADE THE BEST OF THE WORST OF TIMES

JASON VOIOVICH

JAYWALKER PUBLISHING LLC

Copyright © 2025 by Jaywalker Publishing LLC. All Rights Reserved.

No part of this book may be reproduced in any form by electronic or mechanical means, including information storage and retrieval systems or generative artificial intelligence training models, without permission in writing from the publisher, except by a reviewer who may quote brief passages in a review.

First Edition May 2025, BBLHP-A

ISBN 978-1-7370013-6-2 (paperback)

ISBN 978-1-7370013-7-9 (eBook)

ISBN 978-1-7370013-8-6 (audiobook)

Library of Congress Control Number: 2025907349

Published by Jaywalker Publishing LLC

Minneapolis, Minnesota USA

www.repeathistory.com

For Vivian and John

RESOURCES FOR TODAY'S INNOVATORS

"Those who cannot remember the past are condemned to repeat it."

George Santayana, 1905

"Those who study innovation history have the opportunity to repeat that success."

Jason Voiovich, 2025

Many of you reading this book are simply curious about a different perspective on 1930s America—a more positive look back at a challenging time. But some of you will want something more. You may consider yourself an entrepreneur, inventor, innovator, or an all-around creative person. You're reading this book to search for wisdom you can apply to your own idea.

To help you on your innovation journey, I've created several companions to this book. They'll make those lessons more explicit and actionable. Best of all, they're free with the purchase of this book.

Please visit **repeathistory.com/bullfrogs** to download your materials.

TABLE OF CONTENTS

INTRODUCTION	1
1. CLEARLY MAGIC	7
2. NIGHT AND DAY	21
3. IT TASTES LIKE CHICKEN	36
4. DINNER AND A SHOW	52
5. THE GINGHAM GIRL	68
6. THE FIRST FURBABIES	80
7. THE FIRST WONDER DRUG	95
8. MY NAME IS BILL, AND I'M...	112
9. MORE THAN ONE WAY TO PASS GO	129
10. THE FIRST POPCORN MOVIE	145
11. BINGO!	160
12. UNREAL ESTATE	175
13. THE CUSTOMER IS NEVER RIGHT	191
14. "WALT'S FOLLY"	206
15. MANUFACTURED TERROR	221

16. UNTOUCHABLES	237
17. THIS LOOKS LIKE A JOB FOR...	254
18. TRUE GRIT	268
19. THE HERO WE DESERVED?	282
20. AMERICAN MYTHOLOGY	301
21. ART IMITATES LIFE	315
CONCLUSION	330
ACKNOWLEDGMENTS	336
KEY PEOPLE	337
FURTHER READING	352
ABOUT THE AUTHOR	361
ALSO BY JASON VOIOVICH	362

INTRODUCTION
THE MOTHER OF INVENTION

Catholics sure know how to build churches.

Even in tiny Caledonia, a town of only 2,800 souls in far southeastern Minnesota, St. Mary's is impressive. Four generations of my family worshipped under its 50-foot arches, sat on pews glossing with the patina shine of untold services, watched sunlight dapple through stained glass windows, and felt (as much as heard) its thundering pipe organ.

Founded in 1854 by Irish and German immigrants, this towering Gothic specimen stood unchanged until a modest remodel in 2002. (Even a century and a half of tradition has to yield to modern electrical codes.) Despite the grandeur of the building and its modern improvements, St. Mary's basement remains...unimpressive. All the ceilings are low, all the chairs are hard, and all the windows are upstairs.

Negotiating the stairs with my grandmother in the early 1980s reminded me of every other church basement I had ever seen. If they aren't the same everywhere, I have yet to find one. During lousy weather, they serve as multipurpose rec rooms, cafeterias, indoor playgrounds, and, every Friday night, the town Bingo hall.

For the uninitiated, church basement Bingo is a form of religiously sanctioned gambling. Grandmothers often bring visiting grandchildren along—partly to keep them entertained and partly to show off to the other grandmothers. (I always needed a fresh haircut and clean clothes. I never knew why until much later.)

Each player buys into the game by purchasing rows of paper Bingo cards, three to a sheet, and plucking a dauber from their purses to mark spots as numbers are called. (My grandmother always carried spare daubers, so supplying me with one was no problem.)

At the end of the night, as the ladies swapped stories of their winnings—or, more often, how they were "set" for a particular number that was never called—the priest would make a brief statement about how much money they had earned for the church that night. Yes, the game brought people together, but Bingo was (and is) a significant fundraiser for many parishes. In fact, those same churches may not have survived the Great Depression had it not been for a priest in Pennsylvania who adopted and popularized Edwin Lowe's version of the game. Many churches made peace with the ethical issues surrounding gambling so they could keep the doors open and serve needy parishioners during the worst years of the 1930s. Many still do.

You might be tempted to overlook the part about *me* needing to buy Bingo cards so that I could play alongside my grandmother. I was pretty young when she first brought me along, and I didn't have my own money. You might have figured my Depression-era grandparents would have handed over the $5 to $10 cover charge. If you believe that, you don't have Depression-era grandparents. Oh no, I had work to do before we left for church.

My great-grandfather built our family home on a double lot on Marshall Street, which meant my grandmother had plenty of room for her garden. During my summer visits, I worked a couple of hours each day, pulling weeds and harvesting vegetables. As I came in with my basket of goodies, my grandmother would sort them into "eat today," "save in the refrigerator," or "care package for the neighbors." We wasted nothing.

When the downstairs refrigerator filled, the surplus moved into the storage cellar or upstairs to the *spare* refrigerator. (Because this was a multi-generational home, it featured a full kitchen on the upper level.) That refrigerator was older. Much older. In fact, it nearly dated to the time many families purchased *their* first refrigerator: during the Great Depression. Buying one was a bigger deal in the 1930s than it is today—a basic unit cost about $3,000 adjusted for inflation. To them, it was an investment, not a luxury. A refrigerator helped preserve food and reduce waste. Old habits die hard.

But it wasn't all dirty work.

In decades past, the downstairs living room served as an impromptu roller skating rink and library. (Minnesota winters are dark, cold, and long. Kids get bored.) My grandparents had long since put the kibosh on roller skating, but the built-in bookshelves remained, featuring a collection that would rival any library in town. Behind glass doors were the same books that my great-grandfather bought and collected. He enjoyed Westerns and adventure stories, as well as books about the local area. That included the *Little House on the Prairie* series of children's books, published during the Great Depression, about a pioneer family surviving and thriving based on grit, hard work, and family.

However, before I could read, I had to finish my chores. That meant one final task from my grandfather. During the months I was away, he would sort any pocket change he received into four jars—one each for quarters, dimes, nickels, and pennies. My job was to sort the appropriate number of coins into a paper rolling sleeve, which my grandfather would then take to the bank to deposit back into their account. Waste not, want not.

My reward for all this work was to keep whatever value the *pennies* had. That usually amounted to something north of $5 and something south of $10—plenty to buy a couple of Bingo cards. In other words, my grandparents taught me to—quite literally—pinch pennies.

If you were like me, you learned about the Great Depression in school. Specifically, you probably learned about how difficult it was. Families were separated as husbands "rode the rails" searching for work. People waited in endless bread lines. Many went hungry. Some had it even worse; their livelihoods blew away in the so-called "Dust Bowl" regions of middle America. The net result was that we were so psychologically broken that Americans demanded a new social contract with our government, asking it to provide social safety nets in a way it never had before.

Even as a child, that narrative never sat well with me. My grandparents weren't "broken." They were cheerful, generous people. And no, they weren't wealthy, if that's what you were thinking. But there *was* something different about them.

They were resourceful and creative in a way subsequent generations never quite matched. *They had to be.*

I grew up admiring their spirit and inventiveness—so much so that I made a career out of it. For nearly thirty years, I've dedicated my professional life to helping other innovators capture that same energy to launch new products and services.

That's what this book is about—the ingenuity of the average person who made the best of the worst of times. We can learn from our grandparents. We just need to listen.

...

And we're *not* listening.

Historians often use the "hangover" metaphor to describe the Great Depression (partly in reference to *The Great Gatsby* character by F. Scott Fitzgerald), where Americans awoke on Tuesday, October 30, from a decade-long bender. They didn't recognize where they were (Herbert Hoover denied the situation), they couldn't find their car keys (consumers overextended their credit), their wallets were missing (deflation shrunk the average person's buying power), and they had a massive headache (people were scared and psychologically scarred). Some people, both literally and figuratively, found themselves in the gutter.

Just as often, historians deploy biblical language. Their accounts of the 1929 stock market crash more often read like a religious calamity—the destruction of Sodom and Gomorrah or the Great Flood. Americans required divine punishment for the "wickedness" of the Roaring 20s. The election of Franklin Roosevelt was the coming of the savior. His "first 100 days" (the first time that phrase had been used) ushered in a new, brighter era for Americans. His work programs not only got people back on the job and stabilized the banking system, but they also changed the psychology of the average person. *The only thing we had to fear was fear itself.* If that doesn't sound like scripture, I'm not sure what qualifies, and I grew up Catholic.

To be fair, it's not that authors haven't tried to capture the authentic experiences of everyday Americans.

For many, their introduction to the lives of the so-called "Greatest Generation" came from journalist Tom Brokaw in 1998. It retells roughly three dozen first-person accounts of those who came of age during the Great Depression and participated in the Second World War. Basically, people were "great" because of the terrible burdens they faced. Many of the histories you'll read follow this format.

If you didn't read Brokaw's book, you probably read John Steinbeck's. When most people think about the Great Depression, they imagine the heartbreaking scenes in *The Grapes of Wrath*. Steinbeck's novel rips our emotions to shreds through the brutal story of the Joad family on their way from their ruined farm in Oklahoma to rural California, fleeing ecological devastation on the Great Plains. Yes, sometimes fiction can capture emotion better than purely factual accounts, but it paints a simplistic picture that prevents us from seeing the complex reality.

Unfortunately, histories of the Great Depression often serve as a Rorschach test. What readers see in the facts largely mirrors their view of the world *today* and what they feel the current situation requires. The average person actually experiencing those events is a foil—a "non-player character" in today's cultural language—someone who features only as a tool to advance the plot.

It's not that these histories don't have value, but did you notice something about all of them?

They're all *negative*. It's in the name, isn't it? The Great *Depression*. How could there be any positive story there? I don't intend to argue that all other historians are wrong or that it was a blissful decade (I can feel my grandmother's side-eye as I write this), but none reconsider the Great Depression as the Great *Accelerator*. That's a critical additional perspective to add to the discussion because so much of our daily lives still benefit from what our grandparents figured out.

If we want to focus on everyday people's creativity, ingenuity, and resourcefulness during the Great Depression, we need a new history.

. . .

This book explores the Great Depression not simply as an economic downturn or human tragedy but rather as a *catalyst* for innovation in three distinct areas: the products we bought, the entertainment we consumed, and the people we elevated as heroes. Each aspect tells us something important about the development of the American mindset.

We'll travel back in time to our grandparents' homes, gardens, communities, and movie theaters. We'll eavesdrop on their dinner table conversations. It's a world that will seem shockingly familiar. You'll notice Scotch-brand tape on the craft table, gingham patterns on the walls (and clothes), and color photos in their memory books. We'll snuggle up with our first true pets—both dogs and cats—and if we got sick, our grandmothers would give us the first true antibiotics. We'd play Bingo on Friday nights, *Monopoly* on Saturday, and watch *King Kong* on Sunday at the theater. Over dinner, we'd discuss the latest exploits of Eliot Ness (which we probably approved of) or the rants of Father Coughlin (which we probably didn't).

Yes, throughout this book, you'll hear the stories of the stock market crash, the Dust Bowl migrations, political upheaval, world events, and psychological stress. However, they take a backseat, providing context for what *everyday people* needed to do not just to survive but to create a new and better world.

In fact, American culture during the Great Depression is better understood as a *continuation* of the consumer culture born in the Roaring 20s, not a rejection of it. In all these examples, we'll see how everyday people took matters into their own hands. They *chose* hope over fear. Their spirit and ingenuity laid the groundwork for the mobilization required of us in World War II. We couldn't have fought the war and won the peace any other way.

There's an old saying that necessity is the mother of invention. It's also the father of character. It's long past time we learned more about both. Our grandparents (and, for some of you reading, great-grandparents) stand ready to teach us. Let's meet them.

1

CLEARLY MAGIC

If you tried to find a poster child for the gritty practicality of the 1930s, you'd be hard-pressed to find a better candidate than a banjo player from St. Paul, Minnesota. By all accounts, Richard Gurley Drew played quite well. It's lucky for us that his musical career didn't work out. But to tell his story the right way, we need to rewind the clock a decade.

The workplace of the 1920s—bustling and full of promise, though it was—didn't interest Drew at all. St. Paul wasn't (and isn't) a bluegrass mecca, but there were plenty of jazz clubs, and the Roaring 20s gave an aspiring young man plenty of chances to bloody his fingers on the catgut.[1]

By his teens, Drew's calloused fingers had earned him enough money to begin a mechanical engineering program at the University of Minnesota. Drew, however,

---

1. Yeah, gross, huh? It's true, though felines weren't the usual victims. An unfortunate gopher earns inadvertent musical immortality in many cases. They're easier to catch than most cats and they carry just about enough intestine to string a typical instrument. Players claim natural materials add a richer sound than nylon or other synthetics. Sorry, Goldy Gopher. The truth might hurt, but it sure does sound nice.

was more hands-on than sit-and-listen—a performer, not an audience member. After 18 months, Drew dropped out to find work.

With a few engineering courses under his belt and an intuitive understanding of creativity, Drew thought he had a shot when he opened the newspaper. A little company based in Two Harbors, Minnesota, was hiring engineers.

If you don't know where Two Harbors is, you're not alone. As the name would imply, the small town nestles between two inlets about 30 miles northeast of Duluth, Minnesota. If you don't know where Duluth is, imagine the pointy western end of Lake Superior (the greatest of North America's five Great Lakes). That's Duluth. In the mid-1920s, the port city was on track to become the next Chicago. The region is rich in iron ore and other metals, and tons upon untold tons of taconite pellets made their way out of Duluth Harbor to smelting facilities on the East Coast. Industries, not to mention startup companies, tend to cluster around activity like that. Think of Duluth as an early twentieth-century version of Silicon Valley.

Drew probably had never heard of Minnesota Mining and Manufacturing, but who could blame him? No one else had either. It was like knowing which internet company would hit it big in 1990. You could have been forgiven for missing the occasional Google in an ocean of Pets.coms. No matter. Taconite Valley was the place to be, and Drew had a musician's instinct for a good stage.

Musicians also have a way of handling embarrassment better than mere mortals. They get up on stage, after all. Throwing caution to the wind, Drew sent the little startup company a letter.

Here's a taste:

> I have not as yet been employed in commercial work and am eager to get started. I realize that my services would not be worth much until a certain amount of practical experience is gained, and I would be glad to start with any salary you see fit to give…I am accustomed to physical labor, if this be required, as I drove a tractor and did general farm work.

That's catgutsy.

It's clear Drew had no idea what might be required, but he was the kind of guy who would sweep the floors if he needed to. Who knew? Maybe they'd want him to play the banjo on lunch breaks? He probably would have done it. (Perhaps he did. You would have listened, wouldn't you?) However, playing his little fiddle against the devil wasn't destined to be Drew's calling. His new boss, William McKnight, brought on the ambitious young dropout to...deliver sandpaper.

That may not sound like an auspicious beginning, but hang in there. This former banjo player turned sandpaper delivery driver would change our lives forever.

. . .

Sandpaper was big business in the 1920s, and Drew quickly got to know the area's booming automobile body shops and manufacturers. They were his biggest customers. As more people bought cars, companies rushed in to fill the need. Here's where fate (or perhaps McKnight's keen eye for talent) paid off. Stage musicians tend to notice things about their audience. They have to. If the audience isn't grooving with you, you won't get called back for another gig. Musicians are also good improvisers. They're not afraid to give something new a try.

Here's what Drew noticed: Masking was a major problem.

During the automotive assembly process, technicians needed to do much of the painting *after* the car was assembled. Despite what Henry Ford might say, most consumers pined for some color other than black. If you were competing against the Model T—the most popular vehicle on the market in those days—you had better have something special. Paint was an obvious (and reasonably cheap) way to distinguish yourself. Two-toned paint jobs? That's twice as nice. Unfortunately, doubling up the paint was often an exercise in futility.

To protect one color from another (not to mention to protect glass parts), painters masked off the affected areas with butcher paper, old newspapers, homemade glue, and heavy-duty medical tape. Cars looked like they were going into surgery under the care of the world's worst doctor. This hillbilly solution worked about as well as you might think. As technicians removed the tape, chips of *both* paints would come off with it. Worse, they'd need to clean the goopy residue from their homegrown adhesives. Touch-up required sanding, re-taping, re-painting, and re-hoping this time would be better.

From a sandpaper manufacturer's perspective, that was both good and bad. On one hand, more flub-ups meant more demand for Drew's product. On the other, more sandpaper meant more frustrated customers.

What happened next transformed Drew from an opportunistic salesperson to one of the world's most underappreciated engineers. He noticed something no one else had.

The trick was the adhesive, not the paper. How did Drew know about adhesives? Because that's what his company was good at. Sandpaper is, put simply, rocks of varying sizes glued to a backing paper. If you weren't good at adhesives, the little rocks ended up all over the floor when you rubbed them on anything. That's how sandblasters work, but it's not such a good idea if you want to contain the little abraders. As it happens, some of the adhesives worked quite well. Others, not so much. They wouldn't form a permanent bond. Maybe one of those terrible adhesives would work as a *temporary* mask?[2]

Drew went ahead and tried it. Records from the time aren't clear on whether he had formal authorization for his pet project, but he did it anyway. (Hint: That pattern would not only define Drew, it would also define his company.)

Of course, it didn't work out perfectly from the get-go. Nothing does. Back at the company labs, Drew tried plenty of semi-sticky combinations. In one instance, as the legend goes, he didn't want to put too much adhesive on the strip (making it too sticky), so he added adhesive only on the edges of the backing paper. Upon seeing the latest experiment fail on the shop floor, a snarky plant manager shouted at him to "go tell his Scotch bosses that they shouldn't be so cheap with the adhesive and put it on all the way!"[3] In those days, to say someone was being "Scotch" meant they were penny-pinching, miserly, or more charitably, thrifty. Drew was pretty immune to profanity by this point, and calling his Scottish boss Scotch probably wasn't the worst he had heard that day.

---

2. If you're wondering, yes, this is the same way Post-It® notes work.

3. It's one of those racial slurs that doesn't quite generate the emotional heat it once did in the United States. Does it still in the UK? Someone from across the pond, please reach out.

That said, the shop floor technicians had a point. Drew's experiments weren't working, and everyone was losing patience. After months of trial and mostly error, McKnight pulled the plug on the project. Drew, however, would not be deterred. Knowing he had authorization on any purchase order under $100, he ordered his supplies in $99 chunks.

Then he got it. He finally got it. Drew invented the first masking tape—affectionately (and ingeniously named by the marketing department) Scotch® brand tape. That little company in Two Harbors? Minnesota Mining and Manufacturing? You might know it better as 3M. It would not stay little for long.

By the end of 1929, the wheels were about to come off the American economy. To hold it all together, our grandparents would need all the tape they could get. Drew would not let them down.

...

In most history classes, October 29, 1929, more colorfully known as "Black Thursday," marks the opening bell of the Great Depression. On that trading day, the American stock market lost 11 percent of its overall value—a percentage drop that would not be repeated...until the following Monday, when the index dropped nearly 13 percent more...and then Tuesday, when it slipped another 12 percent.

Most retellings stop right there. They don't circle back to the story on Wednesday when a coalition of bankers and wealthy families injected capital (and confidence) into the market. Stocks rallied, regaining 12 percent of their lost ground. In fact, stocks rallied until April, when the metaphorical gas tank ran dry. A longer, slower slide then continued through the spring and into the summer, with the market finally bottoming out in July of 1933 after losing 89.2 percent of its value. From there, stocks would (slowly) gain ground through the balance of the decade. Although it would take 25 years for the market to reclaim its former peak, the climb back began earlier than most people think.

In retrospect, Black Thursday is as good a day as any to mark the beginning of the Great Depression. It's an easy milestone. You were probably asked to remember it for a history quiz in high school. The problem is that no one thought of it that way at the time.

The stock market had gyrated wildly before—even earlier that year. It seemed no worse than the so-called mini-depression of 1920-1921. Many observers at the time wondered why it had taken so long for the market to correct itself. The Florida real estate market had floundered and fallen more than two years before, sending ripples of panic throughout the national real estate market. Although not as many people owned homes then as now, some thought a broader correction was long overdue.

When the bottom began to fall out, Main Street observers noted—with some justifiable satisfaction—that Wall Street was getting its comeuppance for years of ridiculous stock valuations and irrational exuberance.[4] A little serving of humble pie would do them some good.

Neither the President, Herbert Hoover, nor his Treasury Secretary, Andrew Mellon, was particularly concerned. Stock market corrections are necessary to eliminate those companies that no longer effectively derive sufficient value from their capital. Or, to put it in a more straightforward metaphor, an overheated economy is like an overgrown garden. It needs pruning.

Over the coming months, Hoover seemed correct. Although the stock market had not fully recovered, it didn't seem like the weeds had spread to the rest of the garden.

But they had.

Fast-forward two years. By the presidential election season of 1932, the situation was clearly going from bad to worse for the average person. You see, although Main Street might have had the first laugh at Wall Street's stumble, what they failed to realize was that Wall Street did indeed serve a purpose: It allocated capital. That's business-speak for giving money to companies to invest in research and development, buy new equipment, expand into new markets, and hire more employees. The purpose of the stock market is to find the most efficient way to get that money into the hands of businesses with a track record of making the best use of it.

---

4. "Irrational exuberance" was a phrase coined by U.S. Federal Reserve chair Alan Greenspan in a speech in 1996 to describe the overheated tech market in the late 1990s. As you may recall, that market didn't crash until the end of the decade. It captures the sentiment here well.

Sure, there were plenty of examples in the 1920s of the market getting out of whack. Rampant speculation was common, which simply meant that instead of doing its job (allocating capital to well-run companies and starving poorly-run companies into oblivion), Wall Street was like a drunken sailor on shore leave, throwing money at any pretty radio stock that walked by.

In the weak stock market that followed the crash, there was so little money sloshing around that Wall Street could barely function. Even *good* companies couldn't get financing. When good companies can't get money to run their businesses, that's when people start losing their jobs. When workers don't have work (or think they might not have work soon), they stop buying things. When consumers stop buying things, companies have even less working capital and need Wall Street even more.

That was the vicious cycle that took hold in the early 1930s.

How vicious? Stock valuations aren't a good measure of that. Let's look at the numbers average people care about. According to data collected by the U.S. Department of Commerce, *every* consumer spending category dropped.[5] In what would be the worst year, 1933, consumer expenditures for food and beverages, household furnishings, and transportation dropped a staggering 40 percent from their 1929 peak. Clothing and recreation fell even further—more than 50 percent. Housing spending (mostly mortgage and rent) sank 25 percent. Even spending on medical care dropped by a third.

In that same year, unemployment would peak at just under 25 percent. In human terms, nearly 13 million people were out of work. That's certainly bad enough, but it was even worse in two ways. The first is obvious: No one knew if one in four out of work was the bottom. How could they? It didn't look that way at the time. We only know it from hindsight. The second, however, was more insidious: Yes, one in four people out of work is bad, but that number hides the true number—the *underemployment* figure—those people who suffered through reduced hours, reduced wages, or (at best) the ever-present fear that they might

---

5. Search for the "Historical Statistics of the United States: Colonial Times to 1970" published by the U.S. Department of Commerce. Consumer expenditures are found in Chapter G (pages 416-469, specifically).

be next in line at the soup kitchen. Fear clearly wasn't the only thing we had to fear.

We'll cover more of the economic impacts of the Great Depression throughout this book as they relate to our story, but we need to pause here to address an often under-discussed perspective. As bad as unemployment was, by definition, 75 percent of people *did* have jobs during the worst of it. More than that, those people (usually men) who were unemployed or underemployed often were married to women who picked up the slack with part-time or full-time employment of their own. In other words, most people weren't riding the rails, schlepping from town to town looking for work, or packing up their family in a converted Model T to escape the Dust Bowl in the Midwest. Those make for powerful and poignant stories, but that wasn't *most* people.

If that's true, what made this Depression Great?

Think of it this way. You saw neighbors who had worked this morning laid off in the afternoon. You knew people struggling to scrape together enough money to buy food. Everyone seemed to be cutting back. You may not have known any ex-soldiers marching on Washington to demand their bonus pay, but the papers were full of those stories.[6]

And it wasn't just the stories. Newspapers and magazines carried heartbreaking photos of hungry children, proud men in their Sunday best waiting in bread lines, and farmers watching their topsoil (and livelihood) blacken the sky. By 1932, this had been going on for two years with no end in sight. President Hoover, up until recently, had been talking about how temporary this all was. It sure didn't feel temporary.

When we consider the average consumer's perspective, it was not as much the reality of their economic situation as it was the *perception* of their economic situation. The Great Depression was a "depression" in the psychological sense of the word as much as (or perhaps more than) the economic devastation.

---

[6]. The group was called the "Bonus Expeditionary Forces" (or BEF). They were mostly World War I veterans who were promised extra pay for their service. When they didn't get it, they marched *en masse* to the Capital. Although the march (mostly) ended peacefully, avoiding a coup on the government was a near run thing. If you're interested in learning more, the National Park Service has a great article on the subject.

Let's put it more simply. When you put yourself in that time, in that place, with that mindset, would you feel good about going out to spend money? Of course not.

The first thing you'll do—before anything else—is avoid waste. If you could avoid a trip to the grocery store by preserving food or mending torn clothing, that kept money in your pocket for a rainy day. That was especially important during a season when there seemed like no sunshine in sight. Psychologically, it felt better, too. It was empowering. You weren't making do with less; you were simply being practical and smart.

Waste not, want not, right?

Saving food was a good start, and everyone was doing it. Food manufacturers took notice and began working on stay-fresh packaging. However, they couldn't solve the problem of how to seal it. That problem leads us back to Drew, 3M, and the most indispensable product in our homes today.

. . .

Did you know that refrigerator sales went *up* during the Great Depression? It's true. Sales of first-generation refrigerators exploded in the United States during the 1930s. At the beginning of the decade, only eight percent of kitchens had one. By 1939, 44 percent did. And they weren't cheap. Advertisements of the time feature models (without a freezer, it should be noted) starting at $99.50 (and up). That's just over $2,000 adjusted for inflation, not counting the "and up" part. The average inflation-adjusted prices ranged from $2,300 to $3,600.[7]

Today, an entry-level refrigerator might cost $300. A good one, $1,000. A spectacular model that all but cooks dinner might set you back a few thousand.

Certainly, some of the declines in price and increases in quality have to do with a general trend—technology tends to get cheaper and better over time, all things being equal. Also, many people would have paid in installments—a financing innovation born in the Roaring 20s and in full swing by this point. However, that doesn't quite answer the question of why people would spend so much to buy a

---

7. A hearty thank you to the Morris County Library in New Jersey for curating this data from vintage Sears & Roebuck catalogs. Click on the "Historic Prices" section to take a trip down memory lane. Other notable prices include bathing suits for $4, beach chairs for $1.60, and if you didn't spring for the beach chair canopy for $1.40 extra, you could pick up sun burn cream for 35 cents.

refrigerator. The Great Depression was a scary time for American consumers, yet they gladly forked over a massive proportion of their financial security for a home appliance.

That's because they saw the refrigerator as an investment. It allowed homes to dramatically reduce food waste, keeping foods (especially leftovers) fresh for much longer. It only took a few ruined meals to make the return on investment on that refrigerator seem worth it.[8]

However, simply running the math on how many meals it would take to pay for the fridge isn't quite the right way to look at it. Think of the psychology of what the refrigerator represented. With that new home appliance, you were taking an active step to converse and protect your finances. Even if you still threw away food, which most people did, it felt like you were being smart.

Food manufacturers absolutely took notice. They were working on the biggest problem facing food storage and transportation: effective moisture barriers. Luckily, the good folks at Dupont had a brand new solution: cellophane.

Cellophane was a 1930s wonder material for a lot of reasons. We hinted at its moisture barrier properties. That was a big win. Moisture is a key ingredient in spoilage and freezer burn. Even better, cellophane is transparent. Consumers love to see their food—in the refrigerator and *especially* at the grocery store. It helps us know if we're getting bright red steaks or (let's be charitable) grayish-green steaks. In the middle of the Great Depression, struggling retailers might try to sneak one by you.

Unluckily, however, Dupont had a problem: no seal.

Moisture isn't the only issue in food preservation. So is air. That's part of how canning works—you remove the air. (That's why a can should "pop" when you open it for the first time. If it doesn't, toss it.) Cellophane could be melted into a permanent seal, but that's clunky and difficult. What was needed was a fast way to seal cellophane packages of food on demand and in any shape needed. Order one steak; seal one steak. You get the idea.

---

8. Although some commentators point to advertising that claimed the refrigerator allowed middle-class homes to (essentially) hire a servant, this is a case where modern readers might not understand the context and consequently miss the point. Middle-class America wasn't pining for in-home domestics.

If only someone could figure out how to put adhesive on this new backing material. Drew was up to the challenge.

This innovation transformed Two Harbors-based Minnesota Mining and Manufacturing into the global 3M. By this point in the story, masking tape had become such a moneymaker that McKnight had given Drew an R&D workshop staffed with a motley crew of inventors to devise solutions to problems like creating a workable tape out of cellophane.

The first task: Which of the thousands of adhesives in 3M's portfolio would create the perfect backing for cellophane? It wasn't an easy problem to solve.

What they finally came up with is probably the image you have in your mind when you think of the word "tape." It's the iconic Scotch brand clear tape, though they called it simply "cellophane tape" in its first release. (The marketing department would fix that oversight in short order.)

Of course, the food industry loved it, but so did everybody else. Consumers found thousands of creative uses for the new tape. A few of the most notable included fixing torn paper money. When money is tight, a dollar is a dollar. Ripped money is garbage. Taped money is legal tender. But money wasn't the only paper worth saving. Books, magazines, photos, and documents all got the Scotch treatment. Think about it. A clear tape is the fastest solution; sometimes, it's the only solution. Our grandparents used clear tape to fix window curtains, toys, clothes, and shoes.

Scotch tape solved hundreds of seemingly insignificant irritations of everyday life. They disappeared beneath the sticky end of transparent Scotch tape. For example, did you know that dry cleaners used to *glue* tags on your clothing? Yeah, you heard that right. Glue. Scotch tape replaced that.

In the grocery store, transparent cellophane tape sealed bags of cookies and crackers to keep them fresh.[9] At home, it could seal cracked chicken eggs. On the farm, if those were fertilized chicken eggs, the tape protected the developing chick until it was ready to hatch. (Really!)

---

9. Cracker packaging is a more vexing challenge than people give it credit for. Before cellophane wrappers and tape, crackers often were shipped, sold, and stored in giant 50-gallon barrels. As you can guess, you wanted to get into the crackers early before the rats found them. This is the origin of the term "cracker barrel," and it was not a term of endearment (or a kitschy restaurant).

It's hard to imagine life without Scotch tape.

The only problem, in the beginning, was the obvious tape problem that's been with us since Drew gifted the world with clear tape: Where the heck is the end of the roll?!

Enter patent 2,221,213 by John Borden, one of Drew's colleagues at the 3M "funny farm" (officially known as the Pro Fab Lab, but never called that by the inventors who worked there).

The first version of the tape dispenser—which you can still find on eBay—is a certifiable weapon.[10] This monster weighed over seven pounds of cast iron to dispense less than one ounce of rolled tape. It didn't take long to miniaturize this idea into the iconic "snail" dispenser we know and love. The first version was still metal but it was much slimmer and quite the improvement. You can still find one at an antique store, though they're not weapons-grade like the original. (Thankfully, those are harder to find.) The 1940s saw the introduction of plastic versions, which you can still buy today.

Clear Scotch Tape, aka Magic Tape, proved just the right invention for just the right time. It's not only that Drew and his colleagues at 3M found a solution to a technical problem. They certainly did that. However, it was stressed *consumers* who began to get creative.

To 3M's credit, it didn't take long for the marketing department to figure out what people were doing. They were living through the same Depression as everyone else. Advertising of the time celebrated the problem-solving and ingenuity of the average person as well as spread creative uses for the new tape beyond word-of-mouth. Like refrigerators, tape became an investment—a critical weapon in the battle against waste.

Sales of 3M tape exploded. In its first year, 3M sold over $165,000 in transparent tape. That's about $3.3 million adjusted for inflation. By 1935, that number had increased tenfold. By 1940, sales had risen tenfold again to over $14 million, or about $280 million in today's money. That's a lot of tape, all sold during the worst economic period in American history.

---

10. In a game of Clue, the butler did it, in the kitchen, with the tape dispenser.

That's the power of a good idea. American consumers were learning to choose products based on their value, not just their style.

...

Although Scotch tape's utility was evident from the start, it did more than that. In a certain population—our grandparents, yes, but also immigrant communities today—it ingrained a sense of "repair consumerism."

Sometimes, the nature of "wear out, not rust out" is driven by economic necessity. Sometimes, it's also driven by a deep desire to do more with less, be conscious consumers, and protect environmental resources. Sometimes, it drives the "right to repair" movement—a pushback against voided warranties when you break the tape on electronics or require special tools to access the inner workings.

Is that most people? No.

Repair culture swells during economic downturns and recedes in the face of the new and shiny. But there's something about the pride of enacting a simple repair that satisfies a deep craving. It protects your investment. It "sticks it to the man." A humble piece of tape is an exercise in consumer power—albeit tiny, it's a symbol of power nonetheless. With that act, consumers are telling the world's manufacturers that they don't need to buy something new. To get their money, the latest product had to be better than the old product, plus a 1-cent piece of tape.

McKnight's 3M certainly cashed in, but the company realized something important along the way. Its culture of creativity, ingenuity, and grit needed cultivation and support. McKnight summed it up this way:

> As our business grows, it becomes increasingly necessary to delegate responsibility and to encourage men and women to exercise their initiative. This requires considerable tolerance. Those men and women, to whom we delegate authority and responsibility, if they are good people, are going to want to do their jobs in their own way. Mistakes will be made. But if a person is essentially right, the mistakes he or she makes are not as serious in the long run as the mistakes management will make if it undertakes to tell those in authority exactly how they must do their jobs. Management that

is destructively critical when mistakes are made kills initiative. And it's essential that we have many people with initiative if we are to continue to grow.[11]

McKnight was talking about the culture of 3M he was building. He also could have been thinking of the many different, talented engineers and scientists working there. But this description perfectly summarizes his star banjo player from St. Paul.

So, what about Richard Gurley Drew?

He passed away in 1980, age 81, just five years shy of seeing Scotch tape being voted America's most indispensable household product. By the end of his century, 3M would produce 5.5 million miles of tape each year, or about 645 miles of tape each hour. To put that into perspective, you could stretch that length of tape to the moon and back ten times over. His name is on dozens of patents for his company. His innovations spawned a product catalog of over 900 pressure-sensitive tapes for 3M. That includes the ubiquitous Post-It note, which relies on Drew's original innovation for its inspiration. His work nearly single-handedly built the $80 billion global adhesives industry. Today, 3M tapes are used not only in the home but also in electrical work, construction, and even surgery. There might be a piece of 3M tape *inside you* right now.

Would Drew be happy that his little roll of Scotch tape became our first humble mascot during the Great Depression? Sure, he would. That's just the kind of guy he was.

---

11. Yes, McKnight said men *and* women. 3M respected talent and results more than they fretted about women in the workforce. They were far ahead of their time.

2

NIGHT AND DAY

Things were not going well for Leopold Saxe Godowsky Jr. and Leopold Damrosch Mannes.

And no, it's not because people kept confusing them, though you would have been forgiven for slipping up. Both Leopolds were nearly the same age—born only a few months apart—Mannes in 1899 and Godowsky in 1900. And both were accomplished classical musicians.

In the early years of the Great Depression, they could have been doing just about anything rather than sweating it out in a rented New York apartment, stirring toxic chemicals in a row of vats resembling witches' cauldrons. Still, a job is a job, and the symphonies weren't exactly thriving in the mid-30s.

Who would trust a couple of concert pianists to play with chemical vats in the heart of New York City? George Eastman, for one.

About Halloween 1930, the founder and namesake of the Eastman Kodak Company signed a contract with the two Leopolds to work on something very, very special. Did Godowsky and Mannes see themselves as modern-day warlocks concocting a new brew?[1] Well, maybe. In addition to being concert musicians, the two were also trained chemists. These Renaissance men were just the types to attract the visionary Eastman, and he had high hopes for success.

However, as 1930 turned into 1931...and 1931 became 1932...and then, 1933, and...ugh, 1934...the pair were having about as much success as a couple of Medieval alchemists trying to coax lead into gold. Sure, they had an idea for something revolutionary in color photographic film processing, but there's a big difference between an idea and a working product. Heck, there's a big difference between an idea and a working *prototype* for a product, and the two weren't close to either one after nearly five years of effort.

To understand why one of the world's most successful inventors—who made photography accessible to the masses—would support Godowsky and Mannes for years with nothing to show for it, we need to take a step back and consider the state of the photography industry in the United States in the middle of the Great Depression.

...

However, before we can do *that*, we need a brief diversion to explain what, precisely, we mean by "camera." Anyone born before 1980 can skip this part. Anyone younger needs a refresher on the camera as a stand-alone device and its accompanying image processing method, "film."

Today, your smartphone features a better camera (and video camera, for most) than anything built before the year 2000. They're better in nearly every way, but what most people think of as "better" refers to the camera's image resolution—or, in other words, the amount of detail (measured in pixels) the camera can capture in each image. Higher-resolution images mean crisper photos, brighter colors, deeper contrasts, and the ability to zoom in to examine (or crop out) additional details.

However, higher resolution wasn't the big win (at least, not the biggest). Professional analog cameras—the type we're talking about that used film—could capture stunning detail, color, and depth. Many professionals claim digital cam-

---

1. We'll use their surnames in this chapter, but no one else did in casual conversation. They were "Leo and Leopold" to their wives, friends, and business associates.

eras have never caught up. No, the true breakthrough for the average person was the ability to see the photo immediately as it was captured.[2]

To anyone born after President Reagan, being unable to see their photos right away is still sort of mind-blowing. To anyone older, it's...Tuesday.

If you wanted to take a picture, you needed to lug around a dedicated device (the camera) and load it with enough film to capture the number of photos you wanted. Photographic film is a unique material that captures an image when exposed to light. That's what a camera's shutter and internal mechanisms were for—to expose a portion of the strip of film to the image at just the right time. And then, in a fraction of a second, mechanically advance the film away from the exposure and back into the body of the camera, where it won't get re-exposed with new light and ruin the image.[3] Each roll of film had a finite number of exposures—usually 20-30 or so, depending on the roll. Once that roll was exposed, you needed to open the camera and feed in a new one.

If you forgot film, your camera was an expensive paperweight. More to the point, when you ran out of film, you were done taking photos until you bought more.

Capturing photos was only step one. When not housed inside the camera, rolls of film required cute little opaque tubes for protection against errant light until they were developed.[4] Ah, developing. That's the next step in the process. Film captured a *negative* image—simply stated, a picture with all the colors reversed. The development process reversed the colors so that the resulting printed photos would show the image you (hope) was intended. The final step involved printing those photos, which could only happen in specific sizes of glossy paper:

---

2. Careful observers will note that we're skipping over digital cameras with removable memory cards. Despite what business types now think about Kodak—that it lost its way and has become the poster child for missing opportunities—the company holds some of the first digital camera patents. The real issue was that the digital camera was a stepping stone to the camera as the smartphone killer app. Once that happened, the camera as a standalone device was doomed.

3. Photographers would often purposefully "double expose" the film for artistic effect, for most people, this meant there was something wrong with their camera.

4. Those film containers were great for storing...other stuff, too. Ask a Baby Boomer what they kept in there and watch their face turn red.

three-by-five, four-by-six, six-by-nine, and a few others. There's no rhyme or reason behind these other than that they were standardized to the printers of that era.[5]

All of this, of course, costs money. The camera itself was expensive. The film was costly as well, in more ways than one. First was the initial purchase, but then you ran the risk of snapping a photo with the lens cap on, shooting a picture of the floor, or catching just the moment your aunt closed her eyes. Unlike your smartphone, there was no delete button when you flubbed. And people flubbed *a lot*. Exposed film was exposed forever. The worst part? You wouldn't know that until you picked up your developed photos a week later.[6]

Yet, despite all the trouble, people loved photography and couldn't get enough of it. Think about it. Can you imagine your life without the ability to take pictures? We have George Eastman to thank for that.

. . .

Photography before Eastman was not a pleasurable experience, neither for the photographer nor the subject.

When most people think of photography before 1900, they think of one thing: sepia—that odd, antique-tan tone that fills in for white in photos of Civil War generals with spectacular facial hair.[7] The reasons for the dour tone and stilted expressions were technical. Exposures took a long time, so if you moved (or tried to smile that long), the resulting image would turn out blurry.

---

5. The metric-based Europeans have a more logical solution to this. A large sheet of paper, termed A0 (said A-zero) is subdivided by half to form A1. A1 divides into two A2s, and so on ad infinitum, but in practical terms, all the way to A8 (about 2x3 inches, or "wallet sized" as it was known). It's a more efficient way to handle paper sizes, but alas, Americans can't resist going their own way when it comes to measurements.

6. If you took a...well, let's just say "sensitive" photo...you could be pretty certain everyone at your local pharmacy would see it and probably took the opportunity in the darkroom to make their own duplicates. That was another risk.

7. The term "sideburns" refers to the partial beard style for men dating from this era. Its progenitor (or at least the first to sport epic facial hair of this type recorded for posterity) was Union general Ambrose Everett Burnside. Look him up. Epic is the only word to describe it. Such is the power of photography and a catchy name.

In his book *Retromania: The Funkiest Cameras of Photography's Golden Age*, historian Lawrence Harvey describes the opportunity this way:

> By the time 1900 arrived, photography had experienced 60 years of camera production that had generated specimens best described to the untrained professional as bizarre, complicated, bulky, fiddly, and unfathomable. What chance had the world of coming to terms with these hefty constructions that required the use of tripods, knowledge of toxic chemicals, and university qualifications in mathematics and patience?

Photos took so much time and were so expensive that only wealthy people tended to afford them (and put up with the process). The net effect is that old-timey photos are overrepresentative of rich, WASPy New Yorkers.[8] Eastman's insight was that cameras needed to be *much* easier for the average person to use, or they'd never prove more than an expensive novelty.

In Eastman's mind, a better camera design must include a few key features: It needed to be hand-held; tripods must be optional, not required. It also needed to be easy to maintain. The average person wouldn't take a mechanical or chemical engineering course to use or fix it. Most of all, it needed to be simple to operate—so simple that even a child could use it successfully on the first try with no training.

All that was a tall order, to be sure, but Eastman succeeded in 1900. The Brownie was the first product that we recognize today as a modern camera.[9] The simple box design could snap 10 photos without reloading film, and there wasn't much that could go wrong. When you were done, you sent the film to Kodak. They would develop the photos and mail them back.

---

8. Sorry, New Yorkers. You're an easy target here. To be fair, your kin are disproportionately represented in early portrait photography.

9. The name "Brownie" refers to its inventor, Frank Brownell. Contrary to popular suspicion, it's not a reference to chocolate treats just becoming popular about that time. For those wondering about the Girl Scout youth program of the same name, that didn't start in the United Kingdom until 1914.

The Brownie cost $1 and each roll of film cost 15 cents. In today's dollars, that works out to about $30 for the camera and $4.50 for each roll of film. If you're counting by the photo, that works out to 45 cents each before adding development and printing.

That last part about development and printing. Did you catch that?

To be a photographer required *three* purchases—an initial investment in the camera (hardware), an ongoing investment in film (software), and when you wanted to see the photos you took, another charge for development, printing, and mailing (service).[10] Despite the wallet triple dip, no one minded. Compared to what came before, it was so cheap and so easy that anyone could do it.

The Kodak Brownie changed the world. All you need to do is look at the photos. Okay, it would be a bit misleading to say that the *world* had changed. It didn't. It's better to say that we simply saw more of the world than we did before.

North Carolina State University history professor Tammy Gordon makes that case in her book, *The Mass Production of Memory: Travel and Personal Archiving in the Age of the Kodak*. To illustrate her point, she describes Kodak advertisements doing what advertising does: giving people an idea of what to do with their camera. (If you've never used one, it's not necessarily obvious what to take a picture *of*.)

Specifically, she notes the idealized Caucasian, upper-middle-class families doing Caucasian, upper-middle-class things. Picnicking on the beach. Playing in the yard with the dog. Checking out local landmarks. In her reading, the Kodak marketing department had a vision of who would buy the camera and what they would use it for. And by extension, non-Caucasian or lower-income persons weren't invited to put their finger on the shutter.

However, although Kodak *advertising* may have lacked representation, Kodak *customers* did not.

Nearly everyone found a way to afford the camera—the upper and middle classes, sure—but also lower-income buyers, immigrants, minorities, and gender

---

10. Careful business types will notice the similarities to Gillette's "razor/razorblade" business model wherein the razors are given away (or sold at a steep discount or loss) with resulting profits made up in the sale of razors. The key difference here—the smarter one, actually—is that Kodak didn't lose money anywhere in this value chain.

nonconformists. (There were plenty of them back then; they were more common than you might think.) They documented their lives exactly as they appeared to *them*.

What they showed us created the modern aphorism: *A picture is worth a thousand words.*

It's one thing to read a journalistic report on a tenement building. It is quite another to see black mold spidering its way up a wall and cockroaches swarming a crib. (Ick, right?) It's one thing to hear rumors of men and women in homosexual relationships. It's quite another to see a photo of two women embracing in front of the Washington Monument. It's one thing to hear the anguish in the voice of a reporter covering the *Hindenburg* airship explosion.[11] It is quite another to see a photo of the blimp in flames, trapping its passengers beneath it.

Images have a power that verbal descriptions often do not. Or perhaps it's a different power. It's certainly a more accessible power. Words can deceive, but humans are visual creatures. What we see becomes real.[12]

Gordon makes the case that Kodak's marketing department aimed to *convince* people that their lives would be incomplete if they were not documented. One can imagine evil marketing overlords chortling to themselves and twisting their waxed mustaches as they reviewed advertising copy, congratulating themselves on their devious manipulation of our emotions. The more the masses believed them, the more film and photographic processing they would buy. (Bwah, ha, ha, ha!)

---

11. Imagine seeing it live and having the presence of mind to report it. The full text is so shockingly emotional that it bears repeating in full. These are the words of Chicago radio station WLS reporter Herb Morrison: "It's fire and it crashing! . . . This is the worst of the worst catastrophes in the world! Oh, it's crashing . . . oh, four or five hundred feet into the sky, and it's a terrific crash, ladies and gentlemen. There's smoke, and there's flames, now, and the frame is crashing to the ground, not quite to the mooring mast. Oh, the humanity, and all the passengers screaming around here! . . . I can't talk, ladies and gentlemen. Honest, it's just laying there, a mass of smoking wreckage, and everybody can hardly breathe and talk . . . Honest, I can hardly breathe. I'm going to step inside where I cannot see it. . . ." To be fair, those 118 words paint a pretty vivid picture.

12. Images are so powerful, in fact, that publisher William Randolph Hearst remarked, "You furnish the pictures, and I'll furnish the war," in response to the sinking of the USS Maine in a Cuban harbor in 1897. The photos would indeed start a war between the United States and Spain.

However, removing our metaphorical tongue from our cheeks, the evidence clearly shows that consumers didn't need the encouragement.

All humans have a need for significance—a need to show that their lives have meaning and importance. That our birthdays are special. That weddings are magical. That our loved ones live on after they're gone. Photos are powerful connections to the monumental events in our lives, but they're not the whole story. The candid moments—the cat knocking over the Christmas tree, an infant's funny expression, or the first time you met your future spouse on a ride at the fair. All those images—the magical and the mundane—create deep, personal memories.

In other words, we can explain the desire to buy cameras in massive numbers without resorting to manipulative marketing. Did Kodak encourage it? You bet. You would, too, if it were your business. But if photography had not satisfied a deep human need, no amount of marketing would have worked.[13]

From 1900 to the early months of the 1930s, consumers bought cameras in droves and film by the bucketload. But what would happen during the Great Depression?

...

What happened was precisely the opposite of what you would have guessed. Camera sales *increased*. The Great Depression depressed the market for many consumer goods, but photography proved incredibly resilient. Think about it: Photography is a way to document your life—to make it feel meaningful. If you're anxious about things beyond your control, photography is a defiant act of resistance and an antidote to powerlessness.

Despite photography's popularity, innovation *was* slowing down. Remember that the 1930s-era camera was really a three-part *system*: hardware (the camera itself), software (film), and service (development and printing). In the early 1930s, the only part of that equation that was advancing was the camera hardware itself, at least in any meaningful way for the consumer.

Seeing cameras fly off the shelves and noticing the obvious follow-on business opportunity, drug stores and retailers eventually got into the film processing

---

13. This is why, at least as of this writing, virtual reality is nowhere as compelling as actual reality.

business alongside Kodak. That gave consumers more places to develop their photos, but it's not as though the photos were any different. Maybe a bit cheaper due to price competition, but not better.

Harvey's funky cameras book is a love letter to this era in camera hardware innovation, and his affections are not misplaced.

New camera brands entered the market at about this time to give Kodak a run for its money. This competitive pressure forced all manufacturers to specialize in specific customer types and needs. For example, the biggest issue with cameras for the average person was their bigness. Sure, they were smaller than the wheelbarrow-sized cameras of the 19th century, but many were still the size of an American football. That's too large to carry around everywhere. In 1936, Ensign designed its "Midget" camera that could fit comfortably in a man's frocket (front shirt pocket) or a woman's handbag. Kodak responded with its "Jiffy" model a few months later. Both of these set the trend for miniaturization that continues to this day.

On the opposite end of the continuum were professional photographers—especially semi-professional photographers trying to eke out a freelance living from their shutter skills in the worst years of the 1930s. For those customers, Kodak introduced the $5.75 Bantam alongside the $1 Brownie. This new model quickly found a home with portrait photographers, journalists, and artsy weirdos.

Kodak also entered the market for motion picture cameras and film, quickly establishing itself as a triple business threat serving everyday consumers, professionals (semi or otherwise), and moviemakers.

Marketing improved as well. At the height of the Great Depression, Kodak ran a promotion giving away 500,000 cameras for their 50th anniversary to any child who turned 12 years old that year. Think about that for a second. In the United States, there might have been less than two million children who qualified (the numbers aren't reported for only age 12 from the U.S. Census). By definition, that means it won't be only Caucasian, upper-middle-income, WASPy kids who got a free camera for their birthday.

This was all innovation, to be sure, but did you notice something missing from the three-part equation? Perhaps it was the same thing the two Leopolds noticed.

With a couple of poor quality and expensive exceptions, film was available only in black and white.

It's finally time to see the world in color.

. . .

Perceiving color is all about mixing. Cells in your eyes do this biologically, but the same general principle works to reproduce colors in film exposed by a camera. At a basic level, they both do the same thing: convert light into information. To help us understand what the two Leopolds created, we need to understand just a little about how it works. Don't worry. We'll keep the science lesson brief and intuitive.

Most people today are familiar with the term "RGB"—even if you don't know exactly how it works, you've seen those initials somewhere. It's how screens show you colors. The letters stand for Red, Green, and Blue. In a simple thought experiment, if you have 100% of red, 100% of green, and 100% of blue, your eyes perceive white—the presence of all color is white—sort of the opposite of how a prism (or rainbow) splits light. By contrast, if you have 0% of each color, your eyes perceive black—the absence of color and light. Vary the percentages of each of the three input colors, and you get almost any color your eye can perceive.[14]

The first experiments with color photography film in the early decades of the 20th century (and as early as the 1860s) involved just red and green. Instead of making all photos seem oddly festive, the resulting images looked washed out. Everyone looked either sick or dead. Although this was the age when the monster genre started gaining popularity, no one wanted to buy photos where everyone in your family looked like they were patient zero in the zombie apocalypse.[15]

As early as 1917, the Leopolds saw one of the first color motion pictures, *Old Navy*, and the color was singularly terrible. This sort of origin story frequently occurs in the history of many innovations. Someone sees "version one" of some

---

14. For those of you wondering about printing and the initials CMYK (Cyan, Magenta, Yellow, and Black), the principles are the same, but the process is different. That's why there's always a slight difference between how an image looks on screen and how it looks in print.

15. By the way, most Wikipedia entries for most subjects have the basic story right. The entry for color photography, circa early 2024, isn't one of them. The information is spotty and the history doesn't even mention the Leopolds. Check the bibliography of this book for better sources.

product or process and imagines how it could be improved. That washed-out nautical tale was the inspiration Godowsky and Mannes needed.

Their first pre-commercial product—a proof of concept—came later that year. Named "Kromoplastikon" after nicknames they had for themselves, "Kromo" (Mannes) and "Plastikon" (Godowsky), the film and corresponding development process was fiddly, unpredictable, and expensive.[16] Despite that, the two Leopolds (and their wives) believed in the opportunity enough to continue to invest what time and resources they could until they found a commercial sponsor.[17]

That would happen, oddly enough, in a way completely disconnected from any formal business pursuit. Mannes was sailing to Europe for a musical performance in 1922 when he met a senior partner at investment firm Kuhn, Loeb, and Co.[18] If you're unfamiliar with that name, don't worry. It's enough to know they were a fierce competitor with the J.P. Morgan organization of that era—a name most people have heard of. In other words, this was a great stroke of luck. After returning, a few junior partners visited Mannes' home to view the process. They were impressed enough to invest, giving the two Leopolds the breathing room they needed to continue their work and, eventually, cross paths with George Eastman. It should be noted that it helps to have the folks at Kuhn, Loeb, and Co. make that introduction.

Money, however, can't buy innovation success. It helps, sure, but it can't do the work. Note the dates. The Leopolds received their investment over a decade before they would finally succeed. But we're getting ahead of ourselves. Let's circle

---

16. Can we appreciate the spectacular weirdness of these nicknames for a moment? Sure, we can.

17. One of the joys of working with primary sources is learning about nicknames and family relationships. The two had strong family support, with their wives encouraging them along the way. It's a beautiful story. Those sources also reveal how they referred to each other—Mannes was "Leopold" and Godowsky was "Leo." We're simplifying to "the two Leopolds" or using their family names in this chapter, but that's not how they referred to themselves in person or in correspondence.

18. Remember, there were no transatlantic flights during this time, so this meeting happened on an ocean steamship crosssing, which routinely took about 9-14 days, depending on the boat. Go too fast, and...well...the Titanic was still in very recent memory.

back to the beginning of our story with the two inventors struggling to make it all work in a steaming New York apartment.

As we've noted, there's a big difference between an idea, a prototype, and a commercially-ready product. What's more, the process is not necessarily linear. Plenty of ideas never become successful prototypes, and many of those fail to make the leap to commercialization. In fact, very few do.

In the case of color film, a finicky process might be okay in a lab (or even Mannes' spare bedroom), but it wouldn't fly in the hands of half a million children holding their first Kodak Brownie.

The commercial breakthrough finally came in 1935. Kodak was good at making black-and-white film, and that (ironically) proved to be the missing link. The team (by this point, including additional Kodak research scientists) created a triple-coated film—each layer sensitive to only one of the three colors: Red, Green, or Blue. The chemical process that transfers this image to a color print is fascinating, but it is not essential to linger on the details here other than to say that it came out of the minds of two classically trained musicians, not the professional chemists at Kodak. Sometimes, a fresh perspective is what's required.

The result was the first commercially-available color film, named appropriately, Kodachrome.[19] The first commercial application was actually 16 mm movie film (a more professional audience was a logical start for a new product like this), with 35 mm single image film following the next year.

The industry had new *software* for the first time since the beginning of photography. Almost immediately, our world burst into color.

. . .

Of course, the world was colorful before 1935. However, when you read history books, you could be forgiven for thinking the world only came in shades of gray. (It's one of those odd things you need to explain to elementary school kids.) Kodachrome, both literally and figuratively, changed our perception of our history.

---

19. The name had been recycled from an earlier Kodak product, so if you go look it up, be careful you're finding the correct product. (This happens in business more than you might think. Good names are hard to find.)

Do you remember that story about the *Hindenburg* disaster? Most of us watched the black-and-white newsreel footage or grayscale photos of the scene and aftermath because that's what most photographers used. Most. But not all. One photographer carried the new color film and captured something completely new. A bright white smear couldn't quite capture the emotional impact of the scene in the way his orange fireball could. (Look it up. The two photos are, quite literally, night and day.)

On a happier note, color also quickly entered feature films. Metro-Goldwyn-Mayer's 1939 release of *The Wizard of Oz* would be unrecognizable in black and white. Ruby red slippers aren't as magical in gray. Or how about the difference between *Steamboat Mickey*—the first Disney animated short film—and the groundbreaking *Snow White and the Seven Dwarfs* in 1937? There's something engaging about the sparkle of the diamonds in the mines, the brilliant costumes, the greens of the forest, and the red of the evil queen's apple. All black-and-white films end up looking a little moody. Color allowed filmmakers endless flexibility to adjust emotional impact with subtle changes in color and saturation.

Even fashion became more colorful. Coco Chanel's little black dresses started to sport flowers, bright colors, and striking patterns. Remember the famous phrase, "You can have any color you want, so long as it's black?" Consumers of the 1930s removed the second clause. It would be many years before the color black would return as a fashionable choice.

However, perhaps the biggest single unexpected change happened in the travel industry. Photography in general—and color photography specifically—encouraged people to get out and see the world. Black-and-white photos might have captured a memory, but color photos created intimacy. People wanted to see the gritty energy of New York City, the greens of the Redwood forests of California, or the layer-cake oranges of the Grand Canyon.

Even during the depths of the Great Depression, people voted with their wallets and sprang for (much more expensive!) color film. Photography clearly served a need. Several, actually. A need for significance. A need for our lives to have a sense of permanence. A need to tell our stories. A need for a creative outlet. A need to capture a moment. Or a need just to have fun.

. . .

Today, it's difficult to underestimate the power of color photography. We've lived with vivid color memories and images for so long that seeing black-and-white images is jarring and antiquated. Kodak had a lot to do with that; in many ways, it fell victim to its own success.

The traditional story told on business school campuses is that Kodak failed to anticipate the transition to digital cameras in the 1990s, beginning a slow decline to irrelevance and bankruptcy. By the 2020s, Kodak was a nostalgic brand, with its owners trying to figure out if it had value left at all.

However, that story arc is not quite true. Eastman's legacy included decades of innovation in both cameras and film, including some of the first digital camera patents *and* commercially available digital cameras. That said, its film business was so powerful that it was difficult for the company to retool itself fast enough to address the digital change.

While digital cameras still have a place with professional filmmakers and high-end photographers, our smartphone cameras are more than up to the task for the average consumer. What do we do with them? Exactly what our grandparents did; we take a lot of pictures. Why do we do it? For their reasons as well; to remind ourselves (and everyone around us) that our lives have meaning.

It's reasonable to say that our smart*phones* aren't phones at all. They're smart-*cameras* with other goodies tacked on. The camera is, far and away, the most popular app on most people's phones. According to the research site Photutorial, we take about 1.81 trillion photos annually. That works out to about 57,000 photos each second, or roughly 5 billion photos each day. By 2030, the team estimates we'll hit 2.3 trillion photos each year. If anything, their data probably undercounts our snappy habit.

The average smartphone (smartcamera) user has about 2,100 photos stored on their device. Apple's iOS users skew the average upward; Google's Android users downward, but that's more an issue with buyer demographics than the underlying technology. Both platforms feature outstanding cameras by any measure.

In a direct piece of evidence for how photography and travel are joined at the hip, the COVID pandemic reduced the overall number of photos captured by a staggering 25 percent in 2020 and 20 percent in 2021.

North American consumers remain, far and away, the biggest shutterbugs. We take an *average* of 20.2 photos daily, followed by Asians at 15, Latin Americans at 11.8, Africans at 8.1, and Europeans at 4.9.

Every day, we share 6.9 billion images on WhatsApp, 1.3 billion images on Instagram, and another 1 billion in stories and chats.

Despite those staggering numbers, here is the best evidence we have about what photography means to us. The latest best guess is that the internet houses 750 billion images, which is only about six percent of all images ever taken because the vast majority of photos are *never shared*. They're ours. They mean something only to the photographer.

. . .

It's hard to know what the two Leopolds would have thought of all this.

After scoring the win with color photography, Mannes had had enough of inhaling development chemical fumes and returned to his classical music career. Godowsky also kept playing, but he spent more time tinkering and inventing. His name graces dozens of patents for Kodak, but also sketches and proposals for an electric razor, a dry cell battery, a type of aircraft, a baby nursing bottle, and a combination cleaning swab and septic tank activator. (One struggles to imagine how all those inventions fit together, but that's the kind of person Godowsky was.)

In a sad coda to this largely wonderful story, Kodak's founder started to run out of emotional energy. In 1932, after years of struggling with a degenerative back condition, George Eastman committed suicide in his Rochester home. His final note read: "To my friends, my work is done—Why wait? GE."

Would Eastman have made a different choice had he known how close his musician inventors were to changing the world? That's impossible to know.

What we can say for certain is that consumers chose photography over other "necessities" they clearly needed. It's the best evidence we have that Americans might have been hungry and scared, but we were not defeated. During the darkest days of the Great Depression, we still felt our lives had meaning and our memories were worth documenting. And if our memories were worth capturing, they were worth capturing in color.

3

IT TASTES LIKE CHICKEN

"The bullfrog can make a sound like a wailing tugboat or scream like a cat."

That's an apt characterization from a mid-century *New Yorker* magazine article trying to describe in words the indescribable sound of *Lithobates catesbeianus*, otherwise known as the common American bullfrog. Adults can reach six to eight inches from snout to vent—and nearly twice as long when their legs are stretched out—making them one of the largest amphibians in North America.[1] Certainly, the noisiest.

Their size (and more specifically, the size of their legs) will factor strongly later in our story, but for now, try to imagine the din from your neighbor's backyard. That's right; it's 1934. You live in suburban Milwaukee. No, steamships aren't coming into port on Lake Michigan. No, the family cat isn't in heat. You find yourself living next to an honest-to-goodness bullfrog farm.

---

1. However, the American bullfrog has nothing on its African cousin. The so-called "Goliath Frog" weighs as much as a typical housecat. Imagine the sound *that one* makes.

Like many other Americans, your neighbor has been out of work for a few months, and his prospects don't look good. While other local men have resorted to reduced hours, second jobs, and asking their wives to pick up a shift at the local bakery, your neighbor has a "better" idea.

Over the past few months, he's been reading *Frog Raising for Pleasure and Profit*, receiving his book in chapter installments through the mail.[2] At first, you thought this was another passing fad. When a half dozen frogs arrived in the mail a few weeks ago, it was sort of funny. The kids played with them while your neighbors dug their pond. It was cute to watch the smaller male bullfrogs attempt to woo their larger female companions over the course of several nights. It was a welcomed distraction from all the bad news in the papers.

Fast forward 12 weeks, and it's not cute anymore. Now, there are dozens of bullfrogs, and every night is mating night. The cacophony of randy males trying to outshout each other sounds like a freight train in your bedroom.

You've talked with other neighbors to stage some sort of intervention. (The police don't have a law on the books for "frog noise.") During a neighborhood group therapy session, one of the more charitable couples from down the block reminds everyone that just a few weeks ago, there were *hundreds* of frogs, not merely dozens. Most of the brood seemed to catch a fungus, which considerably quieted things down. Though, the smell. *Oh god, the smell.*

Despite all that, your breeder neighbors don't seem to mind. If anything, tribulations have only deepened their excitement. Bullfrogs are all they want to talk about. They're farmers now. Not of wheat, corn, or soybeans, of course. What can you make on those commodities right now? A handful of dollars per acre? This is (what's by now being called) the "Great Depression," and that's nowhere more evident than in farm commodity prices.

In an effort to help farmers, the Federal government tried deploying basic economic principles. In other words, it reduced supply to increase prices. It seems like that should have worked. It did. A little. However, they did this while consumers couldn't afford the higher prices, and plenty of people were going

---

2. In the *Harry Potter* book series, Hagrid refers to a similar book: *Dragon Breeding for Pleasure and Profit*. One wonders if J.K. Rowling read Broel's book.

hungry. If people were waiting for the government to come to the rescue, they'd be waiting a long time. No, his family was charting their own course. They could make hundreds (even thousands!) of dollars per acre raising bullfrogs, and the demand for their massive meaty legs was unlimited and growing!

That fungus? Beginner's mistake. Your neighbor installed an aerator to keep the pond water fresh. And yes, he needed to dig another pond after the adult bullfrogs started eating their own tadpoles. This was all just part of the learning process. You'll see.

Um, what do frog legs taste like? Well, your neighbor's got an answer for that, too. A clipping from the *Tampa Bay Times* all the way in (exotic) Florida. See here: "It tastes like chicken." Everyone loves chicken, right?[3]

When questioned about the "unlimited" market for frog legs and why you've never seen them on the menu in any Wisconsin restaurant, he starts hand-waving about New Orleans, France, and the "Oriental" demand. And you're forgetting about this Dr. Broel guy. He's a genius. He's from Europe, you know!? Royalty, even. The best part? Frog legs are in such demand that his factory will buy every frog you can raise! It's a perfect system. You know, prejudice and jealousy are the only things standing in the way. That's right. You're jealous!

It doesn't *seem* perfect, and you don't *feel* jealous as you look over his shoulder into a reeking, fetid pond full of amorous bullfrogs and their spawn, but your neighbor's sure excited about it. And what's the harm? Everyone's trying to make a living; at least they're doing something constructive. He and his wife (and kids) have never worked so hard. Heck, if what he says about the growing market, the prices he can fetch, and the guaranteed buyer is genuine, it all seems pretty good.

What does he have to lose?

. . .

You might have caught the interesting name in our neighbor's story: Dr. Broel—more specifically, Dr. Albert Broel—who was an authentic medical doctor in the same way a double-stuffed chalupa at Taco Bell is authentic Mexican

---

3. This may be the first time this phrase had been used in popular culture; it was certainly one of the first times it was written down.

food, so this is the last time we're going to honor him with that title.[4] Of all the fantastical people of this era, Broel deserves a spot in the Great Depression Hall of Certified Characters.

A brief backstory is in order. It's worth it.

Albert Broel was born in (what is now) Poland (or maybe Lithuania) in 1888 (or 1889, depending on the source). There's even some scant evidence that Broel was part of Polish nobility—a Count, specifically. Clearly, royal blood did not exempt him from grunt work military service. Like many young men of that era in that part of the world, he found himself carrying a rifle as part of the *Russian* military facing off against the Germans on the eastern front in World War I.[5]

As it turns out, Broel's unit was captured by the Germans. Like most German prisoners, Broel endured a harrowing experience in a prison camp before leading a daring escape in the middle of the...okay, no. This wasn't anything like *Hogan's Heroes* or *The Great Escape*. The guy who caught Broel turned out to be his cousin. While the other men in his unit went to prison camps, Broel and his cousin concocted an escape plan where he made his way to the United States. (*It's good to be the Count...*)

What's notable about this entire improbable tale is that Broel's *noblesse oblige* did not seem to extend to any of the men in his unit or under his "command." Whether or not he could have negotiated their release is unknowable; the military and political situation on the eastern front was chaotic, to say the least. The bottom line is that no one quite knew the whole truth about Broel—a recurring theme, as we shall see. What we do know for sure is that Broel made it to the United States.

Broel didn't land on U.S. shores with a breeding pair of bullfrogs stuffed in his luggage, if that's what you're thinking. Although Broel later claimed that his

---

4. Journalists as late as the 1950s still referred to Albert Broel with the "Doctor" title. He claimed to have a degree in "naprapathy," a branch of wellness aligned with chiropractic that focused on massage and nutrition, though he would never produce evidence to that effect, such as it might have been worth in that era of lax standards and mail-order degrees. In 1923, Broel was convicted of practicing medicine without a license, so that throws cold water on the honorific title.

5. They called it "The Great War" and not "World War I" for obvious reasons. No one knew there would be a second war in less than a generation, though many suspected it at the time.

French mother introduced him to the delicacy of frog legs and that he always wanted to teach the world to raise frogs, that seems like shooting an arrow and painting a target around where it landed. No, Broel's frog husbandry days were in the future. For now, settling in Detroit (a good place to be in the 1920s), Broel and his new wife Olga needed to find a way to make a living.

Oh no, it wouldn't be anything like working in a food processing plant or an auto factory. That would make sense. This was Broel we're talking about. Things were about to get weird(er). They didn't start by breeding frogs. They planned to focus on eligible singles.

Broel, his wife, and his mother-in-law decided to start a matchmaking service.

Yes.

You heard that correctly.

Named, inexplicably, and in no relation to the Quaker religious group, the American Friendship Society, the Broels placed small classified advertisements to attract subscribers. "If you want 'A Rich Wife!' or 'Wealthy Husband!'" it read, "Send for our big (FREE) list of descriptions."

Now that you've identified your future (wealthy) spouse, how do you woo that person into your arms? For $1 (about $20 today), you could send away for a book that would show you how to snare your beau dandy or lonely debutant. Short story: It worked. The classified advertising subscription service boasted over 100,000 subscribers, but it was the instructional book sales that helped Broel see the true potential opportunity. In today's language, we might say that Broel learned how to *monetize his followers*.

What could possibly go wrong? Buckle up.

Let's introduce ourselves to another 1930s swashbuckler: Harry F. Powers. Only he wasn't a pirate of the Jack Sparrow variety. He was a bad man. Christened by the media as the "Bluebeard of Quiet Dell" (a reference to his small West Virginia hometown), Powers used the American Friendship Society to write to dozens of women. Unfortunately, he wasn't looking for love. He was looking for victims.

Asta Eicher, a widow and mother of three, responded. Suspicious bankers flagged at least one forged check before Powers skipped town, but not all of them. She and her children were never heard from again. Massachusetts widow Dorothy

Lemke fell under Powers' spell and disappeared as well, along with $4,000 from her bank account (over $75,000 today).

How many other women were victimized? It's impossible to know. We know about these two because they helped lead the police back to Powers' home, where they found the bodies. In the aftermath of Powers' trial and speedy execution, the American public not only learned these horrid details but also read letters from dozens of other women who were (likely) days away from extortion and certain death.

The publicity put Michigan's law enforcement agencies on the scent of the American Friendship Society, the platform that allowed Powers to select his victims. What they discovered...was not good. In its four years in operation, the AFS had collected over $100,000 in fees (about $1.9 million today) as a registered not-for-profit. That's what accountants call a "tax issue" (aka the only way they could finally bring down Al Capone in 1931.)

It would get worse for Broel. Scrappy journalists started digging into Broel's background—his non-existent "medical" degree and subsequent conviction for practicing without a license, as well as the fact that he may have been a *servant* to the noble Broel family, not a legitimate Count himself.

The worst part? During all the hullabaloo, Broel and his family were on a European vacation. As should be obvious, there was no social media back then that could provide live updates (and a warning about what they were coming home to). The Broels returned to find neighbors carrying figurative pitchforks and (if the stories Broel tells are to be believed) *literal* clubs. After an alleged neighborly beatdown outside of town, the Broels decided Michigan was a bit too hot. Rural Ohio might be better, miles away from anything or anyone.

The perfect place for a bullfrog farm.

...

As you might have guessed by now, Broel's first foray into frog husbandry wouldn't go well.

When you want to set up your own frog farm, it helps to know about two critical things: frogs and farming. Simply eating frog legs and seeing a farm doesn't qualify. Broel may have referenced some earlier works he dredged up in the library or available by mail order—that's impossible to know; Broel doesn't mention it in his book—but even if he could find something, there wasn't much available. Let's also agree that his French mother (if she was indeed French, which also seems unlikely) probably wasn't much help either. No, Broel was on his own.

Even more surprising, Broel didn't simply decide to start a bullfrog farm; he also built a *cannery* to process adult frogs into salable canned goods. That's chutzpah right there.

You might say to yourself: Hey, that's not such a bad idea. If you rely on capturing frogs in the wild (the other way to acquire frogs for your cannery), the breeding population in Ohio might not sustain it, especially in the winter months. Raising your own supply seems like a smart application of the principle of vertical integration. Large-scale industrial livestock production began taking off in the United States in the 1920s after the ramp-up in war production. Frogs aren't like other livestock (as we'll see later), but perhaps he could learn from his rural neighbors.

That...wasn't Broel's idea. Remember where he made his money in human husbandry (and wifery)? That's right: training materials. Yes, Broel would need to raise bullfrogs, but only as many as would be needed to show others how to do it.

Later, we'll learn why frog farming isn't quite as easy as Broel made it seem, but for now, it's enough to know that Broel must have known that, or he quickly discovered it. The entire facility—ponds, technique, canning factory, everything—was carefully concocted to impress the average person, not to raise a commercially viable population of bullfrogs.

What Broel truly perfected was a system that would teach others how to raise bullfrogs on a smaller scale in their own backyards or small plots. That system included the book containing the details of the Broel system—originally published as individual pamphlets you could mail away to receive.[6] It also included training courses where you could travel to Broel's Ohio facility and learn the system hands-on.

---

6. There are very few copies of this book left in print. The one I was able to acquire is a handsome green (duh) hardcover book containing not only all the materials, but some tear sheets with Broel's handwritten notes. It's probably something that I'll donate to a research library someday.

However, Broel knew that the *process* didn't matter if the target audience didn't know about it. That's Marketing 101, of course, and Broel was *very* good at that, owing to his experience as a modern-day cupid. He knew how to place advertisements cost-effectively in newspapers and magazines nationwide. More than that, those publications were happy to have the business. Of the many businesses that struggled to survive in the 1930s, some of the hardest hit were newspapers and magazines. Broel's advertising dollar went much further in the 1930s than it would have in the 1920s.

Great reach is one thing, but getting people's attention is quite another. You don't need to work hard to convince people to care about finding a romantic partner. Bullfrog breeding is...less compelling. He'd need help honing that pitch.

Through sheer serendipity, Broel would find his wordsmith. Local farmer Sylvester Lawrence Schutt used to work at the local electrical company until his job evaporated in the early years of the Great Depression. Luckily for Schutt, his true talent wasn't connecting positive to positive and negative to negative. Schutt had a natural gift for language and promotion—precisely what Broel needed. Between the two of them (Broel providing the system and the chutzpah and Schutt spinning the advertising flair), people began to flock to Broel's bullfrog mecca, seeking financial salvation.

The opening of our story already taught us something about the sales pitch, but why did it work so well? And why was it destined to fail?

. . .

Most histories of the Great Depression focus on the suffering of the average family. Not only are there plenty of factual accounts (Timothy Egan's *The Worst Hard Time* is an excellent example) and compelling images (the forlorn, haunting black-and-white image of Florence Thompson), what really burned the zeitgeist of the era into the collective consciousness were the *fictionalized* accounts. Through the story of the Joads in *The Grapes of Wrath*, John Steinbeck retells through his novel the real stories of many families on the Great Plains fleeing the Dust Bowl and making their way to sunny but not-so-welcoming California. Those stories are dramatic and deeply heartbreaking.

When you consider why those accounts were so compelling, one key fact rises to the top: The average person wasn't out to screw the other guy and make a lot of money. That was the underlying cultural theme of *The Great Gatsby* in the Roaring 20s. No, people of the Great Depression simply wanted to take care of their families. They weren't afraid to do the brutally hard work to make that happen.

That was nowhere better in evidence than the so-called "alphabet soup" of agencies that spawned in the wake of FDR's election. As just one example, the Civilian Conservation Corps (or CCC) employed thousands of men to build parks, dams, and bridges. Others ran telephone and electrical lines out to rural homesteads. Out-of-work artists, photographers, and writers scoured the country to tell its stories.[7] In every case, people worked *hard*.

The impact of all those programs—ambitious as they were—was limited for various reasons. And no, it wasn't that "the government just didn't spend enough money" or "it made wasteful, bureaucratic decisions." (Both left-wing and right-wing commentators are wrong on this one.) Organizing that many people, when and where they are needed, was a task we couldn't accomplish today, much less 100 years ago. Even military dictatorships couldn't (and still can't) pull that off. The United States barely made it work during World War II. Yes, government intervention mattered, but no, it could never be enough. Americans needed to shake off the Great Depression themselves and rediscover their pioneer spirit.

Consider all that and then reconsider Broel's pitch. He didn't promise quick riches with no effort. No, bullfrog farming was difficult. Yes, there was money to be made, but what was so appealing was that it was hard work that you did on your own. You charted your own destiny. Not government. Not big business. *You*. Broel also promised something no one else would (or could): certainty. If you did the work, he'd buy all the bullfrogs you could raise.

The get-rich-quick pitches of the 1920s, like the notorious Ponzi scheme, were all about *greed*. The get-rich-quick pitches of the 1930s, like Broel's bullfrogs, were about *grit*. The pitch worked because it was better aligned with the mindset of the time. Unfortunately, it was still a scheme.

---

7. Incidentally, this is one of the reasons we have so many firsthand accounts of the slavery era in the United States. Many formerly enslaved people gave their stories to these writers before they passed away.

Any experienced animal breeder would have immediately seen the issues with Broel's plan. It's time you did, too. Here's the reality of frog farming.

...

The first thing to know about bullfrogs is that they are amphibians. They need water to breed and to develop young, but they can breathe air and live on land. That means they tend to stay close to water.[8] If you're trying to breed bullfrogs, a source of water is job one.

Not just any water will do. Bullfrogs like ponds and shallow lake beds, so if you don't have one on your property, you'll need to find a way to create one. Fortunately, Broel's book provides detailed pond construction plans, including aeration equipment to keep the oxygen level high. (Bullfrogs can breathe through their skin in the water.) Stagnant water can promote the growth of fungal and bacterial infections, which are largely preventable by aerated water. Frogs are delicious, too, at least if you're a fish, hawk, fox, raccoon, or any of the dozens of other backyard predatory animals. Your pond had better feature barriers against those critters. Fences are great. Nets are better. But it can't be glass. Insects need to be able to get in.

Why is that?

Unlike chickens, which will eat seeds and grain, cows, which will eat corn or graze, or hogs, which will eat just about anything in front of them, bullfrogs have a very particular requirement. Their food needs to be *moving*. They'll eat just about anything they can catch, so long as the prey animal moves. That makes raising captive bullfrogs a challenge. Broel recommends adding lighting to attract insects as food. However, insects are tricky to attract at the right times and in the right quantities to sustain your growing brood, so small fish, crayfish, and other squiggling prey items almost always supplement insects.

You know what's also a squiggling prey item to an adult bullfrog? *Their own tadpoles*. That complicates things. In practical terms, bullfrog breeders need to immediately separate adults and young into different ponds. A female might lay

---

8. Though not always. Some frogs stay buried and dormant in dry deserts until seasonal rains revive them. Then, it's a mad rush to breed and develop young before pools dry out again.

up to 20,000 eggs during a summer breeding season, but the resulting tadpoles will only become perfect wriggly little snacks if you're not diligent.

How long will you need to keep adults and their tasty young apart? Again, unlike livestock animals like chickens—who will grow to adult weight in as little as eight weeks—bullfrogs take up to three *years* to reach full legginess. That's a lot of time for something to go wrong. Theoretically, one breeding pair can produce 20,000 offspring, which is plenty to sell to Broel. However, this is one of those many times when theory doesn't match practice. It's not even close.

When you do all the math and consider the time, expense, and losses to predators and disease, for every three pounds of food your bullfrogs eat, you can expect about one pound of salable frog meat. You don't need to be a calculus professor to know that won't work out long term.

Even Broel knew it. He was chased out of Ohio in the same way he fled Michigan. Regulators there accused him of not *actually* operating a canning operation. (He hadn't produced *one* salable can of frog legs in all the time he ran the business.) There simply weren't enough wild frogs to supplement the utter failure of individual breeders to make his system work. That's why he crossed the country to set up shop in New Orleans. Not only was there a vibrant French population (who appreciate frog legs; you will find them on the menu there), but the nearby swamps could supplement adults when breeders (inevitably) failed.

If this clearly wasn't working, why did bullfrog farming go on as long as it did?

. . .

In part, people wanted it to work for all the reasons we described. Raising bullfrogs was brutal but empowering. However, we can't ignore the fact that it was—at least in part—a scheme that promised more than it could possibly deliver. Eventually, it would lead to Broel's downfall.

Broel and Schutt marketed instructional materials aggressively—too aggressively, as it turned out. Many of us will recognize part of their promotional strategy: Use comments from satisfied customers. The trouble is that Broel's team didn't verify those people's claims before it republished them. In one claim that caught the attention of the Federal Trade Commission (FTC), Broel cited *another* person's calculation that a farmer could make $360 billion growing frogs within three years.

On its face, that number is ridiculous. For one thing, that's quoted in 1930's money and breathtaking in its scope. The entire U.S. economy, measured by Gross Domestic Product, would barely eclipse that number. The Great Depression was bad, but the economy was still bigger than a bunch of horny bullfrogs. Of course, Broel was sanguine:

> 'I assume it is needless to tell you that I made no such statement,' he wrote back to an Ohio journalist. He wasn't necessarily endorsing it. The claim was 'simply published as I publish all other things of interest to people engaged in the frog business. I think you will agree with me that such a statement is so ridiculous upon its face that it could not seriously influence the judgment of anyone deliberating as to whether or not he should engage in frog raising.'

That's...not how it works.

The FTC is tasked with, among other things, ensuring truth in advertising.[9] With newfound authority granted by Congress about this time, regulators were cracking down on this sort of tomfoolery. Eventually, Broel settled with regulators and cleaned up his advertising act, but the damage to his reputation was done.

Finance columnist Kenneth Haas, writing in the *Bowling Green (Kentucky) Park City Daily News*, summed up the situation in an example of epic journalistic snark:

> You must admire the crust of men who can sell saps ten frogs for forty-seven fifty, Broel had never been any more honest than the law required. Haas even joked about how Broel figured out his next line of work after regulators shut down the Friendship Society. Then Mr. Broel probably reached for his dictionary, placed his

---

[9]. Most people don't know this, but advertising (aka "commercial") speech is *not* free speech. Advertisers can use flouncy language and highlight only the good parts of a product, but they cannot lie to you about a material fact. If a product claims to contain X ingredient, and it does not, the FTC has the power to stop sales until the issue is resolved. It's not a perfect system, but I'd trust the average truthfulness of an advertisement against a political speech any day of the week.

finger momentarily at 'friendship' and slowly and sadly moved it down to 'frogs,' he wrote. Frogs! Happy thought. And now the frog business has slumped. What will it be next?

Facing these claims, Broel was bankrupt by 1936, though it didn't stop the frog craze. Given everything we just learned, the obvious question is, *why not?*

Because state governments promoted raising bullfrogs, too.

What most people don't understand about the Great Depression—and specifically the economic aid provided to workers—is that much of it was state-driven. The rationale was simple: States were closer to the unemployment problem. No state, however, had a good solution. Federal government programs get all the attention in our history books but were primarily an adjunct to state-based relief efforts. Some people petitioned the federal government directly (the Veterans' March on Washington is the best example), but most assaulted their *state* capitals for help.

In other words, state governments were in urgent need of something to tell people.

Officials had heard of bullfrog farming (Broel was good at promotion, if nothing else), and they loved it for several important reasons. First, it encouraged self-reliance. Second, it was a food source. Third, it kept people in their homes. And fourth, if they're successful (and the state DNRs knew they probably wouldn't be), they might even see a boost in tax revenue.

Win. Win. Win. Win.

Several state offices began producing their own instructional guides for would-be bullfrog breeders. They're filled with more sober instructions and admonitions than Broel's books, but many bear a striking resemblance to *Frog Raising for Pleasure and Profit*. The real impact, however, was validation. It was one thing to hear about the potential of bullfrog breeding from a shameless self-promoter. Reading a pamphlet from your state's Department of Natural Resources is quite another. Many states competed with each other to attract this new "industry." It tells you more than anything else about how desperate states were for any form of positive economic activity.

Ultimately, it wasn't backyard bullfrog breeders, end-of-their-rope state governments, or even unscrupulous schemers who would inherit the legacy of Broel's best idea. Broel inadvertently invented the business model behind large-scale livestock operations.

. . .

When you read between the lines, Broel's business model becomes clear. In order to keep selling instructional materials, Broel needed to have some believable operation where he could purchase and process bullfrog legs to serve (what he believed to be) a growing market. There certainly was enough of a market in New Orleans.

Yes, his New Orleans canning facility was a bit of a tourist attraction—it featured training facilities and a giant kitschy bullfrog out front—but it was primarily a working cannery, and it needed a consistent supply of bullfrogs for efficient operation.

When neighborhood breeders couldn't meet his demand (and they almost never could), he would supplement supply by paying local hunters to capture bullfrogs from the Louisiana swamps.

As the average person got wise to the challenge of raising bullfrogs and threw in the pond (so to speak), Broel became even more reliant on hunters. For their part, the hunters drove bullfrogs to the brink of local extinction in the swamps, which coincidentally boosted the mosquito population, spreading disease. (To its credit, the State of Louisiana halted hunting during the breeding season to help the population recover.)

So no, this was never going to work commercially.[10] But did you catch the innovation? Broel outsourced the toughest and most unprofitable part of his operation—the dirty, smelly work of raising bullfrogs—to smaller, independent operators where he would buy up their supply. Of course, he'd train them and answer questions, but he wasn't personally on the line if they failed. It was his

---

10. To be fair to Broel, when you read his book, he provides multiple possible sales channels for frogs. In addition to frog meat, he recommends selling frogs for biological research (you dissected a frog in high school, didn't you?), prize breeding stock (like horses?), aquarium use (okay, maybe a few...), amusement and advertising (how many ads have you seen with frogs since Bud-Weis-Er?), and employment opportunities in the frog industry (sort of self-referential). So, no. This was never going to work.

incentive to set up as many as possible so that he'd have enough supply, even if no individual breeder made a lot of money.

That system may not work for bullfrogs for all the reasons we now know, but it would work spectacularly well for poultry.

In the United States, poultry (mostly chicken and turkey) is marketed and sold by just a handful of firms: Tyson, Purdue, Pilgrim's Pride, and Wayne-Sanderson. However, it would be wrong to assume these four firms raise their own stock. No, for the most part, they adapted Broel's business model.

Here's how it works.

A sponsor company sends independent farmer-operators hatched eggs—the cute little chicks you imagine—in cargo trucks, thousands at a time. As the farmer, you pay for your chicks. Over the next six to eight weeks, depending on the variety and the instructions from your buyer, your job is to raise the birds to slaughter weight. Costs for feed and medicine are all on you, as well as the up-front investment, which may run more than $250,000. If anything goes wrong, you had better hope you have insurance. Some of the firms even sell you the food. (Broel didn't do that. It was a rare missed opportunity.)

Of course, your buyer has an incentive to train you. They *want* you to succeed, but if you don't, they've separated themselves from the riskiest part of the process.

Then, your sponsor company picks up the chicks—they were basically on loan—and pays you for your "value add" to the process. Oh, and one more thing. They set the price based on current market conditions when they pick up the full-grown birds. Think about it. This is Broel's business model on steroids. (Sometimes, given the growth hormones used in non-organic poultry raising, quite literally.)

On the one hand, each party gets to focus on what it's good at—farmers raising animals and the sponsor company marketing the finished product. On the other hand, it's pretty clear who has the power in the relationship. That said, growers are consolidating as well and becoming more sophisticated. Power never lasts forever.

Speaking of the average person recapturing power over their own lives, part of Broel's legacy must include the growing movement to produce your own food. That includes raising animals.

According to the American Pet Producers Association, although fewer than two percent of Americans live on a farm, more than 13 percent now keep chickens (mainly for eggs). Author Tove Danovich describes this trend in detail in her book, *Under the Henfluence: Inside the World of Backyard Chickens and the People Who Love Them*. Raising animals clearly means more to people than a simple business transaction.

Whether bullfrogs or chickens, despite all the risks and hazards, they both represent the same desire for the average consumer to take control of their lives. They're willing to put in the work and find the money to make it happen.

For Broel's part, he died in 1966, still being called "doctor" and, despite it all, recognized as America's leading authority on bullfrog breeding. If you're curious, you can still visit his daughter's museum home in New Orleans, where she has dedicated a room to her father's enterprise. Her opinion of her father is what you might expect: a loving tribute to a man who gave her a wonderful childhood and legacy. Her book is worth reading as a love letter to her dad. It's sweet and paints a poignant perspective of the story you just heard from the little girl right in the muck of it.

Bullfrog farming may not have been "America's most needed yet least developed industry," as Broel was keen to say to journalists, but he only needed to swap one word to make it right. *Grit* was America's most needed and least developed industry. Consumers of the Great Depression would not disappoint.

DINNER AND A SHOW

Journalists called it the "bum blockade." Of course, that wasn't what anyone in polite society called it, but that's what it was. Law enforcement used force to prevent poor people from entering Los Angeles, with implicit and explicit support from a majority of its citizens.

In the early 1930s, Los Angeles had a population of just over one million people, about a third of the size of Chicago at the time. Put simply, the region was not what it is today. Los Angeles was facing an influx of thousands (tens of thousands) of migrant families from as far away as Oklahoma. They traveled with anything they had—sometimes beat-up Model Ts, sometimes horse-drawn carts, and sometimes on foot.

The city simply didn't have the resources to accommodate that many new residents without the means to support themselves, but let's not sugarcoat it: Many residents didn't want them there. They worried that these new migrants would outcompete them for the scarce jobs. Everyone was on edge. Given the situation, it's difficult to imagine any community welcoming newcomers with open arms. As other cities posted billboards encouraging migrants to "keep moving" along

Route 66, LA could not. Los Angeles was literally and figuratively the end of the road.

However, if there was one person in Los Angeles who thought differently, it would be Clifford Clinton. He was the kind of guy prepared to put his money where his values were. Clinton saw the same situation, but he decided to do something positive about it. His solution would not only change our perception of what it would mean to serve the needy, but it would also help us redefine (and remind us of) what a meal truly is.

Combining his given name and family name into one word, he created Clifton's restaurant in 1931. It would operate under a unique business model—the so-called "penny restaurant." As the name implies, most dishes cost one cent. Even adjusted for inflation (19 cents today), nearly everyone could find some change in their couch cushions for a meal. Penny restaurants had been around for a couple of decades, mostly in larger urban areas, but were seeing a revival during the early days of the Great Depression.

City planners and LA's smartarati liked that idea. Bread lines and soup kitchens were not only a drain on dwindling city resources, but they also generated unsightly lines that snaked down the street. The serpentine metaphor was apt. Bread and soup lines were a venomous reminder of how bad things were, not to mention how they poisoned the morale of the people in them.

Unlike a bread line, Clifton's was a restaurant, complete with tables, servers, and a menu. But unlike other penny restaurants, Clifton's would not turn away those who couldn't find the coins to pay for their meal. On opening day, his slogan was "Dine Free Unless Delighted," which in practical terms meant that many people ate on the house. Still, Clifton's wasn't a charity; it was a choice. Choice changes everything.

However, why would people choose Clifton's when they could visit another penny restaurant? (His wasn't the only one that opened up in LA that year.) Why would they continue to choose it after things got better? That was Clifton's true innovation: the recognition that a meal was something more than sustenance. He created a dining *experience*.

We'll come back to Clifton's story later. However, to truly understand what made his approach so special, we need to step back and understand the massive transition in mealtime that occurred not only because of the Great Depression but also (relatedly) because of food innovation and government policy.

Be warned. Clifton's was one of the few bright spots in this story. The rest is about to get ugly.

. . .

In the winter of 1929, after the stock market crash, it wasn't obvious that things were about to get as bad as they did.

The states of the United States weren't quite as economically interdependent as they are today, nor did information travel quite as fast—there was no social media where the average person could share their experience. President Herbert Hoover reminded people that the finances of the American government, the American business community, and the American people were on fundamentally sound footing. People believed him, and most had ample reason to.

However, if you lived in New York—the epicenter of the crash—you had a clue something was wrong. There had always been bread lines and soup kitchens in New York. A city that large always faces those issues. Poverty, sadly, was nothing new. That said, most relief efforts were concentrated in primarily immigrant neighborhoods.

But as 1929 snaked into 1930, bread lines started popping up in *middle-class* neighborhoods. Then, upper-class neighborhoods. By the end of 1931, New York had 81 bread lines throughout the city. *Eighty-one.* No one was prepared for that. Not city officials. Not residents. No one.

In *A Square Meal: A Culinary History of the Great Depression*, historians Jane Ziegelman and Andrew Coe describe how middle-class and upper-class bread lines were different than what came before. You've probably seen the photos, and if you looked closely, something seemed...off. These weren't people wearing cast-off rags or traditional immigrant garb waiting for charity. These people might have been queuing for a church service. They were humiliated but would not allow their shame to extend to their outward appearance. At some level, it was as if they simply would not accept what was happening to them.

Despite the dramatic change in the class position of people seeking aid, officials stuck doggedly to their preconceptions of what type of person they must be—and, more importantly, how that would impact relief policy—both in terms of the specific foods offered and the morality that surrounded those meals. Neither was helpful.

Part of the issue stemmed from the definition of food aid itself. Planners never envisioned serving full meals, much less providing those meals for any length of time. These were emergency rations to stave off the worst effects of hunger and prevent starvation. No one was prepared for the same people, in ever greater numbers, to keep showing up day after day. It was a worrying sign.

Perhaps the bigger perception issue stemmed from the image of people needing relief. Social workers of the time didn't understand why people were showing up, and frankly, they didn't care to learn. Even (especially) among so-called Progressives of that era, people who needed aid "deserved" their situation. Needing food aid wasn't simply an economic issue (you lost your job) but spoke to a moral delinquency or defect of some kind. Part of that might have been a way to mentally separate aid-givers from the precariousness of what they were seeing. In many cases, these were your neighbors. They were just like you in every observable way. If a simple case of bad luck could happen to them, bad luck could happen to you. Better to imagine they had some moral skeleton in their closet.

If you follow this chain of reasoning—that these were only temporary stop-gaps for people who needed to correct their own moral failings—the solution is self-evident: Close the breadlines. That's right, by 1931, New York (and cities across the country) were turning people away. Many private charities kept operating, but as you might guess, it was nearly impossible to keep up with demand. The primary reason was that cities couldn't afford to keep them open, but the convenient rationalization was that the "dole" would create dependence on the government. When you're tempted to think this was a case of heartless rightwing moralists in some Dickensian dystopia, remember that Progressives were largely in charge on both sides of the political aisle.

However, one place you couldn't ignore the issue was in school. Thankfully, it would become one of the few bright spots. Kids—a lot of kids—arrived at school hungry. In many schools, it was the majority of kids. Teachers could deal with a *few* hungry kids, but 30 rumbling bellies don't lead to a productive learning environment.

Teachers of the time got creative.

Many of them transformed the first class hour of the day into Food Preparation class, where students learned the basics of cooking, nutrition, and servings. Of course, they ate what they made. Then (as now, in some cases), this was the only solid meal that students would receive, and it took the pressure off stretched and breaking home budgets to pay for and prepare that meal.

However, this bright spot in our story of the official response to hunger does feature a dimmer switch. A mix of Victorian and Puritan morality (especially in the Northeast) also extended to food in the classroom. If you couldn't afford food, you shouldn't afford enjoyment. Therefore, relief food wasn't *supposed* to be enjoyed. It was fuel alone. Bland food was better food for...reasons. That was especially and sadly true with immigrant children. Italians, for example, know how to make simple, cheap foods that taste very, very good. (Dandelions sauteed in olive oil make a spectacular aromatic dressing.) However, the Puritans in charge of the school programs would allow nothing of the sort.

So, it was a bright spot. Not a tasty spot. But a bright spot nonetheless.

All this begs the question: Why was it such a problem to feed people?

. . .

Although some ingredient prices spiked in the 1930s, contrary to popular belief, food was actually very cheap. The problem was that it was *too cheap*, and farmers were going broke. With a combination of rising interest rates on farm equipment and lower commodity prices, many farmers lost money for every acre they harvested. Why? Commodity prices dropped 60 percent from 1929 to 1933. When you make a fraction of what you made just a few years ago, but your mortgage and equipment payments stay the same, the economics aren't difficult to understand.

Government farm policy during that time attempted to help—in some cases, successfully, but in many others, made the situation worse. Official policy, especially once FDR took office, was to buy up commodities from farmers and redistribute that food. That helped somewhat, though distribution was a clunky process. In other cases, farmers were paid not to produce crops, which did put upward pressure on prices (less supply, higher prices), though at the worst possible time in a food shortage. Some prices were so low that it was cheaper for farmers to dump milk in the drain or let wheat rot in the fields. That says nothing about droughts that curtailed production in the mid-1930s (aka "The Dust Bowl") when poorly managed topsoil simply blew away.

All while people in the cities went hungry. While kids went hungry. While bread lines closed.

It's easy to look back with decades of hindsight and come away infuriated at the official responses to hunger—the moralizing, the inefficiency, the third-grade understanding of economics.[1] However, it's important to remember that people were doing what they could, in the best way they knew how, without the benefit of 90 years of future knowledge. That said, people of the time realized quickly that they couldn't wait. No one was coming to save them. Big policy solutions are great, but eating happens today, not in a few months when things get sorted out.

It's time to set government policy aside and learn how consumers solved the problem themselves and how government policy eventually caught up *to them*.

. . .

When people are hungry, they do what they need to do. Many people still lived in rural or suburban areas. The forests, fields, and lakes scattered throughout the landscape made for excellent foraging and fishing. It was like a return to our hunter-gatherer origins. It could never permanently replace a functioning agricultural market, but it would do in a pinch. In addition to wild game protein, all manner of berries, field vegetables, weeds, roots, or fungi were (quite literally) on the table. It's hard to know how many people ate the wrong thing and got very sick, but people learn pretty quickly to avoid *Atropa belladonna* and *Amanita phalloides*.[2]

---

1. As you might guess, there is so much more to the economic picture than this. It's beyond the scope of this book to explore deflation, inflation, the Gold Standard, the Federal Reserve, and monetary policy. All of which had an impact—both positive and negative. If you want to read more about that, be careful. Economists are not dispassionate observers of numbers. Most have an axe to grind—especially the "readable" books of the subject. Most of them are written to influence policy today and in the future, not to explain what happened in the past. A hint: If you want the most unbiased accounts, read the books that seem the most boring.

2. Deadly nightshade (and its berries) and the Death Cap mushroom. The word "death" in the common name gives us a clue that the Latin names do not.

When pre-agriculture strategies failed, people did what you would expect them to do: They planted gardens, raised animals, and preserved food. That explains part of the popularity of bullfrog farming, chicken coops, and bunny husbandry. All are tasty, and rabbits breed like...well, you know. Other forest critters weren't safe either. If a fox shows up to raid the coop, he's just as likely to end up in the Dutch oven as the chick in his belly. People ate raccoons, squirrels, deer, geese, and ducks—if they could catch it, shoot it, hook it, or trap it, they ate it. Not coincidentally, this is the era when angling became much more popular. (If your uncle can't stop talking about fishing lures, blame your depression on the Great Depression.)

Basic economics regressed as well. If your buddy was handy with the rifle and brought down a deer, and you were a better angler and brought in a half-dozen muskies, the two of you would arrange a trade. It's impossible to know what percentage of the food economy devolved into ad hoc barter networks, but the anecdotal evidence—especially from rural areas—suggests a meaningful amount.

You can see why. Not only was meat at the grocery store prohibitively expensive, but the supply was (sometimes artificially) low due to the aforementioned farm policy. It's unsurprising that Americans started giving the ducks in the neighborhood pond the side eye.

Even the way people prepared food changed, and not necessarily for the better. A Utah State University exhibit details several resourceful methods used by families during the Great Depression:

> Liquid from canned veggies could be used as a soup base. Juice from preserved fruit could be poured over cakes. Casseroles were a mix of multiple leftovers: noodles, potatoes, onions, beans, [and] veggies. Margarine wrappers were saved and used to oil cooking and baking pans. Recipes developed at the time may sound strange now: water cocoa, boiled milkweed pods topped with cheese, chicken feet in broth, ketchup sandwiches, gopher, bacon grease sandwiches, and oatmeal with lard. Families that could not afford chicken often turned to an innovative dish called City Chicken.

City Chicken was basically ground whatever-you-could-get, eggs, buttermilk, and spices.

Euphemisms appeared on many menus and did exactly what was needed: They obscured the reality of everyone's predicament. But let's be clear. No one confused "water cocoa" with cocoa.

. . .

All this helps us understand why refrigerator sales exploded in an era of tremendous economic stress.[3] If you were making anything-sausage out of miscellaneous raccoon parts, you certainly were not letting any food spoil. The investment made tremendous sense, especially with department store installment payment plans (an innovation of the decade before).

The federal government wasn't blind to these trends. Hoover's overoptimistic approach wasn't working. He was (wisely, at least for a time) trying to avoid the psychological doom loop we've talked about so much already. However, by the time Roosevelt took office, everyone knew that the ship had sailed. FDR was ready to face the problem head-on, but with an approach that was more similar to what came before than most people realize.

Remember that before Roosevelt won the 1932 election, he was the governor of *New York*—in many ways, responsible for overseeing the "food as fuel" philosophy behind relief programs. What's more, his wife Eleanor was born and raised of the same Puritan moralistic stock.

Eleanor, for her part, wanted to ensure the White House set the right example—especially in its kitchens—even though the Roosevelts were wealthy and the Federal budget did allow for seasonings. If the American people were eating plain meals, so would they. Her mantra, and the message of "Aunt Sammy" on the radio (Uncle Sam's wife, purportedly), was "plain food, plainly cooked." It was a noble sentiment but a terrible execution. FDR *hated* the meals in the White House, and his dinner guests concurred. In one memorable quip from Earnest Hemingway

---

3. In an echo of today's marketing strategies, some refrigerators models were sold embedded with radios. That strategy worked about as well in the 1930s as it does in the 2020s. Not very.

in 1937, the author christened the liquid in the bowl in front of him, "rainwater soup."

The odd morality of that era knew no political boundaries.

Even the name of Roosevelt's food relief agency in New York—the Temporary Emergency Relief Administration—belied its guiding idea: *temporary* and *emergency*. FDR hated the idea of people losing dignity on the dole and wanted to send a clear signal that *jobs* were the only lasting solution. The national version—FERA, or *Federal* Emergency Relief Administration—was the same idea, on steroids.

As you might expect, the twin pillars of "temporary" and "food as fuel" embedded themselves in the program's execution. Let's step down a level. In practical terms, what did that mean for people receiving assistance?

If you were on the program, you'd receive a yellow sheet of paper (like a coupon) that could be exchanged for food at participating grocers. Not all foods, mind you—only certain foods. To protect against fraud (both from recipients and distributors of food aid) TERA (and later, FERA) officials would inspect grocers' records, perform spot checks in stores, inspect shopping baskets, and even follow women back into their kitchens to ensure they weren't buying or preparing food they weren't allowed to have. That would be like "those people" stealing from the government.

Can you guess how well that went over? Of course, you can.

As a rule, Americans bristle at heavy-handed approaches. To be fair, Prohibition should have taught that lesson, but alas, some people never learn. The prior decade—for better and for worse—created a robust "choice culture" in the mind of the average American. He or she expected to decide how things would work for them, even when it came to direct aid from the government.

The natural reaction was pushback. Why shouldn't recipients of handouts need to follow some simple rules? They're only for their own good. That certainly was the attitude of Harold "Harry" Lloyd Hopkins, FDR's righthand man when it came to TERA and FERA administration. (Hopkins followed FDR from New York to the White House.) However, idealism and moralism soon gave way to practicality and acceptance. Many (perhaps most) aid recipients simply ignored the rules; there was no one to inspect every shopping basket, and everyone knew it.

Some even resold coupons when they had a surplus and bought them when they were in need. A secondary market quickly developed, supported by (and often facilitated from) the backrooms of grocery stores. It was like alcohol Prohibition all over again—but this time, it was bags of flour instead of liters of whiskey—and the grocers were the speakeasies.

In the end, and after trying everything else, Hopkins recognized the power of consumer culture (and the average person's knowledge) to make the best decisions for their unique situation.[4] Government strategy shifted from *command and control* to *cash and information*.

Direct cash assistance would allow housewives (yes, mostly women) to make the best decisions with the freedom to choose how to spend their money. But how would they do that? It's one thing to prepare a full meal when you're not struggling to afford ingredients, but how do you prepare a nutritionally balanced meal when you need to make sacrifices? Where could you skimp safely? How could you be more efficient? What techniques were best? That's what housewives needed most: reliable nutrition information. With that, they could figure it out on their own.

The answer was the first government-sponsored (and mandated) nutritional guidance. This wasn't quite the "food pyramid" of later decades or the ubiquitous nutrition labels we see on nearly all food products today. However, for the first time, food manufacturers would need to clearly identify the ingredients in their food, portion sizes, and basic nutritional information. They couldn't hide behind euphemisms and flouncy language.

But that didn't mean they didn't innovate as well.

We haven't talked much about how the food industry responded to the Great Depression, and it's about time we did. After all we've discussed, it's easy to come away with the impression that food innovation ground to a halt after the stock market crash. Nothing could be further from the truth. The Great Depression spawned one of the most innovative eras in food marketing: packaged foods, snacks, and fast foods.

---

4. This is a paraphrase of the pithy observation: "Americans can always be trusted to do the right thing, once all other possibilities have been exhausted." Commonly attributed to UK leader Winston Churchill, there is scant evidence he ever said it. Though, it does sound like something he would say.

. . .

The opportunity was clear. Consumers wanted inexpensive, easy-to-prepare meals that contained adequate nutrition. Now, before we get all indignant about how "processed" foods are bad for us, consider the alternative: starvation. Or raccoon sausages. Or mushrooms that make you feel funny. C'mon now. Can you see the appeal? The 1930s saw an explosion of packaged foods that, well, let's be honest, hit two of those three objectives. They told us more about food and people's relationship to eating than they did about pure physical need. Let's meet a few of them, shall we?

One of the foods that attempted to hit all *three* buttons was Quaker Oats—as one of the first affordable cereals, it was easy to prepare (milk is better, but hot water works in a pinch) and nutritious. The happy old man on the iconic cylindrical package dates back to the 1920s, so the company had a branding leg up when the market crashed. However, the nutrition in pure oats isn't complete, especially regarding vitamins. That's why the Quaker Oats Company began *fortifying* its cereal. This is the first time we see the enrichment of processed foods en masse. Today, that process is commonplace, and it's the reason most people don't get scurvy, rickets, or beriberi unless something is seriously wrong. Today, it's less common to worry about people getting enough to eat (most often, it's the opposite problem), but in the 1930s, many people were malnourished.[5] A fortified breakfast cereal was an important advancement.

This was also the first time Kraft Foods introduced its iconic macaroni and cheese boxed meal. If you could step into a time machine from today to 1935, you'd know exactly how to make it: Boil the noodles, drain them, and add butter, milk, and the (included) fluorescent orange cheese powder. It was also fortified, though no one would (or did, even then) confuse this for a nutritionally complete meal. No matter. The marketing message made it clear who (and what) this was for: "The housewife's best friend, a nourishing one-pot meal." Mac and Cheese

---

5. How much? Depending on what source you use and what methods *they* used, between 11 and 40 percent of all World War II recruits were initially rejected due to malnutrition. That's a big deal. If the Germans are eating well and Americans were not, they were going to win.

was also one of the first meals easy enough to prepare that kids could do it when dad (and mom) were working.[6]

When mom was home and wanted to step up her game from shockingly orange cheese powder, she turned off Aunt Sammy and started reading Shiela Hibben. Hibben was the *New Yorker* magazine's food critic, penning her first column in 1934 after success with *The National Cookbook* in 1932. The Federal Writers Project built on that success with the "America Eats!" series, edited by Katherine Kellock. Sponsored by the Federal government, writers fanned out nationwide to interview home cooks and celebrate local cuisine. It was the first time many American consumers became familiar with the grand diversity of food choices in their vast home country, and they couldn't get enough.

More help came from the kitchen testers at *Good Housekeeping* magazine, who introduced the "question box" and "Good Housekeeping Seal of Approval"—the *Consumer Reports* of Home Economics. They'd try out all the new boxed, canned, and frozen foods, giving home cooks tips on how to prepare these new food options.[7]

American consumers clearly cared about food—how it tasted and how it was prepared—even during the worst years of the Great Depression.

But just when you thought it was all a battle between good nutrition and good flavor (and wondered why no one realized you could have both—or if they did, thought it was somehow the work of the devil), consumers told everyone that they wanted a bit of happiness in their lives as well. And the best form of quick happiness? You know the answer. Chocolate.

The 1930s saw the popularization and marketing of the candy bar in a way that simply hadn't happened before. Yes, there were a smattering of options before the crash, but if you enjoy peanuts, caramel, and chocolate, 1930 was the first time you could enjoy all three in one place: a Snickers bar. Two years later, you could try a 3 Musketeers—sort of Snickers without the peanuts and caramel. Compared to most food innovations, this was hardly creative. Basically, candy

---

6. Was this one of the first meals you learned to make?

7. Many boxed, canned, and frozen foods predate the Great Depression, but the 1930s dramatically accelerated their adoption by American consumers.

makers at confection giants Hershey and Mars kept trying to pour chocolate over tasty stuff to see what people liked. And oh boy, did they sell well.

Sure, chocolate tastes good, but there was a practical reason at play. Nutritional value aside, the candy bar was the cheapest way to consume the highest number of calories. It helped that it tasted good, of course, and that it was shelf-stable for much longer than other foods. Bottom line: A candy bar was a reasonable option if you needed calories. And psychologically, chocolate made things seem a little better, at least for a while.

Speaking of feel-good food, the 1930s also saw the creation and spread of Dunkin Donuts throughout the northeast and Krispy Kreme in the south. Like chocolate, donuts were cheap, calorie-dense, and stayed fresh. But unlike chocolate, they encouraged socialization—either sitting around the table eating donuts and drinking coffee (at Dunkin) or sharing a box of Krispy Kremes with friends.[8] During an economic *and* psychological Depression, those little escapes were welcomed.

What can we say after all the gastronomical ups and downs? Food is much more than sustenance and biology. It's more than resourcefulness and waste management. It's about those things, and it needs to be, or people starve. But the biggest issue with government well-meaners is that they forgot the other stuff it's about: community, heritage, enjoyment, and fun.

Consumers of the 1930s decided those things were just as important.

. . .

With all that in mind, it's finally time to circle back with Clifford Clifton.

Visiting Clifton's Cafeteria wasn't anything like standing in a bread line. Clinton understood that a meal meant so much more to people down on their luck. Did you need a newspaper to check the want ads? It was free. Read as much as you like. Haven't been able to afford anything nice for the kids in a while? They got complimentary sherbet for dessert. Need something refreshing with the meal? Take a cup to the punch fountain and fill it up. Need something to take your mind off it all? Clifton's even offered a free tour bus to show you the sights—like

---

8. Oh, and one more thing. Most people think the fast food craze began in the 1950s with McDonald's restaurants. What they miss is that the fast food industry traces its roots back to the Great Depression when Colonel Harland David Sanders started selling fried chicken from his Kentucky restaurant.

the celebrity tours today, though one thinks much less ostentatious. Lonely? In an echo of Albert Broel, Clifton's offered a "Guests' Exchange Service" to match up lonely people, though no one (to anyone's knowledge) used it to track down people and murder them for their money. It probably helped that anyone coming for a 1-cent serving of vegetables probably wasn't the type. Do you just need someone to talk to? You could even sit down with the staff—including Clinton himself—for an impromptu therapy session. Seriously. Clifton's was the place to be.[9]

But Clinton wasn't done. Not by a long shot.

He traveled to the Pacific Northwest and picked up some massive redwood logs, which he transformed into massive structural pillars in the main dining room of his new four-story dining extravaganza. The bottom floor featured a babbling creek running through it, providing a constant feeling that you were out in the woods. There was even a rocky outcrop where local musicians would sing and play for the diners. The look was completed with a full mural on all the walls.

Other floors featured a waterfall to complement the "Pacific Seas" theme, complete with blazing neon orchids, real tropical trees, bamboo, and exotic birds—a triumph of Polynesian kitsch, as one reporter called it. In the rain hut, it actually rained every 20 minutes. The top floor was a standing-room-only eating area where patrons could mill about and listen to music—like a poor man's (and woman's) nightclub.

If you're trying to imagine this, find your nearest Rainforest Cafe. Or, better yet, go visit one. You'll get the idea.

None of this meant that the dishes weren't cheap or that you couldn't get a free meal. Clinton believed that a meal meant more to people than simply sustenance. It was a communal event. Things were hard enough outside. Your meal should be…something more.

It wasn't just that he fed the modestly able-to-pay or even those formerly well-off on hard times. Clifton's fed anyone who wasn't actively drunk or high, and that included people without homes, or more to the consternation of the

---

9. There were other so-called "penny restaurants" across the country, including one run by fitness guru and publishing icon Bernarr McFadden. He dispensed his brand of health advice along with meals. Interesting story. Weird guy. Look him up. It's worth it.

racist authorities, Black and Hispanic people as well. He was also a bit too evangelical for many of the anti-religious Progressives of the times. It also rubbed them the wrong way that his *restaurant* was more successful than their *programs*. As Russ Rymer put it in a 2003 *Los Angeles Magazine* article: "Where he saw morals, they saw moralism."

That said, Clinton's operation was so efficient that the government swallowed its bigotry and asked Clinton to audit its own food charity programs. However, Clinton did the job a little too well. To this point, we've implied that although some efforts may have been misguided, everyone trying to feed their citizens at different levels of government had noble intentions. They did not.

Clinton didn't just do what many government auditors do and make a cursory inspection of food pantries in Los Angeles, make a couple of token recommendations, and allow things to continue. No. He produced probably the most detailed report ever created to audit a government agency. It ran hundreds of pages. It landed with a literal and figurative thud. Sparing the details, Clinton's report implicated dozens of city officials—including some in the mayor's office—with corruption, mismanagement, and embezzlement of money and resources meant for food relief. (Remember, this is when people all over the country were going hungry.)

The mayor's office, in an act of contrition and acceptance, fully accepted responsibility. They turned themselves in to face the judgment of local authorities and resigned their commissions. That allowed the citizens to elect a new group of people who were better able to accept this crushing responsibility.

Just kidding.

The payback was swift. Restaurant inspectors showed up at Clinton's restaurants *much more often* under the guise of "just doing their job," finding the silliest violations imaginable. He fixed them. City officials then bussed in hundreds of migrants that they had been forcing to camp outside the city and dropped them off at Cliffton's doors. He fed them. They planted "customers" to complain about anything and everything; some even started fights. He handled them. When all that failed to deter Clinton, the mayor pulled the trump card. He dropped off dozens of Black people at the restaurant. (This was not a racially accepting time.) Clifford Clinton fed them, too.

That last one was the true test. Suffice it to say that Clifton's integrated dining room wasn't welcomed by everyone. He would not be swayed. He even published the feedback in his newsletter, *Food for Thot*, so that he could make his position clear. In one letter, a patron wrote: "I have always liked Clifton's, but yesterday two Negroes came and sat at my table. After that the food tasted like sawdust." His response? Epic. "If colored skin is a passport to death for our liberties, then it is a passport to Clifton's." That's the kind of man he was.[10]

If the mayor thought this Christian would simply turn the other cheek and allow corruption to continue, they hadn't counted on Clinton's reading of the parable of the money changers in the temple.[11] Clinton would fight back. He organized the city's first full recall campaign to oust the mayor and force new elections. During the recall campaign, the mayor's office upped the game and bombed his house. This was the severed-horse-head-in-the-bed moment meant to drive Clinton off track. It would not work. Clinton succeeded. The mayor and his cronies were driven out.

Clinton was ready to sacrifice everything for his vision—a better vision—of what a meal meant for people. It's the same vision that Quaker Oats, Kraft, Mars, Hershey, Dunkin Donuts, Krispy Kreme, Colonel Sanders, *Good Housekeeping*, Shiela Hibben, and millions of would-be anglers, hunters, and foragers all understood, too.

A meal is so much more than food.

---

10. Sadly, the note quoted here matches the sentiment, but not the timeframe. This one comes from *1944*. Racism was alive and well, despite Clinton's efforts.

11. This verse occurs in three of the four Christian gospels. Mark, Chapter 11, Verse 15 might be the best, but take your pick.

THE GINGHAM GIRL

Photos from the 1930s show a marked departure from the fashion of the Roaring 20s. It's quite striking.

Not for men, of course. Most men could get away with clothes they bought decades before without too much social judgment. However, women didn't have that luxury, even in the Great Depression. The person most responsible for that transition is Madeleine Vionnet, a fashion designer you've probably never heard of.

The 1920s featured flirty, boxy, and short dresses. They were feminine, certainly, but they also challenged gender roles because they gave women more freedom of expression in dancing and socializing. Clothes also became cheaper and more accessible, mostly due to easier-care fabrics. In all this, Coco Chanel was the queen. Most every woman you know owns at least one of her little black dresses.

As we've seen, the country's mood had changed, though perhaps not in the obvious way you're thinking reading a book focused on the Depression years. Yes, economics mattered, but the change in dominant visual media mattered nearly as much. Motion pictures allowed filmmakers to create their vision on a larger-than-life screen. It's not that boxy, short dresses didn't translate well to the big screen, but they couldn't quite capture the feeling of elegance and glamour filmmakers wanted to show. Movies then, as now, were escapes. Fashion needed to evolve.

This is the "golden age" of movies many people fondly remember. Stars like Greta Garbo, Ginger Rogers, and Judy Garland popularized long, flowing gowns that hugged the length of their bodies in a way Chanel's dresses did not. More than that, because subtlety doesn't work well in black and white, female stars wore high-contrast makeup. Bright red lipstick also showed up well in the first Technicolor films. While not every woman had the figure to match the movie stars, they could easily copy the makeup patterns they saw, especially as cosmetics became cheaper and more widely available in the 1930s.

Although Chanel still played a substantial role in the fashion world, the transition to flowing gowns wasn't her idea. The concept is a simple (but devilishly difficult) innovation in dressmaking: the bias cut.

If you look at many clothing fabrics closely, you'll notice that the direction of the stitching (usually a cross-hatch) is *perpendicular* to the grain. That's easier to see on thicker fabrics (like flannel) than thinner ones, but a small magnifying glass is all you need in most cases. This technique is the most straightforward assembly process because it reduces the chances the fabric will begin to fray before it's stitched into clothing. The result is…well, square. Unless the fabric is very light (and even when it is), it does not flow nicely over the body's natural curves. That's less noticeable in men's clothes or in Chanel's boxier 1920s dresses. Standard cuts were cheaper and easier to produce, leading to a boom in inexpensive personal expression. However, this lack of elegance was quite noticeable in longer, flowing women's dresses—precisely the type becoming popular in the 1930s.

That's where Madeleine Vionnet comes in. Unlike Chanel, she shunned the spotlight. She was a master craftswoman, putting her considerable genius not into self-promotion but rather into opening a new door to fashion design. Simply put, her "bias cut" refers to cutting at a 45-degree angle to the fabric's weave. It's more delicate and difficult because the fabric must be under tension during the entire process. Vionnet's process forced her to reimagine how dresses were constructed—the pieces that make up the pattern before they're sown together.

This allowed her to design those parts from the ground up, like recutting a completed puzzle and reassembling it into a more attractive final picture.[1]

That result was simply stunning. Clothing assembled using a bias cut flows more seamlessly over the body's curves and, in Vionnet's creations, more accurately shows the female form underneath. More bluntly, women could appear nude while fully dressed. The elegance on the big screen was obvious immediately. To many, this was the age of iconic feminine beauty on screen. American women went wild for it.

That's even when the dresses constructed with a bias cut were (and are), speaking diplomatically, unforgiving. Women didn't care. Even during the Great Depression, women expressed themselves in elegant evening wear. They'd even bring some of those touches of elegance into careerwear and homewear. It's difficult to reconcile the graceful images of the 1930s with the economic struggles many of these people faced. Before we're tempted to claim this was a tiny, out-of-touch elite, it was not. Although the fashion and makeup industries took a sharp hit in the early 1930s, they had largely recovered by the middle of the decade.

That said, there is a bias at play—and it's not simply a pun on the bias cut, although the comparison is apt. It's an *urban* bias and a *media* bias. As more people moved into the cities and media became more engaging and pervasive, our history books (and, therefore, our collective cultural memory) focused there. Charitably, American women prioritized their outward appearance and presentation to the world. Less charitably, the bias cut plays into an image of the fickle, wasteful, and exploited consumer.

This is our vision of 1930s fashion. Like most simple explanations, it is incomplete and misleading.

To find the truth and the lasting innovation in fashion of the 1930s, we need to leave the cities and walk out of the movie theater. We need to drive to the still-robust rural communities of the Great Depression. They were struggling, too, but their challenges were different. Flowing gowns didn't make much sense

---

1. Historical fashion expert Betty Kirke attempted to recreate Vionnet's process from scratch and write a book about the bias cut and Vionnet's role in the fashion industry. It took her years and she never quite accomplished it before she passed away in 2016. It was that difficult. If you're interested in the technical details, you won't find a better explanation.

on a farmstead, but that didn't mean women were content to sit back and let the fashion world pass them by. This fashion innovation didn't come from Paris or New York but from the housewives and agricultural supply companies of Minnesota, Iowa, and Missouri. It was pure Midwest fashion that was as iconic in its own way with surprising staying power. In the process, we'll learn something much more important about the character of the American consumer.

It's time we learned about flour sack dresses.

. . .

You've probably never heard of a flour sack dress. Even if you have (or you've worn one), the backstory is helpful.

Today, flour comes packaged in *paper* bags, but that's a relatively recent change. In the 1960s, the price of cotton climbed past the crossover point where it was more economical to package flour in paper sacks—especially in smaller quantities for the home market, but even for bulk quantities shipped to bakeries and rural communities. Why not earlier? Bagging flour isn't a trivial problem. Not just any paper will do. Too thin, and it rips. Too thick, and it's not economical. The bag needs to be sealed well enough to protect the contents but not so well that buyers must destroy the bag to disgorge its contents. Even decades later, it's not quite right. To find the bakery aisle in any grocery store, simply look for the shelves coated in flour dust.[2]

Cotton bags were everywhere if you were a rural homemaker in the 1930s. They carried flour, of course, but also animal feed, sugar, salt, and fertilizer. (Though you might not choose to repurpose that last bag.) You could also find several sizes, all designed to carry different product weights, from five pounds to 200 pounds, though 25- and 50-pound sacks were the most common.

Of course, some industrious homemakers immediately saw the repurposing potential of flour sacks. As early as 1924, Asa Bales patented the "Gingham Girl" cross-hatch design for his company's flour sacks—patent number 1,611,403—primarily to differentiate its bags on the shelf and capitalize on the

---

2. Before cotton sacks, flour came packaged in wooden barrels. Obviously, that had its own economic challenges, and by the end of the 1800s, lumber became too expensive and hit the crossover point with abundant cotton in the southern United States. This is one of the many impacts of mechanization in the southern United States about that time.

reuse market. However, the Roaring 20s was a time of rapidly shrinking clothing prices, so refashioning empty bags into clothing often wasn't worth the effort.

The first substantial use of flour sacks to produce clothing on a massive scale didn't happen in the United States. During World War I, living in Belgium was an unlucky geographic accident. The so-called "Low Countries" were sandwiched between the most massive armies on Earth at the time—the Germans on one side and the French and British on the other. At the outset of the conflict, the German war machine quickly overran Belgium on its way to meet the French.

As many of us learned in high school history class, the speed of the initial invasion ground to a halt quickly. When the armies dug in for the long fight, they quite literally dug in. The resulting line of trenches mostly hugged the French/Belgian border, meaning that Belgium—the most densely populated country in the world in 1914 with 7.6 million souls—found itself *behind* German lines.

Very quickly, food started running low.[3] For Germany, their priority was their troops first, their citizens second, and everyone else (a distant) third. It didn't take long for Belgian citizens to begin to starve. The warring parties certainly chided the Germans for failing to care for occupied populations, but those warnings were largely brushed aside. France, Russia, and Great Britain didn't have food to spare either. Winston Churchill (yeah, *that* Winston Churchill) even suggested that Belgians should be allowed to starve because it would bring international condemnation on Germany and force a quicker end to the war.[4]

The only nation with the industrial and agricultural capacity to address the problem was the United States. However, getting food to where it was needed wasn't easy. Belgium was a war zone behind the lines of an antagonist. Whoever led this effort must have a detailed understanding of distribution, shipping, and logistics. This person must also be a skilled negotiator. Most importantly, this person must have a commanding presence without "official" authority. Everyone—especially German leadership—needed to respect this person.

---

3. There's a terrible logic behind the so-called four horsemen of the apocalypse. *War* leads to *famine*. Famine leads to *disease* (or more commonly referred to here as "pestilence"). Disease leads to *death*. In war, especially long wars, the horrible sequence plays out every time.

4. Yes, Churchill is revered in the United Kingdom for his role in the next war. In this war, he was...less revered.

Enter Herbert Hoover.

Most people remember Hoover as the person who either caused the Great Depression or didn't do enough to address it. However, in 1914, this former mining engineer was one of the most brilliant administrators the United States had ever produced. He singlehandedly coordinated the evacuation of over 120,000 Americans from the war zone at the start of the conflict. When it came to organizing food relief for Belgium, Hoover was the natural choice. How he did it was pure brilliance.

Hoover knew that if he shipped food directly into Belgium through the German authorities, the generals would simply redirect it to their own troops. That wouldn't work. It might actually backfire. Although America remained neutral at the outset of the war, no one wanted to give the Germans an advantage. Instead, Hoover declared all food aid shipments property of the United States until they were handed off to *Belgian* relief workers. In 1914, the Germans wouldn't risk pulling the United States into the war by requisitioning its property. More than that, they respected Hoover and knew he dealt fairly. (It also probably helped that Hoover helped the Germans avoid a citizen uprising behind their front lines.)

That did the trick. Hoover was able to stem the tide of starvation and feed an entire country with *surplus* American exports.

Much of that relief came in the form of tens of thousands of 50-pound cotton flour sacks that read "American Commission" on the front and "Belgian Relief Flour from Toledo, Ohio" (or wherever it came from) on the back.[5] It should be obvious that maintaining the Belgian commodity market for clothing wasn't a priority for German authorities either, so Belgian women started using empty sacks to make shirts, dresses, trousers, and even underwear. As a gesture of defiance, clothing made from the flour sacks kept the "American Commission" label on the front. Sure, it was easier that way, but one thinks it was a giant middle finger to German officials who saw them.

As photos of flour sack clothing filtered back to the United States, they were a clear source of pride in a job well done. However, as the United States entered the

---

5. You can still see examples of these in the Hoover Presidential Museum in Iowa. They were gifts of a grateful Belgian people after the war.

war in 1917 (and suffered a painful recession in the early 1920s after it ended), rural housewives found themselves in a similar predicament to the Belgians. They'd solve it similarly—making stopgap clothing out of surplus feed sacks. However, it wouldn't last long. As prosperity returned in 1922 and the "Roaring 20s" really got going, the need to upcycle feed sacks into shirts faded into the background. However, the need seeded the ground (floured the cake?) for the next time there would be a crisis.

Women would be ready.

...

It's unlikely that flour sack dresses (and all the other upcycled clothing we'll talk about shortly) would have become a cultural phenomenon in rural America without a notably poor marketing decision. To understand that decision (which sure seemed like a good idea at the time), we need to understand the value chain for flour.

The "value chain" is simply business language for identifying the steps needed to turn wheat seeds into a bag of flour you can buy at the store. We'll make it even easier: We can skip the seed to wheat, wheat to harvest, and harvest to mill steps. All that's important to know is that hundreds (or thousands) of wheat farmers would ship all their harvested wheat to a few huge centralized facilities.[6] Those facilities processed wheat into flour, packaged it into the appropriate-sized cotton sacks, and reversed the supply chain back to the communities where it was needed.

By necessity, most of these flour sacks—in fact, all feed sacks—were pretty large: 25, 50, or 100 pounds. That's because most were used for industrial bakeries and livestock feed. These were big operations that demanded efficiency. The only reason bags weren't any larger was that people would have trouble moving them around.

During the Great Depression, millers and packagers (like everyone else) sought opportunities to save money. They came up with an ingenious idea: reuse the bags. Usually, there wasn't anything wrong with them. Thick cotton bags were

---

6. One of the biggest was Minneapolis—originally nicknamed the "Mill City" for its concentration of food processors. By the way, the milling process is inherently dangerous. In 1878, flour dust in the air at the Washburn A Mill along the Mississippi River exploded, killing 18 workers and leaving a crater where the mill used to be. You can visit the factory today as a museum.

quite sturdy and could survive several refillings. The millers already had a distribution network in place. They would ask the final buyers to return the empties on the same trains they shipped the packed bags. Then, they'd clean, refill, and resell them. What a perfect solution, right?

Perfect for everyone except one group: the companies that made the bags.

You can see the problem, can't you? Reusing bags meant you didn't need to buy new ones—at least, not nearly as many. In tough economic times, no company was going down without a fight. The battle was on. The trick was convincing people *not* to return their bags, especially when they could get a small credit when turning them in. Remember, cash was king.[7]

Bag makers, like Bemis in St. Louis, began a marketing blitz. Their first idea was to claim that returning bags for reuse was in some way "unsanitary" or even "evil." The first part is understandable. That's a standard argument. Refill a water mug too often without cleaning it and all you've done is create a thriving bacterial culture. The evil part is...less clear.

The Chase Bag Company even produced a magazine—cringingly named "Bagalogy"—to tout the benefits of cotton bags in general and new cotton bags specifically. In one particular feature, "The Advantages of Cotton Bags for Flour," the editors claim bakers prefer new cotton bags, so do railroads for transportation, and oddly enough, so do millers because new bags ensure "safe deliveries."

Despite the vaguely religious language and self-serving claims about customer preferences, bag manufacturers soon stumbled on their most effective sales pitch, cementing the flour sack's enduring cultural legacy: Homemakers were repurposing the bags. They knew this, of course, but before the Great Depression, it simply didn't carry the same urgency for everyone involved. Families were as financially stressed as the bag makers. Everyone was trying to do more with less, and bag makers decided to go all-in on upcycling.[8] They wouldn't simply accept and ride the trend; they would encourage it.

---

7. Ask a Baby Boomer about refunds on glass bottles. Same general idea.

8. Bag makers didn't use that word, so far as we can tell. McCray's book features an upcycling icon on her cover, which is a nice touch.

As we've noted with Gingham Girl, cotton bags featured basic patterns for decades, so this wasn't a new innovation. Additionally, rural homemakers knew the basics of repurposing bags into clothing and did so occasionally. The industry would build on that. The 1930s saw an explosion of patterns—they're quite striking. New designs included, but were certainly not limited to, Scotty dogs, scenes from nursery rhymes, geometric designs, movie scenes ("Casablanca" is quite cute), and flowers of every shape and description.

New patterns were only the beginning. In *Feed Sacks: The Colorful History of the Frugal Fabric*, Linzee Kull McCray's illustrated guide captures the variety in vivid detail and documents the marketing strategy's evolution beyond simply providing more options.

It wasn't just patterns; it was colors, too. Bag manufacturers learned from their local distributors that many women wanted plain white bags. When asked why, they said the obvious: They dyed the sacks to get the desired color. (Not everyone wanted a gingham dress. Sometimes, you just feel...pink.) Predictably, manufacturers start dying bags at the factory to save women the trouble. They called them "tint sacks," and they would transform boring farm supply stores into the most colorful place on the prairie.

Obviously, the more uses for cotton sacks, the better, right? Absolutely. Manufacturers went beyond colors and started sharing *patterns*. In this sense, we mean die-cut patterns—in other words, how to create everything from dish towels (easy) to aprons (a little harder) and full dresses (challenging). Sometimes, those patterns were stenciled on the bag itself, but more often, bag catalogs and magazines would feature measurements and patterns depending on the desired sizes of the finished items. For example, a young girl's dress or boy's shirt might need one bag, whereas a woman's full dress might need two or three, depending on the style. (These women weren't wearing miniskirts.)

In some rural communities, you could tell who was part of the same family by the pattern of their clothing. They might be cut from (quite literally) the same cloth.[9] Many women insisted on it. In what would become a positive feedback loop, women would send their husbands to the feedlot with specific instructions on the sack pattern they wanted, and god help him if he didn't come home with it. When hubby failed, women would go themselves. It was often the first time women ever showed up at the feed store, and owners changed quickly to accommodate a much tougher negotiator. In a small way, the humble cotton sack transformed women's economic lives in rural communities. They were consumers in their own right and demanded to be treated as such. When they couldn't accommodate these new shoppers, feedlot owners would set up secondary markets for pattern swapping. People who needed empty sack patterns to finish a dress could exchange with others with different patterns.

Speaking of patterns, this trend also led to the development of washable inks. Why? Remember that although the pattern or color made great upcycled clothing, the bag's initial use needed to communicate its contents, manufacturer, and weight. No housewife wanted the Gold Medal Flour logo stamped on her rear end or "Pillsbury's Best" on her husband's crotch. This was probably the first time in history that the package was just as important as what it contained.

In response, bag manufacturers printed the colorful patterns and designs in permanent ink and the brand and content details in semipermanent ink—just durable enough to make it to the sales floor. They provided instructions in their magazines (and also in the same washable ink on the bag itself) on how to soak out the unwanted inks in a tub of water. This was just enough instruction for women already accustomed to washing clothes this way.[10]

As the Depression dragged on, rural women found more uses for repurposed cotton bags. Some were obvious—tablecloths, pillowcases, napkins, towels, and drapery—but some were much less so. If you stop into an antique store and find toys from this era, many dolls (human and animal models) were made from the

---

9. The photos in McCray's book are laugh out loud funny. Men's shirts sometimes sported cute little daisies. It was a...fun fashion era in the country. What's even funnier are the *underwear* made from flour sacks. In an echo of today's logowear, some men wore boxers with a big "Pillsbury's Best Feeds" on the crotch. One wonders if some couples enjoyed the double entendre?

10. Most didn't own a washing machine. This was bicep work. In those days, you didn't pick a fight with a rural woman. I'd still advise against it.

same material. Sometimes, you can even see echoes of the inks that didn't quite fully wash off. (Or, because it was a toy, it received less attention in the tub).

Women even found uses for the string that helped close the cotton bags. You may see needlework artwork in that same antique store or your rural grandmother's living room. The original patterns and ideas date from this era. "Home Sweet Home" was the original "Live, Laugh, Love." Those same bag companies often helped her buy her first sewing machine and trained her to use it.

The positive feedback loop of resourcefulness and innovation—the relationship between rural housewives and the cotton bag manufacturers who served them—is among the most powerful examples of American ingenuity during the Great Depression.

. . .

All that said, the relationship wasn't all Scotty dogs and pastel pink. Families needed time to mix metaphors and make lemonade out of lemons.

How do we know? Washable inks are a great example. Families were proud. Even as their farms (in some areas) were literally blowing away in giant dust storms, they didn't want people to know they couldn't afford new clothes. Sure, there has always been a culture of resourcefulness and DIY on the farm, but refashioning a fertilizer sack into a pair of men's briefs was assuredly *not* ironic. Bag manufacturers understood this, and their innovations helped women hide the fact they needed to sew flour sacks so their children would have something to wear as they grew. Even today, much of what we know about colorfast inks comes from this era. The clothes you're wearing right now are better in nearly every way because of these efforts.

However, what may have started as shame upcycled itself into fierce pride.

Over the coming years, rural America would embrace this spirit of ingenuity in a way the rest of the country couldn't quite match, and still doesn't fully understand. It should come as little surprise that the resourcefulness of rural America ramped into high gear during the war years that would follow the Great Depression. Not only could its agricultural engine feed the United States during World War II, but it also fed Great Britain, Russia, China, and everywhere else that needed feeding. The war effort was grandma's kitchen on a global scale.

To page through McCray's book is to step through the trademark style of the home in rural America. When Americans imagine the best of what makes us *us*, this is what we see.

By the 1950s, however, this specific form of reuse had reached its peak. Although a few thrifty hipsters repurpose cotton sacks today, it's ironic, not practical. By the 1960s, paper bags began to take over as the price of cotton skyrocketed and cheaper clothing could be made overseas.

The enduring legacy of these humble patterns shows up everywhere, however. Fans of the Great British Bake Off (or "Baking Show" on this side of the pond) worship at the "Gingham Alter" during the show's dreaded "Technical Challenge." The same patterns show up in both high and low fashion—for women *and men*—even today. (Walk into the men's clothing section and try *not* to find a plaid, check, or gingham pattern.) Ladies, how many of your clothes feature little flowers?

Even more impressive is how few people were involved in a trend with such far-reaching impact. It's estimated that during the Great Depression, about 3.5 million people (mostly women and children, but many men as well) wore clothing made from repurposed feed sacks. In a country of about 60 million women and children, that's only about five percent.

We can talk about improved agricultural technology and more sustainable soil management born in the aftermath of the Great Depression. Still, we cannot—and should not—discount the gritty resourcefulness of people who made clothing from feed sacks. That small group of people fed the world during the next war, drove lasting innovation in the fashion industry, and created our vision of down-home Americana.

6

THE FIRST FURBABIES

No one was moving.

It was the middle of the Alaskan wilderness, hundreds of miles from anywhere and hundreds of miles to nowhere else. Did we also mention that although it might have been summer, it was cold? Needless to say, the team didn't have time to sit and shiver, but Snookum was indignant.

Snookum was a three-quarter wolf/malamute hybrid (mostly wolf) who would not move if he didn't respect you. That's because Snookum was the pack leader and most certainly did not respect our new friend, Father Bernard Hubbard.[1]

"Better not touch him until you know him better," reminded a kindly Father McElmeel, Hubbard's local guide and on-the-ground companion. This was Hubbard's first time with a dog sled, and if Snookum wasn't moving, neither were Katmai, Nancy, Prince, Warrior, Toxin, Margey, Pete, Bill, or Daisy.

Let's pause for a moment and admire the variety of the names in this motley crew. It's sort of like a roll call of Santa's reindeer...if Santa were tripping on

---

1. Did Snookum harbor some deep resentment about his cutesy name? Was he compensating with extra aggressiveness? One has to consider that possibility.

shrooms. Unfortunately, Hubbard's thoughts regarding his sled dogs' names are not recorded in his first book, *Mush, You Malemutes!* Luckily for us, there are plenty of other details.[2]

But first, back to the dog sled. Sled dogs are, by design and necessity, high-energy. If you don't exercise them enough, they'll take out their aggression on anything in sight. Usually, that's each other. Not good. These are powerful animals that can do serious damage. That happened at least once on Hubbard's first voyage from Nulato to Nenana in Alaska—a distance of over 375 miles.[3] In other words, they needed to get moving.

Father "Mac" (as he was known in those parts) chided Hubbard for being a little wimpy. He encouraged Hubbard to speak up in a commanding tone. The dogs didn't understand spoken language; they understood how it was said. So, Hubbard spoke up. The dogs went. Hubbard stayed put. More specifically, Hubbard promptly fell off the back of the sled as the pack accelerated from zero to 30 miles per hour in a matter of a few seconds. (It's not recorded if Father Mac started laughing, though we must assume he did.) Hubbard neglected to have a strong grip on the sled before he shouted the *MUSH!* command which, as Father Mac explained to a seated Hubbard, was decidedly not a good idea.

Undaunted, Hubbard eventually got the knack of it, gaining the pack's respect and even building a special bond with Katmai. Her shaggy, mottled gray and white fur graces multiple photos in Hubbard's account. Little did she know it, but she'd be a national sensation, but more on that later. Right now, Hubbard needed to keep his head in the game. It was the summer of 1930. There was no GPS, few maps, and no rescue if anything went wrong.

. . .

Before meeting Santa's trippy-named dog sled team, Father Bernard Hubbard was a geology professor at Santa Clara University in California. Not content to sit

---

2. Yes, he spelled "malamutes" with an "e." I have a first edition signed copy I picked up from a used book store. I'm looking at it right now.

3. If you're curious, use Google Maps to locate these two specks of habitation in the Alaskan countryside. It doesn't *look* that far until you realize Google can't calculate driving directions *because even 100 years later,* there are no roads. The best way to get from that particular point A to point B is by airplane, when the weather allows, and dog sled, when it doesn't.

behind the pulpit and convince a worried congregation that everything would be alright after the stock market crash, Hubbard decided to take a more show-me approach. All the best geologists are field workers at heart, and Hubbard was no exception. In the coming years, his "sermons" would reach further than any church congregation.

During the summers of 1930, 1931, and 1932, Hubbard trekked all over Alaska, but it was his harrowing trip into the Aniakchak Caldera that made him famous. *Mush, You Malemutes!* is as captivating to read today as it was when it was first published in 1932.[4] Listen to some of the chapter titles: "Flying the Moon Craters of Alaska," "The Valley of 10,000 Smokes," and "The Heart of Fire Mountain."

In one of his most thrilling stories, Hubbard retells the story of his trip with a bush pilot high above the crater when the single-engine aircraft lost power. (Imagine the most terrifying rollercoaster you can imagine. Got it?) As the pilot struggled to restart the engines, one can imagine Hubbard wondering if he would meet God a little earlier than he had planned in the heart of a still-active volcano. Fortunately for the team—and us and posterity—the pilot knew enough to regain lift by diving *into* the fall, pulling up when he had regained enough airspeed to produce the necessary lift under the wings. By any measure, that's a good story, and the book is full of them.

Some readers might be thinking: Sure, Hubbard spun a good yarn, and the dogs were cute (everybody loves dogs), but is this just another clueless explorer trekking off to "discover" where other people already lived? As a matter of fact, no. Hubbard's stories about the Innuit people are some of the most compelling.

Let's touch on just one of many examples. Hubbard was fascinated with the concept of hospitality among the native people. As they explained to him, it's a self-interested kindness. For anyone traveling out on the ice, you're obligated to provide shelter, food, and rest. It's easy to experience a crisis on the barren plains, even for experienced travelers. A culture of hospitality means that when that

---

4. I was able to get a signed, first edition copy of the book for my personal library. It's faded, worn, and...just wonderful.

unlucky traveler is you, there's a better chance you'll survive to offer hospitality to someone else the next time.[5]

However, there was a catch.

Hubbard and his dog team would approach villages and, upon entering, would be immediately offered food and shelter. But it was a test. Can you guess what it was? Based on what we know so far, sure, you can. The correct response was to deny the request until the *dog team* was cared for—fed, sheltered, and given a place to rest. You might be hungry, but the dogs did all the work. They got you there. Maintaining their strength and stamina would be the only thing that would save *you* next time. The love of dogs is a theme that permeates Hubbard's book. It wasn't just that the dogs ensured his survival, though it was that. Hubbard, and the Innuit he met, loved them like family.

Who wouldn't want to hear more about that?

The folks at *The Saturday Evening Post* certainly thought so. They published a feature article about Hubbard's adventures after he returned from his first summer trip in 1930. The December 13, 1930 article featured the "Moon Crater" story, retelling the tale of Hubbard risking life and limb to descend into an active volcano caldera. The story fit perfectly with the times: Here was someone willing to risk it all, endure the hardships, and low and behold, he'd come out okay on the other side. This was the idea behind *Nothing to Fear but Fear Itself* years before Stuart Chase helped FDR immortalize that phrase in his first presidential inaugural address.

After reading that article, would you pay to hear Hubbard speak live? Sure, you would.

Billed as the "Glacier Priest," Hubbard's Alaska stories captivated sell-out lecture crowds throughout the United States during the Great Depression. Yes, Alaska had been a U.S. territory for a long time, but it wasn't really explored.[6]

---

5. That aspect of culture concurrently evolves in other resource-starved areas of the globe—desert communities, especially.

6. Alaska only became a territory in less than 20 years before in 1912. Before that, the land was (barely) organized as the "Department of Alaska" or the "District of Alaska."

Other than on a map, very few outsiders had ever visited the vast interior. It captured the imagination as wild, untouched, and brutal.

Hubbard wasn't the only explorer popular at about this time. Here are a few: Lincoln Ellsworth, Roald Amundsen, Richard Byrd, and Hubert Wilkins. Even now, however, how many of those names come to mind? Amundsen, perhaps? To be fair, even Hubbard doesn't quite enter the popular consciousness decades later, but he *was* unique. Hubbard leaned into the "Glacier Priest" persona better than his contemporaries, cultivated the media, and perfected the image of the prototype for today's television naturalist.

Although Hubbard was a geologist/naturalist, he conducted few (if any) scientific experiments. However, he was a masterful storyteller and collector of stories from those who lived there. For its part and for its own reasons, the National Park Service was keen to assist Hubbard in his storytelling, even if everything he documented wasn't quite accurate. More about that later.

What were the biggest applause lines in Hubbard's talk? Stories about the dogs and his bond with his pack. Here's a snapshot of one of the best. Hubbard would retell the story of Prince and Warrior. When the pack were puppies, distemper ravaged the litter, and most of them died. Prince fell deathly ill and was not expected to recover, but Warrior would have none of it. The older malamute would spend hours cleaning Prince's little eyes and muzzle to keep the worst of the "poison" at bay. After that, the two were inseparable and the hardest workers on the sled team. (If you're wondering, that's correct. There was not a dry eye in the house.)

Alaska might have drawn the crowds, but stories of Warrior and Prince, and especially the photos of Katmai nuzzling Hubbard to keep him warm on the vast frozen expanse, touched their hearts. Those rugged dogs would help transform America's relationship with pets.

. . .

Companion animals—or animals kept by humans for pleasure or companionship, better known as "pets"—go way back in American life. This draws the distinction between sheep, ducks, poultry, cattle, and hogs that people may have had a relationship with…which abruptly ended, often with a meal. That's also true of *working* dog breeds like sheep dogs, and cats kept for their mousing and ratting abilities. Yes, working animals were a bridge to the idea of pets, but no, keeping six-toed cats on naval ships isn't exactly what we're talking about.[7]

Speaking of bridges, although we read stories about pets as early as ancient Egypt, the boom in companion animal ownership began in Europe and America in the 1840s. Well, that's the best evidence we have. Pet ownership certainly began earlier; it's just that we didn't have a good way to learn about it until an unrelated invention helped show us: the camera.

As we've learned, the camera forces its owner to decide what they want to take a picture of. It's a window into our emotional lives in a way writing simply isn't—at least for most people. People usually write about *important* things. It's a rational, slow, deliberative process—even emotional subjects are treated in rational detail. By contrast, people take pictures of emotional subjects. Even in an era of clunky, fiddly, and expensive cameras, photos capture something important in the moment.

Early photographs clearly show that pets were emotional companions. Of course, 1800s-vintage cameras required subjects to sit still and hold a pose much longer than "point-and-shoot" models of the turn of the 20th century, so not all pets made good subjects. (Puppies and kittens are underrepresented in early photographs for obvious reasons.)

Economics played a role as well. Not only were early cameras expensive (until about 1900, when Kodak released the Brownie), but the resources needed to keep a companion animal were also in short supply. The resulting photos skew towards wealthy people with pure-bred fashionable dogs (and some cats, birds, and other menagerie of show animals). Did people of more modest means keep pets? Certainly, but we don't have good photographic evidence of that, and they probably skewed toward hybrid pets/workers—the previously mentioned herding dogs and mousing cats. However, we know there was an emotional con-

---

7. The trait is referred to as polydactylism. Cats with an extra toe were (or at least, thought to be) superior rat catchers on 19th century naval ships. You can still find their descendants at the Hemingway House in Key West, Florida. These days, they don't need to catch their dinner. They're shockingly well cared for.

nection beyond the rich and famous. How? Some of the most powerful evidence of that emotional connection are pet obituaries and dedicated pet cemeteries.[8]

Bottom line: Pets were a part of American life before the Great Depression. However, for most people, they weren't really family members in the way we think about them today. That transition happened during the 1930s, driven by (seemingly) unrelated trends. Let's unpack them.

. . .

The first was the rise of the automobile in American cities. A famous photo from 5th Street in New York City taken in 1900 shows a thoroughfare clogged with thoroughbreds. A photo of the same intersection taken 13 years later shows one (presumably terrified) horse in an ocean of automobiles.[9] The full transition from horse to car would be complete by the end of the 1920s. There was no going back, especially for veterinarians.

Until the early 1930s, the veterinary profession didn't treat dogs and cats, much less birds, reptiles, or other critters. If you worked in a rural area, you were a livestock vet. If you worked in the city, you were a horse vet. It was as simple as that. In the city, there were a lot of horses to care for because they were the primary means of transportation, so most vets enjoyed a thriving practice. Within the span of half a career, the automobile changed all that.

Cornell University maintains a spectacular archive of interviews with veterinary school graduates from that era. Between 2007 and 2010, Dr. Donald F. Smith, dean emeritus of the College of Veterinary Medicine, tracked down dozens of 1930s graduates to capture their firsthand accounts before they passed away. Reading (and, in a few cases, listening) to the transcripts of the interviews reveals a massive transition in the field. Veterinary schools, Cornell included, simply didn't teach students about canine and feline health. It wasn't a thing. (Universities are often a bit slow to catch on to rapid shifts in the needs of their students. This is

---

8. There are plenty of primary sources for these, but a warning: They are deeply sad. Don't search for them unless you want a good cry.

9. This photo may be found in the George Grantham Bain Collection.

no exception.[10]) Newly minted graduates, however, found themselves unable to earn a living in the city unless they could treat an animal other than a horse. Even rural vets were under stress as smaller livestock operations consolidated, but they could get by. The city vets were in real trouble.

As much as some horses were undoubtedly loved, by and large, horses were working animals. Vets of that era treated them as such—perhaps not quite like a mechanic would treat a car, but perhaps not that different either.

Dogs and cats were, literally and figuratively, different animals. Away from herds of sheep or rat-infested barns, their primary value was emotional. With more people moving from rural areas into cities (and especially suburbs), the number of companion animals skyrocketed in the back half of the 1920s. By the early 1930s, veterinarians would need to shift careers if they didn't find a way to shift their practice.

The first change was the veterinary office—in fact, that there was an office at all. Before dogs and cats, vets came to the horse; the horse didn't go to the vet. Now, vets needed to invest in real estate. Remember, these were the days before the doctor's office most of us humans would visit. (Doctors either worked in hospitals or came to your house.) Vets needed to develop a lot of this office design on their own. They figured out pretty quickly that they needed a nice waiting room—sometimes two, to split up dogs and cats and avoid brawls in the lobby—as well as dedicated exam rooms where the vet could treat an individual animal.

Speaking of doctors' offices, MDs had just started routinely wearing white coats, and vets had picked up the habit. (As you can imagine, wearing a white coat in an urban horse barn is not a good idea, except for your laundry service.) Did MDs look at vet offices to design their own clinics? Sort of like reciprocal learning? That's impossible to know, but one assumes many doctors had a dog at home, took her to the vet, and couldn't help but notice the practical office design.

---

10. In one respect, however, Cornell was ahead of its time. In just one example, Dr, Robert Ferber, who joined in 1936 and graduated in 1939, was part of a class including eight Jewish students, an African-American student from Tennessee, a Chinese national, and three women. This mix of races and genders was not unusual in veterinary schools. Many people found this field much more welcoming than the (human) medical profession.

More than simply a physical location to treat patients, vets needed to learn…well, how to be a vet for dogs and cats. They didn't learn it in school, so they started teaching themselves on the job. It helped that vaccinations for distemper and rabies became available in the early 1930s. Pet owners had a good reason to visit their new vet office, and vets had an easy initial sale to get them in the door. Once they were there, vets could offer some of the very first flea and tick collars. Anyone whose dog brought fleas into the house will know why they were such strong sellers.

The bigger observation is that people rarely dickered on the price. Even during the Great Depression, vets could charge reasonable rates. That tells us that a change had happened. People saw companion animals differently. They weren't simply animals any longer. They were becoming *family*.

...

The next major innovation was dedicated pet food. It's difficult to imagine now, but before the 1920s (especially the 1930s), there simply wasn't such a thing. Dogs and cats ate a combination of wild-caught food and table scraps. Anyone with outdoor cats knows how many songbirds they can catch. They rarely go hungry.

However, industrial food processing became much more sophisticated (and cheap) during the interwar years. That meant many new human food innovations. In addition, farm commodity prices collapsed in the early years of the Great Depression, and ingredients became very cheap. Price pressure also led meat processors to figure out what to do with the parts of the animal they used to throw away: organs, bones, and other edible but not human-palatable goodies. Every food processing company was looking for new sources of revenue, and grinding "miscellaneous" ingredients into commercial pet food was a no-brainer.

The first processed dog food, Ken-L-Ration, debuted in the mid-1920s. However, it was canned, reasonably expensive, and found only a limited audience. The real innovation was shelf-stable dry dog food—otherwise known as "cubes" or "kibble." Not only was it a cheaper option at a time when that was a big deal for most people, but it also took advantage of a unique feature of manufacturing supply chains most people outside the industry don't know about.

The idea was something called (and still called) co-packaging, invented to take advantage of otherwise idle production equipment. Setting aside all the business language, the concept is easy to understand. Here's how it works. Imagine a processing factory that can dehydrate ingredients into some sort of kibble. If that factory produces dog food for only one brand, the amount sold probably won't keep the equipment running at maximum efficiency. Equipment that's not making kibble is costing the owner money. Now imagine that the same factory could produce kibble for several brands. It's not a stretch of the imagination. The base process is the same. The only differences are the ingredients, flavors, shape of the kibble, and most importantly, the design of the package. That's the part the end consumer cares about.

(By the way, this isn't only applicable to dog and cat foods. Pretty much everything you buy at the grocery store fits this model. For example, if you buy the generic version of ketchup, you're probably getting one made on the same line—with only slightly different flavors—as the name-brand ketchup.)

The advantages are clear.

Production equipment is expensive, quality control is challenging, and ingredient sourcing can be a nightmare. These are specialist skills that, frankly, the end consumer can't see, doesn't understand, and pays little attention to.[11] These skills are largely separate from mass marketing tasks: branding, packaging, store placement, pricing, and advertising. By centralizing (and sometimes outsourcing) production, brands could focus on the latter set of skills instead of the former.

The pet food industry was one of the first to take advantage of this arrangement because although pets were becoming more emotionally attached to the family, they couldn't express their preferences in quite the same way a human could.

According to *Pets in America: A History*, historian Katherine C. Grier found that only 12 pet food plants produced over 221 canned food brands—or over 18 per processing factory. That's impressive today; it was even more so in the 1930s.

---

11. I know what you're thinking: People care about where their food comes from. Sure, that's true for a small percentage of people, but not *most* people. In Marketing 101, we learn not to confuse our personal preferences with the market as a whole. Want to know how we know that? Pet food factories aren't always dedicated to making pet food exclusively. The same equipment can process human food as well, and often does.

However, it wasn't just dedicated pet food specialists who got into this game. All food processors were under pressure to find new revenue streams. One in particular—Carnation (yes, the milk products company)—began experimenting with unused capacity in the early 1930s and invented the first true, dehydrated kibble in 1936. They named it "Friskies" and sold it as a "cube-type food that is a complete ration for dogs."[12]

This new kibble had obvious advantages. It was cheap. It was shelf-stable and would last months. It did not need refrigeration. (Although refrigerator adoption grew quickly in the 1930s, most people still didn't have one in 1936.) In an age where table scraps would be saved for the next (human) meal, this new food didn't eat into the people-food budget. Finally, it was ready to eat with no rehydration or other prep. When your family's work schedule amounted to "whatever work you could get, whenever you could get it," easy-to-prepare meals made sense for you *and* your pets.

Still, introducing any new food isn't easy, and pet food is no exception. Who would Carnation get to evangelize its new food?

You can guess the answer, can't you?

...

A feature in the 1936 issue of *The Carnation* magazine pictures a smiling Hubbard snuggling Katmai next to a 10-pound bag of Friskies in the wilds of Alaska. Whether high-energy Katmai was enticed to sit still by discipline or by hopes of tearing into the bag can only be supposed. If kibble was good enough for Hubbard's sled dogs, it was certainly good enough for yours.

What we do know is that sales of kibble-style pet foods exploded afterward. What we don't know is precisely why. Did you notice what's missing from our stories so far? Direct evidence. Only in the 1970s did we start to survey Americans about their opinions and behaviors around pet ownership. We know that the transition from "companion animal" to "family member" was well-entrenched by that point, but we couldn't know (from those data) when it started. We're

---

12. It wouldn't be until much later that veterinary nutritionists puzzled out the obvious: Dogs and cats are different animals. The formulations diverged from that point, but owners fed the first version of Friskies to both dogs and cats. It probably served neither very well.

making the case here that this transition happened during the Great Depression, and so far, we've only provided what lawyers would call circumstantial evidence.

That said, what we *have* presented nearly proves our case. It's time to pile on the evidence. Any one piece of data wouldn't be enough, but taken together, they paint a picture of a mass shift in consumer psychology.

Let's continue our case with the first canine celebrity: Rin Tin Tin. This lovable German Shepard was charismatic enough to overcome America's general distaste for all things Kaiser after World War I. The original Rin Tin Tin got his start mouthing into the void in silent films of the 1920s, but it was his trademark bark on the radio of the 1930s that solidified his claim to fame.

(A brief pause to highlight the person who did the sound effects for the show—the perfectly named Bob Barker. Yeah, *that* Bob Barker. He'll be back later in this episode.)

As the first true non-human celebrity, Rin Tin Tin's radio programs were so successful that his puppies, grand puppies, and great-grand puppies all went on to their own careers, often under the same name.

Speaking of celebrity canines, Disney's 1955 *Lady and the Tramp* retells a story from the 1930s about a down-on-his-luck mutt who finds success through a combination of grit, resilience, and clever schemes.[13] He became the master of his fate. It was the perfect allegory of the Great Depression. Parents who took their children to see this movie in the 50s were no strangers to Tramp's plight. His story resonated with them. They made it through those years the same way.

Consider the popularization of (completely unnecessary) pet clothing. In a move that Coco Chanel or Madeleine Vionnet would have approved, dog fashion became chic. And not just clothes, furniture too. In the 1930s, for the first time, you could buy dog bowls, pet beds, and cat scratching posts that matched your decor. Of course, that meant pet toys, too. They simply didn't appear in large numbers before the Great Depression, but after that, people couldn't get enough of them. Even Santa got into the act. A little something for the family pet (or pets) found its way down from the chimney and under the Christmas tree every

---

13. The pound features heavily as the place-which-shall-not-be-visited. Today, we have "humane societies." There was no such thing then, and very few were "humane." Tramp's fear of the pound was justified.

December. All this supposed frivolity at a time when people were chronically worried about money.

The Great Depression was also the first time some dogs returned to working status, albeit in a completely new way. Dorothy Harrison Eustis founded the first seeing-eye dog training school in New Jersey in 1929 and, by 1933, was exporting those methods to Great Britain and the rest of the world.[14]

Despite all that solid evidence, the clincher is the data from the American Society for the Prevention of Cruelty to Animals (ASPCA). They've tracked surrenders to shelters since the turn of the last century. It's not perfect and admittedly a bit self-serving, but it's the best we have.

Here's what they found. As you might guess, as people moved to cities and suburbs, the overall number of companion animals increased, as did the number of animals surrendered to shelters. (In those days, that was usually a death sentence.) One would expect that during the Great Depression, the number of surrenders would spike. It did not. In fact, it's pretty much the opposite of what happened. While the number of cats surrendered increased slightly in the early part of the decade before trending back down, the number of dogs surrendered decreased.

The American family had a new member.

...

It would take decades for the pet products industry to fully mature. Differentiated food for cats and dogs didn't hit the market until after the Second World War. Other exotic pets didn't become popular until the counterculture 1960s, and even then, iguanas and parrots never quite caught on the same way dogs and cats did.

By the 1970s, not only were marketers beginning to survey American attitudes towards pets, but surrenders dropped sharply as well. In retrospect, much of that decline was due to the reminders from one man on one very popular television game show. From 1979 to his last appearance on *The Price is Right*, the host would end each show with this:

---

14. This is so much more to know about Eustis. She was inducted into the National Women's Hall of Fame in 2011, more than a half century after her death. Yet by all accounts, she has yet to have any dog lover pick up the task of writing her biography. Maybe that will be you?

Bob Barker reminding you: Help control the pet population. Have your pets spayed or neutered. Goodbye, everybody!

The number of unwanted pets plummeted, and at the same time, the number of wanted pets surged. In 2023, 65 million households included at least one dog, 46 million included at least one cat, and most included more than one.[15]

According to the American Pet Products Association, who should know, Americans spent $138.8 billion (yes, *billion*) on their pets in 2023, up 11 percent from just the prior year. The trend shows no sign of slowing down. Pets are the biggest single addition to American family life in the past century. Especially notable is that as families became smaller from a human perspective, they've grown from an animal perspective. We seem to be redefining what family means; they don't all need to be humans.

It's something the Glacier Priest would have understood and approved of. For his part, Bernard Hubbard's legacy is more mixed. When you read about him today from the National Park Service…well, have a read for yourself:

> [Hubbard is] exactly the kind of companion you would want on a camping trip into the Aniakchak Crater, for he was passionate, optimistic, and fun. Hubbard personified our need for wonder, our excitement for mysteries, and our desire for heroes. He brilliantly played upon our need to believe that blank spaces still existed on our blue and green spinning sphere. Perhaps he understood that sometimes fiction fills our societal needs as significantly as fact.

That's what we call damning with faint praise.

The NPS was thrilled to have Hubbard trekking around the Alaskan wilderness in the 1930s and 1940s. It helped them get National Park and National

---

15. In 2023, there were about 127 million "households" in the United States, which makes counting like this a bit confusing. That said, it's a lot of pets. If you're curious, Gen Z are the most adventurous. They are more than three times as likely to keep a turtle, rabbit, or bird.

Monument status secured in Congress for huge areas of Alaska. But once that was done, they seemed done with him. Revisionist articles published since then aren't exactly more flattering than what you've already read. It's probably a combination of his religious activities and the archaic language he used, which doesn't quite fit today's zeitgeist. When you read his books, you'll see some cringy passages, but you'll also read about the tremendous respect he had for the Indigenous people and his awe at the unbroken wildness of the place.

It seems most of the criticism comes from the fact Hubbard wasn't doing *science*; he was doing *marketing*. He was the first prototype of the nature popularizer—the same path David Attenborough, Steve Irwin, and Jane Goodall walked down in the following decades. "Serious" scientists have a love/hate relationship with these types. On one hand, they love the attention (and funding) that comes with increased awareness. On the other hand, they wish people would love nature for the reasons *they* love it.

They might be right, but they're missing the point. David Attenborough isn't doing hard science on his uncountable nature programs.[16] Sharing his passion for the natural world makes the average person care about a place and animals they will (probably) never see. Once people have an emotional connection, they're more likely to choose to protect and preserve it. It's a conservation powerful tool, even if it can irritate purists.

However, none of these trends in pet ownership or explanations of Hubbard's legacy tell us why this transition occurred during the Great Depression.

For that, we need to stop paying attention to the humans and remember the real stars of the show: Katmai, Snookum, Warrior, Bill, and the rest of Hubbard's menagerie of sled dogs—as well as untold millions of dogs and cats who entered our homes during one of the most stressful periods in American life. When you think about how pets are probably the best cure for human anxiety, it finally makes sense.

In the worst years of the Great Depression, our dogs and cats nuzzled up, wagged their tails, purred softly, and reminded us that everything would be okay.

---

16. Wikipedia says 148. That seems low.

THE FIRST WONDER DRUG

Parents in Tulsa could handle a hot summer. They weren't prepared for what happened next.

In September 1937, summer was hanging on tight in Oklahoma. Daily highs routinely peaked above 100 degrees Fahrenheit, reaching a scorching 111 twice in August. Oh, and did we mention it had been raining as well?[1] Mix triple-digit temperatures and high humidity in that region, and...well, you get a sense of what it might be like to live in the devil's armpit.

September wasn't looking much different until the 25th. Then the weather changed. 90s and 100s became 60s and 70s overnight.

Perhaps it was that abrupt shift in temperature that triggered a wave of infections in school-aged children. Perhaps it was simply kids doing what kids do when they head back to school. Either way, parents reached for a new elixir they'd just read about in *Time* magazine. We'll get to the specifics soon enough, but for now, it's enough to know that this medicine could work wonders. Or so they

---

1. The National Weather Service maintains daily weather records going back over 100 years in most locations. Our tax dollars at work. That's how we can be so sure it was genuinely terrible.

heard. Many in Tulsa sought out Dr. Archie Calhoun to get their medicine. They trusted him. They had every reason to.

A few days into treatment, however, and this elixir didn't give anyone the miracle they were looking for.

First, children stopped urinating. That's not so unusual. Sore throats make drinking anything painful, and strep throat can be especially bad. No one was worried just yet. Unfortunately, that fluid had to go somewhere, and parents noticed their children's forearms, calves, hands, and feet starting to swell. That's called "edema," and it's concerning. They called Dr. Calhoun and brought their children back to see him. He couldn't explain it either. What was going on?

Then things took a turn for the worse.

The pain came next. It was bad. It was all over. All kids are a bit lethargic when they're sick, but this was different. They couldn't get out of bed. They didn't know where—or sometimes, who—they were. Dr. Calhoun rushed back. Now, in addition to excruciating, generalized pain, these children were experiencing irregular heartbeats and chest pain. Their kidneys were shutting down.[2]

Within 21 days, all of the patients Dr. Calhoun prescribed this new elixir were dead. That total included five children as well as one of his best friends.

And it wasn't just Dr. Calhoun's patients in Tulsa. The same horror movie played out throughout the southern United States, sending reports flooding into the understaffed, overworked, and underpowered Food and Drug Administration.

Something was very, very wrong.

. . .

Suspicion, as you might expect, focused almost immediately on the manufacturer of this particular elixir: S.E. Massengill Co.[3]

Earlier that summer, an observant salesperson in Bristol, Tennessee, reported to company headquarters that he was seeing demand from doctors for a liquid

---

[2]. This list of symptoms of kidney failure come from the Mayo Clinic, but they are also dutifully recorded in the heartbreaking primary sources.

[3]. Yes, this is the same company best known (today) for feminine hygiene products. Founded in 1897, this family-run company made the move from wholesaling to manufacturing its own products before the ill-fated 1937 formulation we're discussing here. GlaxoSmithKline now owns the Massengill brand.

version of this new substance rather than the hard-to-take powdered form, especially for pediatric patients. Liquid medicines are easier for children to take, and that's especially true of infants. The competition was fierce (we'll get to that soon enough as well), and the company didn't have any time to lose to take advantage of the opportunity for increased sales during the upcoming 1937 cold and flu season.

Staff chemist Harold Cole Watkins was tasked with finding a way to dissolve the stubborn powder in liquid. (Before you ask, yes, they tried water first. Most things dissolve in water; that's what makes it so elemental to our existence. It didn't work here.) After weeks of feverish work, Watkins had his answer: diethylene glycol. With a few tweaks for color, flavor, and smell, Massengill executives called it good, bottled it, labeled it, and shipped it.

(Let's pause here to make an important public service announcement. Diethylene glycol is an antifreeze in the same chemical family as the stuff you put in your car's radiator. It also forms the sweet-smelling puddles in the driveway you don't let your dog drink. It will kill them. It will kill you, too. Do. Not. Drink. It.)

In the company's defense, Massengill probably didn't know that. How could they? They didn't test it. No one else would have, and they were not required to do so. Like most elixirs and patent medicines of earlier decades, they were mostly harmless (or mixtures of alcohol). That's technically what the word "elixir" refers to: a mixture with alcohol as the base ingredient.[4] Massengill swapped alcohol for diethylene glycol. What was the worst that could happen? It was not unreasonable. It was unethical, maybe, but not unheard of based on pharmaceutical practices of the day.

However, the organic chemists at the FDA weren't fooled, and they knew how dangerous that swap could be.

Most of the memos from that era are dense and technical. For clarity, let's invent a simple Q&A-style dialog to help you get the gist of the internal conversation between FDA officials and executives at Massengill:

---

4. In case you're wondering, most patent medicines before the 1930s did *not* contain the radium or cocaine they claimed to. The reason wasn't that people didn't think they had benefits but that radium and cocaine were expensive. For those formulations that did (often purchased by wealthier people), this era is full of stories of people whose faces melted away from tumors from their daily dose of radium.

Q: How many shipments went out?

A: 633.

Q: Did we hear that correctly? Say again. 633?

A: 633. Correct.

Q: Where did you send them?

A: All over the country.

Q: But where, specifically?

A: We're not entirely sure. Each salesperson has their own customer list and they aren't keen to share them, even with us.

Q: Do you mean you have no idea where this product is right now?

A: Correct.

[Expletive deleted.]

. . .

With nearly 100 years of hindsight, it's easy to wonder what on earth would convince parents to give their children some untested potion from a company better known for feminine hygiene products.

Simple. They had every reason to believe it would work. *It had worked*. In fact, it was the first elixir that actually did what it claimed to do. To understand why this was so transformative, we must take a brief step back to the world before the tragedy in Tulsa.

In his 2007 book *The Demon Under the Microscope*, historian Thomas Hager reminds today's readers that the world was largely modern by the early 1930s—we drove cars, visited supermarkets, drove groceries to our suburban homes, stored them safely in our refrigerators, and relaxed in front of the radio. Most of us would recognize that world, with one notable exception: medical care.

Physicians of the early 1930s weren't the respected arbiters of health information they are today. They were more akin to mechanics working on cars, though arguably less successful. If you broke an arm, they could set it properly. They had largely given up barbaric (and ineffective) processes like bloodletting. They routinely washed their hands.[5]

---

5. You have no idea how much resistance there was to hand washing. If you want to know more, check out *The Hand Book: Surviving in a Germ-Filled World*, by Miryam Wahrman.

However, although researchers had deduced the cause of many infections (especially bacterial and parasitic infections, and even some viral infections), they were largely powerless to do anything about them. If you caught a cold, it ran its course...or it ran *your* course. Doctors might be able to offer some basic comfort—rest, fluids, and cool baths for fevers—but they couldn't do much more, and people knew it. Everyone was at risk from what we today would consider minor infections. Children were especially vulnerable. Some estimates show that more than half of all children in that era may not have reached their fifth birthday. While those data seem tragic, they are likely not accurate. But whether the actual number is one in five or one in two—or somewhere in between—a parent's terror at the sound of their child's cough or fever was real.

That's not to say the medical profession had made *no* progress before the 1930s.

Although the actual cause of cholera would not be identified for decades, John Snow and Henry Whitehead didn't need to know the biology of *Vibrio cholerae* to deduce—through tracking deaths on a map—that the disease was related to contaminated drinking water from raw sewage dumped into the River Thames upstream of Victorian-era London.[6]

Although doctors didn't know why the tropics were so dangerous to health, they deduced that mosquitos carried malaria and yellow fever (among other things). By draining standing water near work zones along the Panama Canal route and depriving the little bloodsuckers of their breeding pools, the Americans could succeed where the French had failed.

Speaking of tropical diseases, doctors could treat people with malaria (though not yellow fever) with chloroquine phosphate, the first effective medication that inhibited the parasite's lifecycle. (That malaria was caused by a parasite wouldn't be completely understood until much later.)

Do you have a headache? You could take acetylsalicylic acid, also known as Aspirin. It was developed by Bayer AG, a chemical and dye company in Germany.

So, not nothing. But not great for most people.

---

6. The best book on this subject is *The Ghost Map: The Story of London's Most Terrifying Epidemic—and How it Changed Science, Cities and the Modern World*, by Steven Berlin Johnson.

Researchers in the 1930s understood germs well enough to know that part of the key to success was preventing them from invading patients in the first place. If they could kill microbes on surfaces, surgical equipment, and hands, they could dramatically reduce the number of people who became infected. This insight led to the first disinfectants and antiseptics.[7] They were preventative, not curative, but a vast improvement. Moreover, they led researchers to envision a scenario where they could kill microbes once they entered the body.

The issue was that what worked *in vitro* (outside the body) did not necessarily work *in vivo* (inside the body). To dispense with the Latin and put the difference in real terms, just because an antiseptic or disinfectant killed microbes on a surface didn't mean it would work the same way inside a living system. Well, it probably would work, but you wouldn't want to do it. It's the reason you wouldn't drink bleach to cure an infection. It would kill the microbes, sure, but it would also kill all the living, healthy cells around it...and you. It's like burning down the house to kill the mosquito in your bedroom. Curing the disease by killing the patient isn't a good solution. What was needed were chemicals that would selectively target the pathogen while leaving normal body cells alone. What was needed was an *antibiotic*.

However, knowing what you need and getting it are two different things.

...

The real breakthrough didn't come from the pharmaceutical industry because there was no pharmaceutical industry to speak of. There were *chemical* industries, and the most prominent of those were in Germany in the 1930s.

Surprised? You shouldn't be. In 1909, German chemists at BASF figured out how to extract nitrogen from the atmosphere. (Remember from your 8th-grade science class that the air we breathe is mostly nitrogen, not oxygen.) This was a bigger deal for agriculture than you might think. Farmers, you can skip this part. City folk, listen up.

For thousands of years—since the birth of agriculture in the prehistoric era—farmers had (slowly) figured out that the soil needs to recover periodically;

---

7. Wondering about the difference? Disinfectants kill microbes on non-living surfaces, like table tops, door handles, and surgical equipment. Antiseptics kill microbes on living surfaces, like hands and faces. Don't confuse the two.

otherwise, yields drop. No one knew why, but farmers are a practical bunch, and they would allow fields to rotate and remain fallow for one year in three, or they would plant certain crops (like sunflowers or radishes) that would somehow recharge the land and make it productive again. No one knew why.

That all changed in the 1800s when scientists figured out the key missing ingredient in the soil that resulted from overfarming: nitrogen. If you replenish it, you could avoid fallow fields and increase production. In fact, when farmers started spreading nitrogen-rich guano (bird and bat droppings) on their fields, they not only didn't need to leave a field fallow, but they also increased production everywhere else. It was a stunning improvement that made modern population growth possible. Without nitrogen, there is no modern agriculture. Most of us would starve.

Some islands where birds roost are, quite literally, built from bird poop. Mining, harvesting, and transporting guano were critical industries of that era and made the islands in vast, empty oceanic expanses very interesting to European colonization. (If you wonder why some speck of land in the middle of the ocean was so fought over, now you know.) But it wouldn't last. Even islands literally made of bird droppings couldn't sustain agriculture for long, and the price was starting to go up. Now that people had tasted success (ick), there was a massive opportunity to synthesize nitrogen.

BASF was the first to figure it out and commercialize agricultural nitrogen (in ammonia form) not extracted from bird poo. That breakthrough created the industrial expertise to spawn an entire chemical industry in Germany.

It was that industry, you may recall, that gave the world Aspirin by the turn of the 20th century. The German chemical giants had the expertise, money, and moxie to ask the bigger question: What's next? The answer was obvious: an antiseptic that worked *inside* the body only on the targeted pathogen without (unduly) harming surrounding tissues or systems. Whatever company could answer that question would not only become fabulously wealthy, and not only save millions of lives, but would also create a strategic geopolitical advantage for its home country. Remember, this was an era of intense global competition and tense international relations. In stark terms, whoever had antibiotics would likely win the next global war.

Hager retells the breakthrough story of chemical company I.G. Farben—most famous until that point for making dyes for clothing—and Gerhard Domagk—most famous until that point for a bullet knocking off his helmet in World War I.[8] (A good ring to the head was lucky. His 11 friends from school weren't as lucky.) It was the late 1920s, and the newly minted Dr. Domagk found himself trying to test I.G. Farben's massive stockpile of dyes to see if any would have a therapeutic effect.

And when we say stockpile, we mean literally thousands of combinations. Like most laboratory work, it was years and years of drudgery and failure. Researchers are a special breed—a bit different from the rest of us—and we're lucky Domagk was one of them. After years of failure, the breakthrough finally came with an orange-red dye. Following his standard protocol, he conducted his experiment using lab rats. Both groups received the most virulent strain of streptococcal bacteria he could find. One group received treatment with the dye. The other group did not. Why strep? For one, it was (and is) very common. If something worked on strep, there were a lot of patients who could benefit…and needless to say, a big potential market for I.G. Farben. But the more important clinical reason is that the bacteria infected both rats and humans. If it worked (or did not work) in rats, it had a better chance of working in humans. It's not a sure thing, but it's a better chance.

That said, Domagk wasn't confident in this trial. And no, it wasn't simply because hundreds had already failed. It was because this dye had no effect on strep *outside* the body. In other words, if you mixed this orange-red dye with strep bacteria in a test tube, you'd get orange-red colored strep that can still kill you.

But this time was different.

The control group rats died. Fast. Just like humans did.

The treatment group's skin turned orange-red. And they all lived.

Oh. My. God.

It worked.

---

8. The book dives into the scientific detail. It's fascinating and well-written, even for the layperson, but those details aren't relevant to the story here. If you're interested, Hager's book is the best treatment of this subject. You'll enjoy it.

Domagk didn't know why sample KL487 worked—it just worked. Perhaps the dye somehow "found" and "stained" the bacteria and prevented it from replicating in the body? (Remember, this was a chemical company. It must have something to do with the dye, right?) Whatever the causal mechanism, it was a miracle. No one had ever seen anything like it. There must be something about how the body metabolized the dye that made it effective because, remember, it did not work in a test tube. After years of crushing failure, the feeling of joy, disbelief, and anticipation must have been overwhelming. However, Domagk was a good scientist. He had to be sure. More experiments were needed. Bigger samples. So many questions. However, there was no question more urgent than this one: Would this new treatment work in human patients?

What did researchers do in that era when they wanted the answer to that question? They didn't design and conduct a rigorous clinical trial. They tested it on a real person. In this case, a local doctor was struggling to treat a baby suffering from what, at the time, was a leading killer of newborns: childbed fever—usually a nasty strep infection. KL487 worked. Researchers in Great Britain caught wind of the discovery in scientific journals. A group of doctors there were trying to save 26 women fighting infections immediately after childbirth. They were all hours from death. KL487 worked there, too. They were clearly onto something.

Over the coming months, Domagk and his team would refine KL487 with hundreds of new versions. On Christmas Day, 1932, I.G. Farben filed its patent for KL730—a gift to the world.[9] It's scientific name was para-amino-benzine-sulfanilamide, or "sulfa" for short.

The I.G. Farben marketing department did better, naming the new wonder drug "Prontosil"—the root word "pronto" implying that the drug acted fast. Although that was true, they might have been the first marketing department in the history of marketing anywhere that *undersold* its product.

---

9. The evidence indicates the actual date wasn't precisely December 25, but it made for a great story, and I.G. Farben didn't publicly correct the record. That's a good example of Marketing 101 right there.

Prontosil—a sulfa compound derived from chemical dyes—was the first antibiotic.[10]

. . .

With nearly 100 years of experience with antibiotics, it's a bit difficult to understand what this meant to people at the time.

Finally, there was a legitimate treatment for diseases that sickened and killed people throughout history. We could explore hundreds, thousands, millions of painful narratives, but no two stories—exactly 12 years apart, both featuring sons of presidents—better help us see the transformation in public psychology at play.

Let's begin in 1924 on the lawn of the Calvin Coolidge White House. Coolidge's son Calvin Jr. loved to play tennis on the grounds and, like most strapping young teenagers, had played all day. He received a small blister on one toe, which was just part of the sport. It was nothing to worry about. All teens are invincible, aren't they?

By that evening, someone was wrong. Calvin Jr. began to feel unwell. By the next day, his fever had spiked. Doctors were brought in—the best ones they could find. They even admitted him to the Walter Reed Army Medical Center. This was the White House and the president's son, after all. However, despite the best care available, doctors could do little except bear witness as Calvin Jr. became sicker and sicker. He had blood poisoning, probably from staph bacteria entering the minor blister site. He was dead within a week.

The death shocked the country, but perhaps no one more than his parents and perhaps no one more singularly than his father. Coolidge often gets ribbed for his "silent" persona. He's often criticized for his hands-off approach during the raucous 1920s when the country probably could have used a bit more adult supervision. However, it's funny how we forget that all these people are human and that Coolidge never emotionally recovered. His final years in office were racked with grief. He had to walk by those tennis courts every day on the way to his desk. Think about that.

---

10. Okay, if we're going to get technical, sulfas are *not* antibiotics because they are not biological, they're chemically synthesized. Penicillin, by contrast, is a true antibiotic. Sulfas are referred to as "pro drugs" or chemotherapy. For the purposes of the consumer reaction, that distinction doesn't matter.

The pain, like so many other mothers and fathers throughout history, was without equal, though (sadly) not unusual.

Let's fast-forward 12 years and meet another presidential son. This time, it was Franklin Roosevelt's son, Franklin Jr. (Yes, another "junior." That was a bigger thing in those days. It reminds us to read history carefully.)

The stories are so eerily similar that they might have been a replay. It wasn't tennis this time; it was a sinus infection and sore throat, but the details hardly mattered. Franklin Jr.'s condition deteriorated along a similar path to Calvin Jr.'s more than a decade before. If the infection reached his bloodstream, he was a goner.

But Franklin Jr. would catch a break.

Doctors Perrin H. Long and Eleanor A. Bliss of Johns Hopkins Hospital in Maryland read obscure German medical journals. They learned about a possible new treatment under the trade name Prontosil. The rest of the American medical establishment largely dismissed the German results out of hand—what did a dye manufacturer know about medicine? It wasn't an unreasonable question. Despite that, in contrast to their colleagues, Long and Bliss decided to test it themselves. In 1936, they started treating very sick patients with the new drug (as much as they could get their hands on) and saw the same miraculous results.

It was from them that Franklin Jr.'s doctor learned about Prontosil. It was Elenor Roosevelt who pushed him to use it. And it was that drug that saved her son's life.[11]

The story was so miraculous that it appeared in the December 28, 1936 issue of *Time* magazine. They called it "the medical discovery of the decade."

For once, *Time* was underselling it.

The impact and importance wasn't lost on anyone.

What came next was the sulfa craze.

. . .

---

11. Dr. George Loring Tobey Jr, described colorfully by *Time* magazine as "a fashionable and crackerjack Boston ear, nose & throat specialist" had no idea how much Prontosil to administer. He guessed...probably on the high side. Franklin Jr turned red, and had a *very* long recovery, but he made it.

By this point in the story, you probably have a couple of questions. First, when you take antibiotics today, you don't turn red. Or blue. Or green. Or anything else. (Unless you've got a nasty allergic reaction. If you do, call 911.) And second, who the heck is this Domagk guy? When you read the chapter title, you probably thought we were going to talk about Scottish scientist Alexander Fleming and penicillin.[12]

Both questions are related, so let's tackle them in order.

If you remember, I.G. Farben was a chemical dye company. After the global release of Prontosil, its researchers began working to find additional dyes that might be suitable for other clinical applications. Their progress was, to put it mildly...frustrating.

The worst part from a business perspective was that the dye didn't seem to matter. The formulation worked whenever a dye was paired with a sulfinamide molecule chain. Once ingested, the body would break apart the molecule. The sulfa would do the infection control part (at least, on certain bacteria, and through mechanisms we don't need to describe here), and the dye would turn your skin a funny color.

That would be fine if the sulfinamide molecule were patentable on its own. It was not. Sulfinamide had been a well-known chemical for decades, but no one had thought to use it for this purpose.

Before you're tempted to think that greedy capitalists at I.G. Farben discovered the truth and simply refused to share that knowledge to keep their monopoly, that's not quite how it happened. First off, that's hindsight. No one knew that it was sulfinamide and not the dye (or some combination of the two) that was the secret to its effectiveness. Remember, Domagk and his team tried literally thousands of combinations over several years. Second, Domagk's team was looking for something in its portfolio of chemicals to use for another purpose. That mindset likely slowed the realization that it wasn't the dye at all—when you have a bunch of nails, everything looks like a hammer. Third, that's not how science works. Scientists share with other scientists to validate their work. That's not to

---

12. If you ask ChatGPT 3.5 to give you the first commercially available antibiotic, it will get this answer technically correct (sulfa is not a true antibiotic) but substantively wrong. Let's correct the record, shall we?

say they're not egotistical; it just means that others get to see what you've done. And that's where we need to talk about the geopolitics of the late 1930s.

Don't worry. The history lesson will be brief and relevant. Prontosil, by everyone's reckoning in the late 1930s, would be a blockbuster. If a German company—that had just decided to ally itself with the Nazi party—was the only one that could make it, that was a bit of a problem for everyone else. No one had any illusions that Hitler and his gang would be gracious on the world stage. And let's not forget national pride. A private company from Germany had scooped French scientists at the Pasteur Institute; it should be noted that the two countries weren't exactly friendly after the last war.

However, French commercial interests didn't limit their mindset. Their scientists simply wanted to know how it worked. They eventually discovered that the active ingredient was sulfa, not the dye. With one scientific paper, the Pasteur Institute opened the floodgates to anyone and everyone who wanted to market sulfa.

As you might guess, after an initial phase during which several German curse words were likely to have been spoken, I.G. Farben began marketing "White Prontosil"—basically, plain sulfa—to leverage publicity surrounding its brand name, but no one was fooled. Branding is what Americans do better than anyone else in the world. And because anyone could package and sell it, lots of companies did, very quickly, to meet the demand.

That's the crux of why an American company (it could have been anyone, but it happened to be Massengill) decided to mix sulfinamide with antifreeze to make it more palatable for kids to drink. We'll get to the continued fallout soon enough, but let's answer our second question. What about penicillin?

You may have learned that Fleming discovered penicillin growing on a set of bacterial cultures he accidentally left out too long in 1928. The resulting penicillin mold ate the bacteria mercilessly. Huh, Fleming thought. Maybe there's a use for this mold? Remember, however, that the prevailing thinking at the time was disinfecting surfaces and skin, not antibiotics humans would ingest. He published a paper in 1929 that garnered little interest from the scientific community. Moreover, penicillin didn't grow *that* easily, especially in commercially viable quantities.

It wasn't until 1938, after the world had seen what sulfa could do, that researchers took another look at Fleming's work to see if penicillin worked inside the body and not just on surfaces. And it wasn't until the outbreak of World War II that scientists accelerated their efforts. Since the beginning of human warfare, most soldiers have died from infection, not battlefield injuries. Sulfa drugs were beginning to change that equation, but they weren't effective on everything. The world needed new drugs, and they needed them quickly. Penicillin eventually proved safer than sulfa and more effective against a wider range of infections.[13] By the war's end, most research and development shifted to penicillin, and frankly, people forgot about the funny German dye that started it all.

But all that's big-picture stuff. As a parent in 1937, if a new drug could save your child's life, wouldn't you do just about anything to get it? Sure, you would. You would have picked up a bottle of Elixir Sulfinamide from your doctor and hoped for the best.

. . .

As the tragedy unfolded in the fall of 1937, letters flooded into Franklin Roosevelt's office, mostly heartbroken letters from parents urging action. How painful must it have been to read letters from parents who lost their child only to know that the same miracle drug saved his own?

We can't know which of these letters had the most impact on the president, his advisors, or Congress, but perhaps it was this one from Dr. Calhoun, whom we met earlier in the story.

> Nobody but Almighty God and I can know what I have been through these past few days... Any doctor who has practiced more than a quarter of a century has seen his share of death. But to realize that six human beings, all of them my patients, one of them my best friend, are dead because they took medicine that I prescribed for them innocently, and to realize that that medicine which I had

---

13. About three percent of patients have allergic reactions to sulfa drugs. That's higher than most other antibiotics. Despite that high rate of reaction, sulfa drugs are used today to treat urinary tract infections (UTIs); inflammatory bowel disease; malaria; skin, vaginal, and eye infections; and burns.

used for years in such cases suddenly had become a deadly poison in its newest and most modern form, as recommended by a great and reputable pharmaceutical firm in Tennessee: well, that realization has given me such days and nights of mental and spiritual agony as I did not believe a human being could undergo and survive. I have known hours when death for me would be a welcome relief from this agony.

Largely powerless and underresourced as it was in 1937, the Food and Drug Administration wasn't waiting for letters. All 239 FDA staffers fanned out nationwide, tracking down every ounce of Elixir Sulfinamide produced by Massengill.

The first step was tracking down the salespeople. Remember, Massengill didn't really know who the end customers were; they only knew their own representatives. (There was no email list or instant messaging. Agents needed to physically locate each person.) Once they found the salespeople, they needed to convince them to share their customer lists. That wasn't always easy, but a few stories of what would happen to people who took it (and what had happened already) did the trick. Finally, they needed to find the elixir and convince the customers to give it back to them.

The FDA's authority to do that hung by a thread. They could only seize the property because of mislabeling—a marketing issue, not a safety issue. Why? Technically, an "elixir" was a substance using alcohol as its base ingredient. Because Massengill used diethylene glycol, the product was not an elixir and, thus, illegally sold. Had Massengill said "solution," the FDA would have been powerless.

Ultimately, FDA agents tracked down 234 gallons and 1 pint of the total 240 gallons sold. The remaining product killed 107 people.

How did Massengill react to the tragedy? Let's just say it was everything you hoped it wouldn't be. Leadership "regretted" the deaths but noted (sadly and correctly) that the company did nothing illegal and that the product was indeed manufactured correctly. Harold Cole Watkins, however, had a functioning conscience. Distraught over his role in the deaths, he took his own life. One wonders if Massengill's management regretted the 108th death as much as the previous 107.

However, the American consumer would not be content with regret, and the FDA would not remain powerless for long.

. . .

In the wake of the tragedy, Roosevelt signed the Food, Drug, and Cosmetic Act (FDCA) in 1938. There's plenty of legalese, but in short, it established the modern FDA.[14] If you wanted to launch a new drug (or medical device of nearly any type), you needed to ensure the product was safe *before* marketing it. The act also gave the FDA broad power to remove an unsafe product from the market if it was found to be unsafe *after* they had given the *initial* okay.

The act also indirectly created the modern pharmaceutical industry. Why was that? Before 1938, any douche company could slap a label on its antifreeze concoction and try to sell it. That was fine when most of these "patent medicines" and "elixirs" didn't work...and everyone knew it. But sulfa changed everything, especially consumer expectations that a new medicine would be effective. To meet this demand and satisfy new FDA gatekeepers, only the most sophisticated companies stayed in the drug-making business. Developing and releasing a *safe* drug took (and still takes) years. Only the largest and most well-funded organizations can do it.

Sadly, however, this approach hasn't been a panacea. Look up the "thalidomide disaster" for a horrifying echo of this a generation later in the 1950s. You won't need to search far if you want a list of failures. However, given the number of new drugs released each year, the number of true disasters is quite rare. That doesn't make them okay, but American consumers recognize the difficult balancing act between releasing a potentially life-saving drug quickly and waiting until it is absolutely safe. There is no perfect answer.

The act also indirectly created the image of the modern doctor. Before the 1930s, doctors would come to you, and they really couldn't do much other than explain how you were likely to suffer. After sulfa, *you* went to the *doctor*. The 1938

---

14. The modern FDA has plenty of issues, but it provides a stunning amount of information for consumers, healthcare providers, and industry.

law formally put physicians in control of medications. To get one, you needed a prescription. It was no longer optional. Otherwise, the pharmacy wouldn't sell you lifesaving medications. It transformed the image of a doctor from a glorified mechanic of moist machinery to a literal and figurative lifesaver. They remain among the top respected professions in the minds of most Americans.[15]

Perhaps the most surprising aspect of the sulfinamide disaster is that it had the opposite effect you might expect—it primed the market for new antibiotic discoveries. That might seem odd given everything we've just discussed, but not if you imagine yourself as a patient or parent in the 1930s. For the first time, something worked. A 2009 National Bureau of Economic Research study examined the change in life expectancy before and after sulfa drugs. How could they isolate the impact? Sulfa drugs could treat some conditions but not others, notably tuberculosis. Deaths from TB stayed steady, while maternal mortality and deaths from pneumonia and scarlet fever declined sharply.

So yes, sulfa really did work. The hype was real.

Maybe sulfa wasn't the miracle cure for everything, but maybe, just maybe, we had turned the corner.

---

15. Depending on what data you look at, doctors and nurses battle it out for the top spot. No other profession quite comes close. Firefighters, maybe. That's it.

8

MY NAME IS BILL, AND I'M...

What must have been going through Dr. William Duncan Silkworth's mind as he turned the corner into Bill Wilson's room? Sadness? Hopelessness? Resignation? Caregivers' emotions often parallel their patients, almost like a psychological reflection. That's especially true in alcoholism treatment, and Dr. Silkworth had seen it all before.

It was the summer of 1934, and Dr. Silkworth was making rounds. This was not a pleasant place. No hospital is, of course, but this institution was particularly heartbreaking. This hospital treated alcoholics suffering from the final medical complications before their eventual death. His patients experienced heart failure, loss of kidney function, and even brain damage.[1] That last one is the worst. It makes late-stage alcoholism exceedingly challenging to treat. Near the end, alcoholism is the only part of the patient's personality that remains.

But this patient was different. He was awake. And he had quite the story to tell.

---

1. Several reputable medical sources describe the "stages" of alcoholism. It often begins (seemingly) harmlessly—an increased tolerance for alcohol or missing a day or work. The earlier you intervene, the more successful treatment can be. If you even suspect you *might* have a problem, it doeesn't hurt to call.

"...a wave of depression came over me," Wilson recalls. "I realized that I was powerless—hopeless—that I couldn't help myself and that nobody else could help me. I was in black despair. And in the midst of this, I remembered about this God business. And I rose up in bed and said, 'If there be a God, let him show himself now!'"

One can imagine Dr. Silkworth's reaction. Did he look up from his chart with a curiously raised eyebrow? Or was he simply jaded from hundreds of bizarre, otherworldly stories coming from the mouths of late-stage alcoholics? It's impossible to know in his recollection of this story. All we do know is that he allowed Wilson to continue.

"All of a sudden, there was a light," Wilson continues, undeterred, "a blinding white light that filled the whole room. A tremendous wind seemed to be blowing all around me and right through me. I felt as if I were standing on a high mountain top..."

"I felt that I stood in the presence of God. I felt an immense joy. And I was sure beyond all doubt that I was free from my obsession with alcohol. The only condition was that I share the secret of this freedom with other alcoholics and help them to recover."

"Ever since it happened, I've been lying here wondering whether or not I've lost my mind."

"Tell me," Wilson pleaded. "Was it real? Am I still...sane?"

Once Wilson finished, Dr. Silkworth looked down, gathered his thoughts, and got ready to change history.

Had it been any other doctor at nearly any other time in human history, the answer to Wilson's question would have been a resounding *no*. Alcoholism wasn't well-understood in that era. Sure, people knew it was a problem—even an intractable problem for a certain group of people.[2] However, no one understood why or how some people could drink and stop and others could not. It was one of the main points the temperance advocates in the United States used to push

---

2. That list included former U.S. president and Civil War general Ulysses S. Grant. Once he started drinking, he couldn't stop himself.

through Prohibition more than a decade before. Sadly, even an outright ban on alcohol didn't work for this group.

Luckily, this wasn't any other time, and Dr. Silkworth wasn't any other doctor.

"Yes, my boy. You are sane. Perfectly sane, in my opinion," Dr. Silkworth continued.

Wilson clearly had a conversion experience, a divine intervention, or a psychic upheaval. As a "man of science," he didn't fully understand it. However, he encouraged his patient:

"Whatever it is you've got now, hang onto it, boy. It is so much better than what you had only a couple of hours ago."

In other words, Bill Wilson asked for God's help, and God *showed up*. God told Bill that he must share this revelation with others. It's the closest thing to a modern prophet in the old-school, biblical sense you'll meet in this book. Wilson would heed the call.[3]

This is the story of the movement that would be called Alcoholics Anonymous.

...

We need to take a brief detour here to clear up some misconceptions about alcohol and alcoholism. Without that, it's difficult to understand the urgency for a specific group of people and why most others don't quite get it.

First, let's clarify what we mean by "alcohol." When we talk about the alcohol we drink, that's technically ethyl alcohol (also known as ethanol), distinguished from wood alcohol (methanol) and isopropyl alcohol (isopropanol, for cleaning and disinfecting). They're all related, but only ethanol is "safe" to drink.

We use scare quotes on the word "safe" because the human liver can process undistilled or distilled ethanol in small doses without resulting in near-immediate death. (Don't drink the other kinds.) In teeny doses, we're pleasantly buzzed. In slightly higher doses, we're drunk. Much higher than that, our livers can't keep up. Untreated, we'll develop alcohol poisoning and risk death. That's because

---

[3]. The stories differ. This one comes from *Not God: A History of Alcoholics Anonymous*, written by Ernest Kurtz and published by Hazelden Pittman in 1991. (Careful observers will recognize the name. Hazelden is one the nation's premier substance abuse rehabilitation centers based in Minnesota, USA.) Although this conversation was certainly not written down or recorded as it was happening, it gets the storyline right.

ethanol is toxic. Over time, sustained ethanol use can damage the liver, brain, and other organs and can lead to psychological and physiological addiction.

That's what drove Bill Wilson (and so many others before and since) to the hospital. His body and mind were poisoned by years of chronic alcohol abuse. It can happen to anyone, but we'll circle back to why it's such a problem for people like Wilson.

That begs the question, doesn't it? If alcohol is indeed a poison and destructive in many ways, why haven't we simply phased it out? Societies tend to remove behaviors and ideas that don't produce successful outcomes in a Darwinian process. It may take a long time, but it happens.

Well, some societies have done that. Muslims and Mormons come immediately to mind as two with outright prohibitions on alcohol use. Additionally, some cultures and subcultures tend to drink much less than others. During the early part of the 20th century (the so-called "Progressive Era"), several governments enacted prohibitions on alcoholic beverages, not just the United States. However, those examples are the exceptions that prove the rule. Why is restricting alcoholic beverages so difficult?

As Griffith Edwards describes in his book *Alcohol: The World's Favorite Drug*, it's not as simple as that. Drinking alcoholic beverages has been wrapped tightly in societal rituals ever since humans learned to ferment, brew, and distill.

In ancient times, many workers were often paid in beer.[4] Why? For one, it was safer. Have you seen the Nile River in Egypt? Floating crocodile dung and decomposing plant matter don't exactly encourage taking a long drink. Although the Pharoah's staff didn't understand why the brewing process made water safer to drink, they understood that it did. Healthier workers meant faster construction. That said, the typical alcohol by volume percentage (or ABV) was much lower than it is today. At two to three percent ABV, pyramid block movers would have to down a lot of warm Egyptian hooch even to get a mild buzz. Additionally, beer is essentially liquid, shelf-stable bread. If you need to feed a lot of people in a hot desert, you could do worse. In fact, it wasn't until the modern era—and really,

---

4. Including the workers (and to be clear, enslaved people) who built the Egyptian pyramids. To the best of our knowledge, no extraterrestrials were needed, just a lot of beer.

only the past 100 to 150 years—that water was generally safe to drink in most industrialized societies.

Over the long arc of historical time, Edwards describes how alcohol sluiced its way into all sorts of rituals and meals. Religious observances were especially notable; the Christians, in particular, have an entire ceremony in which the wine served becomes the "blood" of their savior.[5] How do you turn down God when He gives you the gift of His son's life force? Not easily, that's for sure. You might get away with that in a modern church. You'd be likely to be tried as a heretic and burned at the stake if you did it a couple of hundred years ago.

It's not just church services. Think of Sunday brunch, the wedding toast, or the college football game. They're all powerful social rituals in their own way. To paraphrase American management consultant Peter Drucker: Alcohol drinks culture for breakfast.[6]

In essence, that's why giving up alcohol is so tricky for societies. It's not just that it can be fun in small doses (as is the case with many drugs we don't need), or that it helps lubricate social relationships, or that it could have mental health benefits we don't quite fully understand. The deeper reason is that drinking alcohol is woven into the fabric of our culture.

However, for a small subsegment of the population, the integration of alcohol into our culture presents a major problem. To better understand the idea behind Alcoholics Anonymous, we need to distinguish casual drinking (even the frat party variety) from alcoholism, the disease. As you've likely experienced in your own life, most people can have a drink—even multiple drinks—without alcohol taking over their lives. They drink, but they are not *addicted* to drinking.

Alcoholics like Bill Wilson are different. Researchers suspect, quite strongly, that there is a genetic component to how certain people's bodies react to alcohol. Genetic alcoholics cannot stop themselves once they begin drinking. Even one drink leads, inevitably, to a drunken stupor. You can think about it like an au-

---

[5]. The process is called Transubstantiation. The same ceremony also involves bread transforming into the "body" of Jesus.

[6]. His original observation was that organizational culture eats strategy for breakfast. If you're trying to enact change in an organization, and that change goes against its culture, you are *very likely* to fail.

toimmune disease—the same way people with Celiac disease must abstain from all gluten-containing foods. Alcoholics like Wilson must abstain from alcohol.

Dr. Silkworth was one of the first people to suspect this link. No, he didn't understand genetics as we do today, but he did observe that some people simply couldn't stop. He deduced that it tended to run in families, and he reasoned that abstinence was the only workable solution. Even then, he struggled to call alcoholism a "disease." We simply didn't understand enough about alcoholism in the 1930s, and being a good scientist, Dr. Silkworth wasn't ready to go that far. In practical terms, that meant people like Wilson would get limited help from the medical community. They would treat them, but only after they began to show physiological symptoms. By then, it was often too late.

Although Dr. Silkworth didn't use this definition, since then, the medical profession has codified what alcoholism entails. It's a useful definition so that we're all clear on what we're talking about. You'll notice several elements that Dr. Silkworth identified and that Wilson needed to address in any treatment approach.

According to The Diagnostic and Statistical Manual of Mental Disorders, Fifth Edition, more briefly known as the DSM-V, alcoholism:

1. is is a primary Illness not caused by other illnesses nor by personality or character defects;an addiction gene is part of its etiology;
2. has predictable symptoms;
3. is progressive, becoming more severe even after long periods of abstinence;
4. is chronic and incurable;
5. persists in spite of negative consequences and efforts to quit;
6. changes brain chemistry and neural functions, so alcohol is perceived as necessary for survival;
7. produces physical dependence and life-threatening withdrawal;
8. is a terminal illness;
9. can be treated and can be kept in remission.

In other words, alcoholism is not just a regrettable wild night at the club. For alcoholics, there is no safe dosage. Therefore, complete abstinence must form the foundation of Wilson's mission. He had his work cut out for him.

...

The origins of what would become Alcoholics Anonymous began in the church basement of the Oxford Group, a non-denominational Christian organization focused on addiction recovery. Wilson's drinking buddy attended, so that's the first place Wilson tried.

The Oxford Group approach featured many of the so-called "12 Steps" that would form the foundation of AA—submission to a higher power, admitting that you are powerless over alcohol, and a fellowship with others as critical to the recovery journey. However, in one important respect, the approach was quite different, and perhaps not in the way you might think. It wasn't the religion that was the problem; it was the preaching. Leaders of the program weren't alcoholics themselves. Yes, their heart was in the right place, but they couldn't quite empathize with the group members.

Wilson noticed that although the program had some success, the preaching approach often fell on deaf ears. Yes, submission to a higher power was important, but it was clear that it didn't matter which higher power it was or how precisely you defined it. Yes, admitting you were powerless over alcohol was important, but it was easier to admit that to someone who also faced powerlessness. Yes, the fellowship was important, but the most important relationships were those between people on different stages of their journey—someone who had been sober for many months knew what a person was thinking in the early days of just trying to put down the bottle. A pastor's counsel just wasn't the same.

It's impossible to know precisely how long these thoughts and impressions percolated, but in AA lore, the founding moment happened during a business trip to Akron, Ohio.

Wilson needed a drink. He was alone, away from his support structure at home. He knew he wouldn't be able to resist. He knew he was about to relapse. It was an emergency. In desperation, Wilson found the contact information for another person in the Oxford program in that city, dialed the number, and begged to meet him right away. Wilson knew he needed to talk with someone who understood. It was the only way.

Dr. Robert Holbrook Smith—a prominent local surgeon and struggling alcoholic—didn't want to meet.

At least, that's what his wife said. Eventually, she persuaded her husband to meet with Wilson, but he would only meet "for a few minutes" and nothing more. Whether it was his wife's persuasive ability, Dr. Smith's sympathy for another struggling alcoholic, or divine intervention —take your pick. Wilson showed up on Dr. Smith's doorstep.

What happened next transformed them both.

As Wilson told his story, Smith couldn't believe what he was hearing. It was as if Wilson was in his head, replaying his own terrible thoughts and rationalizations.

The one facet Wilson couldn't relate to was Smith's ability to obtain alcohol during Prohibition. That's what started him down the path. As we mentioned, Progressive activists used people like Smith to help justify banning alcohol entirely. However, in practice, it was very easy to get a drink illegally and even easier for medical professionals. In one of the most bizarre exemptions to the law (and there were many), doctors could write prescriptions for alcoholic beverages. Yep, you heard that right. You could visit your doctor for a shot of whisky. Imagine what that was like for Smith. He had protected access to alcohol anytime he wanted it. For most doctors, it was a way to earn extra money. For Smith, it was the worst possible enabler. By the time Wilson and Smith met in person in Ohio, Prohibition was in the national rearview mirror, but Smith's addiction was not.

The two spoke for hours, shared stories, and saved each other from picking up their next drink. That was the spark. That was the missing element. It was alcoholics helping other alcoholics. Over the course of the next few years, Wilson and Smith (among a handful of others) would codify this process into the 12 Steps of AA.

You can read about this story (and many others) in the so-called "Big Book" of Alcoholics Anonymous, originally authored by Wilson in 1939. It's still in print today. In fact, you don't even need to buy a copy. You can download the full text from the AA website.

We'll pull several stories from the book, but it's time to describe the 12-Step program Wilson and Smith put to paper in the back half of the Great Depression. These come verbatim from the Big Book, but we'll break them up into sections to help understand the context and why each one is important to the whole.

1. We admitted we were powerless over alcohol—that our lives had become unmanageable.
2. Came to believe that a power greater than ourselves could restore us to sanity.
3. Made a decision to turn our will and our lives over to the care of God as we understood Him.

Notice what AA owes to its religious origins. The first three steps are direct references to powerlessness before alcoholism. That's a critical point. Alcoholism is a condition that defies the rational brain. In fact, rationalizations are a key feature of alcoholism and must be addressed. However, notice the subtle distinction in the third step: "...as we understood Him." What AA is saying is that how you understand God isn't important. What's important is that you *surrender* to that deity. Over the years, people have expanded this step to include God, god, gods, spirits, ancestors, nature, or "the universe." The specifics don't matter. In other words, you don't need to envision a guy with a beard touching another clean-shaven guy on the ceiling of a cathedral in Rome to make it work.

4. Made a searching and fearless moral inventory of ourselves.
5. Admitted to God, to ourselves, and to another human being the exact nature of our wrongs.
6. Were entirely ready to have God remove all these defects of character.
7. Humbly asked Him to remove our shortcomings.

The next four steps are a reckoning, not a rationalization. Alcoholics must stop making excuses for their drinking. Instead, they must complete a detailed accounting of how alcohol has negatively impacted not only their own lives but also the lives of people around them. More than that, they must share that accounting with (their concept of) God as well as another person—usually first, another alcoholic. We'll get to that. And finally, they must be ready to change. It's one thing to realize something is harmful. It's quite another to be ready to do something about it. (That's something we all can relate to, right?) Remember, though, the alcoholic accepts their own powerlessness. That's why surrendering to God is an important precursor to these admissions. If it were possible for the alcoholic to make the changes, they would have done it already. Self-help isn't going to cut it. According to AA, only God can make it happen.

8. Made a list of all persons we had harmed, and became willing to make amends to them all.
9. Made direct amends to such people wherever possible, except when to do so would injure them or others.

Steps 8 and 9 are all about taking action. It's not enough to accept responsibility for the harm your drinking caused; you need to take action to remedy those harms. This is where the healing process transitions from an internal monologue between the alcoholic and their concept of God and becomes a dialog between that person and those impacted by their behavior.

10. Continued to take personal inventory, and when we were wrong, promptly admitted it.
11. Sought through prayer and meditation to improve our conscious contact with God as we understood Him, praying only for knowledge of His will for us and the power to carry that out.

Steps 10 and 11 remind the alcoholic that recovery is a journey, not a destination. Remember what we learned about alcoholism: there is no cure. In short, you're always an alcoholic (at least, from a medical or genetic perspective), even if your last drink was 35 years ago. We see this in how people introduce themselves at the beginning of an AA meeting. They'll say, "Hello, my name is Bill, and I'm an alcoholic," not "Hello, my name is Bill, and I *was* an alcoholic."

12. Having had a spiritual awakening as the result of these steps, we tried to carry this message to alcoholics and to practice these principles in all our affairs.

The final step is, perhaps, the most important point. From a religious perspective, it's easy to read this as evangelism. Not quite. It's a very specific call to action. The twelfth step requires assisting someone else on their journey to sobriety. It recognizes that, at a certain point, an alcoholic can only be truly successful when they help someone else. For one, it allows them to stop focusing so much on themselves, their own condition, and their own situation. For another, teaching someone else always ends up teaching the teacher as well. Something about that person's experience will enrich the resolve of the mentor, too.[7] But mostly, mentorship defines the Alcoholics Anonymous approach—it's alcoholics helping other alcoholics. Yes, medical or psychological professionals may be involved when needed, but they take a backseat. People help *each other* through this because they're the only ones who truly understand.

That's the Alcoholics Anonymous people know...or at least have heard of. The notion of "12 Steps" has bound itself into pop psychology, only matched by the likes of Dale Carnegie's "How to Win Friends" and Emile Coue's "If you believe it and conceive it, you can achieve it." You're probably wondering if these 12 Steps actually work. The short answer is a surprising "yeah, pretty well," for people who stick with the program. We'll get into a more detailed description of the medical efficacy of AA (as well as its drawbacks) shortly, but before then, we have to understand another aspect of the program that most people don't know. These next 12 Steps are just as important.

Alcoholics Anonymous calls this next group the "12 Traditions." These traditions—guidelines, really—have defined the program's long-term success. Let's have a look.

---

7. There's plenty of research on this concept in the "mentorship" literature. The mentor/mentee relationship ends up transforming both people, albeit in different ways. If you've ever participated in a high level in a martial art, you know this from personal experience. At a certain point, you only continue to advance by teaching others.

1. Our common welfare should come first; personal recovery depends upon AA unity.
2. For our group purpose, there is but one ultimate authority—a loving God as He may express Himself in our group conscience. Our leaders are but trusted servants; they do not govern.
3. The only requirement for AA membership is a desire to stop drinking.
4. Each group should be autonomous except in matters affecting other groups or AA as a whole.
5. Each group has but one primary purpose—to carry its message to the alcoholic who still suffers.
6. An AA group ought never endorse, finance, or lend the AA name to any related facility or outside enterprise, lest problems of money, property, and prestige divert us from our primary purpose.
7. Every AA group ought to be fully self-supporting, declining outside contributions.
8. Alcoholics Anonymous should remain forever non-professional, but our service centers may employ special workers.
9. AA, as such, ought never be organized; but we may create service boards or committees directly responsible to those they serve.
10. Alcoholics Anonymous has no opinion on outside issues; hence the AA name ought never be drawn into public controversy.
11. Our public relations policy is based on attraction rather than promotion; we need always to maintain personal anonymity at the level of press, radio, and films.
12. Anonymity is the spiritual foundation of all our traditions, ever reminding us to place principles before personalities.

Look at what they do there. To read these is to see a laser focus on the mission; there is only one criterion for membership. They protect privacy (even though the relationships are not legally privileged). They don't get involved in anything else. And most importantly, only alcoholics counsel other alcoholics. They might hire an accountant to keep the books or a web developer to maintain the website, but those people are not involved in treatment or meetings.

This focus has kept the message and the mission pure over decades. From a consumer marketing perspective, this organization has completely structured itself only to serve that market with only that issue. AA's focus is unmatched in almost any organization, anywhere. It's a lesson most could learn from.

. . .

Now that we know more about the Alcoholics Anonymous method and its organizational structure, let's explore why it works and why it's generated its fair share of criticism. To do that, we need to read a bit more from *Alcoholics Anonymous: The Story of How More Than One Hundred Men Have Recovered from Alcoholism*—or, as it's better known in AA circles, the Big Book.

The Big Book begins with personal narratives, specifically Wilson's, along with a series of others. It describes the 12 Steps and the journey to recovery. However, to stop there risks missing the broader point. What you can't help but notice is a shift in focus from internal to external—from the alcoholic to their negative impact on others. That includes their spouses, children, community, and even their employers.

To be clear, the Big Book does not ask that outsiders share the *blame* for the alcoholic's behavior and choices, but it does ask that others accept *responsibility* for assisting their loved one or colleague in the healing process.[8] In some cases, the situation is irreconcilable and must result in the end of that relationship. It's often easier to forge new relationships once the recovery process has sufficiently progressed, but the Big Book doesn't let anyone off the hook. Even the effort of repairing a hopelessly broken relationship will help everyone move forward.

In an unexpected twist, that responsibility extends to employers as well. The Big Book suggests that managers learn how to spot alcoholism in their ranks and actively encourage them to seek treatment. Wouldn't it be easier to simply fire them? Perhaps, and sometimes, that's necessary. But alcoholics tend to be hard workers—they work hard to find a way to drink—and it's something that makes them good salespeople, effective leaders, and all-around get-it-done people. In

---

8. It should be noted that one of the real heroes in Wilson's story was his wife, Lois. Not only did she support her husband's journey, but tolerated housefuls of raging drunks arriving at all hours of the day or night. In 1951, she founded Al-Anon, a 12-step program for the *families* of alcoholics to support them on their journey. If there is a better criterion for sainthood, it's hard to imagine one.

other words, selfishly, from the employer's perspective, they're worth the investment.

Think about how surprisingly modern that perspective is. It flies in the face of the uncaring scientific automaton images of Depression-era workforces. To be clear, not everyone bought in, but not everyone had to. Companies with managers who accepted this responsibility outperformed those who didn't, especially after the 1930s when labor became scarce. No one today would argue corporate culture doesn't have its share of heartlessness, but it's nothing like it was before the Great Depression. AA played an important role in that change.

Speaking of the broader community, you might have been wondering how AA addresses the "ritualistic" aspect of drinking. In other words, what do you do when drinking alcohol is part of the fabric of your social life? Good question and you probably can guess the answer: the AA meeting.

Alcoholics Anonymous understood from its beginnings that you cannot treat alcoholism in isolation. Alcoholism is as much an individual problem as a social issue. Successful treatments must involve both. In short, you need a new friend group of non-drinking buddies. AA provides that. In many ways, AA is its own sort of "church"—simply redefining church as a group of people who share a common belief and mission. During AA meetings, participants introduce themselves, share their stories (or not), discuss aspects of the Big Book, and note milestones. Members who maintain sobriety for certain lengths of time receive rewards (coins and other mementos) to mark their progress. It sure sounds like a church, doesn't it?

The insular alcoholics-only approach has led some commentators to criticize AA as some sort of cult, but the characterization quickly slips down the drain. A cult requires fealty to a charismatic leader—a person, and ideally, someone alive—rather than a set of ideas and ideals. In that sense, Alcoholics Anonymous is more like a true religion than a cult.

But we're skirting around the heart of the matter. None of our descriptions of the mechanics of AA, its 12 Steps, its 12 Traditions, its holistic approach, or its substitution of drinking pals with sober friends address the true questions we must ask: Does Alcoholics Anonymous work? More to the point, does it work better than other approaches? Finally, what is the program's long-term impact on our society and other substance abuse treatments? Let's do that.

...

Surprisingly, the first two questions are the easiest to answer.

The best long-term review of the effectiveness of alcoholism treatment approaches might be George Valliant's 1995 study, *The Natural History of Alcoholism Revisited*, published by Harvard University Press. His group explored multiple treatment options, including Cognitive Behavioral Therapy (CBT) and pharmacological approaches, and came to this (depressing when you think about it) conclusion:

> Formal treatment, *with the exception of attending Alcoholics Anonymous*, did not appear to affect the men's long-term outcomes.

Other studies have shown similar effects on women.[9] Valliant's team also confirmed several facts AA already knew: Abstinence is the only long-term solution. True alcoholics cannot return to "occasional" drinking. How do they know that? Over two-thirds of the members in AA develop some other sort of compulsive behavior—gambling, sex, eating, or smoking—but they'll also abuse positive habits as well—exercise, nutrition, or religious observance. There's clearly a genetic underpinning driving this behavior, although recent research shows multiple genes are likely involved.

More interesting, Valliant's team asked the next logical question: Does Alcoholics Anonymous work more effectively for everyone, or does it work because the type of person most likely to benefit from that approach pre-selects into that type of program? It's the same question that tries to connect marriage and happiness. Are married people happier, or are happier people more likely to get married? It's hard to tease apart cause and effect. The answer to that question, however, seems to be positive as well. Put simply, AA works.

---

9. As many women will note with justifiable frustration, there are fewer long-term studies of *most conditions* with women, or even a balance of men or women. Even more sadly, that's true of issues that impact women directly. As of this writing, the only notable exceptions are childbirth and breast cancer.

It may surprise you to know that other researchers and commentators believe AA—on the whole—has done more harm than good.

Stanton Peele was the first among many with his 1999 book *The Diseasing of America: How We Allowed Recovery Zealots and the Treatment Industry to Convince Us We Are Out of Control*. The basic idea is that Alcoholics Anonymous convinced us that poor personal choices were, in fact, "diseases" to be "treated" by the medical community and pharmaceutical industry. Now, before we dismiss Peele as the first in a long line of tinfoil hats, seeing conspiracy in every bottle of beer (which his online reviewers are quick to do), his argument should not be dismissed out of hand.

Peele makes the case that Alcoholics Anonymous was the progenitor of this "diseaseification" trend—from food addictions to shopping addictions to pornography addictions. AA allowed people to externalize the cause of their own poor decisions. When you are the victim of some external force, it's only natural to look for an external solution. Predictably, the pharmaceutical and medical industries profit by naming this new disease, convincing people they have it, and then marketing (often ineffective, but always expensive) treatments. It's difficult to tell who's victimizing whom.

Peele's book fits comfortably into a victim/oppressor worldview whose popularity has ebbed and flowed over the past 100 years. What's interesting is whether or not you believe Big Pharma created shopping addiction to sell you prescriptions (ask your doctor about Noshopatall™), it's a stretch to claim Alcoholics Anonymous was somehow responsible for it.[10]

Wilson, for one, never saw it that way. Alcoholics Anonymous is all about personal accountability for a very specific group of people. For that small group, AA is life-changing and life-saving. That's the secret, though. AA is not for everyone. It only resonates with a particular type of person: an alcoholic. For everyone else, it's like going to a church service for a religion you're not a part of, in a town you don't know, spoken in a language you don't understand. That's why Alcoholics Anonymous is so hard for everyone else to understand and so

---

10. That's not to say people don't try. The Wikipedia page for Alcholics Anonymous has been edited over 10,000 times since it was created. That's more than any other topic in this book. It clearly strikes a nerve.

important for the people who do. In the end, the only person who could help an alcoholic was another alcoholic.

A final note:

For a small number of you reading or listening to this chapter, what you just read or heard might have struck close to home. If you believe you have a problem with alcohol, please seek help that feels right. There is hope. Alcoholics Anonymous can connect you with resources near you. Visit them today at aa.org.

MORE THAN ONE WAY TO PASS GO

In 1932, Richard Darrow caught strep throat. Unlike his older brother, "Dickie" didn't seem to shake it. Within a few weeks, the infection had progressed to scarlet fever—so named because of the distinctive rash that blooms over the upper torso. It's a dangerous complication. Scarlet fever can cause lasting brain damage, especially in children.

Sadly, the antibiotics that might have halted this progression from strep throat to scarlet fever to irreversible brain damage were more than half a decade in the future.[1] Once the fever finally broke, the new reality was grim. Dickie would need round-the-clock care for the rest of his life.

Can you imagine what was going through the minds of his parents? Like millions of other working-age men in 1932, his father, Charles Darrow, was unemployed. Unlike millions of other wives, Esther Darrow could not find odd jobs to make ends meet; someone had to care for Dickie. That part was clear. Even keeping up with other children his age seemed beyond him now. When a group of

---

1. If you're thinking penicillin, you're partially correct. Penicillin likely could have treated Dickie Darrow, but what we're referencing here are sulfa drugs. You can learn more about those in Chapter 7.

children were playing near a lake, Dickie simply kept walking into deeper water. What would have happened had another child not spotted Dickie floundering and pulled him out? All young children need some level of supervision, but most children will grow out of the need for continuous monitoring. Dickie would not.

Imagine the crushing pressure on Charles Darrow in the dark winter months in Pennsylvania. The so-called "Community Chest" in Philadelphia quickly exhausted its meager relief funds. Everyone knew the mayor's assertion that "no one was starving" in the city was a lie. Worse for the Darrows, resources for persons with mental disabilities were nearly non-existent. Institutions of that era largely deserved their terrifying reputations. The handful of better options cost money—money the Darrows did not have.

The Darrows were broke. Charles had no prospects. He couldn't "ride the rails" looking for work and abandon his family, not with a child with special needs. There was no social safety net to speak of. It was all on him. No father should ever face that creeping terror, but he did.

In most modern retellings of the story of the game *Monopoly*, Charles Darrow is cast as the villain. He stole the idea from the woman who created (and patented it) years before, twisted it against her intentions, sold it to game manufacturer Parker Brothers, and never even acknowledged her—much less paid her—for all her work. For decades, she was ignored and forgotten.

A 2015 book review in the *New Republic* sums up the current mood with the title, "An Anti-Capitalist Woman Invented *Monopoly* and a Man Got All the Credit."

It sure sounds like an open-and-shut case. The desperation of Darrow's plight might make him a sympathetic villain, but he was a villain nonetheless.

Could it be that simple? As you might guess, no. It isn't.

. . .

We'll return to the legal and ethical questions later. For now, let's rejoin Darrow and his wife at the dining room table in the winter of 1932. Like most people that year, they had plenty of time to ponder their situation. They passed that time playing a board game with their friends, the Todds. Things were bad for pretty much everyone. Frankly, they could all use the distraction.

The foursome could have been playing any number of games—cards, dominos, or Mahjong. Simple games have always been popular, but that was especially true in the dark early days of the Great Depression when people needed cheap (or even better, *free*) escapes from the day's news.

This wasn't that kind of game, though. It was a new one. It was a so-called "board game," meaning it was played on a game board, usually printed cardstock. Yes, similar products were on the market before then, but none really took off. This new one didn't even have a name people agreed on.

The Todds owned a one-of-a-kind copy *they copied* from someone else. Unlike most board games of that era, this one didn't necessarily "begin" in one place and "end" in another. You looped. On each turn, you moved around the board based on the sum of the two dice you rolled.[2] The idea was simple: As players moved around the board, they could purchase the spots they landed on. Any subsequent player who landed on that spot needed to pay you rent. Each rent payment was a bit different, just like actual real estate.

This version featured Atlantic City landmarks, but the Todds mentioned it wasn't always that way. The local Quakers did that. The original game came from New York, so the story went, but no one knew for sure. That was based on an earlier version they saw that featured "Wall Street" instead of "Boardwalk." No matter. It was basically the same thing. There was even a version where you could "improve" the property by investing in houses and hotels. The Todds thought the Quakers added that feature, but it was hard to say.

The game ended when one player bought enough property and drove others bankrupt by charging ever-higher rents. You might get lucky and land on "free spaces" on the board, but that would only last so long. A good game could last a few hours—perfect for fun after-dinner entertainment and discussion.

Everyone they knew was playing it, though everyone seemed to have their own shabby oil-cloth copy, their own variations of the rules, and their own story on how they got their hands on it.

---

2. Using dice was a bigger deal than you'd think. Dice were associated with gambling and debauchery. To use dice in a board game made it risqué and likely increased its popularity. Sinfulness tends to do that.

What was going through Charles and Esther's minds as they walked home that first evening?[3] There must have been a twinge of guilt having fun while they left Dickie at home (presumably under the care of an older sibling). Despite that, having a few hours of a mental break from their household stress must have been refreshing. We might be able to empathize with them and make educated guesses, but we can't know their conversation. However, unlike most families facing that situation, we can piece it together based on what happened next.

The Darrows saw an opportunity. They would not waste it.

. . .

Contrary to the instinct that people would not want to play a game where the object was to ruin other people financially—especially during the Great Depression—that's precisely what made it so engaging. People may not be able to control their circumstances in real life, but in game life, they could see what it felt like to be a ruthless tycoon, if only for a few hours.

Over the coming weeks, the Darrows and the Todds played this game. *A lot.* In fact, they played so often that the Todds started to think it was a bit strange. More than anything, it was the *way* the Darrows played. Charles and Esther asked innumerable questions about the game's rules, strategy, and mechanics. They even asked for a copy of the instructions. When the Todds told them there weren't any, the Darrows asked them to write them a copy.

Even the game's name had a sketchy past. It seemed like the original version was called "The Landlord Game" or "The Landlord's Game." (No one could decide if the apostrophe was supposed to be there.) Another version was named "Finance." Could you buy that version in a store? Some people seemed to think so, but no one knew for sure. Other versions of the game had been played on college campuses all over the East Coast, especially among economics students. Students often called it by its catchier name, "Monopoly." That would be the name the Darrows would run with.

This is where the story starts to get a bit morally ambiguous. The Darrows, so far as anyone knows, never told the Todds (or anyone else) what they were up

---

3. Most biographies only focus on Charles because he would be the "inventor" named in the eventual Parker Brothers marketing plan. However, we know that Charles and Esther worked together on the game. They were a team. That's why we're elevating her role here.

to. That said, did they need to? Clearly, people had been making (and, in some cases, selling) this game for at least the past 25 years. Maybe longer. There was no "internet" where you could easily search for the game, nor was there easy access to a patent or trademark database to check if someone else owned the rights to the creation. Besides, if the game was as old as people said, patents only protect an invention for so long. What's more, with all the different variants in play, who was to say who owned what?

And one more thing. The game might be fun, but it was also…well, unattractive would be the polite term. Transcribing from oilcloth version to oilcloth version—*by hand*—will do that. Most boards were rife with misspellings, including one that would feature prominently in a legal dispute later: *Marvin* Gardens instead of *Marven* Gardens. All that said, if *Monopoly* was going to be a commercially viable product, it needed a major facelift.

. . .

The first idea involved rethinking the cloth gameboard's square shape. Most people the Darrows knew owned *round* dining room tables, not square ones, so a round game board should better fit the table without leaving awkward half-moon-shaped empty spaces in front of each player. Well, "awkward" is one way to put it. Another way would be to say this is the perfect place for drinks, snacks, play money, and other goodies. Although Darrow's first game board design was round, he quickly abandoned it.[4]

The Darrows would make smarter decisions from here. After the circular false start, Darrow "Passed Go" and tried again.

It was time to focus on the design aesthetics—the artwork that would make the game come alive. Though nearly broke, the Darrows scraped together the money to hire a local illustrator to spruce up the game. He brightened the colors (some versions already distinguished the different groups of properties by color; others did not) and added illustrations for the "jail," the "police officer," and "Rich Uncle Pennybags," who would become the game's mascot. Darrow also formalized the initial set of game tokens each player would use to mark their progress around

---

4. Historian Thomas Forsyth has perhaps the best collection of historical artifacts on the evolution of the early days of the *Monopoly* game, including an image of Darrow's first round game board. You can find it at landlordsgame.info.

the board: A cannon, thimble, top hat, iron, battleship, and boot.[5] Finally, he did away with the dull oilcloth in favor of bright white cardboard emblazoned with the title "MONOPOLY" in distinctive all caps in the center and Copyright 1935 by C.B. Darrow underneath. Later that year, December 31 to be precise, the U.S. Patent and Trademark Office awarded Darrow patent 2,026,082.

It's the game we would still recognize today, nearly a century later.

But *should* he have received a patent? We'll revisit that question later. Just because you were awarded a *patent* doesn't mean you automatically have a successful *product*. With the work he had put in, the Darrows had something with potential. Now they had to sell it.

. . .

Like most entrepreneurs of that era (and many today), the Darrows sold their game to friends, family, and acquaintances door-to-door. And sell, it did. Darrow's *Monopoly* sold so well, in fact, that sales quickly outpaced the ability to produce games one-by-one in their home. They needed to contract a printer to boost production capacity and quality.

As sales increased, Darrow approached the most significant player (pun intended) in the board game business: Parker Brothers.

They turned him down.

Twice.

In the same year.

Luckily, the Darrows had enough time (and guts) to take advantage of the 1935 Holiday Shopping Season. (And yes, people still bought presents during the Great Depression. You'd be surprised. It was a welcomed break from the bleak news, and people sacrificed to give gifts.) Charles convinced FAO Schwartz—one of the nation's biggest toy retailers—to carry *Monopoly* in its stores. It sold so well that Parker Brothers ate crow and returned to the bargaining table.

Although consumers were still buying games, it wasn't as though the going was easy for Parker Brothers. They were in a tough spot and needed a big hit to

---

5. Wondering about the race car and purse? Those were added later in the first year, but were not part of the original set. Some vintage sets still have generic tokens, so if you're going to buy one of the originals, make sure you check.

turn things around.[6] The Darrows had done the hard work of demonstrating market demand; that's what Parker Brothers was worried about when Charles first approached them. In other words, the Darrows proved it would sell. Had Parker Brothers bought it the *first time* Charles asked, they probably would have paid much less. However, the risk reduction was worth it. *Most new products fail*, even today, and products were failing hard and fast in the Great Depression. The company couldn't afford to make a mistake.

The deal would not only revive Parker Brothers but also make the Darrows wealthy beyond their wildest dreams. The initial payment of $7,000 certainly was a nice boost. That works out to roughly $132,000 in today's money. But it was the residuals that *really* mattered. The Darrows would receive a small percentage of every game sold.

And *Monopoly* sold a *lot* of games.

It was a great story. It was a true story. But it was not the *whole* story. (You probably guessed that already.) It's time you heard the rest of it.

For that, we need to rewind the clock nearly 40 years.

However, before we shift to that narrative, it's important to give credit where credit is due. Not to the editors of the *New Republic*. They were simply writing a book review on Mary Pilon's 2015 history, *The Monopolists: Obsession, Fury, and the Scandal Behind the World's Favorite Board Game*. It's a well-written history, but without the work of Dr. Ralph Anspach in the 1970s, it's unlikely any of this story would have been known.

Anspach was a San Francisco State University professor in the early 1970s who had an idea for a game. The concept was simple: Instead of attempting to buy up all the properties on the *Monopoly* game board, his game would *start* with monopolies. Players then work to break up the monopolies into smaller, discrete units. In short, *Anti-Monopoly*.[7] He published his game in 1973 and ran straight

---

6. In her book, historian Mary Pilon recounts the story of one of the wives of the Parker "brothers" (there were indeed brothers who ran the company) who convinced them to take a risk on the game. We often forget about the behind-the-scenes characters, like Esther Darrow, who often play critical roles. I'm glad Pilon included her. It's a fun story, although too much detail for this retelling.

7. Want to play *Anti-Monopoly*? You can buy a copy on Amazon. You can choose to play as a monopolist or a free-market competitor.

into a challenge from the Parker Brothers legal team over his use of the name and concept with authorization or licensing from the trademark owner.[8]

He wasn't about to go down without a fight, and like most academic types, he wasn't afraid to do the research.

Here's the story he uncovered.

...

Elizabeth J. Magie (later, Phillips) was about as different as it was possible to be from Charles Darrow.

"Lizzie," as her friends would call her, was born in 1866 and grew up idolizing her father. He was part of the cadre of journalists following the Lincoln-Douglas debates before the Civil War. It was a historic time, a historic place, with historic people.

As Magie grew up, her father's journalistic subject matter shifted from the icons of the war years to the most massive transition in American life to that point: the beginning of the migration of people from the vast rural interior to the newly prominent cities. As agricultural technology improved, commodity prices dropped. That made it less economically viable to farm small plots of land. In short, their children could not simply divide a single homestead and make a living as families grew. They would need to move. At the same time, those growing cities were home to massive industry (and hence, jobs) born of rapid industrialization. Add to that the surge of immigrants from varying parts of Europe in the two decades from 1880 to 1900, and you have all the ingredients you need to catalyze a significant cultural upheaval.

Cities simply couldn't build housing fast enough to meet demand. Hastily built tenements sprang up, owned by...well, let's just call them what they were:

---

8. You might be wondering, was this a patent or trademark violation? They're both intellectual property protected by U.S. law, but they work differently. To oversimplify, a patent gives its owner exclusive commercialization rights to an invention *for a limited period of time*. They expire, on purpose. You don't get to exploit your invention forever. Trademarks are different. So long as you're using it to market your product, you can keep using it indefinitely. Let's say you invent a better mousetrap, patent it, and call it "Mouse-Be-Gone"—a name you also trademark. The patent will expire in 15-20 years, depending on the specifics. At that point, others can make your product without licensing it from you. However, no one else can use the trademarked name. (That's why store brand acetaminophen can't use the brand name Tylenol.)

slumlords. The ignorance of rural and foreign migrants meant that unscrupulous landlords had a ripe opportunity to take advantage of people with a combination of crippling rents for barely-standing hovels.

This is the cultural change Magie's father reported on. It's no surprise that it shaped her political and economic beliefs.

The late 1800s marked the birth of several schools of economic thought, all largely in response to the turmoil we just mentioned. Karl Marx is the one everyone remembers. He defined economics largely as a struggle between the owners of capital and the "proletariat" who provided the labor. Eventually, as the theory went, the working class would take control of the means of production and usher in the communist (or socialist) revolution, which was marked by equality and equity.[9] We've already hinted in this book that people who came of age during the 1920s were highly influenced by these ideas being put into practice for the first time in the new Soviet Union. When the American economy crashed, it was seen by many in those circles that the time for the predicted collapse of capitalism and the rise of the working class had indeed arrived. Many of these people now held positions in FDRs cabinet and influenced his policies.

But Magie wasn't a Marxist. *She was a Georgian.* There's a big difference. She wasn't anti-capitalist; she was anti-*giant/exploitative*-capitalist. In other words, small capitalism worked well. However, as organizations grew and consolidated, the inevitable power imbalance became harmful. Georgian economics seeks to remedy that problem.

Never heard of Georgian economics? You're not alone. Henry George (hence, the name) put pen to paper in 1879 with a simple idea: a single tax. Basically, your labor and value-added services should not be taxed; only *land* should be taxed.[10] It harkened back to the Indigenous idea that the land (and the resources it contained) belonged to everyone; the government's role was to hold those assets in public trust. Because communal ownership was impractical and didn't extract

---

9. Obviously, there's more to know about Marx and his ideas that are beyond the scope of a book covering the consumer response to the Great Depression. If you're interested, read *The Communist Manifesto*, written by Friedrich Engels and Karl Marx in 1848.

10. That idea of land is broader than physical property. George meant *intellectual property* as well, like patents and trademarks, which is more than a bit ironic given how Magie's story played out.

maximum value from the land, land owners would pay taxes for the privilege of exploiting those resources. Excess payments above and beyond the government's need would be returned to the citizens as distribution payments. In short, only landlords paid taxes. (Remember the word "landlord.")

It's easy to see the appeal of the Georgian approach in the late 1800s and early 1900s. The kindest way to describe landlords was "exploitative." Slumlords is more accurate. All other descriptions involve profanity, and this is a family book.

Henry George passed away in 1897, but a small group of intellectuals, economists, professors, and journalists on the East Coast picked up the Georgian banner and worked to further the cause. Magie was one of those, but how would she make her mark? Women didn't have as many options at the turn of the century, and certainly not in economics. She needed to get creative.[11]

Eventually, Magie decided her contribution to the cause would be an educational game. Of course, adults would play the game, but she had hoped children would play it with their parents. Through play, they would see the plight of the renter and how unfair it was. In fact, her biggest boosters would be college professors assigning their students to play her game.

Games, especially board games, weren't as ubiquitous as they are today. In the early 1900s, most were games of chance, played with dice or cards. A few, like Parcheesi, were popular from immigrant communities (in this case, the Italians) who brought the game with them. Board games that existed had none of the familiar mechanics of play we're used to now: the path a player took on the board, how dice rolls worked, or complex game strategies. She had to come up with that all on her own.

In trying to teach an economics lesson, Magie invented complex board games.

. . .

---

11. We're skipping over Magie's strong role as a feminist and suffragist around the turn of the century. Like most of them, she wasn't afraid of controversy. In one notable example, she took out a classified ad offering to "sell herself" into marriage, comparing the institution to chattel slavery. The responses ranged from creepy to helpful to useful. Poet and activist Langston Hughes gave her work as a contributing journalist. She wouldn't marry until age 44, and only then because her income options were limited. Her marriage to Albert Phillips was more like a business arrangement than loving embrace.

The first version of *The Landlord's Game*, patented in 1904, would seem familiar to a modern *Monopoly* player.[12] The board was divided into 40 spaces—four larger corners with nine locations between each one. "Jail" and "Go To Jail" dominated two corners. Railroads (though unnamed) took up spots on each of the four sides' center locations. A player might land on a "Luxury" square, although it was not explicitly called a "tax." Property values increased as you went around the board, from $1 rent for the cheapest spot to $22 for the most expensive. Owning those properties increased proportionately, from $10 to $220, or ten times a single rent. Players rolled two dice to advance. As they progressed, they paid rent to the property owner if they landed on a purchased spot. Otherwise, that player could buy the property.

The game's object would also make sense: The player with the most money at the end of five loops of the game board wins. It wasn't necessary to bankrupt a player, though that certainly could happen.

That's where the similarities ended.

In *The Landlord's Game*, players don't "Pass Go"; they start on a square named "Labor Upon Mother Earth Produces Wages"—a reference to how labor and the land are connected. Looking for "Boardwalk" or "Baltic Avenue?" Named properties don't exist in this version, nor were they grouped meaningfully (by color group, for example). Although all patent drawings look austere (usually just line drawings), this one is exceedingly plain, especially for a game.

Magie had the germ of the idea, but to reach a wider audience beyond people interested in economics, the game needed to evolve...and that's where ideas like "who owns the game" get tricky.

...

Almost immediately after it was patented, the game began to change.

A 1906 version of the game, published by the Economic Game Company in New York, included several new features. Color was the big one, though not in the way you're thinking from future versions of *Monopoly*. Colors distinguished properties you could purchase from railroads, taxes, and other utilities. Players

---

12. The first patent was number 748,626, granted on January 5, 1904. Magie received her first patent before she could vote legally in federal elections.

could choose four "jobs"—timber, farming, oil, or coal—each with different wage rates and tax requirements. Finally, properties took on familiar New York City names, such as Broadway, Madison Square, and Wall Street.

As the game spread along the East Coast, it wasn't long before thrifty college students (and their professors) started to make additional changes. They sometimes copied the game from the original board game onto oilcloths. Those oilcloth versions spawned other oilcloth versions. It was a sort of "copy of a copy" situation, where it didn't take long for unique versions to arise and for new players to forget where the original version came from. It was a group of Quakers in Pennsylvania, as you'll recall, who added the color groupings and the Atlantic City street names.

This modest level of success proved a mixed blessing for Magie. On one hand, she wanted the game in the hands of as many people as possible. That they adapted it to their needs is a sign that the basic idea was sound. However, that same adaptation made it more difficult to protect her creation.

As the first two decades of the new century wore on and the game spread far beyond her control, the original patent expired. Her *second patent*, awarded in 1923, marked a modest refresh for the game and, more importantly, extended her protection well into the timeframe in which Darrow discovered it and Parker Brothers acquired it.

What's more interesting than the cosmetic changes to the game board was the expansion of the rule set. Players could choose which style of the *Landlord's Game* they preferred: "monopoly" or "prosperity." The first is played as already described. That's the version most people played, but Magie wanted to formalize the alternative. In the prosperity version of the game, instead of trying to amass the most wealth and bankrupt other players, participants could decide to cooperate and work to lift all players. The winner in this scenario was a team win: How long did it take to boost the poorest person to double the wealth they started with? Magie hoped that players would choose this version as they learned the evils of the rent-focused monopoly approach.

It was a nice thought…but it wouldn't work.

Both Magie and, later, Professor Anspach wanted to use a game to impart a moral lesson, like a religious parable or literary fairy tale, but one you would teach yourself through a fun experience. It's one of those things that *seems* like it should work but often doesn't.

At their core, games are entertainment. They can communicate lessons, but balancing fun and education is challenging. If the player gets the sense they're being taught something, the illusion shatters. So-called *edutainment* requires subtlety, and Magie was anything *but* subtle. Adding the prosperity rules was a sign that the Landlord's *Game* was becoming the Landlord's *Lecture*. It would have been better to develop and promote the prosperity option as a "secret" set of rules—like the secret menu at certain restaurants—that players could discover on their own.[13] That feeling of secret knowledge builds engagement and circumvents our resistance to being "taught" something.

Instead, Magie's new rules implied players of the "monopoly" version were "bad." And do you know what people love to be more than anything else…at least in a game? You guessed it. They don't simply want to amass the most wealth in five turns around the board. They want to crush their friends and family into poverty.

The Darrows understood that. Parker Brothers understood that. Magie (and later, Anspach) did not.

. . .

Despite that, Magie did not go quietly into the night once she saw the Darrow's version.

By 1936, it was clear Parker Brothers had a hit. It was also clear they had some legal trouble. Although the U.S. Patent and Trademark Office awarded Darrow a patent, they clearly didn't do enough research. Additionally, and not unexpectedly, Darrow wasn't the only one to market some version of this game. Another version, named "Finance," had been on the market for a couple of years and sold modestly well. These were serious problems. Executives at Parker Brothers needed to act quickly.

First, Parker Brothers needed to better understand where the idea for the game came from. Was it Darrow's idea? Did he take "inspiration" from anyone else? In

---

13. Ever been to an In-N-Out Burger on the west coast of the United States? If not, make sure to ask for your Double-Double "Animal Style."

other words, did the company need to worry? When asked by the Parker Brothers legal department, here is an excerpt of Charles Darrow's response:

> The history of monopoly is quite simple. Friends visiting our home in the later part of 1931 mentioned a lecture course they had heard in which a professor gave his class scrip to invest and rated them on the results of the imaginary investments. I think the college referred to was Princeton University. Being unemployed at the time, and badly needing anything to occupy my time, I made by hand a very crude game for the sole purpose of amusing myself. Later friends called and we played this game, unnamed at that time. One of them asked me to make a copy for him which I did charging him for my time four dollars. Friends of his wanted copies and so forth. By mid summer of 1933 it was obvious that we should cover a valuable product with a copyright so applied for on October 24 of that year. The publication upon which the copyright was asked came out on July 30th, though the actual game had been in circulation some time. At least two months prior to the date of the application of the copyright. So much for the history of monopoly.

That's sure so much…something.

If that doesn't sound like the whole truth to you, you would be correct. Parker Brothers didn't think so, either. They took matters into their own hands.

Buying the rights to *Finance* was easy. Assuaging Magie was another matter. She was keen to go public with her frustration (and did so, at least once). In the end, Parker Brothers agreed not only to give her a one-time $500 cash payment—better than $12,000 today—but also agreed to publish two additional games she created. Remember, Magie wasn't out to become wealthy. She wanted to teach. Having the most prominent game company in the world publish and market two of your games was a major success. Magie would continue teaching economics until she passed away in 1948 at the age of 81.

In the end, Magie *was* compensated for her ideas. In fact, she received more than most, although much less than Darrow's $7,000. Nonetheless, Parker Brothers chose to bury her story in favor of Darrow's.

Why?

Two main reasons. One that made sense for Parker Brothers and one that's more broadly true.

To help promote *Monopoly*, Parker Brothers used the story of a down-on-his-luck everyman from Pennsylvania who not only came up with a great idea but also found a way to make it happen when the company turned him down. It was a "rags to riches" story that American consumers desperately wanted to hear.

But wouldn't adding the narrative of Magie's contribution help? Not really. As much as we might appreciate her contributions, it's taken us about 4,000 words to get to this point. The average consumer (like it or not) simply doesn't have the attention span. Throw in a complicated economics lesson and a firebrand personality...and that complicates the message. Could Parker Brothers have found a way to tell a better story, like the one you just read? Maybe, but the fact is, they didn't.

The second reason is the difference between *invention* and *innovation*. Inventing is a purely creative act. It's what happens when you pull a fresh idea out of your mind and describe it for the first time. If it meets a series of criteria, the U.S. Patent and Trademark Office will even grant you exclusive rights to bring your idea to market, albeit for a limited time. That's how patents work. They give inventors the space to do the (arguably) much harder job: Get consumers to purchase and use their invention. That's what *innovation* means. It's a two-part dance between the inventor and the user of a product or service.

In short, Magie *invented* the game by creating the idea but struggled to bring it to a wide audience. Darrow *innovated* by finding a way to sell that idea to the mass market. Both are worthy of admiration.

In the end, Magie's story faded, and Darrow's story stuck because of unlucky timing. The mood of the late 1930s had changed. The crippling psychological and economic depression was being replaced with the genuine threat of another global war.

It's easy to understand why consumers would want to escape into *Monopoly*, isn't it? The game provides hours of fun with family and friends. It takes them away from the swirling stress of the world around them. And maybe, just maybe, you can make it big...if only on the game board.

In the intervening decades, after millions of "official" games have been sold, many people still make up their own rules or play variants of the game—licensed or unlicensed—in a sort of homage to the game's messy history. If you're playing a bootlegged version, know that people have been doing that for over 100 years. You're in good company.

If, after all this, you find yourself sympathizing with Magie's legacy and want to honor her creation, you may want to consider playing *her version* of *Monopoly* with the "prosperity" rules. You can find them online, and they adapt well to the game you probably already have in your closet. Perhaps her lesson will finally sink in? Who knows? You'll have to play it to find out.

10

THE FIRST POPCORN MOVIE

In the long history of bad ideas, this one certainly ranked near the top.

Meriam Cooper and Ernest Schoedsack found themselves at the bottom of a pit covered only by a few rough-hewn planks. They had to hope wood cut from trees in a perpetually-drenched jungle could support the weight of what was coming their way. The two men (and one woman we'll meet in a moment) were the first in a long line of nature filmmakers—then referred to as "natural dramas." They weren't content with filming magnificent jungle animals at a distance. Oh, no. That's why they dug the pit.

It was 1926, still well within the silent film era. Despite the name, silent films weren't without musical scores, sound effects, or narration. Those elements were simply added later. Audio and video weren't synchronized, so the camera work needed to sparkle. Great visuals and scenes were one of the hallmarks of that era. Most of the principles of action filmmaking we know and love today were born in those early days when you couldn't rely on sound (or color, for that matter) to help tell your story. Making a movie took a lot of technical skill.

Back to the pit.

On Cooper's signal, local villagers would trigger a stampede of elephants in their direction so that the pair could film them trampling overhead. (What the villagers thought of two Americans digging a pit and trying to get elephants to run over them *on purpose* was, sadly, lost to history.) You have to admit, though, that *would be* a great shot…if nothing went wrong. And to be clear, things had already (nearly) gone terribly wrong.

In an earlier shot, Cooper decided to film a Bengal tiger from the (presumed) safety of a high hide. Villagers taunted the tiger until it was thoroughly pissed off and then sent it in Cooper's direction. Suffice it to say, Cooper miscalculated how high an angry tiger could jump. He nearly became lunch. One has to imagine the side wagers the villagers took on how long it would be before one of the three Americans got eaten or trampled.

Oh, we said three, didn't we? That's because unlike most expeditions of this type, which feature stupidity only of the testosterone variety, Ruth Rose went along as well. We'll learn more about her later, but for now, she was a jack of all trades, keeping her bosses from dying and local villagers from laughing too hard.

Back to the elephants.

As instructed, villagers triggered the stampede. Miraculously, the planks held. It worked! It actually worked. What a great shot! Congratulations all around!

Wait?

What's that?

Is one of the elephants coming back?!

Curious about the odd covered pit they just ran over, one of the elephants decided to stop, turn around, and have a closer look. And by "closer look," we mean using its massive feet to smash the planks apart. Only after getting its foot stuck (and destroying more of the setup in a rage trying to extract its foot) did the pachyderm rejoin its herd.

Battered and bruised, but none of the worse for wear, Cooper and Schoedsack emerged victorious. Within a few weeks, they had all the shots they needed to create a world-class nature documentary named *Chang,* after the local word for the animal that nearly trampled them.

They wanted to show American audiences not the docile and defeated animals they saw behind bars in Victorian zoos, but the wild and dangerous creatures those zoos only hinted at. Cooper even embarked on a side trip to capture photographic evidence of giant "dinosaur-like" lizards on a nearby island.[1]

While Cooper was chasing down Komodo Dragons, Schoedsack and Rose had fallen in love. The two left Cooper to hunt for lizards while they returned to the United States to get married. Alone but elated, Cooper had plenty of time to think on the steamship ride back across the ocean to New York. He conceived a new type of movie involving all the drama he had just experienced: amazing animals, unexplored jungles, native people...and a larger-than-life gorilla.

Oh, and airplanes. Don't forget airplanes. In the 1920s, airplanes were still pretty cool.

...

Airplanes are an appropriate place to start our story about the movie that would eventually become *King Kong*. As many of you know (or perhaps heard from parents or grandparents), propeller-driven, bi-wing fighter aircraft shot down the title character after he climbed to the top of the Empire State Building in New York.[2]

Of course, airplanes were the *tech du jour* in 1920s and 1930s movies, but Cooper and Schoedsack were uniquely qualified to incorporate them into their film. Both men were pilots at a time that *really* meant something.

Let's start with Cooper. He was born in Jacksonville, Florida, educated at a fancy school in New Jersey, earned an appointment to the U.S. Naval Academy, and was kicked out for "raising hell" and championing aviation as the future of warfare. Undeterred, he made his way to Minneapolis, where he did a stint as a reporter. Then, that same year, he migrated to Iowa and Missouri for the same job. This was a guy who didn't let the grass grow under his feet.

Always the adventurous type—hellraiser is an excellent word to describe him—Cooper joined the *Georgia* National Guard to help track down Poncho Villa in *Mexico*. (Still following along?) After being called back from the chase,

---

1. The Smithsonian's National Zoo & Conservation Biology Institute website maintains a fascinating page on these unique animals. They are the world's largest lizards, with males reaching more than 8 feet long and weighing more than 200 pounds.

2. Haven't seen the movie? Not the so-called "Monsterverse" remakes from Toho, the original? You're missing out. You can stream it on all the major platforms.

he wanted to do what most adventurous people of that era wanted to do: learn to fly.

In 1917, Cooper crossed the Atlantic to France to fight as a bomber pilot in World War I. In some of the first "dogfights" ever recorded, his plane was shot and caught fire. Cooper spun the plane to extinguish the flames but could not prevent its inevitable crash behind enemy lines. Suffering burns across much of his body and disfiguring wounds to his face, he was presumed dead. The Army (who had authority over the Air Force until 1947) even made out his death certificate and sent it to his parents. However, Cooper caught a lucky break when the Germans caught *him*. Their plastic surgeons expertly repaired his damaged face and cared for him until the end of the war.

(As it turned out, the death notice from the Army *and a letter from Cooper himself* from a German convalescent hospital both reached his parents at the same time. One suspects they weren't surprised he could do his own impression of Schrodinger's Cat.[3])

As if that wasn't enough, Cooper's time in Europe wasn't over. A natural leader, Cooper caught the attention of Herbert Hoover, who was still organizing relief efforts after the war. Hoover had prevented the Belgian people from starving during the German occupation, and he was doing his best with the rest of the continent after the armistice was signed in November 1918. Hoover put Cooper in charge of Polish relief efforts and promptly sent the young hellraiser across the Polish frontier.

You can't make this stuff up. A fictional story would sound (oddly) more believable.

Let's move on to Ernest Schoedsack.

Ironically nicknamed "Shorty," the 6-foot-5-inch Schoedsack also played a crucial role in World War I. He was an expert photographer and videographer and, yes, a pilot who flew bombing missions over Germany.

---

3. This refers to the famous 1935 thought experiment attempting to describe the indescribable weirdness of quantum superposition. The cat in the hypothetical box is presumed *both* alive and dead *until* the observer opens the box. Make sense? No? You're not alone. Quantum theory was just being worked out in the 1930s and only a handful of people understood it. (Not many more do now.)

A California native by way of Iowa, this farm boy was another one of those types who simply wouldn't let tall corn obscure his grander vision. (It helped that he could see over most of it.) At war's end, Schoedsack traveled to Poland to fight the good fight, trying to prevent its territory from being carved up by its larger neighbors.

That's where he met another pilot with a crazy backstory. You already met him. There was probably no one else alive who would have no trouble believing the odd series of events that led them together, and they both recognized fate when they saw it.

It wasn't long before the pair were globetrotting across the planet, collaborating on film projects. We already know about elephants, tigers, and dragons (oh, my!), but it was on a stopover project in the Galápagos Islands where they met the indomitable Ruth Rose.

Rose was already an accomplished Broadway actress when the New York Historical Society tapped her to head off to the islands as its official historian. Why was she chosen and not a *trained* historian—or, in that sexist era—a man?

Rose was the adventurous type, not at all in the mold of the delicate creative industry starlet, even then becoming stereotypical in Broadway and Hollywood. She had real field experience, which many of the male historians in New York did not. (Mostly, they were what was politely referred to as "library naturalists.") Years before, Rose had been stationed in British Guyana, cataloging wildlife of all kinds—often scientifically interesting, often deadly, and sometimes both. She was also an outstanding organizer, administrator, and, most notably for their later collaborations, a writer.

Schoedsack was smitten almost immediately. Cooper might have been less taken with her initially, but everyone stood in awe of her indispensableness. Even during the Great Depression, this trio had no trouble finding work. It certainly helped that Cooper's airline stocks didn't skip a beat during the 1929 crash and kept him financially secure when most others struggled. However, that likely didn't matter. It's tough to imagine three people better suited to crafting the first great American adventure blockbuster.

. . .

If you were a betting person, a "monster" movie wouldn't be what you would have predicted in the early 1930s.

All movie studios were struggling, and RKO certainly was, too. Like most Hollywood studios, the company that would eventually produce *King Kong* was reeling under the weight of both expected and unexpected trends.

The first was the obvious cause: the Great Depression. It should come as little surprise that the early 1930s were a tough time to be a movie studio. It's not that people didn't want entertainment (they certainly did) or wouldn't go to movies (they did that, too, albeit with a bit of a dip in attendance). It's that ticket prices slid downward. From 1933 to 1937, the average cost of a ticket *fell* by about half. It doesn't take a finance professor to understand that less money at the box office will lead to lower studio revenues.

The real horror double-feature for the studios and the theaters, however, was that this drop in revenue happened at the same time that they needed to invest in a lot of new equipment. In 1927, Warner Brothers released one of the first so-called "talking pictures," or "talkies," as they would be known.[4] The innovation was quite striking—sound, especially actor's voices—could now be synchronized with the visuals on the screen. With synchronization, you could have what most people now take for granted: dialog. Audiences went wild for talkies, and if studios and theaters didn't invest in the equipment to show them, they wouldn't be in business for long. The golden age of silent films was over.

This was an important transition for our dynamic trio. They had cut their teeth on some of the best-regarded natural dramas of the 1920s, but they were all silent films. Yes, there was music, but you couldn't hear the animals. A tiger isn't a tiger if you can't hear it roar. They would need to up their game, but it wouldn't be an easy sell to the studios.

Why was that? Didn't we just say that's what people wanted to see (and hear)?

The studios also discovered that while investment in the equipment was expensive, investment in the production of the films was (surprisingly) less so. If you think about it, it makes sense. Simply having actors on screen with limited

---

4. We're referring to *The Jazz Singer*, which was an appropriate choice for one of the first synchronized movies. There's some debate about the "first" movie of this type, but the debate isn't relevant here. Warner Brothers' success with this film sparked the transition away from the silent film era.

sets and props was a way to save money. Sure, you needed to pay big-name actors and have them dress in attractive clothing, but you didn't need to send intrepid explorers to the far corners of the earth to capture footage of a tiger almost eating your director. Studios in the early 1930s produced a lot of talking *dramas*—partly out of necessity and partly out of playing with their new toy.

It wasn't long, however, before the novelty started to wear off. By the mid-1930s, audiences began to expect talking pictures and wanted something a little more than 90 minutes of talking heads.[5] The studios were in a pickle. They needed a big win. To get it, they needed to show the audience something they had never seen before.

But what would that be?

Luckily, Cooper had an idea.

. . .

> I got to thinking about the possibility of there having been one beast, more powerful than all the others and more intelligent…Then, the thought struck me: What would happen to this highest representation of prehistoric animal life in our materialistic, mechanistic civilization? Why not place him at the pinnacle of the tallest building, the symbol in steel, stone, and glass of modern man's achievement and aspiration, and pit him against modern man?

This excerpt comes from a studio press release that promoted the film in 1933, but Copper had mulled over the idea for a long time. Later in the release, he admits that this image of the giant ape on the tallest building in the world was the *climax* of the movie, not the beginning. Cooper needed to work backward from the movie's end to trace what would happen first. In other words, the team wrote the story arc in reverse.

---

5. Wondering how this could possibly happen. Remember the first time you saw WiFi on an airplane? People cheered. Now, if the WiFi is broken, passengers moan. Consumer expectations are funny like that.

Let's follow that, shall we? If it's been a while since you saw the movie (or never saw it), this part will catch you up.

The first question: If Kong was destined to climb the tallest building in New York and wasn't hiding in Brooklyn all this time, how would he get to New York?

Well, the human protagonists would need to visit Kong first. They'd need to see *his* world. They'd need to meet the people who worshipped him. What were they like? What were their motivations? One also presumes Kong wouldn't sit down for tea, discuss the situation, and ink a 10-city tour deal with some American in a pith hat. Kong would need to be captured. Once he arrived in New York, he would need to escape this confinement. Cooper didn't have to have it all figured out now. Rose would take care of those details.

Perhaps, but that does beg the question: How do you capture a 50-foot gorilla? A few rifles wouldn't cut it, and the aforementioned tea negotiation wasn't realistic.

The answer: Kong needed a love interest. In fact, the team had received that critique on their earlier film (the one with the tigers and elephants). It was exciting, but...where was the romance? To his credit, Schoedsack thought the idea was utterly ridiculous. And to *his* credit, Cooper realized that's how the movie would get made and why audiences would flock to it—especially women, who might not want to watch a monster movie, no matter how great the cinematography was. To *her* credit, Rose was able to find a way to write a Kong love story that didn't seem *too* campy. Never having seen a *blonde* beauty before, Kong would be swept away by his animal desires.

If that sounds like Rose didn't quite uncampyfy this enough, consider a few things. One, it could have been worse. Plenty of love stories of the time were cringy enough to make your face stay like that. And two, she worked in the adventure scenes where Kong was protecting her from the dinosaurs and other mega-critters on the island, only being captured after becoming exhausted after kicking a T-Rex's butt.

Swept up in the publicity of their "find," the expedition wouldn't be able to resist putting Kong on display as the "eighth wonder of the world." He'd promptly escape, grab his love interest, and climb the Empire State Building—which had just been completed in 1931.[6] That helped add to the appeal.

Here's where we get to the part where the airplanes shoot down Kong. Ultimately, it was a struggle between raw nature and modern technology, and technology would win.

The story arc was pretty clear from the beginning. Now, they just needed to find a way to make it.

Let's recap.

Cooper had a great idea and a compelling storyline…but no idea how to bring it to the screen. Schoedsack knew what the camera needed to capture…but had no idea how "real" and "imaginary" elements would come together. Rose understood what made crisp writing that kept the action moving…but had never written anything like that.

And that was all okay. Better than okay, actually.

That's because this team had the *right* experience to create this type of film. All three understood how animals moved and interacted with the natural environment—especially the jungle. They also had firsthand experience with indigenous people who called those areas home. This film would (almost) be more like a documentary than a drama, where the audience would follow the team as they explored, made discoveries, and handled problems.

However, no one knew how to put a 50-foot gorilla or dinosaur on the screen *with* live actors. That…was going to take some work.

Today, we're accustomed to simply prompting a generative AI program to "show me a video of a giant ape fighting a T-rex." That technology didn't exist in the 1930s. Even getting animatronic creatures to interact with live characters on the screen was beyond most filmmaking techniques of the day. Once RKO Studios agreed to make *Kong*, they didn't need to make only a movie; they needed to invent something called "special effects."

. . .

---

6. The iconic art deco Chrysler Building had been the tallest building for just two years until the Empire State Building (and its iconic spire) took the title at 1,250 feet. Originally, the spire was meant to serve as a docking station for airships. You have to admit, that would have been cool.

Most people who enjoy special effects (and even plenty of people who love the craft) don't realize the debt they owe to an Irish immigrant named Harold O'Brien.[7] Authors George Turner and Orville Goldner detail the full story in their cinematic history *The Making of King Kong*, which, unlike other retellings, doesn't omit O'Brien's pivotal role. Although stop-motion animation wasn't his original idea (it was invented by a French filmmaker a few decades before), O'Brien perfected it.

In basic terms, stop-motion animation exploits an optical illusion. You can try it for yourself with a notepad and paper. Draw a stick figure on the first page. On the next page, alter the drawing *just a little*...perhaps moving its hand as if starting to wave. On the next page, move the hand position a little more. You get the idea. Each page features a distinct, separate image, but something magical happens when you flip through the pages quickly. Your eye fills in the gaps, and it appears like the stick figure is running, jumping, or whatever you drew it to do.

O'Brien used a 16-frames-per-second film speed to create the optical illusion in his first film. In practical terms, that meant capturing 16 still images for every one second of footage. Do the math. If you wanted a three-minute animation, you'd need 8,880 stills. (By the way, that's about the length of the Kong versus T-Rex scene in the original movie.)

Albeit tedious, this process works with stick figures, watercolor paintings (as we'll see later with the first animated feature-length film, *Snow White and the Seven Dwarves*), or clay models. Clay models are what's important here. Why is that? Clay models allow filmmakers to manipulate *scale*.

What's scale? Let's say, for example, you wanted to film a giant gorilla emerging from a group of trees. First, you're probably not going to build a full-sized,

---

7. Most biographies note O'Brien's excessive drinking. However, we can't discount the fact these reports were written by people who hated the Irish with a racial animus we can't quite understand today. In the so-called "racial hierarchies" popular in that era, they were near the bottom. O'Brien's level of alcohol use hardly seems relevant here given what he accomplished, so we're going to leave it out. However, be warned that if you read more about him, you'll see some ugly stuff.

50-foot model gorilla.[8] You might build a head or hand for close-up detail shots, but a full-scale model certainly wasn't practical in the 1930s. (It's hard to do *now*.) A "scale" model simply refers to the ratio of your model to the real thing. A 10:1 scale would mean your 50-foot gorilla would be five feet tall. A 100:1 scale is a five-inch model. Either one is much more manageable. (The *King Kong* team actually used a variety of sizes and models depending on the scene.)

If you're creative, you can use a bonsai mini-tree approach to place your mini-Kong in a mini-jungle.[9] Get everything right, and the viewer would believe Kong was as large as a full-sized tree. Another trick to enhance the illusion was to include "reference objects" of known size—a car, building, or mailbox—that would serve as a visual anchor point for the size of the objects in that scene.

This all sounds straightforward, but the details were anything but trivial. For example, let's say you added real (miniature) plants in your 20:1 scale "jungle." Real plants are living organisms that *move* as the day goes on. You might not notice in photo 72 of 8,880, but you will notice in photo 7,200 of 8,880, especially when you see thousands of shots flick by in mere seconds of a motion picture.

O'Brien's skill was making sure you *didn't* notice.

Plants were one thing. People were another. There was no way to use clay-modeled people; the difference would be too noticeable. Kong needed to interact with actors in the *same scene*. Sometimes, the audience might see Kong's hand grab the lead actress Fay Wray. That was a life-sized model hand, so it was comparatively easy to film. The only trick was ensuring the perspective change wasn't too jarring.

No, the real challenge was overlaying the animated shots with the human shots—*at different scales*—so that it appeared that humans and giants were interacting. O'Brien's true innovation (with Schoedsack's help) was combining the

---

8. Filmmaker Steven Spielberg would use this technique with both *Jaws* and *Jurassic Park*, and it was enormously difficult even decades later. In the 1930s, it would have been impossible. Instead, filmmakers build the occasional full-sized or half-sized models for close-up shots. The team did its work so well in fact, that some reviewers believed *all* of the shots used life-sized models. It's a testament to how well the team was able to shift perspectives from scene to scene.

9. Bonsai mimics the image of a larger tree in miniature. There's no evidence the *Kong* team thought of it this way, but that's the idea.

two shots into one final visual. O'Brien would create the stop-motion animation with "spaces" where the human actors would appear in the scene. The human actors would be filmed "interacting" with the animals...or, more precisely, where the animals *would be* in the final scene. Today, it's commonplace. In 1933, it was the first time it had been done.

We're skipping over a fair number of other fascinating details. Turner and Goldner detail the switch from 16 to 28 frames per second, nearly doubling the workload but dramatically smoothing the animation. Or how Cooper would borrow set pieces and other actors from other pictures that happened to be shooting on sets nearby to save money. Speaking of saving money, plenty of animation ended up on the cutting room floor to shorten the running time. Longer films not only cost more to produce (they took more reels), but they also meant the theaters could have fewer showings per night. This could have made for an awkward story experience, but it's where Rose's writing and editing shined. In the end, the shorter film was a *better* film.

Despite all the technical wizardry, one innovation stands out: the decision *not* to reveal Kong too early in the story. Some at RKO questioned this writing decision. Why wouldn't you show off the exciting camerawork early in the film? Wouldn't audiences get bored? Two reasons to delay the reveal—one technical, one narrative. Cooper and his team understood that while the special effects were impressive, they weren't...perfect. Clearly, these were models; if you looked too closely, you'd see the flaws. Rose wrote the story to draw in the audience, allowing them to become invested in the narrative and suspend disbelief *before* the big reveal. By that point, audiences were so captivated that they went along for the ride.

Timing, perhaps more than any other innovation, would define what it meant to successfully incorporate special effects into a film.

After months of work, *King Kong* was finished in March 1933, one of the darkest, most frightening months of the Great Depression.

Why would people go see a monster movie? They were already in one right now.

. . .

To be fair, RKO supplied film critics with 10 minutes of footage. They were blown away. They knew this would be groundbreaking, but without showing an audience that "preview," the average person would not know what they were getting. Studio executives waited nervously for opening weekend.

They wouldn't need to wait long.

In its first three days in theaters, *King Kong* made $89,921. That's about $2.1 million today. That might not sound like much, but remember two things: First, this was during the Great Depression when ticket prices were *dropping*, averaging about 25 cents. More than 350,000 people saw the movie in the first few days. Again, that may not sound like that many people until you remember that the total U.S. population was about one-third the size it is today. That would be equivalent to about 1.2 million people now.[10] The movie would go on to make over $5 million on a budget of about a half million dollars. That's outstanding, even by today's standards.

Everyone had their own pet theories on why the movie had done well.

While many of the reviews seemed to get the point (the *New York Times* called it a "fascinating adventure"), others seemed almost upset that a "monster movie" had done so well. John Mosher of *The New Yorker* wrote that Kong was "ridiculous" but had to admit that "many scenes in this picture are certainly diverting." In an unintentional play on words, the *Chicago Tribune* attributed the success to its "mammoth novelties."

A 1933 *Time* magazine review went with a more cerebral explanation. It struggled to explain why audiences would like the movie, somehow deducing that people didn't take Kong seriously:

> It might seem that any creature answering the description of Kong would be despicable and terrifying. Such is not the case. Kong is an exaggeration ad absurdum, too vast to be plausible. This makes his actions wholly enjoyable.

---

10. The math gets a little complicated based on population expansion, movie ticket prices, the number of theaters, and additional entertainment options, but *King Kong* did comparable sales to *Jurrasic Park* in 1993. No one quite seems to agree on how much money *King Kong* made, exactly. There are different ways to calculate the overall number. It doesn't matter. It was a big deal.

Where *Time* thought Kong was ridiculous, Cooper, for his part, saw the film as a throwback to a bygone era. Nostalgia explained the appeal.

> The world is getting smaller every year. I mean, it's becoming too civilized. I can remember when the world was a grand old place—filled with unexplored lands, choked with adventure. In those days, Schoedsack and I used to run away to the ends of the world, confident of finding real motion-picture material. But now, what's a fellow to do? Where is he to go?

None of these explanations—its technical prowess, Kong's buffoonery, or nostalgia for a world gone by—seems to capture the magic the audiences felt when they saw it. On one level, *King Kong's* success was simple: No one had ever seen anything like it.

Here is a list of other notable films from that year: *Roman Scandals, I'm No Angel, Gold Diggers of 1933, She Done Him Wrong, The Bowery, Tugboat Annie, Footlight Parade, Dancing Lady, 42nd Street,* and *Dinner at Eight*. These films earned more money than *King Kong*, by the way. Do you remember any of them? No? A year later, neither did anyone else.

Kong was unique. Unique has staying power.

However, on another level, people identified with *King Kong*—no, not the literal monster—the *figurative* one. The Great Depression was full of real monsters—economic hardship, job losses, bank runs, starvation, and despair. Seeing a giant gorilla on screen was about as close of a metaphor as you could imagine to the terror people felt daily.

But perhaps that's simply trying to overintellectualize it. The simplest explanation might be the closest to the truth. *King Kong* was utter escapism, pure and simple. It was the first popcorn movie. For 100 minutes, audiences would leave their dreary, frightening world and enjoy the ride.

Audiences voted with their feet. *King Kong* redefined what a movie could be and the stories it could tell. Without Kong, there would have been no Snow White. No Dracula. No Frankenstein. No Godzilla. No Jaws. No Aliens. And no Jurassic Park. In fact, many of today's biggest movies owe their special effects legacy to Cooper, Schoedsack, Rose, and O'Brien. Without them, our entertainment lives would be somehow...less spectacular.

More than anything, however, *King Kong* was the perfect movie for its time. FDR had just taken over. The weekend after Kong's release, Roosevelt ordered a bank holiday to halt the panic in the financial sector. It was a fitting metaphor. Yes, the monster was at our shores. Yes, it was scary. No, it was like nothing we had ever seen before. But in the end, we would defeat it.

11

BINGO!

Father Jacob Kowalewski had a problem. Like most small Catholic parishes in the early days of the Great Depression, donations were down—not just a little down—w*ay down*. At the same time, the need for charitable assistance was up—w*ay up*.

As bad as it was, tiny St. Mary's Polish Church in Wilkes-Barre, Pennsylvania, probably fared worse than most. The Scranton area as a whole wasn't doing well, but if you were a community that mainly catered to recent Polish immigrants…well, that could be bad. Newcomers often aren't welcomed in a community and economy where jobs are scarce. Whether immigrants actually "took" jobs from current residents wasn't the issue. People were looking for someone to blame for their predicament, and the broader community's mood was on the verge of ugly.

Of course, Kowalewski knew that. He also knew that not everyone was under actual economic stress. (We'll talk more about the Catholic response in general later, but seeing the impact on a small scale is, in some ways, much more important and instructive.) Here's the funny thing about this or *any* economic downturn. In 1930, when we met our intrepid priest, unemployment wasn't (yet) that bad. Parishioners heard stories of people jumping off skyscrapers in New York, food prices collapsing, and massive layoffs at formerly bustling factories. However, the Great Depression hadn't reached the average person in Wilkes-Barre.

But that's not how fear works.

Fear made the nine in ten people who still had work in 1930 hold onto their money more tightly. Who knows what tomorrow might bring? Things were getting worse; it was just a matter of time. However, none of that changed Kowalewski's mission to help those who needed it now. How could he get comparatively well-off people to loosen the purse strings? Imploring parishioners from the pulpit on Sunday wasn't working fast enough or well enough. Kowalewski needed a game-changer.

As it turned out, "game" was precisely the correct word. People have always loved to play games, and the Great Depression would be no exception. In fact, the 1930s saw the birth of board game culture in the United States with *Monopoly*, *Sorry!*, and *Scrabble*. However, Kowalewski didn't just want people to play games in the church basement; he needed them to spend money, and no one would pay a cover charge at a church.

If you're wondering why we're dancing around the obvious solution, it was tricky for a priest to talk about the *positive* values of gambling. Kowalewski knew what every casino knew: In the end, the house always wins. Gambling is profitable because the basic statistics *always* work against the gambler over the long run. But just because it would solve the problem didn't mean he could do it. Card and dice games (the most popular and well-understood games of chance) were something the Catholic church predictably and routinely railed against. Kowalewski couldn't just set up his own card tables and roulette wheels. That was too close to *the ends justify the means* for his taste. He needed a different option.

By chance (and by intended pun), he came across another Polish kindred spirit—Edwin Lowe. He was Jewish, not Catholic, but strange times make for strange bedfellows, and Kowalewski was desperate. Lowe had an intriguing new game.

A very brief diversion before we continue. Do we know for sure *the priest in this story was Father Kowalewski? No, we don't. At least, not exactly. No one had conducted this research before. Here's what we do know. Edwin Lowe was approached by a priest in the Wilkes-Barre area. Data from the Catholic Diocese of Scranton shows only 19 priests active during that time in that township. That narrows things down. Add to that the reasonable assumption that one Polish immigrant might seek out another Polish immigrant, and the priest pool shrinks to three. The three in question are Vincent Jakubowski, Chester Kolokowski, and Jacob Kowalewski, all of St. Mary's Polish Church. The best guess is that some combination of all three of them made the decision.*

Back to the game.

The rules were simple. Each player was issued their own playing card (or cards) with a unique set of numbers arranged in a five-by-five grid with one "free space" in the middle. The *possible* numbers could range from 1 to 75, so there were multiple 24-number combinations, but Lowe didn't know (yet) how many there could be. A "caller" would announce numbers at random. As players saw that number on their card, they would mark that spot. What was great about the game was that there were several possible goals: get all numbers in a row, make a "T" shape, make an "L" shape, make an "X" shape, or even "fill the card."

However, the best part was that it was a *social* game. It only made sense to play as a big group. One person playing one card at one time was possible, but it wasn't very fun. The more people, the better the experience. It helped that the game was easy, too. You simply needed to watch the numbers. And that moment when someone won and yelled out. It was so exciting!

Kowalewski approached Lowe, who had just started marketing a version of the game, and asked if he could use it for his church fundraiser. Lowe, the consummate entrepreneur, immediately saw a massive target market needing precisely what he had.

We might say Lowe had a "Bingo."

. . .

Just to be clear, Bingo wasn't Lowe's original invention. That's a common theme in all innovation history; this game is no exception. What made him special was his ability to recognize a good idea, identify a target market, and execute a plan to bring them together.

The original game wasn't called "Bingo," either. Our best records (and they're not great) chart the origins of a game called "Lotto" in 16th-century Italy.[1] Similar to the gameplay that would define Bingo, Italians played the game using horizontal cards printed with random numbers in groups of 10—1-10, 11-20, 21-30, and so on up to 90. When a number was called, players placed a token (a bean, chip, or something else) on that number. Depending on the specific rules of the game—and there were many—the player (or players) would win.

If you're wondering—*Hey, the word "lotto" sounds like "lottery"*—is there any connection? The answer is *yes*. You can still find places in Italy to play it to raise money for various local projects.[2]

Over the next few centuries, the game made its way to Napoleonic France, where it became *Le Lotto*. You don't need to know Italian or French to deduce that this was, basically, the same game, played with the same rules, just in a different language. In both cases, the game was a useful way to fund small, local projects. When the game spread northward into Germany in the 1800s, the ever-so-practical Germans used a variant to teach their children vocabulary words. (If you're wondering why you played Vocab Bingo in grade school, now you know who to thank...or blame.)

However, the game *really* started to take off when it crossed the English Channel.

The British loved (and still love) this game with a passion that's hard to describe. In typical Brit fashion, they didn't call it *Le Lotto*, even though soldiers picked it up from the French in the trenches of World War I. If you were wondering, they didn't call it "Bingo" either. No, it was called...wait for

---

1. No, it wasn't "Italy" then. The game started in Florence and spread to Venice and Genoa. Formal Italian unification wouldn't occur until the 19th century.

2. Here is a bit more detail from the official Lo Giuoco del Lotto website: "The 'Ambo' pays off at 250 times your original bet while the 'Terno' pays off at 4,250 times. The 'Quaterna' and the 'Cinquina' pays off at 80,000 times and one million times whatever you bet, respectively. For example, if you decided to wager one euro (about one US dollar) on a 'Terno' of 22, 68 and 90, and those three numbers are among the five drawn, you win €4,250 (€1 x 4,250). Lo Giuoco del Lotto draws are held every Tuesdays, Thursdays and Saturdays between 8.00 and 8.30 p.m." Now you can feel like a local on your next European vacation.

it…"Housey-Housey." Apparently, when they first learned it, they would arrange multiple playing cards in the shape of a house.

The strangeness doesn't stop there. The Brits developed an entire mythology around each number from 1 to 90.[3] A few of the fun ones include: "5-0, 5-0, it's off to work we go" (in reference to the Disney movie *Snow White*), "Keir's Den" (aka "10," referring to the current Prime Minister and occupant of 10 Downing Street, Keir Starmer…or whoever the PM happens to be), and the admittedly randy "Meal for Two" (referencing the number 69). Parents, you get to explain that last one to your kids when they're old enough.

"Housey" halls started popping up throughout the United Kingdom in the early 20th century. However, although they didn't call the game *Le Lotto*, the game still featured 90 numbers and a horizontal playing card. The game wouldn't take its 75-number form until it crossed the pond.

The credit for that transition wouldn't belong to Lowe; it would go to a prominent *Australian* stage actor named Hugh Ward. Why did we just travel around the world from England to Pittsburg, Pennsylvania, by way of the land down under? That's because Ward was quite the globe-trotter. Ward picked up the game from his home base in London and traveled to Australia, where he made a name for himself in the farthest-flung reaches of the then-British empire. (It's easier to make a name for yourself as a big fish in a smaller pond.) During an acting trip to the United States, he not only married a Pennsylvania woman, but he also introduced his new game to local carnival goers.[4]

Ward likely changed from the horizontal 90-number game card to the familiar 75-number square card format we use today for his "Beano" game. You heard that correctly—*Beano*, not *Bingo*. Ward noticed resourceful Americans covering the empty spots with whatever they had on hand—at the carnival, that was dried beans. Beans were convenient because the cards could be emptied and played again, hence the name.

---

3. The best place to find this outside of the U.K. is the "List of British bingo nicknames" page on Wikipedia.

4. The information we have here is sketchy to say the least. There is no authoritative history on the origins of the Bingo game, only plenty of anecdotal stories. We're piecing together the likely moves based on agreement among several sources.

(Try to sing B-E-A-N-O with the famous melody you're thinking of right now. It doesn't quite roll off the tongue, does it? Good names are *so* important to a new product.)

That's the game Lowe saw at a carnival in Atlanta, Georgia, in 1929.

. . .

In just a few months, Beano had traveled down the East Coast of the United States from Pennsylvania to Atlanta.

If you're getting the places confused, don't worry. It's enough to know that promoters and entrepreneurs would often follow the carnival circuit. It was a great way to earn money, sell your wares, and learn about innovations in the days before shopping malls and online portals.

Edwin Lowe was the son of an Orthodox Rabbi, educated in the Middle East, and hit the toy sales circuit in December 1929. As you might guess, carnivals are natural places to sell toys, so Lowe was keen to notice anything new that met that general description. What he noticed was a line of people waiting to pay a nickel to play this new game. That was worth investigating.

In an obituary for Lowe, the *Los Angeles Times* noted that his "deep south" sales territory was one of the worst in the nation. It seems reasonable that Lowe would be looking for something that could juice sales or, failing that, a way to strike out on his own and change his circumstances. Keep in mind that this was just after the stock market crash but well before anyone started panicking about the state of the economy.

Lowe couldn't have known how bad it *would get* in just a few years, but as it turns out, his anemic sales territory was giving him an unplanned preview of what was to come. In a pattern other entrepreneurs would follow in the next several years, Lowe turned lemons into lemonade...or, more fittingly, made Bingo out of Beano.

Traveling back home to Brooklyn after the carnival season, Lowe started introducing this new game to his friends. So the legend goes, one of his guests was so excited to win, she yelled "Bingo!" instead of...well, it wasn't clear *what* you were supposed to say in the original game. Whether that story was true, false, or a little of both is impossible to know. It seems just as likely that he came up with the new name and invented the story to make it sound more serendipitous and authentic—like shooting an arrow and painting a target around where it landed. All we *do know* is that Lowe could recognize a bad name when he saw one. Beano sounded vaguely food-like…and a noisy, smelly food at that.

However, it wouldn't take long for serious issues with the rechristened game to surface.

The big problem was something you wouldn't notice standing in line to play the game one person at a time. The original game only featured 12 cards with unique number combinations. If you think about it, that's a major problem. If there are only 12 cards, your group size is limited to 12 players. That might work for dinner parties, but it couldn't handle…say, a sizeable congregation—exactly what Kowalewski was asking about for his church fundraiser.

Lowe finalized the game board into the familiar five-by-five grid we see today, with numbers 1-75 divided into columns headed by the letters B-I-N-G-O. To simplify it for players, the 'B' column contained only numbers 1 and 15, the 'I' column 16 through 30, the 'N' column 31 through 45, the 'G' column 46 through 60, and the 'O' column 61 through 75. Obviously, there were more than 12 possible combinations because each column only contains five of the possible 15 numbers (and the N column only has four possibilities because of the "free space" in the middle of the card).

How many more? Lowe was out of his depth when it came to figuring it out. He'd need help. But before we tackle that math problem, we need to talk about timing.

...

Timing matters.

We all know that intuitively, but it's worth noting that there were plenty of immigrants from the European continent in the decades before the 1930s. Many of them likely played some version of *Le Lotto* or Housey-Housey. Yet none of those versions caught on in the United States.

What was special about the 1930s that made it a ripe environment for new games, especially those that involved gambling and fundraising?

To understand that, we must take a brief detour to examine the history of gambling in the United States. Gambling, as you might expect, goes way back in American life. Lotteries and gambling were a part of the Colonial period in

American history, but perhaps not in the way you might expect. Games of chance (especially those that involved money) were seen as gauche and lower-class. Anything played with cards or dice was considered immediately suspect by respectable society. Horseracing, by contrast, was generally accepted by polite society. That's probably because horses were (and are) beautiful animals requiring expensive care. Only the wealthy could afford to set aside part of their stable for racing, not working, so the entire practice seemed more respectable.

Beyond horseracing, it's not that elites didn't enjoy dice and card games; it's simply that they clucked their tongues while they did it. That's a common theme in all consumer history—moralism by elites rarely extends to their actions. Despite that hypocrisy, many colonies were formed on strictly religious grounds, so a patchwork of legislation determined what games were "legal" in different areas. In general, more strict communities and states meant less (legal) gambling, whereas cosmopolitan areas such as New York and New Orleans featured much more of all types.[5]

Fast-forward from the Colonial era to the decade before the Civil War, and the mood had changed.

This was the time of the so-called "Third Great Awakening" in American life—a strong religious revival that gave birth to the Progressive movement. Most of us learn about this as a catalyst for the Abolitionist movements in the northern states that pushed the country into a war (in large part) to end the practice of

---

5. We tend to think of the colonies founded on religious freedom as bastions of tolerance. They were not. What Massachusetts and Maryland meant by "religious freedom" was freedom to worship as they decided you should worship. They were more concerned with freedom from the state-sponsored Church of England than letting citizens do as they pleased. That's why the First Amendment to the U.S. Constitution was so important.

chattel slavery in the United States. However, less well-known is the evolution of attitudes toward all forms of vice, including gambling.[6]

Newly emboldened moralists targeted gambling wherever they found it, but as you might guess, the approach differed depending on the status of the gambler. In elite communities, a quasi-chivalrous code developed surrounding horseracing. This set of rules dictated who could bet, in what amounts, and when it was acceptable to do so. You can see echoes of that code embedded in the modern "Triple Crown" races; the Belmont Stakes (1867), Preakness Stakes (1873), and Kentucky Derby (1875) are the most famous, but you can see the traditions in place at nearly every track in the United States.[7] Think of it as a societal control so that gambling doesn't get out of hand and that the animals aren't abused. It worked…sometimes. Betting was routinely restricted or banned in that era, depending on the time and location, yet it found a way to happen anyway.

By contrast, restrictions on working-class forms of gambling—poker, dice, and other games played in clubs, bars, and back alleys—were much more punitive and, in the end, much less successful.

Outright bans depended on the strength of the local churches and religious figures, so the result was a patchwork of rules where gambling might be legal on one side of the street and illegal on the other. Most of the time, they settled for bans on Sundays—the origins of many similar laws still on the books today.[8]

---

6. This is also where we see the first rumblings of a Prohibition movement for alcohol. It would take decades to come to fruition, but its roots stretch back here. The first two "Great Awakenings" are better known—the two that predate and coincide with the American Revolution. Some scholars debate the existence of a third, but that seems silly. The cultural impacts were profound—abolitionism, prohibition, gambling restrictions…the list goes on. If you want to read more about it, be careful. Many of the histories are written with a clear pro- or anti-Christian bias. Many others *really* are talking about *today's* political climate. Sadly, it's better to find books on the specific subject (e.g. abolitionism) than the broader concept of religious revivalism.

7. Horseracing for sport (not simply for transportation or farm labor) goes way back. In the Western world, the chariot races in Rome are the most famous, but they got the idea from others further East. There, horses were an integral part of life on the vast plains of central Asia known as the Steppe. Maybe that's where the idea for the spectacular hats came from? It's worth looking into. Those are *great* hats.

8. For example, as late as 2024, you can't buy a car on Sunday in my home state of Minnesota. My adopted home state of Florida (a looser moral state throughout its history) has no such restriction.

Many of these laws either didn't understand (or, more likely, didn't respect) gaming traditions embedded within immigrant communities. In that era, it was the Irish, Germans, and Italians. Later, it would be Cubans and Russians. However, multi-generational Americans needed little encouragement to play games of chance.

...

Of course, gambling came with its vices. The moralists clearly had a point. However, their solution was more moral than practical...and just about as effective. Gambling always seemed to find its way back into American life. Whack the gambling mole in Baton Rouge, and gambling would pop back up in New Orleans. Whack it there, and it moves to a riverboat. Or Galveston. Or Atlantic City. Or, most often, out of sight completely.

By the time we get to the Prohibition era in the 1920s, gambling (like alcohol) was largely illegal or tightly restricted in most places. It also happened everywhere. With local, state, and national Progressive politicians firmly in place in the 1920s and national leaders (Coolidge, then Hoover) either unwilling or unable to adjust those rules, the status quo prevailed. No one was willing to admit to the widespread open secret that restrictive policies weren't working—and in fact, they were encouraging a variety of unintended consequences.

Things were stuck...unless something major happened.

The Great Depression was the "major" thing.

In a famous remark from the Oval Office, newly-elected President Roosevelt quipped that "what America needs now is a drink." It was part of his "First 100 Days" initiatives and marked the beginning of the rapid end of Prohibition.

What's less well documented is the positive impact the end of tight restrictions had on the finances of local and state governments. Even Progressive leaders needed to meet payroll, and there were only so many places to get it from citizens pinching every penny. The pennies they were *not* pinching—to visit a local speakeasy and play a game of poker—weren't being taxed.

Can you guess what happened next? Of course, you can.

By 1933, cities and states sought to extract much-needed tax revenue anywhere they could to fund relief efforts. Remember, the Federal government was only part of the response to the economic collapse. To paraphrase 1980s political icon

Tip O'Neill: *All economic relief is local.* Yes, programs such as the Civilian Conservation Corps (CCC) offered direct employment by the Federal government, but only about 300,000 people served at any one time. That was a lot of people, and it helped, but unemployment peaked at around 25 percent. That meant over 12 million people were out of work. Do the math. Most relief, such as it was, came from local and state agencies.

Even in the worst days of the Great Depression, people spent money on alcohol and gambling, which "rationally" makes no sense but makes perfect sense to anyone stressed out. The idea of the so-called "sin taxes" was born in this era. The reason is simple: Even in economic downturns, they provide reliable government funding.[9]

The effect was swift.

After years of horse races with no (legal) gambling, new tracks started sprouting nationwide. The state of Nevada was the first to take advantage of the new revenue source on a grand scale, legalizing gambling in 1931. The recently completed Hoover Dam provided a reliable power and water source to Las Vegas, an otherwise climate-limited site. Construction crews had already built the roads, so the city was ripe for an explosion in pilgrimages to the first gambling mecca. Despite valiant attempts to slow the growth of "Sin City," by the time the dam was completed in 1935, Las Vegas was well on its way to being the world's gambling capital.

In short, progressives and moralists hated gambling, but they couldn't stop it. However, legislators (in many cases, progressives themselves) were pragmatists. They needed the money. And everyone else? They were going to do it anyway.

...

That was Father Kowalewski's dilemma. Catholics are, by definition, a pretty moral lot. However, they also needed the money to help people, and people were gambling anyway. Could he channel that impulse into something that might

---

9. Fair tax advocates would say that this is terrible tax policy. The idea is that you can't rely on revenue from a tax where you're encouraging people to stop the behavior. Logically, that's at cross purposes. For example, if you fund preschool programs with a cigarette tax, and you're successful getting people to stop smoking (which the tax is meant to do), you'll lose funding for preschool programs. This is one of those many examples where rationality doesn't match reality.

achieve both goals—give people the social experience of gambling and, at the same time, provide a revenue source for the church? It was worth a shot. Lowe's game seemed like the perfect solution, but there was still that tricky issue about the number of possible playing cards.

Leave it to the Catholics to get into the details. Let's say you could fill a church basement with 144 players. (That 144 becomes important for the math in a second.) Remember, you only have 12 card possibilities. That means you'll need 12 copies of each card. (12 times 12 is 144). Bingo isn't very fun when 12 people—*the same 12 people*—win each time. No one wants to split the kitty 12 ways.

Lowe knew he needed to find a solution if he would have any luck selling his game to the priests of America.

He approached Carl Leffler, a retired mathematics professor from the University of Columbia. It was a math teacher's irresistible puzzle: Come up with more playing card combinations for this game. Leffler did just that. He devised over 6,000 card combinations—enough to satisfy priests nationwide for generations.[10] But even that number wasn't the true potential. The European 90-number game has over 24 *quadrillion* possible combinations. More staggering than that astronomical number, because of a quirk in how the 75-number Bingo game is designed, the American version has 23 billion *times* that number in additional combinations—about 5.52 with 26 zeros after it. That's more than the estimated number of grains of sand on every beach on Earth (7.75 with 17 zeros after it). It would take longer than the history of the known universe for all the churches on Earth, playing continuously, to run out of playing cards. That would try the patience of even the most gentle Catholic grandmother.

The churches of the United States had exactly what they needed: A game that encouraged contributions but didn't seem *too much* like gambling. Of course, that was a polite fiction. Although players didn't bet on the outcome of a single call, people purchased a card, and the game continued until at least one person

---

10. Leffler also checked himself into an assylum soon after. Was it the Bingo math challenge that caused his decline or an undiagnosed mental illness...or something else? We will never know.

won. Bingo is an odd combination of a card game and a lottery ticket while simultaneously being neither.

More to the point, Bingo didn't feel like gambling. Unlike poker nights, which feature a dozen players at most, or horseraces, where players make individual, private bets, Bingo is a social event for the entire community. Not only would the game raise money for the church, but it would also attract people to the building outside of traditional service times.[11] Priests and other church aide workers could also get a good sense of the needs of the community—who hadn't eaten recently, who needed a new pair of shoes, and who just needed a hug.

In other words, Lowe had a hit.

In 1933, he registered his copyright and wrote the first American Bingo rule book.[12] Lowe's description is fitting:

> Bingo, a modern game adapted to commercial use, to advertise merchandise and to stimulate sales.

Bingo had a clear purpose, distinct from other "fun and games" of the 1930s. By 1942, Lowe created a new company to market the game nationwide.

. . .

Well, it wasn't all fun and games.

Father Kowalewski's polite fiction didn't fool everyone. Gambling was gambling, and the city of New York (for one) was concerned. Mayor Fiorello La Guardia (yep, *that* La Guardia) went so far as to place a temporary ban on Bingo in 1938. He feared (perhaps rightly; perhaps wrongly) that the mafia would get involved in the game.

If it sounds bizarre that the mob would get involved in church basement Bingo, you must understand what a strange time this was.

---

11. Catholics, and many other faiths, would say that whenever people are gathered in God's name, it *is* church. The priests certainly understood that doctrinal point, and perhaps even used it to justify the activity, but most people just wanted to have fun and spend time with other people.

12. This is another place Ward is sometimes mentioned. The history here is a Grade-A mess. The scholarship is sorely lacking, but like other games like it, the history of Bingo's copyright likely involves a game of "who got there first, wins."

Prohibition was a *boon* for the American mob. The money they could make from bootlegging dwarfed all other illicit revenue streams. As odd as it may seem, there just isn't that much money to be earned breaking kneecaps, running protection rackets, and all the other naughty industries the mob gets involved in. Selling illegal hooch was far more lucrative because there were many more potential customers. Nearly everyone wanted a beer; comparatively few wanted to hire a prostitute.

When Prohibition ended, so did one of the mob's primary revenue sources. It wasn't unreasonable to assume the Italian mob (who were, by and large, Catholics) wouldn't try to find an angle into the Bingo games.

In fact, Bingo seemed positively logical compared to other businesses the mob attempted to corner. La Guardia and the New York mob had recently gone to war over...artichokes. The mayor actually banned the sale of the spiky vegetable best known today for its collaboration with spinach to make a tasty dip. The three-day ban was just long enough to spoil the produce, kill the investment, and break the mob's hold on the supply chain. It wasn't unreasonable for La Guardia to try a ban on Bingo, though it's hard to see how the same dynamics would apply to a game as to perishable food.

Suffice it to say the ban didn't last long.

In short order, the New York state legislature recognized the *fait accompli* and put some rules in place. Probably trusting religious leaders to keep everything above board, New York limited Bingo to churches and synagogues so long as the proceeds went to a charitable cause. By definition, parishes doing relief work were all considered "charitable," so it basically gave churches a *monopoly* on Bingo. (Pun partially intended.)

That's why Bingo has such a powerful association with Catholics even today. However, that exclusivity wouldn't last long.

Las Vegas started offering Bingo games almost as soon as they heard about it and could get playing cards printed. Casino operators quickly discovered what Father Kowalewski knew intuitively—Bingo didn't feel like other forms of gambling. The game also didn't attract the same type of gambler. Bingo players appreciate the community aspect of the game in a way that slot machine, poker, and roulette players do not. Even today, most Bingo games are at odd times—at least for Las Vegas—mornings and middays when most other gamblers are still sleeping off last night's hangover. Native American casinos offer Bingo as well, as do church basements of all faiths nationwide.

Yes, Bingo is gambling, but the mechanics of the experience control some of the worst impulses. A large group of people is a great way to reign in the behavior of those who might otherwise (individually) gamble to excess. More than that, you purchase all your cards at the beginning of the game; there's no way to "ante up" and allow the excitement of the game to encourage risky betting.

Bingo's psychology works. The game also remains a solid moneymaker.

Estimates are hard to come by, but the U.S. Internal Revenue Service tracks Bingo revenue as its own category. In 2023, that number was roughly $10 billion, with 22 to 50 percent profit margins. (Profit is defined as game revenue minus all expenses *and* paying off winners.) Today, you can even play Bingo with an online community; it's the fastest-growing way to play. Will online playing change the community nature of the game? Perhaps. Time will tell.

For his part, Lowe did well for himself. He would supply miniature chess and checkers sets for soldiers heading to World War II. In 1956, he bought the rights to a game an eccentric couple played on their yacht, rechristened it *Yahtzee*, and grew it into one of the most successful dice games in history. Despite a failed hotel project in Las Vegas (the 450-room Tallyho hotel) in the 1960s, Lowe still sold his company to the Milton Bradley Company in 1973 for $26 million, or about $184 million in today's money.

Not bad for a guy who helped millions of people do some good, have a little fun, come together as a community, and maybe, just maybe, get to yell "Bingo!" once in a while.

12

UNREAL ESTATE

Union Pacific Railroad Chairman William Averell Harriman and business school dropout John Garnet Carter didn't know each other. As you might guess, they were probably about as different as two people were likely to be.

What bound them together wasn't as much time or place; it was a common problem with *real estate*. However, if you asked them, they probably wouldn't have seen the connection. During the Great Depression, everyone was trying to figure out how to extract value from any asset they owned, and real estate was one of the most obvious choices. If you owned property, you wanted to find a way to make money from it.

One helpful thing about looking back with nearly a century of hindsight is that we can see how two very different people used very different approaches to solve a very similar problem in a very similar way.

But we're getting ahead of ourselves.

We need to meet both of the characters in this drama, get their backstories, and understand the problems they thought were unique to them.

Let's start with Harriman. He was the sort of guy who used initials in everyday conversation. Depending on the historical record, he was either "W. A. Harriman," "W. Averell Harriman," or more formally, *Chairman* Harriman.

The Harrimans had a long history in the railroad business. His father, Edward Henry Harriman, rescued the Union Pacific Railroad from insolvency in 1898 (albeit with financial help from Kuhn, Loeb & Co.). His son Averell would go on to a successful diplomatic and political career, serving as a U.S. State Department diplomat in the Truman administration (primarily negotiating with the Soviet Union) and serving as the 48th governor of New York, among several other high-profile roles.[1]

It seemed both Harrimans had a knack for being in the wrong place at the wrong time when it came to railroads. (Or put another way, perhaps they were just who was needed at just the right time.) W. Averell Harriman started work at his father's railroad in 1915 and took over as Chairman just as the Great Depression was spiraling downward in 1932. For the history buffs reading, you probably have a sense of how singularly *bad* it was for railroads in this period of history, but for the sake of everyone else, let's briefly recap the situation.

In the 1800s, railroads were a miracle. Since humans first started migrating out of Africa in pre-history, the fastest they could ever hope to travel was limited to how quickly the slowest member of their group could walk. After humans domesticated horses, smaller groups could move more rapidly, but they were limited in how much their horses could carry or pull. Before the transcontinental railroad in the United States, wagon trains took weeks—or even months—to cross the vast continental interior. Living near a river (or later, canal) made things easier, but only if geography was in your favor.

The United States is a big place—bigger than any single country in Europe—so although railroads weren't invented there, Americans adopted them with a pas-

---

1. If you want to know more about the younger Harriman, read Rudy Abramson's 1992 biography, *Spanning the Century: The Life of W. Averell Harriman, 1891-1986*. There are some ugly stories you may also read about his purported connections with a German financier who, in World War II, supported the Nazi party. Financial types in that era saw themselves as somehow "above" global politics, and *most* big business interests in that time were under Hitler's thumb, whether they liked it or not. This isn't an excuse; it's just context.

sion that's difficult to understand now. Passenger railroads allowed people in the middle-to-late 1880s to finally get from point A to point B in hours or days versus weeks or months. From the end of the Civil War to the outbreak of World War I, railroads were the only option for most people and most destinations.

Railroads meant more than just shorter travel times. For the first time, Americans thought of the United States as *one place* rather than a collection of separate regions. We had an unshakeable passion for the rails.

That is...until we started building *roads* for cars and trucks. The success of the Model T—about 15 million sold from 1908 to 1927—meant serious competition for the railroads for the first time. The automobile had several advantages over railroads, but the biggest is the most obvious: People could go where they wanted *when* they wanted. That same logic held for transporting cargo by truck. Trains, by contrast, ran on *their* schedule.

Of course, plenty of people still rode trains (and still do today), but the die had been cast. Railroad passenger and cargo traffic declined sharply as automobile adoption and road construction increased. That's an especially acute problem for infrastructure-intensive businesses like railroads. Empty passenger cars, freight cars, tracks, and stations still need expensive maintenance and payments on their loans. The Union Pacific was worth more than a billion dollars before the Great Depression but wouldn't be after the 1929 crash. The younger Harriman faced the same challenge his father did a generation before: How could he save the UP?

When you boil it down, railroads had a *destination* problem. Passengers and freight wanted to get from one place to another, and in the era of increasing access to *all* locations by road, railroads were losing out. If passengers could get there by car, on their own timeframe, why would they take a train? Perhaps the railroads could market to passengers who couldn't afford cars, but that's not a viable long-term option. The best consumers (then and now) can buy premium fares, meals, and other services. It's tough to make money on bargain shoppers. Only a few companies have ever done so successfully—that's why Sears, Walmart, and Amazon are household names. Most others fail.

No, Harriman needed destinations trains could go that cars could not (or, not yet, or at least not for a long time to come). He also needed passengers who wouldn't quibble about pricey fares. If he couldn't find any, the UP's days were numbered.

. . .

Garnet Carter had a scrappier and much less privileged upbringing. His challenge wasn't trying to figure out how to save a billion-dollar railroad on its way to insolvency. He was just trying to make a living.

Like many people in the first years of the 1900s, he dropped out of high school to make his way in the world. After a few years of wandering and odd jobs, he decided to take a business course—the sort of practical education many self-made people seek once they've seen a bit of the world. Carter had seen enough to know there was money to be made; he just didn't know how. His business course focused his mind on real estate.

Fast-forward a few years, and everyone in real estate was swooning over Florida. In the Roaring 20s, the Sunshine State quickly became the vacation capital of the country due to its warm weather, sandy beaches, free-flowing (and illegal) alcohol, cruises, hotels, and scantily clad people. (Those are the same reasons it's popular now, minus the illegal alcohol.) Surely, there were opportunities to be had.

Carter embarked on a grand tour not only of Florida but many areas of the deep South, including Georgia, Alabama, Mississippi, and Tennessee. He eventually settled not on Miami or Tampa but on a spot in the Chattanooga area near the border of Tennessee and Georgia, right in the heart of the Smoky Mountains of Appalachia.[2] It might not be as sunny, and there might be fewer bikinis, but Carter saw an opportunity where others focused elsewhere.

It was a smart move. Carter declined an offer from an early partner to build a 15-story hotel in the area, much like the ones he saw going up in Miami Beach—sort of a "go big or go home" approach to real estate. However, Carter

---

2. The area around Lookout Mountain is stunningly beautiful, but in a different way than the beaches of Miami. If you go, make sure to visit the Great Smoky Mountains National Park.

had more modest ambitions, and by 1926 (when we catch up with him), the Florida real estate bubble was already popping.[3]

Carter settled on a small property in the Smoky Mountains that had been a popular picnic site for locals. However, its prior owners (trying to earn a little money on their property, per the theme of this story) had fenced it off and charged admission. Sure, that small fee could be a reasonable source of ongoing income—at least during tourist season—but tourists were just as keen to find free spots nearby than pay for this one. At this point in the story, we're still before the crash of 1929, so many families remained flush with cash. But people are people, and a bargain is a bargain.

Bottom line: Charging a few pennies for a smattering of people to picnic in your space versus somewhere else wasn't what Carter went to business school to do. However, a giant hotel wasn't a sound idea either.

It might not seem that Carter's situation was the same as Harriman's, but at a certain level, it was *precisely* the same. For Harriman, it was the legacy of a proud company. For Carter, it was his first true test as a businessperson. Both men needed to figure out what to do with underperforming real estate.

. . .

When we reconnect with Harriman, he hadn't identified his issue as a real estate problem just yet. Yes, the problem is easy to spot with nearly a century of hindsight. It's less obvious when you're in the thick of it. To be fair, he started with a reasonable solution: Union Pacific train cars were, politely, "long in the tooth." Less politely: dumpy. Commentators of the time used the word "appalling." You get the picture.

Consumers with the means to travel how they pleased could either get in their own car on their own timeline or board a smelly, hot passenger car on a noisy train. It was no contest. By the early 1930s, it was clear that cars and buses would

---

3. We cover the Florida land bubble in more detail in this book's precursor: *Booze, Babe, and the Little Black Dress: How Innovators of the Roaring 20s Created the Consumer Revolution*. Another great source is *Bubble in the Sun: The Florida Boom of the 1920s and How It Brought on the Great Depression*, by Christopher Knowlton. However, blaming the Florida land boom for the Great Depression is sort of like blaming a single straw on the proverbial camel's back. Poor camel. Why aren't there better metaphors?

be the *primary* mode of transportation for most people. It also was clear that commercial air travel wasn't far behind.[4] Americans are an independent-minded bunch. Give them a chance to choose, and they'll take it. The flexibility of the automobile was unmatched.

If passenger train cars were going to compete with passenger *cars*, they needed to be decidedly less...appalling.

Despite the economic uncertainty of the Great Depression, Harriman went to work, directing his design and engineering team to rebuild passenger cars—quite literally—from the wheels up. The new cars were constructed from aluminum instead of steel, making them both strong and (more importantly) much lighter. Lighter train cars require less fuel, which means less cost, which also means a greater profit margin—and the ability to lower fares as necessary without losing money on each rider.

However, Harriman's biggest improvement from the customer's perspective was something else entirely: air conditioning. The Union Pacific invested in *comfort*. Think about it. We take AC for granted today, but in 1933, precisely *zero* automobile manufacturers offered air conditioning.[5] Theaters and department stores were the first to offer AC in the mid-1920s, and consumers loved it. Trains with AC had a major advantage over sweaty cars in the summer—especially with overnight, cross-country trips.

Short story: It worked. In 1934, Union Pacific passenger traffic jumped 21.4 percent. 1935 saw even better improvement: 34.7 percent. Obviously, that was good news. Harriman and his team were able to reverse the downward trend, but it was like slowing the inevitable. What's more, Union Pacific was likely capturing business from other *train* operators, not automobiles. For long-haul

---

4. Boeing launched the "Model 247" passenger aircraft in 1933. There's no agreement on the first scheduled passenger air service (or even exactly what that meant), but it started *very* early—1914 by some accounts. By the early 1930s, there were several short-haul routes within and between states. Remember that the Wright brothers made the first heavier-than-air powered flight in 1903. That's less than 30 years from the first flight to regular, reliable passenger air service. It wasn't much of a mental leap to believe air travel would be a major transportation option within a few short years.

5. Packard was the first to offer factory-installed air conditioning in 1939-1940, but it was unreliable and expensive. It would take until the late 1960s before air conditioning was standard on a majority of new cars sold.

cross-country routes, serious competition from commercial air travel was not far off. That was especially true for the well-off customers in Harriman's target audience.

(It's worth noting that this flies in the face of our impression of consumer behavior in the Great Depression. Although even well-off people were nervous, air conditioning was worth it.)

Harriman might have won the battle, but he was still at risk of losing the war. Put simply, his trains needed somewhere to go. Ideally, somewhere only the Union Pacific could go. Harriman needed to create a new *destination*. But where would that be? And more importantly, what would passengers do when they got there?

. . .

Where to build his destination was less of an issue for Carter. He knew exactly where it was: a pleasant yet unremarkable picnic area surrounded by a new fence. But considered another way, Carter faced the same question as Harriman. A destination is only a *destination* if people think it is. There needs to be a reason to go.

Big open rolling grass fields are suitable picnic spaces, but they're also good for another activity: golf. Unfortunately, this particular space wasn't quite spacious enough for a complete golf course—18 holes, a half-course with nine roles, or even a driving range. Maybe a putting green? Hmm.

For the past ten years, designers had been working on smaller versions of the standard golf course, but mostly, they had worked on the obvious solution: Instead of 18 holes, nine. Instead of nine holes, three. Instead of 300 yards, 100 yards. You get the idea. They fit in what they could into the space allowed. However, from a business perspective, simply building a smaller course on his property wasn't an ideal solution for Carter. Here's why.

On an 18-hole golf course, you can (logically) have 18 groups of golfers all going simultaneously, so long as you stagger their start times. Assuming a standard foursome on each tee and no playing through, you could have 76 paying customers on the course at any given time. (Let's ignore pro shop sales and any restaurant income. Carter didn't have the capital for those additions.)

That sounds pretty good, right? But remember, Carter didn't have space for 18 holes. If he had to shrink to three holes, that changes things, doesn't it? At that size, only 12 players could occupy the course at the same time.

A golf course seemed like a good idea, but the business angle wasn't going to work. For three holes (at best), the investment might not yield much better returns than simply charging access to the park for picnics. There *had to be a way* to make an 18-hole golf course work. But how?

. . .

Harriman was also thinking of "sports," though, by necessity, a different one.

The Union Pacific owned tracks in the vast interior of the American West, primarily above the snow line. In other words, golf could be an option...for half the year. For the other half of the year (or more), golf doesn't work. It's no fun to find a white ball in a field of snow. It's even less fun to try to hit it. Getting the ball to roll through a foot of snow into a hole is positively diabolical.

Besides, Harriman was paying attention to a new trendy sport coming over from Europe at the end of the 1920s: skiing. One of the benefits of being part of the "old money" scene in New York was seeing what trendy people were excited about before the rest of the country found out. In the 1920s, fancy types would board an ocean liner and head off to the Alps for their skiing fix. However, after the crash, even wealthy patrons felt the economic stress. They may not be wondering where their next meal was coming from, but they were open to having less costly recreational experiences a bit closer to home.

A little background on the origins of skiing. People have been skiing as a mode of transportation (especially in Scandinavia) for hundreds—perhaps thousands—of years. They used flattened pieces of lumber to move across long distances of generally level terrain, much in the same way people "cross-country" ski today. Skiing was more efficient (and much faster) than snowshoes.

Further south, the Alps offered its residents a different opportunity: *downhill* skiing. Over the decades, European downhill skiers had developed basic techniques and equipment to minimize (though not eliminate) the possibility of *dramatic and catastrophic* injuries resulting from unintentional contact with a tree or boulder at speeds of more than 40 miles per hour.

Because they're older (and smaller) mountains, the major ranges in New York (the Adirondack Mountains, the Catskill Mountains, and part of the Appalachian Mountains) are better practice grounds than the very steep Alps. Regardless, as newbies started hitting the slopes, there were still plenty of injuries—primarily broken bones. Instruction was key, and the best clubs brought European instructors to protect their customers.

That said, skiing wasn't very fun. *Check that.* Skiing was only fun in one direction. The other direction—getting back *up* the mountain—was not fun. In those early days, a day of skiing involved spending four hours on an uphill hike carrying gear, briefly interrupted by 20 minutes of racing back down the hill. If you were a novice hoping to make it to amateur, 20 minutes of practice a day wasn't going to cut it.

So, skiing was trendy, fun in spurts, and had potential. Although the Union Pacific didn't own lines from New York City to upstate resorts, they *did* have tracks to much bigger and better mountains. Moreover, skiing was becoming popular in Seattle, so Harriman knew his railroad lines also had potential in the West.

A ski resort was the obvious solution, but what could make Harriman's resort stand out from the growing competition?

. . .

While Harriman ponders that question, let's check in with Carter.

Remember, golf seemed like a good idea, but only if he could build a "miniature" course. However, just building a shrunken ordinary golf course wasn't going to work. That's because the entire point of golf is the challenge of *distance*. Yes, players may have obstacles in the way—sand traps, rough patches, water, or trees—but so long as the player hits the ball straight enough and long enough, it's only a matter of how many strokes it will take to get the ball into the hole.

On a teeny version of that same course, there's no challenge. The game becomes (essentially) 18 putting greens. That might be nice practice for avid golfers, but most families with children aren't going to remain interested for long. Carter needed to find a way to make the smaller course fun for the entire family, especially those with no experience playing golf.

Pure serendipity intervened just at the right moment. These were the early days of the Great Depression, so all manner of abandoned construction equipment, including lumber, pipes, and supplies, were lying around the site—free for the taking. Carter also chose a site in the backcountry, so there was no shortage of grass, boulders, and logs—again, free to repurpose as he saw fit.

What if he could make his version of golf...a bit more interesting?

What if he put a boulder between the tee box and the hole? Or what if players needed to putt the ball through a length of pipe? What about a small hill made from repurposed landscaping? There was plenty of lumber and paint...could he build a windmill that ran on a small motor? Players would need to time their putt to avoid the spinning blades. In short, Carter developed a new set of obstacles that didn't rely on distance; they relied on skill.

Carter didn't stop there. He knew that if kids were excited to visit, they'd drag their parents along. Carter created all manner of fantasy characters—like trolls, wizards, and toadstools— from fairy tales and books. Now, there's something for everyone.

The best part is that the clubs didn't need to be "good" clubs. A cheap putter would do the trick. Free from the constraints of golf course design, Carter could create 18 unique experiences to keep everyone entertained. "Miniature Golf," as it came to be known, is a completely different game.

Carter thought he had a winning formula, but would people show up?

. . .

At least Carter had fun gnomes to draw people in.

Harriman, as we'll recall, actually *had* two problems. The first was precisely where to put this new ski resort. As it turns out, that answer was straightforward. It might be surprising for many people in today's car-centric world to learn, but the *railroads* were the first major boosters of the National Park system. Simply look at a map to understand why. Places like Yosemite, Yellowstone, and the Grand Canyon are not close to *any* major population centers. Trains were the easiest way to get there, allowing Americans to get out and see the natural wonders they saw in photographs from Carleton Watkins or Ansel Adams.

(Automobiles simply weren't reliable enough in that era for most people to risk breaking down hundreds of miles from the nearest human settlement.)

In short, the railroads already had a business model for "destination travel," though this was the first time *they* would need to build the destination. The only conditions were (a) that it was on (or near) an existing line and (b) that it had good potential for skiing—oh, and one more thing: (c) the new resort needed to have a "swanky" factor. If wealthy people were going to forego closer resorts in upstate New York or the beaches of California, it had better be worth the trip. For the new celebrity class in Hollywood and New York, that meant attractive people, famous athletes, movie stars, singers...a who's who list of attendees. Harriman would need to ensure photographers and editors were on hand to capture their antics and goings-on for an eager public reading about them in newspapers and glossy magazines.[6] Harriman also knew that ordinary people would flock there to catch a glimpse of their favorite celebrity or to see for themselves what all the fuss was about.

The location would be a pleasant little nook about halfway between Salt Lake City, Utah, and Boise, Idaho, near today's Ketchum, Idaho. They named it "Sun Valley," somewhat ironically for the signature sport they hoped to promote there.

There was just one problem: How would they get all these beautiful people up the mountain?

. . .

Just as Union Pacific was crafting advertising campaigns for its Sun Valley resort, the rest of the country was flocking to mini-golf courses.

Notice that we didn't say *Carter's* mini-golf course. Yes, people loved his course. It was a big hit, and a neat tourist attraction, but it was just one course in one little corner of the Great Smoky Mountains. The true opportunity was much grander than that.

To understand what happened, we need to learn the concept of "unreal estate." Unreal estate refers to any place that isn't being used for something productive. Untouched wilderness counts (the Union Pacific thought so, as did the U.S. government and the National Park system), but usually, unreal estate refers to abandoned commercial or residential property. There's always *some* of that space

---

6. The business of celebrity is "being seen" and remaining in the public eye. However, it's just as critical that celebrities are "seen" in the right context. In other words, it's a highly-staged environment. Harriman understood this intuitively and created a celebrity's paradise.

in every urban area, but during the Great Depression, empty lots were *everywhere*. Not only were they public eyesores, but they were not generating economic activity (and subsequent tax revenue) that could help local governments.

Local entrepreneurs did pretty much exactly what Carter had done. In fact, they just copied his idea. The result was a patchwork of "Tom Thumb Golf" courses tucked into abandoned lots wherever they would fit. It was a perfect solution. The courses required little space, and the developers could use materials on hand to create the necessary obstacles.[7]

According to just one account from the Jacksonville Historical Society:

> The goofy game offered a plethora of crazy courses. Players navigated through a maze of traps & contraptions and putted past pools, geysers, castles, sunken gardens, petrified forests, Taj Mahals, White Houses, Great Walls of China, fairytale characters, Wild West icons, and Rube Goldberg-like devices. Wildly enough, one course even boasted a trained monkey which grabbed the ball from unsuspecting players!

It didn't take Carter long to realize that his opportunity wasn't in selecting sites and building courses. That was happening at a frenetic pace all around him. He could never keep up. Instead, Carter focused on supplying the *materials* for others to build courses. He offered a range of building items, including logs, pipes, buildings, fairy tale characters, motorized obstacles, and an innovation—artificial turf—that was easier to maintain than real grass.[8] Sure, developers could make their courses, but it was faster and easier to simply buy Carter's equipment. The faster you could open your course, the faster you could earn some money.

---

7. More than one popular magazine called Tom Thumb Golf the "madness of the 1930s"—that's how popular it was. Even restaurants got in on the act. They converted extra dining room space into one or two mini-golf holes to entertain patrons while they waited for their meals.

8. The more commonly-known brand, AstroTurf®, was invented by James M. Faria and Robert T. Wright at Monsanto, in the 1960s. However, commercially-available artificial turf predates their invention by a few decades.

The business press of that era wondered aloud if the trend could possibly continue. One suspects Carter wondered about that too, though if you were lucky enough to own a successful, growing business in the Great Depression, you didn't think too hard.

Unfortunately, part of mini-golf's enduring legacy would be something…not quite as nice. It was certainly not what Carter would have anticipated.

. . .

Before we ruin Carter's fun, let's head back out west. People were coming to the new Union Pacific Sun Valley resort with its reliable winter snowfalls. However, they were less than thrilled with the janky tow rope that would unceremoniously drag skiers back up the mountain. It was better than nothing, but resorts out east had tow ropes. Harriman needed something better.

Luckily, it was the summer of 1935, and the engineering team had some spare time. (Did they play a few rounds of mini-golf? Probably.) The team set up a "garage" incubator to develop ideas to get people up the mountain easily, quickly, and safely. Even more luckily, one young member of the engineering team, Jim Curran, had an idea.[9]

Curran was a globetrotter, and he had seen a hook-and-pulley system in Central America designed to grab bunches of bananas and load them onto a train car, boat, or truck. One person on one end hooked the bunch of bananas on a hook on a line. A motor ran the line in a continuous loop as long as there were bananas to hook and load. Curran thought that the bananas looked like little…chairs.

His idea is based on the brilliance and simplicity of this flash of insight: develop a pulley system with a continuous loop of steel rope. Attach chairs to the rope at regular intervals. Run the rope continuously up and down the mountain. Skiers would simply pick a chair at the bottom of the loop and ride it to the top in comfort in just a few minutes. What could possibly go wrong?

To the other engineers on his team, *everything*. If a bunch of bananas fell a few feet to the ground, someone would simply pick them up. If a skier fell from

---

9. Curran worked for the American Steel and Wire Company, based out of New Jersey. Ironworks and railroads worked hand in glove for over a century—railroads were often their largest and most reliable customers. It's no surprise that the engineering teams knew each other and worked well together to solve problems. American Steel and Wire registered many of the original patents for the chair lift system.

a couple of dozen feet up...that would be bad. And they had more practical questions: How would people get on a *moving* chair with skis on? Would they have enough time? How fast could the rope move? Or more to the point, how slow? How much force would be exerted on that hook as skiers got on and off?

To find the answers to all these questions, the team built a live test track. Because it was summer, they couldn't use skis, so the team tested the idea with...wait for it...roller skates. Eventually, they figured out the optimal angle of the chair, the hook's design, and the pulley system's maximum speed. The result was a series of patents and a complete revolution in skiing. In 1936, the first ski lift in the world was installed in Sun Valley, Idaho.

Skiing had been popular before, but now, it went through a "mini-golf" level growth spurt.

. . .

Speaking of mini-golf, Carter did well for himself. Although the outbreak of World War II dramatically slowed the growth of new mini-golf courses, the trend didn't stop. Carter eventually sold his business and used the proceeds to fund the Rock City Gardens resort. Today, the World Minigolf Sport Federation (yes, there is such a thing) puts the "official" number of U.S. courses at over 900. If you're nostalgic, you can visit Rock City, near Chattanooga, across the border in Georgia, near Lookout Mountain. Sadly, you can't play mini-golf, but there are plenty of family activities.

The real legacy was unreal estate.

People would build mini-golf courses just about anywhere, including *inside* residential neighborhoods and abandoned lots. It makes a lot of sense, doesn't it? Use your unused property to earn a little money. However, in 1934, the U.S. government got into the business of guaranteeing mortgages with the Federal Housing Administration (FHA). It was a good idea in many ways—it helped people afford a home at a fixed, reasonable interest rate, paying over 30 years. It was a response to the housing market collapse of the Great Depression and one of the signature programs of the New Deal.

However, if the government was going to guarantee mortgages, it needed to understand more about the value of property in a certain area. The result was a series of maps that highlighted the level of riskiness of loans. And do you know what was *especially* risky? An unplanned, impromptu commercial business on an abandoned home lot. FHA regulations meant the end of *laissez-faire* property rights in most areas of the country. In other words, no more neighborhood mini-golf.

Unfortunately, certain areas of cities were outlined in red (quite literally *red-lined*) on FHA maps, especially those with lower property values. Over the decades, many of those neighborhoods featured covenants limiting the purchase of property to people of color. Although the red lines are gone, this legislation's enduring legacy remains.

In its own small way, the popularity of mini-golf courses popping up in residential neighborhoods (and other business types as well) helped to catalyze large-scale social engineering from the Federal government. Whether you approve or disapprove of that policy depends much on your politics, but it's worth remembering that there are no solutions to social problems, only trade-offs.

. . .

Harriman didn't need to worry about zoning regulations in the same way, of course, but it was another example of unreal estate.

Managing a National Park is one thing; managing the environmental issues of a private party operating a wilderness resort is quite another. The Federal government struggled (and still struggles) to balance ecological problems with private property rights. For example, can the Federal government perform a controlled burn on private property? What about mineral rights? What about rights-of-way for highways and railroads?

Did Harriman care about that? Did he even foresee those issues? No, probably not. He was simply trying to save the Union Pacific from bankruptcy or a forced merger. In the short term, he succeeded not only in that objective but also in creating a model for ski resorts all over the United States. Downhill skiing at the 1936 Winter Olympics in Germany certainly gave the sport a publicity boost and worldwide attention. After that, Sun Valley was the place to be. Even today, it may not rank up there with Vail or Park City, but Sun Valley remains a destination.

Many people visit it for skiing, of course, but also because (at least, during the summer) Ernest Hemingway loved to fly fish in the rivers.[10]

It's hard to imagine the Roosevelt administration thought that far ahead, either. FDR was a massive proponent of outdoor recreation, directing the Works Progress Administration (WPA) to build the infrastructure needed to support ski resorts, parks, and golf courses—the full-sized kind, not the mini versions.

The legacies of both activities—mini-golf and skiing—are complicated. But remember, people weren't thinking about any of those consequences. Entrepreneurs were simply trying to solve urgent problems; they saw underutilized resources and refashioned them to create something new.

---

10. And, morbidly, because Hemingway committed suicide in Ketchum in 1961.

13

THE CUSTOMER IS NEVER RIGHT

On May 20-21, 1927, Charles Augustus Lindbergh did the unthinkable.

Alone in his single-engine aircraft, named *The Spirit of St. Louis*, Lindbergh stayed awake for over 33 hours—all the way from New York to Paris—a flight distance of about 3,600 miles. Just imagine it. These weren't the days of seven-and-a-half-hour nonstop flights from JFK to Charles de Gaulle. There were no lay-flat business class seats. There was no beverage service. No bathroom. *No co-pilot*.

Speaking of the "co" in co-pilot, Lindbergh's plane didn't feature the multiple redundant systems that even today's smaller aircraft enjoy. (Long-haul passenger jets often feature triple or quadruple redundant equipment for critical systems.[1]) What's more, even private aircraft can communicate via dedicated radio links with other aircraft and ground control.

---

1. The U.S. Federal Aviation Administration (FAA) calls this "Surviveability of Systems." If you're curious, check out Advisory Circular 25.795-7. There's even a specification for how to calculate the physical distance between two redundant systems. Needless to say, Lindbergh didn't have anything like that.

If anything went wrong on Lindbergh's flight—*anything at all*—he was a dead man flying. Well, probably a dead man *sinking* if he survived the crash into the ocean. His only hope would be to land the plane on the water gently enough to survive, and then crash in an area with a nearby boat, and then be able to signal that boat, and *then* for the boat to arrive before he sank or succumbed to hypothermia in the cold Atlantic. Not exactly reassuring.

Did we mention Lindbergh was 25 years old? He was young, good-looking, and certainly brave.

When he completed the trip, he secured the $25,000 Orteig Prize for the first person to make the journey and became instantly wealthy to boot. (That's about $450,000 in today's money.) Lindbergh also emerged as an instant hero and the prototype of the first modern American celebrity.[2] He was honored by the President of the United States. He was inducted into the *Légion d'Honneur* in France. He even received honors from Hitler's Germany. (Air commander Hermann Göring was starstruck, spilling all sorts of secrets about the capabilities of the Luftwaffe in the 1930s.) He was the subject of too many newspaper articles, magazine stories, newsreels, banquets, and parades to count. Lindbergh, almost singlehandedly, jumpstarted the aviation industry.

"Lucky Lindy," indeed.

Americans were justifiably proud of their native-born hero. A Midwestern boy and son of a congressperson from the 6th Congressional District of Minnesota (also named Charles), his flight meant the beginning of more than a century of American dominance of the skies.

Except...it wasn't quite true.

No, Lindbergh did cross the Atlantic. There's no doubt about that. The question was whether Lindbergh was the *first* person to do it.

The answer to that question, oddly enough, was no.

...

In a nondescript corner of the New York Public Library, just above the bustling corner of 42nd Avenue and 5th Street, Norbert Pearlroth sat at his desk. He

---

2. There's much more about the creation of the modern celebrity in *Booze, Babe, and the Little Black Dress: How Innovators of the Roaring 20s Created the Consumer Revolution*. Lindbergh features prominently in Chapter 9.

was surrounded by a pile of books, pamphlets, and newspapers from around the world. Six days a week, every week, Pearlroth would scour the globe for the interesting, the odd, and the surprising. As he put it, this was his "dream job."

Pearlroth grew up in what is now Poland (then part of the Habsburg Empire) around the turn of the century. Like many of his generation in Europe, World War I ended any hope of finishing his university education in Kraków. By 1920, Pearlroth made his way to the United States. He was promiscuously curious, interested in everything, and spoke 14 languages.

In front of him this day was a story about British aviators John Alcock and Arthur Brown. In 1919, they flew a modified World War I bomber from St. John's, Newfoundland, Canada, to Clifden, County Galway, Ireland. Winston Churchill, then Secretary of State for Air, named them the winners of the £10,000 prize for the first transatlantic flight in less than 72 hours.

That last detail was crucial. Other pilots had "puddle jumped" across the Atlantic over several days, landing at waypoints to refuel and rest. Alcock and Brown were the first to do it in one trip.

And what a trip it was!

The plane barely made it over the treetops on its initial ascent. Things would go "downhill" from there. Not long after taking off, the plane's wind-powered electric generator failed. That meant no heat, no radio communication, and no pilot-to-pilot intercom. The last failure might not have been so bad, except after an exhaust pipe failed, the pilots could barely hear themselves scream to communicate with each other. They flew through thick fog, lost their way (they recovered by using stars as navigation aids), and recovered twice from deadly spins. If that wasn't enough, the team ran into a snowstorm that threatened to ice up their equipment and scuttle the entire flight. After 16 harrowing hours, the pair landed not on the intended gentle green Irish field but rather on a sticky, dangerous, murky Irish bog. Cold, tired, and lucky to walk out of a wrecked plane, Alcock and Brown had done it.

Pearlroth read an interview (the first one given by the pair) from Tom 'Cork' Kenny of *The Connacht Tribune*. As he dug further, he came across the front page of *The New York Times*, dated June 16, 1919. Its top headline read:

> Alcock and Brown Fly Across Atlantic; Make 1,980 Miles In 16 Hours, 12 Minutes; Sometimes Upside Down In Dense, Icy Fog

Did you catch that date? June 16, 1919. That was nearly eight years before Lindbergh made his famous flight. Alcock and Brown even carried a small amount of mail, making it the first transatlantic air mail delivery. Others would follow, as would regular postal deliveries. No, the flight wasn't exactly routine. And yes, Lindbergh's flight was the *longest* transatlantic flight to date—by about 1,600 miles. However, it wasn't *that* big of a deal; it was just that people in the United States weren't paying attention.

Pearlroth didn't need special knowledge or secret government clearance to learn about Alcock and Brown's flight. He simply needed to pay attention and look where other people overlooked.

It was just the sort of story his mercurial and adventurous boss, LeRoy Robert Ripley, was going to ask his readers to, *Believe It, Or Not!*

. . .

Ripley knew a winner when he saw one.

For the past decade, Ripley had slowly and steadily built a reputation as a collector of the odd and unusual. We'll get to his background in a minute, but suffice it to say that this bit of trivia was precisely what he wanted to cover in his syndicated cartoon. He was no slouch for details, but Pearlroth's persnicketiness allowed Ripley the confidence to poke the bear.

After Lindbergh's flight in 1927, Ripley penned a simple comic in his straightforward style. It featured a line drawing of *The Spirit of St. Louis* with the following caption:

> Lindbergh was the 67th man to make a non-stop flight over the Atlantic Ocean![3]

---

3. The facts are on Ripley's side. Later in 1919, the same year Alcock and Brown made their flight, a lighter-than-air craft (aka blimp) carried 31 people from Scotland to the United States. In 1924, another blimp carrying 33 people traveled from Germany to Lakehurst, New Jersey. Do the math. That's 66.

Since his national syndication in 1924, most of Ripley's cartoons featured obscure facts from forgotten corners of the world—Sumatran women who used rings to elongate their necks or the natural geography of the highest lake in South America. Readers would glance at the simple drawings, read the one-to-two-sentence descriptive headlines, find them fascinating, and move on with their day. Only a handful of people on Earth would be able to question the accuracy of the statements. Most people didn't bother. It was a neat distraction.

This cartoon generated a...different reaction.

Thousands of readers flooded newspaper offices with angry letters berating Ripley for insulting an American icon. *Everyone knew* Lindbergh was the first to cross the Atlantic by aircraft. This was just beginning to be seen as the "American Century," and heroes like Lindbergh were leading the way.

To be clear, Ripley wasn't saying that Lindbergh *had not* crossed the Atlantic, nor did he say the goal wasn't worthy or that the flight wasn't a spectacular achievement against dangerous odds. He simply stated a fact: Lindbergh wasn't the first. Or the second...or the third... Ripley could have left out the "67th" part, but he had a knack for courting controversy. Being accused of lying—especially about someone as prominent as Lindbergh—was probably the best publicity he could hope for. Instead of shying away, Ripley leaned in and took the high road:

> The men that American people admire most extravagantly are the most daring liars; the men they detest the most violently are those who try to tell them the truth. I think mine is the only business in which the customer is never right.

In other words, Ripley dared people to prove him wrong. Ripley checked his facts. He trusted Pearlroth. And he had traveled the world well enough to know fakery when he saw it.

But this isn't really the story of telling the truth or even the appeal of cartoons as an art form. Ripley's choice to poke the American bear would catapult *Believe It, Or Not!* from a daily cartoon of curiosities to the first multimedia platform. In the 1930s, Ripley's empire blossomed into books, radio, and theme parks. He helped create the business model that Walt Disney would follow over the next few decades. To understand how we got there, we need to understand one of the strangest people in an era that produced more than its fair share of characters.

...

It probably shouldn't surprise anyone that Ripley, the collector and popularizer of the world's oddities, was an oddity himself. Described by more than one biographer as having a "bottomless, off-kilter curiosity," Ripley didn't begin life with much of a leg up.

Born on February 22, 1890...wait. Was he born on February 22? Perhaps not, remarks historian Neal Thompson in his biography *A Curious Man: The Strange and Brilliant Life of Robert "Believe It or Not!" Ripley*. Later in life, he'd never admit to an exact date because of a (possible) pre-marital pregnancy. That was a big deal in those days, and it was *still* a big deal in the first half of the 20th century, especially if you happened to be a public figure.[4]

Back to the story. Ripley was born and spent his childhood in Santa Rosa, about as far northwest of San Francisco as San Jose lies southeast. In other words, not far. He never really fit in. Although Ripley would become athletic and even dapper in his adult life, as a child, he had a pathological fear of girls (even more than most young boys). His late start in the dating world led to some...odd choices later. We'll get to that in due course. It seems reasonable to assume that Ripley loved odd things because, well, he looked a little awkward himself. Even as an adult, he sported a bigger-than-average head, pronounced buck teeth, and a goofy smile. Imagine trying to make friends as a school-aged kid.

Speaking of school, Ripley struggled to pay attention in class and, even more so, struggled to learn to write. Most elementary and secondary school teachers failed to reach him, *except one*. She recognized how hard it was for him to write, and after he turned in a drawing instead of a writing assignment (a good drawing, by the way), she allowed him to draw cartoons to illustrate his writing assignments from then on.

(If you wonder what teachers can do for someone's self-confidence and life trajectory, here's another example.)

---

4. One wonders how many birth certificates were forged or altered before the modern era. It's an interesting thought. It's yet one more way historical records are only *so* reliable.

Ripley even got up the courage to send one of his drawings to a newspaper in New York. To his shock and delight, they sent him a check for $5.00. In today's money, that's not quite $85, but it was a start. Maybe, just maybe, he could make a living drawing. It wasn't an unreasonable thought. The news industry was booming around the turn of the century. Ripley left high school without graduating and talked his way into a job at a San Francisco newspaper.

Why the rush? Ripley felt a keen urgency to make something of himself. His father, his mother, and one brother all died prematurely. Today, we might be able to identify the genetic condition and treat it, but in the early 1900s, medicine was grappling to get all its "doctors" on board with the germ theory of disease and washing their hands regularly.[5]

Remember that job he talked himself into? Well, Ripley got himself fired (twice, actually) within a few months. It wasn't his work that was poor; it was his interpersonal skills. Down, but not out, Ripley decided to risk it all and move to New York. He had a handful of contacts in the Big Apple from selling cartoons as a freelancer, but it's not as if he had a job lined up.

As you might guess from the story thus far, even his landing in New York was a story worthy of an oddball cartoon.

Unfamiliar with the train stations, Ripley exited the train one stop too early *in New Jersey*. It was getting dark. He only had enough money for a cheap place in New York, not a hotel across the river, so he accepted the offer of a stranger who offered to bring him across. That person turned out to be a human trafficker. Luckily, the situation dawned on him in time. Ripley slipped away under the cover of darkness, found a cheap hotel, and hid there until he was sure he'd given them the slip.

After that auspicious beginning, Ripley started to climb the ranks. He was able to land jobs with papers run by now-household names Hearst and Pulitzer, but he never seemed to want to leave the cheap hotel attached to a boxing gym. With no romantic prospects and only cartoons to draw, Ripley worked out constantly. In fact, it was only an injury that stopped him from playing (at least) minor league

---

5. Ripley turned out to be correct. He died in May of 1949 at (probably) age 59. He made it longer than his parents and siblings, but still died of an early heart attack. If they had statins back then, he might have been a major television star as well.

baseball—perhaps even with a shot at the majors. He became a "guy's guy" in exactly the mode you're thinking, discovering women in his 20s with no prior experience to draw on.

It...did not go well.

You'll read some strange things if you dig into Ripley's biography. He was sued *multiple times* by *multiple women*, including his ex-wife, a 14-year-old dancer. (*Believe It, Or Not!*) Yeah. It was *that* weird. At any other time and in any other place, Ripley would have been an outcast. A laughingstock. An utter failure.

But this was not that kind of time or place.

. . .

If you're going to be a bit "off-kilter," New York is the place to do it. It helped that the newspaper industry was *exploding* in the city when Ripley showed up. This is the time in history when sharp-elbowed moguls jostled for position in the most demanding market in the world. They didn't care about weird personal quirks; they needed results. *Now*. Here's why.

One of the most critical driving factors in the newspaper industry, especially in New York, was the arrival of nearly 15 million new immigrants between 1900 and 1920. To put that in context, the entire country's population in 1920 just broke 100 million. If you were to jump in a time machine back to the beginning of the Roaring 20s, about one in every seven people you'd meet would not have been born in the United States. That's a lot. It's a proportion that's never been equaled since. What's more, immigrants did not spread out evenly across the country. They tended to congregate where others spoke their language and followed their customs. New York was one of those places. In the Big Apple, nearly *half* of all residents might have been foreign-born.

For the newspaper titans, millions of new residents meant millions of new *readers*, and a much larger circulation base to sell to advertisers. However, many of those new immigrants didn't speak English—or if they did, not well enough to wade through 2,000-word complex stories. In addition, many new arrivals worked long hours at multiple jobs to make ends meet. They didn't have the extra time or energy, even if they wanted to read. On many factory floors in the days before radio, one person would read aloud from the newspaper while people worked. That was nice for the newspapers while it lasted, but by the mid-1920s, managers found it cheaper to buy a radio and put the reader back to work. The newspapers needed a better answer.

Cartoons were a natural fit.

The idea of the *political* cartoon is quite old in the United States. Ben Franklin's "Join, or Die" was perhaps the most famous, but cartoons played a role in political discourse throughout the 1800s. The appeal is obvious in politics—simple, clever ways to think about big, broad issues. It may seem oversimplified, but the old saying about how many words a picture is worth applies here. Besides, many of the newspapers' new customers wouldn't read the necessary "thousand words." Images would always win.

The cartoonist's skill is capturing the essence of the message in a small space. In the early days, that also meant black-and-white line drawings. Color printing was expensive, and most papers didn't bother. As a final constraint, newspaper printing quality in the 1920s and 1930s was…not great. When you see images of newspapers in that decade, they're often a bit smudged and slightly out of alignment. That's not simply an artifact of age (looking at them decades later); text was generally okay, but printing subtle images was tough. That meant cartoonists needed to be very good at provocative, simple drawings.

In other words, precisely the thing Ripley was good at.[6]

However, Ripley's first column did *not* feature general-purpose weirdness; his "Champs and Chumps" cartoon focused on sports. Given his lifestyle at the time, it made sense. It also helped that the 1920s saw a rapid rise in sports enthusiasm in the United States—especially boxing and baseball. This was the age of Sammy Mandell and Babe Ruth. Even better, new immigrants *loved* sports, especially when one of their native sons was in the ring or on the field. Sports were easy to understand and widely popular.

Ripley's angle (no surprise) was capturing odd facts and statistics. It was during the run of this cartoon that we first see—largely as an afterthought from Ripley's telling—the phrase "believe it or not" appear in print. It wasn't fully capitalized and didn't feature the exclamation point that it would in later years, but like

---

6. Though not *great*, at least at first. Ripley's new bosses in New York sent him to art classes to hone his talent.

many happy accidents, it started to catch on. Although his sports column would continue for a few years, Ripley became known by that new catchphrase.

That's about the time Ripley discovered Pearlroth and offered him a job as his research assistant. There was no way Ripley could keep up with the demand; he knew *sports*, but he couldn't know *everything*, at least not fast enough to keep up with the schedule of a daily column.

With Pearlroth's help, and especially after the Lindbergh cartoon, Ripley's popularity skyrocketed. His cartoon was syndicated in nearly every newspaper in the country—syndication being an innovation by the newspaper industry to license the best writing, photography, and cartoonists to a national audience.[7]

However, Ripley's newspaper bosses saw a bigger opportunity than simply a quirky cartoon.

. . .

Thompson begins his biography at precisely this moment in Ripley's life.

The powers that be in New York saw fit to send Ripley on a round-the-world odd-finding trip. If he could accomplish this much with a research assistant in the library, what could he find in the field? In addition to cartoon fodder, his editors wanted dispatches from the field, and Ripley obliged them gleefully.

To be fair, his first trips allowed him to escape the Prohibition regime in the United States. For a guy like Ripley, that was too good to pass up. He tried Hawaiian moonshine (like a sweetened white rum, also known as Okolehao, and also known as *very strong stuff*), drank "gin to keep warm," drank "beer to cool down," and took liquid lunches in Singapore. American audiences ate (drank?) it up.

Ripley also played with the prudishness of American high society in his dispatches. After one trip to a beer garden in Java, Ripley told readers that he "went to bed and slept with a Dutch wife." It wasn't until the *next day* that he explained that a "Dutch wife" was a sort of oval pillow and "not as romantic as it sounds."

---

7. Some historians have attempted to make the case that it was *really* Pearlroth's work, and not Ripley's, that deserves the credit. That might court controversy (of which, Ripley would have likely approved), but isn't really justified. Pearlroth was an outstanding researcher, but remember, this was a cartoon, not an article. Ripley needed to decide which facts were best *and* capture them in a compelling image. Simply listing facts wasn't enough.

Ripley was more than just a cartoonist; now, he was also a travel correspondent. It was the second brick in Ripley's multimedia house, but it would not be the last.

Lest we think Ripley was content with the tourist version of traveling, remember two things. First, this was well before many areas of the world were accessible by anything more than trading posts on the coasts. Second, and more importantly, Ripley had a pathological loathing of the ordinary. To find truly unique things, he needed to venture off the beaten path. In many cases, he would unintentionally *beat* that path for future travelers.

On one such overseas adventure, Ripley decided he wanted to visit the Soviet Union.

Remember, this wasn't many years after the Russian Revolution, and Joseph Stalin was still consolidating power. Nevertheless, Stalin understood public relations was critical to his reputation on the world stage, and he invited American journalists to tour his new communist utopia. Of course, the journalists saw only what Stalin wanted them to see. They toured model farms, vibrant cities, and modern laboratories; they saw happy citizens everywhere they looked. In a few short years (so it seemed), Russia had emerged from decades of backwardness to lead the world in a grand new social experiment. For many who would go on to roles in the Roosevelt administration, this—well, let's call it what it was—*indoctrination* would have a profound effect. That was especially true in the dark days of the Great Depression when the Soviet Union's system seemed vastly superior to the capitalist West.

What they did *not* see were the tens of millions of "political prisoners" sent off to Siberia for "reeducation" who never came back. Or the lack of actual productivity of any of those factories or farms. Or people waiting in lines for basic supplies. *That* was the Soviet Union that Ripley saw because he didn't ask Stalin to enter the country; he simply talked his way in. Suffice it to say, he couldn't wait to leave.

However, Southeast Asia made the most profound impression on Ripley. The sights, smells, alcohol, drugs, animals, and—*everything*—but mostly, the humanity on display. He witnessed human pincushions in India, a man with clawlike hands in China, and people (purposefully) hanging from hooks in a show of religious devotion.

If you were still envisioning cartoons in the mold of "Garfield" or "Peanuts," that was *not* this.

While Ripley cataloged oddities and sent home dispatches, Pearlroth was hard at work collecting his own share of subject matter for Ripley to illustrate when he returned home, such as that birds had no sense of taste or smell or that the dental nerve of an elephant weighed twelve pounds.

What started as a sports cartoon evolved into a catalog of general oddness. What began as an oddball guy evolved into a traveling newspaper personality. In a sort of ironic oddity itself, everything was going right for Ripley. But that was all before the stock market crashed in 1929.

There was no guarantee that Ripley's off-kilter style would translate from the Roaring 20s to the Great Depression.

...

As it turns out, Ripley might have been one of the luckiest people to be alive when the economy crashed.

It helped that Ripley was popular, but plenty of other popular entertainers found themselves out of work in the early 1930s. What made his situation unique was something we already mentioned but bears a bit more explanation: *syndication*. When a publisher syndicates a cartoonist, photographer, or writer, their work appears in multiple outlets. For smaller newspapers across the country, purchasing access to Ripley's cartoon meant that readers wouldn't have to buy a New York paper to see it—this was high-quality work that would help the brand image of the newspaper carrying it, keeping readers hooked to the *local* paper. For the publisher, syndicating their best work meant regular license fees from smaller papers around the country.

When the Great Depression took hold, smaller papers quickly realized that they needed quality syndicated content for their pages not only because their readers liked it, but also because it was cheaper than hiring their own staff. For the publishers, syndicated content was a consistent revenue stream that likewise did not depend on hiring more people.[8]

---

8. Other publishers attempted to copy Ripley's quirky trivia cartoons, but none of them caught on. What they didn't realize was that it wasn't just the odd factoids, it was Ripley's personality that drew readers in.

In other words, Ripley's New York overlords were more dependent on this quirky cartoonist than ever. It helped that the Great Depression was tailor-made for distractions, and *Believe It, Or Not!* was nothing if not pleasantly distracting.

Completely comfortable with being panned as "the world's biggest liar," Ripley challenged readers to send him odd facts he might not find on a globetrotting adventure or library reference room. The result was a flood of mail from all over the world. One of the net effects of Ripley's rising popularity and influx of what we would call today "user-generated content" was that there were more factoids than could ever get into a daily cartoon. (Many cartoons featured as many as six bits of trivia, but even that density couldn't handle the volume.) Ripley could stop work for *months* and still have enough material for his daily cartoons...*or* his publishers could find a way to take advantage of all that extra material.

Can you guess what happened next? Sure, you can.

The first collection of cartoons, published in 1930, was a runaway success. Priced at $2.50 (about $45 in today's money), it was a meaningful chunk of money for anxious people worried about where their next meal might come from. No matter. It was fun for the entire family—the first "coffee table book."

The success of his cartoons, dispatches, and books made Ripley one of the most sought-after speakers of the 1930s, despite (or perhaps *because* of) his awkwardness. When people saw him live, Ripley's unpolished, stilted style was precisely what they expected. This wasn't an act. He really was *that* strange. His mannerisms made him more believable and relatable to the average person. People *loved* him.

So much, in fact, that Ripley got his own radio show. Now, everyone could hear his nasal voice and halting speech. Despite the economic conditions of the early to mid-1930s, Ripley traveled more than ever. He was quickly becoming the first multimedia brand.

There was just one thing missing.

. . .

It's difficult to envision a world without theme parks, isn't it?

Circuses, fairs, and carnivals aren't quite the same thing. They come and go. They're an event, not a destination. Families (and plenty of adults) could visit Disneyland in California as early as 1955, and later Disneyworld in Florida, Sea

World, Six Flags, Harry Potter World, and dozens of other theme parks across the country and around the world.

They all owe their appeal to Ripley's Odditorium. (Get it? Like "auditorium." Clever, huh?)

This one wasn't Ripley's idea. The idea for a *Believe It, Or Not!* theme park came from the mind of C.C. Pyle—a promoter in the mold of P.T. Barnum a generation before. To those in the know in the business community, "Cash and Carry" Pyle was *persona non grata* and wise to be avoided. Ripley, however, was furiously busy and content to take a hands-off approach to the whole thing. Pyle's idea wasn't a permanent theme park—at least, not at first. The Chicago World Fair was coming soon in 1933, and Pyle's idea was to create a temporary exhibit to capitalize on Ripley's popularity.

The exhibit would be a live walkthrough of "curiosities" taken directly from the pages of the books, comics, radio interviews, and trips. In a time when most people didn't travel that far from home, this was a way for people to see these oddities for themselves.

However, the first exhibit didn't attract visitors. Frankly, it wasn't much different than seeing the cartoons "live." Pyle's concept was basically blown-up versions of the cartoons with some additional explanatory plaques. After a brief surge of curiosity, the hall largely stood empty. It was in danger of being closed altogether. It certainly wouldn't be invited back next year.

To his credit, Pyle understood that the exhibit needed to take it up a notch. There was a certain subset of oddities that "showed better" live than they would on the pages of a cartoon. To put it callously (and in the language of the time), he needed to give visitors a *freakshow*. However, unlike Barnum's traveling shows, these weren't fake oddities; these were real. This is what people wanted to see. The Odditorium became so successful during the Great Depression that Ripley decided to open his first permanent attraction in Manhattan in 1939.

By the end of the decade, there was no media that didn't ask consumers to *Believe It, Or Not!* Ripley was a staple of newspapers across the country. He sold millions of annual collections in book form each year. He was an in-demand speaker. His radio show was among the top performers. He traveled the world with an expense account filled with blank checks.

More than that, Ripley charted the path to multimedia success for everyone who followed. Consumer expectations of entertainment had changed forever.

. . .

Although Ripley's story doesn't end with the outbreak of war in Europe in 1939, it's as good a place as any to stop. The escalating conflict and changing mood meant Ripley was grounded—quite literally. Without the ability to travel, his idiosyncrasies caught up with his unlimited checkbook, and things...got weird. Ripley partied, drank, stopped exercising, and started slipping on his deadlines.

That said, he saw the emergence of television in the 1940s as a way to rejuvenate his lagging fortunes. He even recorded his first television episode in 1949, only to die of a massive heart attack two months later at the age of only 59.

However, *Believe It, Or Not!* was bigger than any single person, even its founder. Decades later, you can still visit Odditoriums worldwide—a total of 18 in all. Ripley Entertainment (now owned by the Jim Pattison Group in Canada) continues to deliver family-oriented experiences. They've even expanded into franchising. For a few million dollars, you can even open your own Odditorium.

Pearlroth, for his part, continued with the Ripley organization until 1975. As Ripley's sole researcher during that time, reading 10 hours per day, six (or seven) days a week, a *conservative* estimate puts his reading total at nearly 300,000 books.

In the end, what was it about LeRoy Robert Ripley, an oddball of a man, that captured the hearts and minds of Americans during the Great Depression? His biographer, Neal Thompson, might have put it best:

> The shy, awkward, misfit loner had become the champion of the freakishness of others. By celebrating weirdness, he made it mainstream...More than entertainment, [Ripley] gave people hope.

14

"WALT'S FOLLY"

It was late October of 1937, about two months before Walt Disney's first feature-length film was set to hit theaters, and things were *not* going well.

Disney was reasonably well-known in the early 1930s. His "Silly Symphonies" cartoons (often shown before feature films) introduced Americans to Mickey and Minnie Mouse as early as 1928. Today's audiences get previews for other movies, but in the 1920s and 1930s, audiences saw cartoons. (Not all things change for the better.)

The bottom line was that although popular, these "shorts" weren't really that profitable. According to Disney biographer Neal Gabler, by the mid-1930s, each short film cost about $30,000 to make—about twice what it cost other film studios. Sure, they were better, and audiences liked them more, but theaters were under tremendous pressure to reduce costs as ticket prices *dropped* during the Great Depression.

To make matters worse, theater owners expected a new short film every few weeks to draw in new audiences. People weren't content to see the same cartoon too many times. Combine rising costs with shrinking revenues, and you can see the predicament Disney found himself facing. It would take a long time to earn enough extra revenue to produce anything more ambitious than an eight-minute cartoon—if it could happen at all. And Disney was nothing if not ambitious.

Walt Disney believed people *would* want to see a feature-length animated film with a deeper plot line. However, most smart people in the entertainment business thought it was a stupid idea for a variety of very smart-sounding reasons. Publicly, they called his project "Walt's Folly." Privately, they called it worse.

Animated shorts were one thing. They featured funny, slapstick humor and simple dialog. After about five to seven minutes, audiences had had enough and were ready to get on with the main event. Disney made appetizers, not main courses. Also, animation wasn't a serious art form. It was "funny" and "for kids." Would people care about what happens to drawings on a screen? Children, perhaps, but certainly not adults. Marketers were just starting to wrap their minds around the concept of children as full-fledged consumers in their own right, but even among those who saw their potential, a full-length feature film targeting only children was a bridge too far. Film industry experts didn't believe in it. Advertising executives laughed at it. Even Disney's employees were skeptical.

But Walt Disney believed in it, and he kept production moving forward by sheer force of will.

However, there was one group he could not simply ignore or bully: the bank. Initially, Disney convinced Bank of America to lend him $250,000 to finance the project. That's about $5.5 million today—a modest sum by the bank's standards but a massive risk for Disney's company. (It had made about $600,000 in 1934 from distribution fees. The quarter-million dollar loan accounted for nearly half its budget.) A few months later, Disney returned, asking for $630,000 in *additional* funding. Bank of America executives agreed. In October of 1937, when we catch up with the budding filmmaker, Disney asked for *another* $650,000. That would bring the total budget to $1.5 million—six times the original estimate—and the film wasn't even done. Oh, and it was set to release to theaters in December of *that year*.

Before the bank would agree to the final loan, BoA chief Roy Rosenberg paid Walt a visit. Rosenberg was not content to wait for the premiere, so he forced Disney to screen the unfinished film privately in his bank's offices. In Disney's later retellings, Rosenberg was "all manly" about the budget until it crossed the

$1 million mark. However, it's clear from the subtext that it was *Disney* who was sweating it out.

During the next 90 minutes, Disney would repeatedly interject to explain how this scene wasn't quite finished or that scene needed better coloring. Rosenberg, stone-faced, said nothing. When it was over, Rosenberg rose, grabbed his coat, and walked to the door without a word. Disney followed him, likely terrified that the creation he had invested so much blood, sweat, and tears to bring to life—*Snow White*—would never see the light of day. Without the additional financing, production would stop *immediately* at the 11th hour. Check that, at *11:59*. Disney's heart must have been racing.

Seated in his car, Rosenberg finally looked up at an expectant Disney and deadpanned: "This thing is going to make you a hatful of money."

. . .

Rosenberg had a reasonable concern. Walt Disney wasn't exactly unknown, but he had no experience producing a full-length feature film, much less a full-length *animated* feature film. However, there was a bigger reason making movies was more challenging in the 1930s: the Hays Code.

The Hays Code refers to the director of the Motion Picture Producers and Distribution Association, William Harrison Hays. A voluntary set of guidelines, the Hays Code was written in response to a series of scandals in the previous decade. When most people think of the "Roaring 20s," movies often don't top the list of concerns about loosening moral standards. They remember these "old" movies as tame compared to what we see on screen today. In the television program *I Love Lucy* in the 1950s, the titular main characters, Lucy and Ricardo, slept in separate beds, even though they were married. How much debauchery were we talking about here? And how could this possibly impact Disney's animated film project about a princess and some little people? Stay tuned.

We'll get to the specifics of the Hays Code soon enough, but films made before the industry's self-censorship regime were *very different* than those made after. Bluntly, they were much more like movies made in the last 30 years. They featured much more foul language, sexual content, and violence than most people would expect. They might be tame by today's standards, but to the moralist types—many of them devout Catholics—movies were a bad influence on the spiritual well-being of Americans.

The trick was to come up with a *national* standard that did not involve the *national* government. During the 1920s, numerous state and local governments devised their own standards for what could be shown on screen, making it nearly impossible for movie studios to comply. What's more, if the studios didn't act, the Federal government might. During America's involvement in World War I, President Woodrow Wilson's Committee on Public Information controlled media in a way largely unthinkable at *any* other time in the nation's history. Although Warren Harding and Calvin Coolidge (Wilson's successors) weren't as keen to use the CPI to censor media after the war, studios were under no illusions that a future President—like the progressively-minded Hoover or the *very* progressive Roosevelt—might not revive the practice. Movie studios were businesses; they wanted a free hand to act. To ensure they didn't get that hand slapped, they would censor *themselves* rather than risk the government stepping in for them.

The tough part about this self-censorship plan was that although (some) people would complain (loudly) about any real or perceived slip, those movies tended to be popular—in other words, the movies with sex, drinking, drugs, violence, and foul language. Studios needed to walk a fine line to give the public what it wanted and stay on the right side of the tut-tutters.

Luckily (unluckily?), the Hays Code was *very* specific. This was well before the now-familiar G, PG, PG-13, R, and X ratings, which wouldn't come until the 1960s. Starting in 1934, the "Code" divided the creative world into "Don't" and "Be Careful." We don't need to memorize the lists like studio executives needed to do; a brief sampling is all we need to get the intent.[1]

The "Don't" list was clear: "Those things which are included in the following list shall not appear in pictures produced by the members of this Association, irrespective of the manner in which they are treated."

---

1. Want to read it? The technical title to search for is, "A Code to Govern the Making of Motion Pictures, the Reasons for Supporting It, and the Resolution for Uniform Interpretation." See why we refer to it as the "Hays Code?" Easier. The document includes 11 "Don'ts" and 25 "Be Carefuls."

Profanity of all kinds was off the table. That certainly included the so-called "seven dirty words" made famous in 1972 by comedian George Carlin, but many more besides.[2] In this case, they meant profanity in the *Biblical* sense of the word. So, no blasphemy...at least not of the Christian God. Additionally, all sex was off the table—showing it, of course, but also suggesting sex, silhouetting sex, sexual diseases, relationships between different races, and "perverted" sex (which included homosexuality). The same rules applied to childbirth. We can quibble about definitions and the difference in morality between then and now, but at least the rules were clear.

(By the way, the Catholic clergy primarily responsible for writing the Hays Code carved out a special clause in this section to make any criticism of the clergy off-limits.)

The "Be Careful" list was *much* more problematic: "Special care [must be] be exercised in the manner in which the following subjects are treated, to the end that vulgarity and suggestiveness may be eliminated and that good taste may be emphasized."

Some cautions make sense—at least from a 1930s perspective. If you're going to use the American flag, it should be shown in a respectful or reverent manner. Flag-patterned clothing was iffy; flag burning (even if by enemy fire or accident) was not. But most of the cautions in the list of 25 "Be Carefuls" had to do with one thing: crime. That included smuggling, arson, gunfire, train robbing, fights, or police actions. You could show it, but you needed to be careful (no "blood and guts"), and you *absolutely* could not "glorify" violence or criminals. If there was a bad guy, that bad guy was caught and punished in the end.

To understand why, we need to understand a unique feature of the post-Prohibition era. Gangsters and mobsters of the Roaring 20s were the ones who, in the words of Al Capone, "gave the public what it wanted." Anyone who drank alcohol during Prohibition (with a zillion exceptions) was supporting criminality, too. The unintended consequence was to put everyday Americans in the same group as the career criminals. It made the mobsters...well, if not upstanding

---

2. No, we're not going to name them all. This is a family book. Though I'm not sure "piss" really ever belonged in that group.

citizens, at least Robin Hood-style rogues. Once Prohibition ended, however, the mob had become much more powerful (and dangerous) to law and order. The Hays Code guidelines were in direct response to this threat. Movies could be a persuasive tool to change hearts and minds, but only if they stuck to the good guy/bad guy script.

Speaking of unintended consequences, despite a few obviously brilliant films, the Hays Code restrictions and guidelines led to a watering down of creativity during the next 30 years. Film critic Katharine Coldiron summarized the difference between pre-Code and post-Code filmmaking clearly:

> ...pre-Code movies often prove revelatory to audiences that bear with them. The people in these films have the same problems we do, nearly a century later: mixed emotions around family bonds, lovers who want too much or too little, jobs that ask more of us than we want to give. These characters struggle with money, make mistakes and muddle through them, and cope with competing life priorities. The Hays Code—although this was not its stated purpose—flattened out these vibrancies and transformed realistic human characters into paper dolls that pushed plots around the studio backlot like uneaten vegetables on a dinner plate. This may sound like an exaggeration. But because the Code was so grounded in moralism, rather than realism, it discouraged ambiguity of all kinds. Families were usually loving and whole, rather than disappointing or healthier after splitting up. People presented in a positive light, particularly women, rarely had vices or lost their tempers. If a protagonist made mistakes, he earned punishment, not a lesson. The colors of real life cannot be developed on film stock imbued with such black-and-white morals.

Again, we might be left wondering how on Earth all this applies to an *animated cartoon*. Was Disney *really* going to show a sex scene in *Snow White*? How violent could a cartoon really get? It's probably important now to understand where Disney drew his inspiration. It's time to meet the Brothers Grimm.

Buckle up. It's about to get dark.

...

The Brothers Grimm (Jacob and Wilhelm) wrote the story "Little Snow-White" in 1812 as a German fairy tale.[3] If you know anything about the Grimms...well, "grim" is an operative word. Let's run through the major plot points and see if *you* can tell where the story might run afoul of the Hays Code.

Our story starts in a castle, where we meet Snow White's mother, the current queen. As she sews, the queen pricks herself with a needle. A drop of her bright red blood falls onto a black wood frame. Reflecting on the image below her, the queen says:

> If only I had a child as white as snow, as red as blood, and as black as the wood in this frame.

(Can we pause here for a moment? Is that a weird thing to say? "As red as blood." Yeah, that's weird. Let's continue.)

The queen got her wish, but unfortunately, she would not live to see her "Snow White" grow up. The queen died in childbirth. That part was, sadly, quite common in the days before doctors and midwives washed their hands. Bearing children was shockingly dangerous for mothers until the 20th century.[4]

Although grief-stricken, the king eventually remarried. The new bride was, as the kids would say, quite the looker. (The Grimms used the term "fairest in the land," and they didn't mean generous and just.) Despite her beauty, the new queen was chronically insecure and would ask her magic mirror to validate her status as the "fairest" each morning.

---

3. The original title was *Sneewittchen*. Because these stories are old enough, they're out of copyright. You can read them in several print and online anthologies. Bookseller Barnes & Noble publishes a nice "classics collection" hardcover version.

4. The doctor who championed hand-washing as a basic practice to lower infant and maternal mortality worked not far away from the Grimms in Vienna, Austria. Read up on Ignaz Semmelweis if you'd like to know more. He was largely ignored during the 1840s and 1850s when he insisted that doctors coming back from the autopsy room needed to wash their hands before they delivered babies.

One morning, however, the magic mirror dropped a bomb. When asked, the mirror replied:

> You, my queen, are fair; it is true. But Snow-White is a thousand times fairer than you.

Not just "prettier." A *thousand times* prettier. Yikes. You can imagine how this deeply insecure person might react. Let's just say "not well" doesn't begin to describe it. The queen's first plan was brutal, albeit a bit impersonal. She hired a huntsman (basically, an assassin) to drag Snow White into the woods, murder her, cut her open, and return with her lungs and liver.

(In Disney's version, the huntsman is supposed to return with her heart. That's...a bit more romantic, right?)

Well, the huntsman couldn't bring himself to do it. He warns Snow White, encouraging her to run away into the forest to escape her stepmother's vanity and wrath. For his part, he killed a boar and brought *its* lungs and liver back to the queen instead.

As she escapes into the forest, Snow White encounters a house inhabited by seven dwarves (not individually named) who make a deal with her. She can stay with them if she does the housework. In return, they'll house and protect her. Presumably, seven bachelors living alone in the woods aren't the most clean people. Who would have guessed? That's the most realistic part of the story so far.

Back at the palace, the queen happily received her gruesome prize and thought she was in the clear. However, the mirror outed the huntsman. Enraged but determined, the queen took matters into her own hands. *Literally*. Disguising herself, the queen's first gambit involved selling Snow White a beautiful corset. (The dwarves were away at the time.) As the queen helped Snow White lace it up, she tied it so tightly that she suffocated and collapsed. Luckily, however, the dwarves returned, saw what happened, and cut Snow White out of the restrictive clothing. The princess was (shockingly, given the lack of oxygen to the brain) none the worse for wear.

The dwarves chided Snow White for being so careless, but in classic Grimm style, she kept up the "foolish" behavior. (Foolishness was a common theme in all these classic fairy tales. They were meant to instruct children on the dangers of trusting strangers, going off alone, etc. This story is no different.) In the next try, the queen sold her a poisoned comb, which would have killed her had the dwarves not removed it. They told Snow White she was not to allow *anyone* inside nor accept *anything* that *anyone* might give her.

To her credit, when the disguised queen showed up with a poisoned apple, Snow White would not let her in and would not accept it. However, the queen was crafty. She had poisoned only *one-half* of the apple—and she took a bite of the opposite side. Trusting that the apple couldn't be dangerous if the woman took a bite herself, Snow White promptly bit into the poisoned half and collapsed.

This time, the dwarves couldn't fix it; they didn't know what had happened. So...of course...they put her in a glass coffin and kept her body in their living room. (That's what you do, right?) Over the course of this three-day vigil, again inexplicably, a "prince" visits the dwarves' home, wanting to see the beautiful woman in the glass coffin. The dwarves—and you won't believe this part—decided to give it to him. (The details of this strange transaction are not disclosed.) As they were moving it, however, one of the dwarves stumbled. The motion jostled Snow White's body, and the piece of half-chewed poisoned apple flung out of her mouth.

After waking and recovering, Snow White immediately loved the prince and returned with him to his castle. (Again, the reasons for this instant attraction are not disclosed.) Within a short time, they decided to marry. For their wedding, the bride and groom invited everyone...including *her* family...which included the queen.

Let's let the Grimm brothers finish the story:

> The wicked woman uttered a curse, and she became so frightened, so frightened, that she did not know what to do. At first she did not want to go to the wedding, but she found no peace. She had to go and see the young queen. When she arrived she recognized Snow-White, and terrorized, she could only stand there without

moving. Then they put a pair of iron shoes into burning coals. They were brought forth with tongs and placed before her. She was forced to step into the red-hot shoes and dance until she fell down dead.

You read that right. They tortured and murdered the queen *at their wedding*. Not very cheery, is it?

Since the story was published, multiple screenwriters had attempted to bring it to the stage, with different variations, some more and some less faithful to the original. The story enchanted Walt Disney, but he knew he needed to make changes. There was *no way* this story would pass muster with the Hays Code, and Disney wasn't a big enough name to try to challenge them. More than that, this story is more than a little nightmare-inducing. Can you imagine showing *that* story as an animation? No amount of cute forest critters will make up for the image of the newlyweds cheering on as they tortured her stepmother.

The trick was transforming this dark, creepy story into a charming tale that would birth a new art form. Let's see how Disney did it.

. . .

Snow White wasn't Disney's first idea.

Actually, he considered Bambi, Alice in Wonderland, and even a remake of the Greek epic, *The Iliad*. The first two would eventually become Disney films, but at the time, he didn't feel the technology was ready to bring those stories to life. Additionally, it just so happened that the copyright for *Snow White* had recently expired, so he could do whatever he liked with the story without paying royalties to the Grimm's estate. Given the company's financial position and the resources needed to make the film, Disney needed to pinch every penny he could find.

However, the story had a deeper meaning for Disney. In his biography *Walt Disney: The Triumph of the American Imagination*, historian Neal Gabler recounts how the themes of parents letting go and the dangers of trust resonated with a young man who struggled with the same issues...though, presumably, he and his wife didn't own a pair of iron dance shoes reserved for his in-laws. Perhaps a less Freudian reason, Disney had tangible evidence that *Snow White* would play well with audiences. A few years earlier, a theater production ran to sold-out crowds in Kansas City. It was precisely the kind of proof Disney was looking for—popularity in middle America.

Once he had his story, he needed to refine it. That's part of what made Disney special—his storytelling ability. Most histories of Walt Disney make him out to be a demanding taskmaster. He certainly was that, but those histories often miss Disney's ability to motivate his team by giving them a crystal clear vision of what was in his head. For *Snow White*, that meant telling (and retelling) the story to anyone who would listen. The Grimms may have written the original, but Disney was rewriting it for a new time, a new audience, and a new medium. He knew precisely the emotions he wanted to create.

But there was a difference between desire and execution. Disney's vision would require a small army, and a well-trained army at that. If you happened to be an out-of-work artist during the Great Depression, you might have found yourself working on the "in-between" drawings made by the principal animators.

What were "in-between" drawings? To create the appearance of a moving picture, the film must advance fast enough so that your eye can't distinguish between the individual frames. At a film speed of 24 frames per second, you need...you guessed it, 24 full-color drawings for each second of film. Or 1,440 every minute. Or more than 100,000 drawings for the entire film. That's...a lot. The principal artists would complete a main drawing every few seconds to indicate the basic action, and the assistants would create incremental drawings between them.

(It's unlikely Disney would have been able to hire so many illustrators, so quickly, and so cheaply, had so many of them not been out of work.)

Not only was it more efficient to divide the labor this way, but the principal artists were busy with research. Disney insisted that the artists study live animals in zoos to understand how they moved. They watched dancers perform, especially how their clothing would react to their movements. Animation was a new art form, and if Disney expected audiences to suspend disbelief, accuracy was critical. Awkward, unnatural movements would ruin the magic. That level of detail extended to voices as well. The team auditioned hundreds of actors to find exactly the right personality to match the visuals.[5] That attention to detail included the dwarves, who would each get their own name, voice, and personality.[6]

Even color saturation received careful attention. *Snow White* was the first film to use the intensity and realism (or lack thereof) of color as a storytelling tool. In this case, Disney chose to increase the saturation of the red in the apple, making it appear more intense and "real" than the surrounding background. Characters were also more vibrant. Otherwise, the team chose muted, realistic colors wherever *less attention* was called for.

Speaking of backgrounds, Disney faced the same challenge Merian Cooper did in creating *King Kong*. The characters and backgrounds were designed and animated separately. In Disney's case, the backgrounds not only needed to capture (and hold) your attention when no "actors" were on screen, but when they *did* interact, they needed to interact seamlessly.[7] For example, when the wind would blow through the trees, it also needed to blow Snow White's dress. If it didn't, it would snap the user back to reality, realizing they were watching a cartoon instead of immersing themselves in a film.

The most evident place to see Snow White's impact on filmmaking is simply to read the credits. *Snow White* credits 104 animators, more than half of *all* the people who worked on the film—more than all the directors, writers, cast, music, editing, and assistants combined.

By December 1937, Disney was ready to show the world the first example of a completely new film genre. Would it work?

. . .

---

5. It's often disconcerting to see the voice actors behind animated characters. For example, Nancy Jean Cartwright has played the voice of "Bart Simpson" for decades.

6. The story behind the creation of a unique personality for "Dopey" was telling. At first, this dwarf was meant to have an "idiot" personality, but Disney hated the idea. The eventual idea was to make him more "dog-like"—simple, lovable, and friendly—rather than overtly stupid.

7. The term for this type of separate background animation is "side-scrolling." If you ever played a 1980s Nintendo video game, you've already seen it. The background is a fixed image that video game characters interact on top of. It was a big deal in the 1990s when technology advanced to the point where players could interact with the backgrounds. That's how technically difficult this is.

With the benefit of hindsight, we know the answer. Still, it's instructive to understand just how big of an impact *Snow White* had on the American public.

Walt Disney's four-year-old daughter Diane was one of the first people to see the film. (She was in the target demographic after all.) She bawled when she saw Snow White "dead" on the bier in the dwarves' cottage. She wasn't the only one. Children cried. Women cried. Men cried. It was a level of emotional connection with the characters that even Disney didn't expect. Heck, audiences even cheered the *backgrounds*. People had never seen anything like it.

Even the usually-reserved *New York Times* film critics were beside themselves. Frank Nugent wrote:

> Let your fears be quieted at once: Mr. Disney and his amazing technical crew have outdone themselves. The picture more than matches expectations. It is a classic.

Snow White was "important cinematically," an "authentic masterpiece," and would be "beloved" by audiences for generations.

The film wasn't only a critical success but also a financial boon. Lines stretched down the block outside theaters showing *Snow White*. Within a few months, it made back its $1.5 million budget, going on to earn $6.7 million by May 1939, making it the highest-grossing movie to date. Remember, ticket prices were low and *falling* in many areas of the country, and children often paid even further discounted rates.

For the first time, success extended beyond the movie theater itself. Gabler cites research from the time that counted over 2,000 *Snow White*-themed merchandise items, netting the company over $4 million.[8] Gobsmacked, the *New York Times* wondered if animation would be the ticket out of the Great Depression.

Walt Disney had reinvented storytelling, the medium of animation, and launched a merchandising empire. Perhaps the most significant result of the entire effort was how Disney demonstrated that people *would care* about ani-

---

8. "Merchandising! Merchandising! Where the *real* money from the movie is made!" Extra points if you know who said that and in what movie. Hint: Kids loved the flamethrower.

mated characters. Over the years, Disney would make emotional magic again and again—Bambi's mother, Simba's father, and Carl's wife, among dozens of others.

Concerns about the Hays Code melted away. Disney had so deftly avoided the problem areas that no one even mentioned it. We tend to focus only on Disney's impact on moviemaking and storytelling, but that doesn't mean the morality issues disappeared. They simply changed form.

. . .

Today's equivalent of the "Hays Code" is a moral re-evaluation, a reckoning, an awakening. Like *many* other people in this era, Walt Disney held views that today we could consider extreme, unconventional, offensive, antisemitic, racist, and generally unworthy of attention. The real question becomes: Is it acceptable to enjoy an artist's work we now find morally objectionable?

In his book, *Drawing the Line: What to Do with the Work of Immoral Artists from Museums to the Movies*, philosopher Erich Hatala Matthes explores these complex questions. There's no right or wrong way to address these issues, but Matthes provides a helpful framework. He separates the larger question into three parts: moral criticism of the person, moral criticism of the artwork, and aesthetic criticism of the artwork. In simpler language, is the person immoral? Is the art immoral? Is the art of good quality?

In Disney's case, we can certainly argue that he held views that were objectionable by our standards but that were mainstream in his time. That doesn't necessarily make them *correct*, but Matthes (and, to be fair, many historians) cautions us to be careful in judging past figures by our standards. In a legal context, we (usually) don't prosecute people for breaking a law that didn't exist when they committed the now-illegal action. We recognize that as unfair. Although not the only way to look at morality, it's a useful reminder. On the other hand, it's fair that our standards change over time—that's often a good thing. It allows society to progress and improve.

Moving on to the art itself, Matthes asks us to consider whether Disney's views would lead him to produce immoral or low-quality art. In this case, we can sidestep the question of low quality and focus solely on morality. For example, if Disney held particular views about the role of women in society, did that view find its way into his films? One could argue, yes, they did. Matthes encourages us to understand the *person* so that we can better understand the impact on the *art* we consume.

Finally, we should consider our place in society and influence on others. Watching a Disney film in private is different from public endorsement. Additionally, those with more influence (celebrities, politicians, business leaders, religious clergy, etc.) should exercise even more caution.

In the end analysis, Matthes asks us to be careful with our condemnations. First, we are social animals. Excommunication or banishment of people was the most severe punishment for its social cost. Today's term is "canceling," which seems less severe until you consider the ability to earn a living. According to Matthes, we should reserve that punishment for only the most egregious cases. Second, how will people judge *us* for things we do today that humans 100 years from now will find objectionable? Think back on the discussion we're having right now. It's unlikely our great-grandchildren will be more understanding than we are.

But most importantly, it's simply not reasonable to go through life exploring the background of every person in every situation. That's not required to live a moral life. We must *choose* which standards mean the most to us and act accordingly. In other words, there are no answers—just better questions.

Seen another way—a more practical way—did any of these questions impact consumer behavior in the decades that followed *Snow White*?

It's hard to find evidence that they did. Consumers during the Great Depression voted with their wallets and have continued to do so for decades. G-rated animated movies are the most reliably profitable films studios can make. Of the top 10 top-grossing G-rated films of all time, Disney accounts for *all ten* and a majority of the top 100.

Disney created a fantasy world, and consumers of the Great Depression were happy to get whisked away. Despite wrestling with the occasional moral issue, we've been content to travel with him ever since.

15

MANUFACTURED TERROR

1937 was not a good year. In fact, you could make the case that it was the worst year of the Great Depression.

"Black Monday"—October 28, 1929—is the date most people point to when they think of the beginning of the troubles. That's the famous day the stock market crashed. *Surely, that was the day the terror set in.* The problem is that most people alive then didn't think the market losing 13 percent of its value was that big of a deal. Yes, it was serious, but it didn't seem more serious than other stock market gyrations in recent memory.

Alternatively, people remember the thundering cadence of Franklin Delano Roosevelt as he reminded Americans that "the only thing we have to fear is...fear itself" in his first presidential inaugural address on March 4, 1933. The three and a half years between October 1929 and March 1933 had seen not just the stock market, but also the entire economy and banking system, teeter and collapse. Yes, that was scary, but mostly, it was fear of the unknown. Uncertainty was rampant. Job one for FDR was to calm everything down so that solutions could work.

1937 was different.

After spiking in 1933 at 25.6 percent, unemployment had begun to fall. FDR's first 100 days (the first time that phrase had been used) had injected some much-needed optimism. However, it wasn't long before the shine started to wear off.

Initial attempts to stabilize wages and prices through the National Recovery Administration (NRA) buoyed initial confidence, but opinions (and compliance) quickly soured. Restrictive food aid coupons—which dictated what consumers could buy and how food would be prepared—were met with frustration and underground resistance. The Works Progress Administration (WPA) had put hundreds of thousands of people to work, but the economy needed to produce *millions* of jobs.

Americans still reeled from the implications of the previous decade's technical changes—automobiles, telephones, radio, movies, and hundreds of other consumer products. Booze was back after the formal repeal of Prohibition, but the windfall of cash the mob earned from bootlegging over the past dozen years meant they were posing a clear and present danger.

In addition, Americans needed to adapt to a media landscape where suffering anywhere was not only amplified (to sell subscriptions and advertising) but also felt more immediate. It was one thing to read a news report weeks after the event; it was quite another to get live dispatches on the radio. In 1900, something happening in Oklahoma wouldn't have bothered many people in Pennsylvania or Wisconsin. In 1937, all that had changed. Media had evolved into a national business.

And if all that wasn't enough, the rest of the world was—quite literally—going to hell. Fascist dictator Benito Mussolini had tightened his grip on Italy. To the north in Europe, an unremarkable World War I soldier and failed painter from Austria was doing the same thing in Germany. Despite the occasional celebrity or politician with an ambivalent (or even slightly admiring) view of Adolf Hitler, no one in America's military establishment was fooled. Another war in Europe was only a matter of time. Often overlooked in American history classes, Japan and China were *already* at war. However, it was a largely one-sided affair, with the Chinese people bearing the dragon's share of the suffering. In the geography in between, whatever halo Joseph Stalin may have earned with his grand communist experiment in the Soviet Union had faded by 1937. Reports were starting to trickle out that Russia's economic progress was so much smoke and mirrors. (Not to mention all the people shipped off to forced labor in Siberia.)

The stress was taking its toll, and artists started reflecting that anxiety. Sinclair Lewis published *It Can't Happen Here* in 1935, exploring the fear of an American fascist takeover. *Could* it happen here? Today, we're a bit jaded by political hyperbole, but in 1937, it truly seemed that the entire American way of life was at stake.

FDR wasn't doing so well either. As his domestic agenda stalled, he attempted a "court-packing" scheme to add friendly Supreme Court justices. This gave his opponents in Congress the first real political weapon to use against him. In the end, Roosevelt's gambit did encourage change, but it left a bad taste in people's mouths.

And then, in 1937, economic conditions took a decisive turn for the worse. Unemployment spiked, the stock market stalled, and momentum seemed to run out. Would we be mired in the Great Depression forever? Was this the "new normal?" Would America be strong enough to withstand growing global threats? With the benefit of hindsight, we know the answer to those questions. But try to imagine what it was like for people living through it—waking up each day to a bone-deep fear that had taken root.

Then, one night, on October 30, 1937, a day before Halloween, you heard on the radio that America was being invaded.

. . .

George Orson Welles wasn't always famous for his broadcast adaptation of *The War of the Worlds*.

Before he was feted as one of the "greatest filmmakers of all time" with *Citizen Kane,* Welles was a high-drama kid in Kenosha, Wisconsin. Don't know where that is? You're not alone. Today, it's part of the in-fill of suburbia between Milwaukee and Chicago on the coast of Lake Michigan. Then, it was nowhere.

Welles *should* have had an easy start in life. His father invented a popular model of bicycle lamp and earned a fortune in royalties.[1] However, like many people of that era, he struggled with alcoholism, stopped working, and squandered much of his money. His mother was an accomplished stage musician who trained with concert pianist Leopold Godowsky (also a co-inventor of color photography film). The young Welles knew which of his parents he wanted to emulate. But in 1924, his mother died of hepatitis, just after his ninth birthday.

Nine.

That meant Welles found himself alone with an alcoholic, broken man for a father.

Biographer Frank Brady remarked, "During the three years that Orson lived with his father, some observers wondered who took care of whom." Roger Hill, one of Welles' lifelong friends and mentors, observed, "In some ways, he was never really a young boy, you know." Put more simply, young Orson had a tough childhood.

If we do the math, Welles lived with his father between the ages of nine and 12, finally cutting his father out of his life when he refused to stop drinking. He would not see him in the next three years. And then, one day, the 15-year-old learned that his father had died alone in a cheap hotel room.

No child should suffer through that. It changed him. Welles was determined to make something more of himself. He would stop at nothing.

By the time we catch up with him again in the early 1930s, Welles was having mixed success with his own production company. He had traveled to Europe with a small inheritance from his father's estate. After returning to New York, he parlayed that into a creative concept: Mercury Theater Group would adapt classics for a modern audience.

Welles' first hit stage production was a remake of the classic Shakespeare play *Romeo and Juliet*, retold in the modern era. All the storyline elements remained,

---

1. It's difficult to imagine how popular bicycles were in the days before mass-market automobiles. They were one of the first higher-speed alternatives for transportation (other than a horse), and you didn't need to clean up after it. Bicycle owners were one of the major advocate groups for better roads in the early 1900s. Ironic that they need to fight for their right to (safely) use our roadways today. Check out *Two Wheels Good: The History and Mystery of the Bicycle* by Jody Rosen if you want to know more.

but the characters and situation mimicked Europe on the eve of a new world war, not the medieval Montagues and Capulets.

Although Mercury found a niche for sophisticated theatergoers who appreciated the effort, *Romeo and Juliet* was a rare early success for Welles. Most adaptations received a ho-hum response from the New York theater community. Despite his struggles, Welles generated interest from CBS executives looking to fill broadcast time for their syndicated stations. It sure sounded like a good idea; Welles certainly had the voice for it (even then). However, *Mercury Theater on the Air* performed so poorly with audiences that it failed to attract sponsors. (Campbell's Soup turned them down flat. "Mm! Mm! ... Nope!") It was more than a bit frustrating for a 20-something Welles with a lot to prove to himself.

Without a steady source of sponsorship income, his show lost its prime-time slot. (That time change will factor into our story later.) Still, Welles' show had diehard fans—not many, but they were loyal. It was not nothing, but it could have been better, and it was clearly not the success he was looking for.

Part of the issue was there were only *so many* classics to adapt. Well, check that. There are plenty of classic works of literature, but only so many that modern audiences would recognize, and even fewer that would adapt well to a modernization approach. Adding to the pressure was the reality of the broadcast schedule. Welles and his team had only a week to adapt a story, write the script, and perform it on air—complete with different voice actors and sound effects. *One week.*

Welles often gets criticized for his intensity; he was not a nice guy to work for. But with a one-week turn time, it's not unreasonable. Things needed to happen quickly, and that lends itself to a demanding, top-down, rapid-fire decision-making style.

By 1937, it wasn't obvious that Welles had another 30 *days* on the air, much less the "legendary" career we associate with him today. It might have been that pressure that forced him to look in an unlikely place for the next adaptation. Maybe the tense mood of the era encouraged him to look to a science-fiction story about an invasion by H.G. Wells.[2]

---

2. Wells, not Welles. No, the two were not related. Students get the spellings wrong on high-school history tests all the time. I was one of them.

. . .

Herbert George Wells (we'll use H.G. Wells from here on out to avoid confusion) was a prolific writer in the United Kingdom. He wrote over 50 novels and more than 100 short stories—both science fiction and nonfiction. He's known for multiple classics in the science fiction genre, including *The Time Machine*, published in 1895, and 1897's *The Invisible Man*. However, H.G. Wells is perhaps most influential for his 1898 novel *The War of the Worlds*.

Here's the basic storyline.

After using up all the resources on their smaller-than-Earth home planet, the Martians decide to invade our homeworld. It's written from the point of view of Victorian London in the late 1890s, but one presumes the rest of the world was getting its fair share of conquering as well. In Part 1, the invaders quickly overpowered late 19th-century defenses and began capturing humans to serve as food and fuel. In Part 2, survivors work to resist the invaders, but most simply hide to survive. The novel ends with the Martians succumbing to Earth-bound pathogens to which they had no resistance in their new environment.

If you're thinking, *hey, that sounds like an allegory for 19th-century British imperialism*, you would be correct.

After the Industrial Revolution (spearheaded in the U.K. in the 18th century), the limited resources of the empire's home islands quickly ran thin. This forced the Brits to expand their overseas colonies, specifically to exploit them for raw materials to feed their growing industrial machine. Local people were captured and forced to work; they could even be said to have been "consumed" by the invaders. On the flip side, the Brits had no resistance to tropical diseases they encountered. (The average life expectancy for a British person in Africa or the Caribbean was measured in weeks.) Both populations—invaders and invaded—died by the thousands.

Beyond the social critique, H.G. Wells explored several other themes—the idea of space travel in capsules (although no one quite knew how just yet) and the implications of Darwin's idea of natural selection and survival of the fittest. For the latter, H.G. Wells observed that the British focus on rational, intellectual power left their bodies physically weak and minds emotionally stunted. They could develop deadly weapons that could overwhelm local populations (as the

Martians did), but their bodies were vulnerable, and their minds were incapable of empathy with their victims.

More ominously, H.G. Wells was one of the first authors to describe the concept of "total war." His heat rays, smoke weapons, and aircraft were all preludes to what the world would see in the "Great War" about two decades later. Like the best science fiction writers, H.G. Wells allowed people to see into the future—not necessarily the specific inventions (although sometimes, they're eerily accurate), but rather what those changes will mean to people living with them.

However, by the time we fast-forward three decades *through* the era H.G. Wells warned Britain about, the novel seemed...well, dated and obsolete. No one needed a prediction of the horrors of the Great War; that terror was now (sadly) history. That's true of most science fiction. Once you live through the "future" era, the impact of the message blunts. In that way, science fiction *always* says more about the era in which it was written than the era it describes.

To adapt H.G. Wells' work for a new generation, Orson Welles had his work cut out for him. The novel was too long, too detailed, and too tied to British culture and places to work well as a short-form broadcast radio adaptation. However, the biggest issue might have been the general appetite for science fiction as a genre in the 1930s.

. . .

Science fiction experienced a significant decline in popularity during the Great Depression. The best the genre had to offer in that decade were two novels: Aldous Huxley's *Brave New World* (published in 1931) and Sinclair Lewis' *It Can't Happen Here* (published four years later). Both were dystopian fictions of a future in which technology had outpaced humanity. They were a reaction to the monumental global changes since the Industrial Revolution and especially the Consumer Revolution in the 1920s.

Huxley's novel opens in the "World City of London" in 632 AF—"After Ford"—a clear reference to the Model T's explosion in popularity in the Roaring 20s. These 26th-century Brits are created in artificial wombs to serve specific, predestined purposes.[3] The novel follows the protagonists' fight against forced conformity and happiness-producing drugs provided to keep everyone in line. Again, this novel (like all science fiction) says more about Britain in 1931 than it does "London After Ford." The historical aristocracy in the United Kingdom was collapsing under its own weight, while new consumer comforts were seen as pacifying its citizens. Would a new caste structure emerge based on the planned communist/Soviet model? It was a genuine fear in the United Kingdom in those days.

Across the pond, Lewis' novel explores an American brand of the same fear—the rise of a fascist regime in the United States and an "American Hitler." This one sticks much closer to the present day. In 1936, Senator Berzelius "Buzz" Windrip used a populist platform to win the presidential election from FDR, returning the country to "prosperity" and "greatness" through "traditional" values and a focus on the "forgotten man." We don't need much explanation to understand the direct parallels between fascist Italy and Germany in the 1930s.

In both cases, the dystopian perspective fit the mood but didn't lift the imagination. Both were political novels that happened to be set in the future—less science, more fiction.

What we think of today as science fiction—aliens, transporters, spaceships, and laser swords—was largely the domain of children's books and short stories. They were fantasies, certainly not serious literature. Remember, the Consumer Revolution of the 1920s had put gadgets in people's homes that would have been science fiction only a decade before. Beaming electromagnetic signals through the air was more magical than anything sci-fi writers of the past half-century had come up with. Science fiction seemed irrelevant.

In short, if Welles was going to choose to adapt any novel for his radio show—especially one that he hoped would turn things around for his struggling production company—a science fiction novel might have been his worst possible choice. In fact, *The War of the Worlds* was a worse choice than most. *Frankenstein* might have been a better choice, but Mary Shelley's science fiction/horror classic

---

3. Haven't read that one since high school? It's the same idea put forward in the 2013 film "Man of Steel." Obstensively, it's about Superman, but it's the same plot arc. Simply substitute Kryptonians for Brits. Did Henry Cavill, a Brit himself, know the connection? One suspects so.

had already seen its way to the big screen in 1931. A radio broadcast would seem...less than that. There was no way H.G. Wells' novel (as originally written) could condense into 60 to 90 minutes. This new adaptation would need to be nearly a complete rewrite.

Remember that a complete rewrite must be finished in one week. That's right. *One week.*

For those not involved in the creative process, it may seem like you can enter a prompt into a generative artificial intelligence tool and get something to pop out, but (a) that's not how it works now, and (b) that's certainly not how it worked then. Orson Welles needed an entire team working around the clock to have any hope of making it happen.

To make matters worse, the first rewrites were...not great. The story was modernized, but it lacked energy. Welles was the only creative team member with an eye for drama, and it was his idea to take advantage of timing. This episode would broadcast the night before Halloween, so playing up the scary angle made sense. The question was, *how* could they scare people?

Let's follow along on the night of October 30. Try to imagine being alive in the fall of 1937 with everything that meant but *none* of what we know now.

. . .

First, Welles retold the story as if it were happening now—as in, *right now.* That meant a certain amount of realism in the broadcast tone and programming. After a brief introduction from Welles himself, the performance started innocuously:

...for the next twenty-four hours not much change in temperature. A slight atmospheric disturbance of undetermined origin is reported over Nova Scotia, causing a low pressure area to move down rather rapidly over the northeastern states, bringing a forecast of rain, accompanied by winds of light gale force. Maximum temperature 66; minimum 48. This weather report comes to you from the Government Weather Bureau. We take you now to the Meridian Room in the Hotel Park Plaza in downtown New York, where you'll be entertained by the music of Ramón Raquello and his orchestra.

Good evening, ladies and gentlemen. From the Meridian Room in the Park Plaza Hotel in New York City, we bring you the music of Ramón Raquello and his orchestra. With a touch of the Spanish, Ramón Raquello leads off with "La Cumparsita."

If you didn't happen to catch the introduction or didn't happen to know the types of adaptations the Mercury Theater Group performed, it might not be obvious what was about to happen next. Remember, no digital title was displayed next to the Spotify playlist or podcast.[4]

Next, instead of a third-person omniscient narrator (like many science fiction books), Welles structured the performance as a series of interruptions to the regularly scheduled programming. The broadcasters would interview local scientists and officials to help explain "what was happening" to listeners. Here's an example:

PHILLIPS: *Good evening, ladies and gentlemen. This is Carl Phillips, speaking to you from the observatory at Princeton. I am standing in a large semi-circular room, pitch black, except for an oblong split in the ceiling. Through this opening, I can see a sprinkling of stars that cast a kind of frosty glow over the intricate mechanism of the huge telescope. The ticking sound you hear is the vibration of the clockwork. Professor Pierson stands directly above me on a small platform, peering through a giant lens. I ask you to be patient, ladies and gentlemen, during any delay that may arise during our interview. Besides his ceaseless watch of the heavens, Professor Pierson may be interrupted by telephone or other communications. During this period he is in constant touch with the astronomical centers of the world ... Professor, may I begin our questions?*

PIERSON: *At any time, Mr. Phillips.*

PHILLIPS: *Professor, would you please tell our radio audience exactly what you see as you observe the planet Mars through your telescope?*

PIERSON: *Nothing unusual at the moment, Mr. Phillips. A red disk swimming in a blue sea. Transverse stripes across the disk. Quite distinct now because Mars happens to be the point nearest the earth ... in opposition, as we call it.*

PHILLIPS: *In your opinion, what do these transverse stripes signify, Professor Pierson?*

---

4. You can read the full script at Wellesnet.com, a site dedicated to Welles' legacy.

PIERSON: Not canals, I can assure you, Mr. Phillips, although that's the popular conjecture of those who imagine Mars to be inhabited. From a scientific viewpoint, the stripes are merely the result of atmospheric conditions peculiar to the planet.

PHILLIPS: Then you're quite convinced as a scientist that living intelligence as we know it does not exist on Mars?

PIERSON: I'd say the chances against it are a thousand to one.

PHILLIPS: And yet, how do you account for those gas eruptions occurring on the surface of the planet at regular intervals?

PIERSON: Mr. Phillips, I cannot account for it.

PHILLIPS: By the way, Professor, for the benefit of our listeners, how far is Mars from Earth?

PIERSON: Approximately forty million miles.

PHILLIPS: Well, that seems a safe enough distance.

Over the coming minutes, the broadcast is again interrupted to announce a "shock of almost an earthquake" near Princeton, New Jersey. This was the first indication that something was happening that might impact us. The location was no accident. Remember that the original story was set in London, and Welles was broadcasting from New York. Having this event occur across the river made it more immediate and relevant.

To make it more convincing, the writing team drove the supposed "invasion route" to ensure the details were correct. That might not mean much to someone listening in Ohio (though specifics always seem more credible than generalities), but it would seem *very real* to those who knew the area.

We'll fast-forward through some of the details. The "earthquake" was the Marian fleet touching down. Observers in the area (all with specific place names) seemed to believe meteorites caused the impacts. Regularly scheduled programming continues to cut in and out as announcers interview "witnesses" and events progress.

Over the course of the next 30-to-40 minutes, the announcements become ever more strained and urgent. Once the military gets involved, events move quickly:

OPERATOR ONE: *This is Bayonne, New Jersey, calling Langham Field . . . This is Bayonne, New Jersey, calling Langham Field . . . Come in, please . . .*

OPERATOR TWO: *This is Langham Field . . . Go ahead . . .*

OPERATOR ONE: *Eight army bombers in engagement with enemy tripod machines over Jersey flats. Engines incapacitated by heat ray. All crashed. One enemy machine destroyed. Enemy now discharging heavy black smoke in direction of —*

OPERATOR THREE: *This is Newark, New Jersey . . . This is Newark, New Jersey . . . Warning! Poisonous black smoke pouring in from Jersey marshes. Reaches South street. Gas masks useless. Urge population to move into open spaces . . . automobiles use Routes 7, 23, 24 . . . Avoid congested areas. Smoke now spreading over Raymond Boulevard . . .*

OPERATOR FOUR: *2X2L . . . calling CQ . . . 2X2L . . . calling CQ . . . 2X2L . . . calling 8X3R . . . Come in, please . . .*

OPERATOR FIVE: *This is 8X3R . . . coming back at 2X2L.*

OPERATOR FOUR: *How's reception? How's reception? K, please (PAUSE) Where are you, 8X3R? What's the matter? Where are you?*

(BELLS RINGING OVER CITY GRADUALLY DIMINISHING)

ANNOUNCER: *I'm speaking from the roof of the Broadcasting Building, New York City. The bells you hear are ringing to warn the people to evacuate the city as the Martians approach. Estimated in last two hours three million people have moved out along the roads to the north, Hutchison River Parkway still kept open for motor traffic. Avoid bridges to Long Island . . . hopelessly jammed. All communication with Jersey shore closed ten minutes ago. No more defenses. Our army wiped out . . . artillery, air force, everything wiped out. This may be the last broadcast. We'll stay here to the end . . . People are holding service below us . . . in the cathedral.*

To the rational observer, the dramatization was absurd in the extreme. Within half an hour, we went from unknown meteorite impacts to the entire U.S. military mobilized to the entire force wiped out by Martians. Thirty minutes. Not likely. Despite that logical absurdity, the performance was slow-building and a brilliant piece of theater...if fiction is what you thought it was.

As part of the drama, at least one station announcement (usually broadcast at the bottom of the hour) was omitted. In fact, it wasn't until *after* this bit of apocalyptic drama in New York that the announcer finally broke in to remind listeners this was a dramatization. The entire reminder is a scant 43 words. Broadcast, it lasted a few seconds. It was easy to miss. Many people did.

The story continues to its climax. Like the original narrative, the Martians succumb (very quickly, we might add—within about an hour) to our diseases, leaving only a trail of destruction and terrified citizens in their wake.

At the very end, Welles finally lets people in on the secret:

Orson Welles: This is Orson Welles, ladies and gentlemen, out of character to assure you that The War of The Worlds has no further significance than as the holiday offering it was intended to be. The Mercury Theatre's own radio version of dressing up in a sheet and jumping out of a bush and saying Boo! Starting now, we couldn't soap all your windows and steal all your garden gates by tomorrow night. . . so we did the best next thing. We annihilated the world before your very ears, and utterly destroyed the C. B. S. You will be relieved, I hope, to learn that we didn't mean it, and that both institutions are still open for business. So goodbye everybody, and remember the terrible lesson you learned tonight. That grinning, glowing, globular invader of your living room is an inhabitant of the pumpkin patch, and if your doorbell rings and nobody's there, that was no Martian. . .it's Hallowe'en.

(MERCURY THEATRE THEME UP FULL, THEN DOWN)

Announcer: Tonight the Columbia Broadcasting System and its affiliated stations coast-to-coast have brought you The War of the Worlds, by H. G. Wells, the seventeenth in its weekly series of dramatic broadcasts featuring Orson Welles and the Mercury Theatre on the Air. Next week we present a dramatization of three famous short stories. This is the Columbia Broadcasting System.

It was brilliant—the creative approach, the pacing, the details, the intensity. Just to read it is jarring. To listen to the broadcast—complete with sound effects and terrific voice acting—is terrifying. No one had ever heard anything quite like it.

But remember, *very few* people did. As we discussed, this show was struggling to find an audience. The initial reports from the handful of people who heard it afterward showed that listeners were impressed. It was a good scare and a well-done production. Aside from a *very small* number of outliers who freaked out, it didn't have much of an impact at all.

So, why do we remember *The War of the Worlds* as a watershed moment in media history?

. . .

The objective evidence doesn't support our collective memory.

According to A. Brad Schwartz, in his history of the "panic," *Broadcast Hysteria: Orson Welles's War of the Worlds and the Art of Fake News,* CBS received only 115 calls, while the Federal Communications Commission (FCC) received only 353 letters. Yes, many of those were concentrated in the New York/New Jersey area, but that wasn't surprising. Compared to a population of about 130 million people, that's not that many, and certainly not a "nationwide panic."

Much of our current *misperception* about the public impact of the broadcast comes from a deeply flawed academic study conducted by psychology professor Hadley Cantril in 1940.[5] These were the earliest days of public opinion polling, and this study would fail on several levels.

First, Cantrill interviewed a small cross-section of people—much too small, as it turned out. Worse, he failed to choose a representative cross-section of people, with too few subjects selected as "controls" (people who didn't hear the broadcast) to serve as a reaction benchmark. Second, he knew the conclusion he wanted before he began the interviews. How do we know? Upper-class people (like him) did *not* "believe" the broadcast, while working-class people (who weren't smart enough to tell the difference) *did* believe it was real. Because most people in the United States were working-class, that's the basis for the idea that Welles had sparked a mass panic.

In addition to the tiny fraction of people who wrote or called in (and assuming they were writing or calling to express *displeasure* with the broadcast),

---

5. There's some debate over who truly authored the Princeton study "The Invasion from Mars." It would seem, given its lack of quality, that the fight should be about who *didn't* write it. It was *so bad*, in fact, that it spurred the development of quality controls and standards in this type of research.

Cantrill's own data don't support his conclusions. Yes, a few people thought the invasion was actual Martians, but most "believers" believed what they wanted to believe—or at least, what they feared. Of those who believed the broadcast, most either missed the introductory remarks about Mars or quickly ignored them. For them, the invaders were Germans, a natural disaster, or a religious rapture. Again, Cantrill lumped all those people into the same group of simpletons, but any *competent* psychologist would see—quickly—that the broadcast triggered whatever deeper fear that individual possessed.

By the way, children seemed to handle the situation far better than adults. That should have been another tip-off. They're easier to "jump scare" but harder to fool. They don't have the same ingrained fears and biases adults do, so they are more likely to take new information at face value (in this case, fiction) than to allow that information to strengthen beliefs or fears they already hold.[6]

In other words, the effects (such as they were) represented well-understood psychology. However, just like the subjects he disdained, Cantrill saw the panic he wanted to see.

To be fair, he wasn't the only one. It's almost as if this research justified the epic level of mismanagement from the major media. In the days following the broadcast, journalists tripped over each other to find (and tell) the most salacious stories. Whether they were true or not mattered little. No careful fact-checking took place when there was so much outrage to be had. In Schwartz's words, the media's "narrative was almost as fictitious as the Martians themselves."

No matter.

Headlines in nearly every newspaper around the country excoriated Welles, asking him to explain himself for this trick he pulled on the American people. Smartly backpedaling and offering humble apologies, Welles understood that it was better to ride the wave than attempt to fight it. He had the instinct every celebrity learns; any publicity is good publicity...especially when your company isn't doing well. In the end, his Mercury Theater Group wouldn't survive, but his career certainly would.

---

6. This is called *confirmation bias* and it's one of the nastiest defects in our mental hardware. It's tough to recognize and even tougher to defeat.

However, Welles was a scapegoat for something bigger—the creeping terror and hopelessness we discussed earlier.

Everyone understood that war was coming and the radio would play a major role. In that world, would Americans be able to tell real news from "fake news?" Would they fall victim to hoaxes and hysterias—some, perhaps, perpetrated by foreign propaganda or subversives within their midst? Would a convergence of technologies make the situation worse? The radio, combined with the telephone, could spread rumors and misinformation faster than ever before. As scholar Herta Herzog put it in 1941: "Radio seems to have taken the place of the neighbor." Or, on the positive side, would this be the wake-up call Americans needed to face down the Nazi threat? By the end of the decade, there were more questions than answers. It was all pretty scary.

Broadcasters felt the anxiety, too, albeit for different reasons. As we've seen in the film industry, broadcasters understood what unchecked public fear might mean: government control and censorship. Even more urgently, advertisers might withdraw their support from broadcasters that angered their customers. Sponsorship was the only viable business model in those days, and broadcasters knew it.

Before the FCC could step in or advertisers could step out, broadcasters clamped down on free expression on their airwaves—gone were edgy dramas and fictionalizations, and in their place were milquetoast programs that "everyone" could like…or, at least, no one would complain about.

In the end, this new adaption of *The War of the Worlds* simply served as the lightning rod for our collective anxiety. It said more about us than it ever did about Martians. Perhaps that's what Orson Welles had in mind.

16

UNTOUCHABLES

Chester Gould was not having much success as a cartoonist.

Born in Oklahoma in 1900, Gould spent much of the 1920s eking out a living drawing comic strips for the *Tulsa Democrat* and *Daily Oklahoman*. However, if he was going to have a bigger future, he needed to make a bigger move. Heading north, Gould landed in Chicago to finish his college education at Northwestern University and, he hoped, impress someone at the *Chicago Tribune*.

Despite the change of scenery, Gould sputtered. Yes, he achieved syndication for a spoof strip on silent films, *Fillum Fables*, and another about a family of cats fascinated by the radio. But no, no one thought *Radio Catts* was the next *Little Orphan Annie*.

However, Gould's luck would change as the gang wars in Chicago heated up in the final years of the Roaring 20s and the beginning of the Great Depression. Listening to a radio dramatization of a Sherlock Holmes story (new Holmes stories were being published as late as 1927), Gould had an idea: What if he could create a comic strip featuring an American version of the famous detective? Okay, not bad...but who would be Professor Moriarty to this American Holmes? That part was easy. His name was all over the papers—the most famous mobster to that point and perhaps, for all time—Al Capone.

Of course, Gould couldn't name the characters "Sherlock Holmes" and "Al Capone." As we'll learn, Capone might have gotten a kick out of it. He was a master of publicity. On the other hand, Sherlock Holmes was copyrighted and...well, *British*. No, his protagonist would need to be American through and through. He would be more like the soft-spoken Federal investigator he was also reading about in the papers—the so-called "incorruptible"—Eliot Ness.

Gould had made 60—*six-zero*—unsuccessful submissions to Chicago Tribune New York News Syndicate boss Joseph Patterson. But his 61st, "Plainclothes Tracy," had potential. The name, though...needed some work. Tracy was fine, but "Plainclothes" was too long. It didn't fit. It was Patterson who came up with the name "Dick Tracy"—police detectives were called "dicks" in those days, and the name didn't carry the (awkward) connotation it now does. Dick Tracy would use smarts and grit to track down gangsters and clean up corruption wherever he found it. Although the strip would evolve over the years, the core message was the same: The good guys would win in the end, and the lawbreaker would get what was coming to him.[1]

Dick Tracy was a bigger hit than anyone could have imagined. Gould would pen the strip from 1931 to 1977—a 46-year run—making it one of the most successful comic strips in the history of the genre.

The bigger question for us is, *why* was Dick Tracy so popular? The Prohibition decade (roughly corresponding to the 1920s) had created a "nation of lawbreakers" and a decidedly low opinion of law enforcement. What had changed?

To answer that question, we need to step back to understand not only the main characters in this drama—Al Capone and Eliot Ness—but also other innovators, August Vollmer and George E.Q. Johnson, who transformed the art and science of law enforcement. We also need to understand the forces that created Capone and Ness. In many ways, this isn't their story at all. It's the story of unintended consequences, strategic publicity, and a new breed of cop.

---

1. You can find beautifully bound collections of the *Dick Tracy* comic strip wherever books are sold, but to get at more of the backstory and evolution of the strip, read *Dick Tracy and American Culture: Morality and Mythology, Text and Context* by Garyn G. Roberts.

. . .

Alphonse Gabriel Capone was a product of Prohibition.

Of course, that's not what the advocates of alcohol restriction—the so-called "drys"—had in mind. However, like so many other aspects of the constitutional amendment and subsequent regulations, Capone was a predictable (albeit unintended) consequence.

To be fair, alcohol abuse had been a major social problem in the United States since its founding. Germany had its beer. France had its wine. But the United States had its rum. Rum is a *distilled* spirit. Beer and wine might range from three to fifteen percent alcohol by volume, but distilled spirits are *much stronger*—averaging 40 to 60 percent ABV or more. More important than the percentage of alcohol itself was the culture that grew up around it. Distilling spirits (e.g., moonshine) was considered a patriotic act of rebellion. Put simply, alcohol has been part of the American experience since the beginning.[2]

Unfortunately, so was rampant alcohol abuse. Although accurate figures are impossible to know (public health records weren't reliably compiled until the 19th century at the earliest), the evidence of broken homes, spousal abuse, child neglect, and financial ruin were impossible to ignore.

The "temperance" movement involved a coalition of religious leaders, social progressives, and women's suffragists who banded together (each with their own reasons) first to restrict alcohol locally and then nationally. The resulting 19th Amendment didn't ban *buying and consuming* alcohol (oddly—most people don't know that); it banned the production, transportation, and sale of alcohol. It also allowed for religious exemptions and home consumption of ciders and other brews, which, on the surface, seemed reasonable. It allowed people to retain the freedom to eat and drink what they chose. However, this is perhaps the most vexing of all the hypocrisies and exceptions to the law. When you think about it in basic economic terms, it makes sense. The *demand* for alcohol remained, but the *supply* was severely restricted. Most "honest" businesspeople would not meet

---

2. For much more on Prohibition—including its historical, legal, and cultural impacts—read *Last Call: The Rise and Fall of Prohibition*, by Daniel Okrent. We'll only briefly touch on Prohibition here as it relates to the battle between Al Capone and Eliot Ness.

this demand. In fact, the vast majority would not.[3] But some would—especially those groups already operating outside the law: the mob.

Prohibition was the best thing that could have possibly happened for organized crime. They were already good at operating in secrecy, but Prohibition gave them a "product" (unlike prostitution, gambling, and extortion) that nearly everyone wanted. Not only that, most people—especially in places like Chicago that voted overwhelmingly against Prohibition—didn't see alcohol as a crime at all. Speakeasies in Chicago operated with an openness almost unheard of everywhere else, which is saying something. What was worse for the moral character of the city (and again, an unintended consequence) was that politicians and police thought the law was silly, too. *They* wanted a drink and saw the same opportunity the mob did: to cash in. To "protect" a watering hole from police harassment, police would offer to look the other way…for a cash consideration. Most of the Chicago political and law enforcement establishment was "on the take" during the 1920s, solidifying a reputation for the windy city as hopelessly corrupt.

Any mobster in Chicago would have done well during the 1920s, but Al Capone had the skills to be even more successful than most. In the end, those would be precisely the skills that would be his downfall, but in the "Roaring" 20s, they were a perfect match. Business was booming, creating a level of growth and sophistication unheard of before. Al Capone used many of the same tactics and strategies to become the Henry Ford of bootlegging—mass production, cost reductions, efficient distribution, and competitive consolidation.

What's more, mass media had created a new "celebrity" culture where savvy businesspeople could craft and cultivate a public image. Al Capone used the media like no other gangster ever had—he was a big man (over six feet tall and weighing more than 200 pounds) with a distinctive scar and immaculately tailored clothes. In other words, he looked the part. Unlike other mobsters who shunned media attention, Capone understood how his public persona would draw people to him—like a sort of anti-hero—and also to his businesses. Why

---

3. Strangely, not all. Because of the religious carve-out in the Volstead Act (the regulatory and legal framework that operationalized the amendment), there was an explosion in the number of "pastors" and "congregations" offering "spiritual" experiences. Yes, the scare quotes are warranted here.

wouldn't you go to *Capone's* establishment if you could drink at any speakeasy? It's the same strategy "influencers" use today. They learned it from him.[4]

As long as Capone kept the ugly side of the bootlegging "racket" away from the public eye, he'd be okay. When a gangster shot another gangster, that didn't impact John and Jane Q. Public...in fact, it seemed a little exciting and dangerous. Paradoxically, it *increased* Capone's appeal. When innocent bystanders *were* caught in the crossfire, he would go out of his way to help them—paying medical bills, making personal visits to the hospital, and (bluntly) killing the people responsible for such sloppiness.

To be fair, mobsters all over the country were taking advantage of Prohibition, making a mockery of the underfunded, underpowered, and largely corrupt Federal and State law enforcement meant to combat them. But no one understood how to leverage the power of the media like Capone. His organization was rolling in cash—earning an estimated $100 million annually (or $1.3 billion today). To put that in perspective, *General Motors* made $177 million in 1926. If he had been a "legitimate" CEO, Capone would have been among the top 10 executives in the United States.

As the 1920s came to a close, Capone's organization seemed utterly untouchable.

. . .

In his own way, Eliot Ness was just as much a product of Prohibition as Al Capone.

Ness was the child of Norwegian immigrants. His father ran a thriving bakery in Chicago around the turn of the century. While Al Capone grew up on the rough and tumble streets of Brooklyn, learning the ruthless efficiency and glory for attention that would define his life, Ness learned a very different lesson in his childhood. The fifth and last of five children, he was...an "oops," as we would call it today. He was ten years younger than anyone else in his household, which crafted a young man who was comfortable in his own head—quiet, reserved, street tough, hard-working, wicked smart, and utterly fearless and determined.

---

4. We cover the birth of celebrity culture in much more detail in Chapter 9 of *Booze, Babe, and the Little Black Dress: How Innovators of the Roaring 20s Created the Consumer Revolution.*

The key difference between Capone and Ness might have been their use of the spotlight. Both used it strategically (as we'll see), but Capone *enjoyed* it. To Ness, it was only a tool.

Capone's father plays little into the man Al would grow up to be. Not so with Eliot. During the Pullman Strike in the summer of 1894, Eliot's father sided with the *workers*, continuing to feed them from his bakery out of his own pocket so that they continue to hold out for better wages and working conditions. Although the Federal government would eventually intervene and put down the strike (because the railroads carried mail—a Federal responsibility), no one forgot the elder Ness's generosity and courage, his son perhaps most of all.

Ness grew up, went to college, and joined law enforcement before he was even of legal age. Because Ness was born at home and did not have official records, he fudged his birthday one year earlier so that he could pass for 25—the cut-off—instead of 24, which he was. It was the first of many "bends" in the law Ness would endorse for the higher purpose of professionalizing law enforcement and bringing down organized crime. We'll get to that in due course.

Before we do that, it's important to introduce the second man who would influence the young Ness: August Vollmer.

Often called the "father of law enforcement," Vollmer created the first professional police program at the University of California at Berkeley. He was disgusted by the rampant corruption he saw (especially in the Los Angeles Police Department) around the turn of the century and was determined to do something about it.

In those days, policing was more of a trade—and barely one at that. It was low-paid, low-skill work that should have been a major tip-off that enforcing an unpopular law would not go well. That was "okay" when people lived in rural communities; law enforcement wasn't as much of an issue when most people lived miles apart from each other. But as people moved to the cities, and especially as new immigrants flooded in (including the Capones and the Nesses), law enforcement became rife with corruption, payoffs, and violence.

Now, fast forward to 1919, when Prohibition took hold in a country that already scoffed at the law (especially in the big cities), featuring a corrupt and low-skilled police force, and a thriving organized crime community. Can you guess what happened next? Of course, you can. Where that corruption was the worst—the biggest cities and especially Chicago, the mob (quite literally) took over.

Vollmer's rigorous reforms were just what the country needed, and they deeply influenced Ness. Vollmer insisted police officers have both street smarts and book smarts—a college degree and experience walking a beat. Although he taught that certain races and cultures contributed to crime, he encouraged hiring African American and female police officers. He instituted bicycle, motorcycle, and automobile patrols (in addition to walking the streets) to allow police to respond more quickly. He encouraged centralized information sharing in the department as well as the use and application of new technologies—fingerprinting, ballistics, forensic accounting, and crime maps—to focus police attention on key areas.[5]

Ness ate it all up. This was precisely the type of career that suited his mix of diligence, toughness, and raw intelligence. He would use all these techniques in the most famous cops and robbers game ever played.

However, it wouldn't be until a confluence of events at the end of 1929—some you know, some you may not—that would catapult Ness into Capone's world.

. . .

On February 14, 1929, seven members of the so-called "North Side Gang"—a rival of Capone's interests in Chicago—were brutally gunned down inside a garage in Lincoln Park. Almost immediately, the press christened it the Saint Valentine's Day Massacre. And even quicker than that, everyone "knew" who had given the order.

Max Allan Collins and A. Brad Schwartz use this scene to open their book and paint a bloody picture of the era: *Scarface and the Untouchable: Al Capone, Eliot Ness, and the Battle for Chicago*. Unlike other, more general histories of the gangster era, Collins and Schwartz focus on the interplay between these two larger-than-life figures. It reads more like a novel, which makes sense given the collaboration between Collins (a historical novelist) and Schwartz (a historian.)

---

5. You may be surprised by Vollmer's views on Prohibition and other "vice" crimes. He is quoted as saying: "Like prostitution, and like liquor, drug use was not a police problem; it never has been and never can be solved by policemen." His views are surprisingly modern, but the moralistic Progressive movement of the day would hear nothing of it.

This event, more than any other, shocked the nation into action. Chicago was out of control...well, to be fair, it was *in control*...just in the hands of the wrong people.

Citizens were scared. One gangster shot was shocking and maybe even a bit scandalously intriguing. Seven people executed in a neighborhood garage was an escalation. It was the difference between seeing a shark from the safety of a boat or seeing a shark while swimming in the ocean. Two different things. When would innocent people start getting hurt? (Chicago, sadly, would not need to wait long.) The Chicago business community had trouble convincing associates to travel to the city; no one wanted to take the train ride home in a coffin.

Moreover, the city was hosting the World's Fair in just a few years. Would anyone come? The outrage reached all the way to Washington. Newly-elected president Herbert Hoover was disgusted with the situation and started to ask his advisors to come up with solutions.[6]

At the heart of the matter with any law enforcement solution was the utter corruption of not just the Chicago Police Department but also (and more importantly) the "agents" of the Bureau of Prohibition. The use of scare quotes is apt. Of the 1,500 (or so) agents, only a handful—maybe ten—were "incorruptible." Eliot Ness was one of those people. It would take him months to hand-pick the very few people (and by the way, not the *best* people, just the ones who weren't obviously in the mob's pocket) who would accept a nearly impossible mission: Take down Al Capone and the bootlegging business that gave the mob its power.

Just ten men.

Against the mob.

In Chicago.

[Expletive deleted.]

Here's how they did it.

. . .

---

6. The situation for Hoover would become politically dire after the stock market crash in October 1929, and especially after the economy didn't quickly recover. Hoover needed a win. He needed to show that he could clean up Chicago and put the criminals who were terrorizing the streets and, more to the point, not paying their taxes, behind bars.

Collins and Schwartz chart the progress of the investigation and tactics in month-by-month detail. It reads more like a thriller and less like a historical artifact (although it is both). For our purposes, we can dispense with most of the tit-for-tat detail and focus instead on the change in perspective of who was a "hero" in the minds of the American public—the lawbreakers or the law enforcers.

Contrary to the popular image of the dapper crime busters on daring stakeouts, much of the work in modern law enforcement—and certainly against the mob in the 1930s—obeys a simple rule: *Follow the money.*

Most people remember that Al Capone eventually went to prison for *tax evasion*, not bootlegging or murder. That's true, but incomplete. Eliot Ness went after Capone's bootlegging racket. George E.Q. Johnson, the United States Attorney for Chicago, devised the strategy to go after Capone for tax evasion. The two-pronged strategy was like a military pincer movement to catch Capone in the middle.

Let's start with Ness and bootlegging.

As you might guess from the success of modern liquor companies and bars, alcohol production, bottling, and distribution are *very* profitable. But how much so? In the 1920s, a barrel of beer (equivalent to 288 pints, give or take) sold for about $55. That's about $1,100 in today's money. It only cost the mob about *$3* to make.

You read that correctly.

Calculating the profit is pretty easy math, isn't it?

However, the $52 profit for each barrel didn't wind up directly in Capone's pocket. Just like any other business, the mob incurred costs. The obvious ones included brewery workers (bottlers, coopers, etc.) and drivers, trucks, equipment, and maintenance. It's pretty dull stuff. The obvious ones *missing* are marketing, branding, and advertising. For what should be obvious reasons, Capone couldn't take out an ad in the newspaper for his beer or ask people to come to his clubs using radio spots.

(Though it should be noted that many speakeasies used standard promotional techniques. They simply advertised their legitimate business—usually entertainers, musicians, and comedians.)

What Capone's organization *did* need to pay (that legitimate businesses did not) was a vast network of bribes and kickbacks—police to inform them in advance when a "raid" would occur, politicians to look the other way, judges to provide lenient sentences to people who managed to get caught, journalists to write positive stories, and the list goes on. Those were significant investments, and again, for obvious reasons, there aren't great bookkeeping records on the full profit and loss statements. But needless to say, bootlegging was still spectacularly profitable.

(But there were *some* records...we'll explain why that was important soon enough.)

That $52 profit on each barrel of beer, along with other profitable bootlegging and illicit activities, explained how Capone could afford to live such a legendarily lavish lifestyle while also being so generous with anyone he encountered.

Ness targeted that fantastic profit margin.

Let's say that after *all* expenses (legitimate and not), Capone earned $20 on each barrel of beer. Ness had a couple of strategies he could use to impact that profit margin. He could put pressure on corrupt police and politicians. That would have the effect of *increasing* the amount Capone's organization would need to pay to keep them pliant. He could also raid speakeasies, unmasking the everyday citizens (wittingly and unwittingly) supporting the mob. However, both were risky strategies. Exposed and humiliated people could just as easily turn *on Ness*, making it more difficult for his group to operate.

The other strategy—and the one he used—was to target the operation's soft underbelly: the production and distribution networks. Part of the reason came down to return on investment. Ness would need to track down and expose literally *hundreds* of corrupt officials and *dozens* of speakeasies all across the greater Chicago area. Remember, he had ten people. However, also remember that Capone (by necessity) adopted mass production techniques to produce beer so cheaply. That meant his production facilities would need to be *large*—industrial-sized. Large brewing facilities were difficult to hide, especially once Ness and his team knew what to look for.[7] If Ness's team could find and shut them down, he could make a significant impact with each raid.

Taking advantage of new technology—wiretaps, specifically—Ness and his team (through diligent deciphering and careful listening) would discover where trucks were going and, more importantly, where they were coming from.

As Ness and his team succeeded, Capone's "expenses" increased to compensate for stopped (and confiscated) trucks and, even worse, inoperable production facilities. Throughout the early 1930s, Ness not only cost Capone money in aggregate, but they would also create supply chain disruption at the local level. It became difficult for the mob to fill orders for specific areas when a bust had just gone down. Once customers learned they couldn't get a beer, they might not return to that club, forcing the owners to boost entertainment expenses to avoid losing customers.

Speaking of public reaction, Ness didn't just go after Capone's bottom line—he would also go after his *brand*. That brand allowed the mob to (cheaply) buy off police and politicians. Taking the shine off Capone's halo would also increase *bribery* expenses without targeting the recipients themselves. In short, if Capone were less popular, corrupt officials would demand higher payoffs.

Ness certainly understood Capone had publicity on his side—he was utterly quotable, courted the media, and came off as a modern-day Robin Hood. Although the Great Depression would start to eat away at that "greed is good" image, Capone knew how to read the room. As the economic conditions worsened, he set up soup kitchens in Chicago that ended up feeding a lot of hungry people. And he wasn't humble about it. He would take every advantage of boosting his name in the papers.

To counter Capone's popularity, Ness got help.

The first strategy we've already hinted at. Ness didn't name his group the "Untouchables," but he understood the power of a good brand when he heard

---

7. And often, *smell for*. You might be able to hide a brewery in a large building, but it's much harder to hide its yeasty smell.

one.[8] Recognizing Capone's success with journalists, Ness would also cultivate those relationships. He wasn't as "quotable" as Capone, but he didn't need to be. Even more than a quote, journalists wanted a *scoop*. Ness would sometimes give journalists early (but not too early) notice of raids so that they could show up and get the best stories and photos.

The second attack on Capone's public image was even more on-the-nose. The team rebranded Capone and the mob "Public Enemies"—with Al Capone at the top as "Public Enemy #1." Even filmmakers and cartoonists (like Dick Tracy) turned against him, creating fictional accounts that allowed the public to see beneath the big smiles and flashy dress and witness the brutality and murder beneath.[9]

Why did it work so well? Ness and the team could also read the room. The country's mood had shifted *dramatically* from the 1920s to the 1930s. The Great Depression changed what was considered "good" and "acceptable" behavior. Flamboyant was out. Frugality was in. Selfishness was out. Selflessness was in.

When you're skimping on meals…and you learn Capone gave away $14,000 diamond belt buckles as party favors from his Miami mansion…well, it's not difficult to turn public opinion. Capone never fully changed strategies. He made the classic innovator's error—what made you successful *then* might not be what makes you successful *now*. He never quite knew what to do with Ness.

Ness was as coordinated, intelligent, and ruthless in taking apart the bootlegging operation as Capone was in building it. But if he didn't know what to do with Ness, he was utterly flummoxed by George E.Q. Johnson.

Where Ness did the boots-on-the-ground work, the United States Attorney for Chicago pursued a different and utterly novel strategy. Here's where the handful of ledgers Ness found during raids would come in handy.

---

8. Charles Schwarz of the *Chicago Daily News* was the first journalist to coin the name in print. It would become the team's unofficial nickname from then on.

9. The filmmakers' unofficial self-censorship rules (the so-called Hays Code) stipulated that. Under no circumstances were criminals to be glorified or celebrated. Bad guys would always "get theirs" in the end. It was a major shift from the 1920s to the 1930s in film. When you watch movies from both eras, the difference is profound.

In 1913, the United States instituted the first (permanent) Federal tax on income as part of the 16th Amendment to the U.S. Constitution.[10] Originally, the law was interpreted to mean that the Federal government could levy taxes on all *legitimate* income. However, in 1921, Congress clarified that *illegal* income was taxable, too, and the Supreme Court affirmed that interpretation in 1927.[11]

It wasn't enough that you didn't pay Federal income taxes. Attorneys could (and do, to this day) argue that ambiguity in the law means their client wasn't aware that a particular income stream was subject to income tax. Once clarified, the taxpayer pays the back tax and a fine, and that's the end of it. To qualify as a criminal felony, the taxpayer must also *know* they are supposed to pay taxes *and* fail to do so. In other words, Johnson needed to prove Capone not only failed to pay his taxes but also that he *intended* to fail to pay his taxes.

As any attorney will tell you, proving intent is *very* difficult. So, even with a few captured transaction ledgers, why did the Feds charge Capone with tax evasion (Johnson's strategy) versus bootlegging (Ness's strategy)?

Penalties.

Bootlegging carried a two to three-year sentence and a modest fine. Even if they could tie Capone to multiple bootlegging crimes (and it was by no means obvious they could), he'd be out of prison by 1934. Capone even thought that was a good outcome. He had done a short stint in prison before and could run his criminal empire from behind bars—especially for so short a time. What's more, maybe the Great Depression would be over by then.

Tax evasion, by contrast, carried much stiffer penalties—ten years or more—that the judge could stack *consecutively*. The bootlegging charges were a

---

10. There were other income taxes levied, notably during the Civil War, but they all expired as scheduled. Prior to the 16th Amendment, tariffs provided the bulk of government tax revenues.

11. You might be wondering if the need to declare illegal income in the 16th Amendment violates your 5th Amendment right not to incriminate yourself. The Supreme Court has ruled "that requiring a person to declare income on a federal income tax return does not violate an individual's right to remain silent, although the privilege may apply to allow the person to refrain from revealing the source of the income." This is what Capone attempted to do. His money came from "gambling winnings or losses" or "gifts from 'supporters'." Um...no one believed that.

sort of insurance policy. If anything went wrong with the tax evasion case, they could hold Capone on bootlegging charges.

We'll spare the court case details—Collins and Schwartz did an excellent job recounting them—but suffice it to say Capone was found guilty before he walked into court.

The judge didn't like Capone (and he made it clear). The jury didn't like Capone (and was intent on putting him away no matter what). And Capone's (otherwise outstanding) attorneys performed so poorly (as in, not questioning the *obvious* prejudice noted above or that the statute of limitations should have expired) that it seems obvious in retrospect that they had been paid off.

That last part is important. They *were* likely paid off. That's because the rest of the mob understood what Capone did not.

The mood had shifted. The "G-men" were the new heroes. The mobsters' days in the spotlight were over...as long as they wanted to be successful. If the mob operated out of the public spotlight, they only had to worry about the police. If they operated in the public eye, they risked an angry citizenry. The police, they could handle. Public opinion, they could not.

The mob, almost certainly, hung their most famous member out to dry.

. . .

Isn't it funny, don't you think, that in all this conversation about Al Capone and Eliot Ness, we've only talked about how crime is *perceived* and not what crime actually is?

Prohibition was the law—a constitutional amendment, no less...there's no higher law in the United States than that—yet millions of people patronized illicit businesses to drink alcohol. (Or became small-time bootleggers themselves.) The mob violated the law, but Capone was considered a "dashing rogue" by most average people. Flawed, yes, but so long as he kept the violence between bad people, it was like watching a gangster *movie*.

In his book, *The Roots of Violent Crime in America*, criminologist Barry Latzer challenges the "reality" of crime and highlights the importance of public perception in law enforcement:

Now, you are probably thinking that Prohibition and the booze gang wars were responsible for the high murder rates in the 1920s. Actually, Prohibition had a mixed impact. On the one hand, it spurred shooting wars between organized crime gangs, which increased murder rates in the biggest cities. On the other hand, Prohibition made beer and other alcoholic beverages very expensive, resulting in less public drunkenness and fewer incidents of associated crimes. It also closed down the saloons, which were centers for young male violence.

Prohibition may have actually *reduced* the crimes that concerned most average citizens. As he points out from data going back more than 100 years, there is "no consistent relationship between general economic conditions and violent crime." In fact, "rises and falls in violent crime are less affected by general economic conditions than by demographics (the size of the young male population), weakness in the criminal justice system, the migration or immigration of groups with historically high rates of violence, violent youth gangs, and the widespread availability of firearms."[12]

In other words, actual crime doesn't mean as much to the citizens living in a society as the *perception* of those crimes. Do people feel safe? Can legitimate businesses operate? Does the government seem to have control of the situation? If those things aren't true, citizens will demand change.

Ness and Johnson intuitively understood this. Although they may not have had Latzer's data, they knew they needed to step up their game. That meant a professional, educated police force using all the tools available—the law, of course, but also technology, forensic accounting, psychology, and a dose of street smarts and toughness.

Add to that the fact that public perception is fickle and temperamental. Take what happened in the aftermath of Capone's conviction.

---

12. Latzer's book *will challenge* your conventional wisdom of crime and its root causes. Some findings are decidedly politically incorrect. One finding that's consistent however: Crime rates tend to be the highest when the proportion of young men is higher than it should be demographically. Sorry, guys.

Al Capone was remanded to custody just before Thanksgiving 1931 after being found guilty and sentenced to 11 years in Federal prison. Finally in prison for the long haul, Capone's promiscuous lifestyle caught up with him. In the days before penicillin, syphilis was an incurable venereal disease that would eventually cause mental decline and mood swings.[13] For Capone, already the manic/depressive type, the disease would cause a marked decline over the coming years. He died in 1947 at age 48.

Did Ness fare...better? Not personally. After a surge of publicity, Ness and his Untouchables unit largely faded from the limelight after Prohibition was repealed in 1933. He continued in law enforcement in the Midwest—chasing down the mob—but succumbed to alcoholism and suffered through two failed marriages. He died of a heart attack, largely forgotten, in 1957 at age 54.

Luckily for his legacy, Ness had just finished his autobiography, *The Untouchables*.[14] The book sold 1.5 million copies and (more importantly) spawned the famous television show of the same name, starring Robert Stack as Eliot Ness in 1959. Without that show, there's a good chance we'd only remember Capone.

For its part, the mob went through a sort of Darwinian evolution. Those who wanted publicity in the mold of Capone were imprisoned—victims of their own "success." The remaining mobsters were smarter—*much smarter*. They (largely) kept the violence in check and hired their forensic accountants and lawyers to obscure their business interests. Even more brilliantly, they *allowed* the public to believe that Capone was the "head" of a top-down hierarchy when the mob never operated that way. Organized crime is structured more like a disconnected web of loose alliances and marriages of convenience. That loose arrangement makes it much more resilient and difficult to combat. However, the public feels satisfied when a "big bust" or "big arrest" happens. Often, the mob stages these events. They've learned how to manipulate public psychology, too.

As we've seen, the media—newspapers, magazines, radio, television, and movies—worked hard to craft the image the mob exploits. It was a "good guy/bad

---

13. Sulfa drugs (the first effective antibiotic) *could have* been used to treat Capone, but they weren't widely recognized until the late 1930s. By that time, the damage was done.

14. Originally, the book was criticized for being inaccurate, but later research has vindicated Ness.

guy" dynamic that (from what we've just read) isn't quite accurate. Who was the "bad guy" in Chicago? Capone, sure. But what about the politicians who accepted bribes? The citizens who patronized businesses they *knew* contributed to crime? It's not so simple. That said, the simplistic cops and robbers media portrayals (that would last for decades—until the 1970s) gave the public what it psychologically needed—what Collins and Schwartz call "poetic justice" when the actual justice was less than satisfying. Seeing a brutal mobster gunned down on screen seemed more "fair" than seeing him sent to prison on a tax technicality.

Law enforcement changed, too, though it never wholly shed its unprofessional image before the 1930s. It's a tough job—there's no doubt about that—and law enforcement continues to struggle to balance professionalism, technology, and accounting with the toughness and street smarts needed to combat criminals.

But in the end, we see a new type of hero emerging in the Great Depression—a person who puts the needs of others and their community ahead of their own. People didn't want a martyr. They wanted someone to look up to. A role model. Someone not influenced by the temptations around them. Someone…untouchable.

THIS LOOKS LIKE A JOB FOR...

Bill Dunn was down on his luck.

Like many in the Great Depression, our story opens with Dunn waiting in an endless breadline—psychologically defeated, desperate, and downcast. But today, fate would grant him a reprieve. By random chance, Professor Ernest Smalley made him an offer he couldn't refuse. Dunn needed a good meal and a new suit. Smalley needed a human subject to try a new drug.[1] It was that simple.

It all sounded too good to be true.

It was.

Though it didn't seem like that at first.

The concoction Smalley asked Dunn to swallow worked. It *really* worked. It gave this down-on-his-luck vagrant telepathic superpowers. Aware he could now read the private thoughts of those around him, our protagonist does (sadly) what you might expect him to do. Dunn almost immediately uses his newfound powers

---

[1]. The early 1930s were the days before the modern U.S. Food and Drug Administration, so this request wouldn't have seemed so far-fetched. It was still dumb to accept, just not uncommon.

to pick winning stocks and make himself ruler over other, lesser people. It was indeed a case of power corrupts.[2]

Speaking of corrupting influence, Smalley wasn't using Dunn as a human guinea pig out of the kindness of his heart. He was *testing* the formula on a "nobody" before taking it himself. You'll remember, however, that Dunn now possessed telepathic powers—the ability to read minds. Frankly, that's a pretty stupid superpower to give someone you're looking to double-cross. Enraged by this cowardice and not wanting to share this newfound gift with anyone else, Dunn kills Smalley.

Unfortunately, the elixir's effects proved only temporary. Even more unfortunately, Dunn's newfound superpowers didn't also include a genius intellect. He killed Smalley *before* he could torture the formula out of him. (If you're looking for a hero or a villain in this story, you'll only find two bad guys.)

As Dunn slowly loses his newfound genius and powers, he attempts to recreate the formula without success. By the end of the story (and it should be clear that it's a fictional story by now), we find Dunn returning to precisely where we found him—defeated again, waiting in the same bread line.

The reader is left to wonder if it was better to have had—*and lost*—great power or never to have had it at all. Dunn and Smalley helped teach a universal lesson in a modern context. It's a simple story (about a dozen pages) that is entirely in keeping with the tragic zeitgeist of the Great Depression. New scientific advancements may have promised a better tomorrow, but today's reality was brutal and grinding.

Appearing in the self-published collection of stories, Dunn's angry, balding head jumps off the title page of the first edition of *Science Fiction: The Advance Guard of Future Civilization*. This was one of many early attempts at a new art form—the graphic novel, more commonly known as comic books. It was hand-drawn, typed instead of lettered, black-and-white, and...a complete flop. But despite its flaws, there was something more hidden under the surface.

---

2. It was 19th century British historian John Emerich Edward Dalberg-Acton (better known as simply, Lord Acton) who coined the phrase "Power corrupts, and absolute power corrupts absolutely." He certainly has plenty of examples of corruption all around him in Imperial Britain of the 1800s.

Bill Dunn might not instantly remind us of Clark Kent. Wasn't the bald guy supposed to be the bad guy? Speaking of hairless villains, Ernest Smalley probably doesn't remind you of Lex Luthor, does he? Worse, there was no good guy. No cape. No "S" on the chest. No outerpants. But this 1933 short story, "The Reign of the Super Man," was the first tentative exploration of the idea of the modern superhero from two of the most famous people in comic book history: writer Jerry Siegel and illustrator Joe Shuster.[3] They were teenagers then (only 18 years old) and just beginning to create a partnership that would birth the hero of all American heroes.

...

All fictional characters share something with their creators, and this creation is no exception. We can't understand the Man of Steel without understanding the two creators who were anything but "men" (yet) and certainly didn't have bodies of "steel." Despite that, see if you can start picking up some of the details that would make it into the mythology of Superman that you might recognize.

Neither Siegel nor Shuster had a lot going for them. Both were awkward, skinny kids from the Jewish ghettos of Cleveland, Ohio. Siegel's family emigrated from Lithuania; Shuster's from Toronto, Canada. Antisemitism was rampant in American public life in those days, and the pair faced their share of bullying and hatred. To be fair, they weren't alone. Millions of Jewish, Italian, Irish, and Eastern European immigrants faced tension to assimilate into the "American Way" while at the same time retaining distinctive subcultures. Many would have a dual—or "secret" identity—one face in public and another in private.

Not surprisingly, both scrawny kids admired the bodybuilders and health culture that grew up in the Roaring 20s. One of the most famous was Bernarr (yes, *Bernarr*) Macfadden, snarkily nicknamed "Body Love Macfadden" by *Time* magazine. Along with his fit family, he posed nearly nude in his many publications, causing all sorts of consternation among the moralist authorities of the day.[4] But to Siegel and Shuster, those men and women represented everything

---

3. The first comic would split the words "Super" and "Man." Because the title spanned two comic book pages, Shuster included a dash between the words. Sometimes, the title is referenced with this dash. It would disappear in subsequent versions.

they *could be*—strong and confident enough to stand with their hands on their hips and thrust out their chest. Does that pose and physique sound familiar?

Being bullied, awkward immigrant kids wasn't all that brought Siegel and Shuster together in grade school. Both of them lost their fathers, and Siegel's died tragically. His father, born Mikhel Iankel Segalovich, suffered a fatal heart attack in 1932 during a robbery at his clothing store.[5] His son Jerry was 17 years old. The idea of being able to come to the rescue and defeat the bad guys was never far from either of their minds. (Remember that last part. It'll show up again.)

Speaking of Siegel, he was the pair's leader, but that's not saying much. If you're thinking of a charismatic storyteller in the mold of a young Ernest Hemingway, lower your expectations. However, compared to Shuster, Siegel was a regular Don Juan. He was, however, bold enough to ditch Shuster after the 'Reign' comic, reasoning that the teenage pair weren't getting much attention from publishers because of Shuster's illustrations (and not Siegel's writing). Okay, perhaps "bold" is the wrong word. *Egotistical* might be a better choice, but both were still children. Who hasn't made bad decisions at that age?

The new partnership (with a more seasoned illustrator) would also fail to generate much interest. It seems Siegel again wouldn't accept that it might be something about the writing that wasn't quite right. Still, he was smart enough to realize that Shuster's straightforward drawings and his direct storylines probably were the right pairing...they simply hadn't found the right story. The two reconciled.

The pair penned and inked dozens of short stories, but none captured that special *something* that would capture attention. During all those hours of failed attempts, Superman—the *idea* of Superman—was never far from their minds. They simply needed to keep at it.

It's a good thing they did. The market was ready for something just like what they were working on. Little did they know that forces were beginning to align to bring their superhero to life.

. . .

---

5. Many immigrants in that era Americanized their names, including my own great-grandparents. Our family name was Alivojvdec, a Croatian surname roughly meaning "Son of Duke." If yours arrived in the United States around that time, they probably did too. You should check.

It might seem strange today, but there were plenty of super men before Superman. Journalists and writers often referred to politicians, military figures, or business leaders using that superlative.[6] In other words, Siegel and Shuster's use of the word "Super Man" didn't carry the singular image we have today of a costumed guy in tights and a cape. There was no trademark protection around the word or phrase—that would come later in response to the success of the Superman comic.

The idea of heroes (obviously) wasn't new either. Siegel and Shuster would derive inspiration from the Greek sources—Heracles, Zeus, Ares, and their Roman counterparts—but also from their native Jewish mythology. That makes sense. Both were Jewish, growing up with stories about David (who slayed the giant Goliath) and Samson (the tough guy with the magic hair).[7]

More modern precursors to what would become Superman included John Carter of Mars (created in 1911 and made into a terrible movie in 2012), Buck Rogers, Flash Gordon, Hugo Danner, and Doctor Savage. All featured a mix of sci-fi and whimsy in their writing, but the common thread was the combination of physical strength and intellectual cleverness to propel their adventures and outsmart the bad guys.

Despite those elements, all the characters and stories that would inspire Siegel and Shuster were *simple*. There was no ambiguity on who the good or bad guys were or what was right and wrong. The protagonist's solution to the challenge at hand could be clever, but the outcome was never in doubt. It's the reason the first Super Man story (separating the words here just as they did in their first story) never caught on. It was more of a *tragedy* than a *hero's journey*, and heroes are what America needed in the Great Depression.

However, that doesn't quite explain how Superman has remained an icon well into the 21st century while Hugo Danner and Doctor Savage faded from

---

6. There wasn't an equivalent term for super women in the Great Depression. Those who rose to prominence in that era were aligned to the struggle for equal rights in the wake of the still-fresh 19th Amendment granting women the right to vote. Female superheroes wouldn't be far behind, however. We see the first ones, like Fantomah and Miss Fury, in the early 1940s.

7. Samson's story comes from the Book of Judges, Chapters 13-16. David's fingerprints are all over the Jewish and Christian Bibles, including most notably, the Book of Psalms.

memory. They had their day, but once the space race got going in the 1950s and 1960s, and *real* people started doing what their heroes did in the comics, the appeal of Buck Rogers and Flash Gordon dwindled, replaced by Neil Armstrong and Buzz Aldrin. Siegel and Shuster's creation, however, would endure. There was something different about Superman, but it would be hard to guess that he would rise to the top of this crowded field.

It would take some additional colorful characters to see that potential—an Army major made famous chasing bandits across the Mexican border and two publishers better known until then for peddling smut.

. . .

Malcolm Wheeler-Nicholson (aka "the Major") is a well-known figure in comic book lore. His idea was to buy the rights to repackage newspaper comic strips into a cheaply printed magazine, usually selling for a nickel or a dime. (That's where we get the term "pulp" fiction, by the way. Pulp refers to the grayish paper used for these early publications.) In 1935, however, he would take that idea a step further, including all fresh material instead of simply reprints of what people could read in the newspapers already. Wheeler-Nicholson's first such effort was the 10x15-inch pulp magazine titled *New Fun*. He still printed it on cheap paper, but it featured all-new material, full-color pages, and engaging stories written for the youth audience. Priced at just a dime, most kids could afford to pick up a copy on their way home from school.

However, Wheeler-Nicholson faced a dilemma. There was a reason kids bought reprinted comic strips. *They were good*. Newspaper publishers worked hard to select the best strips and build an audience through daily repetition. Additionally, the collections appealed to anyone who missed a day or two somewhere along the way. Although buying republishing rights cut into his profit margin, he knew store owners and newsstands would stock his product.

There was no such guarantee with new material, and he still needed to pay artists—specifically, artists who would work on the cheap and, even more specifically, a team just like Siegel and Shuster. Wheeler-Nicholson couldn't afford to be choosy. He'd take whatever they could produce, and the variety of comics they sent (none of which, yet, were Superman—they guarded that idea for now) gave the pair the first *inconsistent* income they'd ever had. We say "inconsistent" because managing the financial end of the business was *not* one of the Major's strong suits.

To be fair, it wasn't an easy business to run. Yes, *New Fun* and its subsequent publications featured all-new material, but newsstands hesitated to fill valuable shelf space with work from unknown artists. The newsstands were businesses, too. Sometimes, Siegel and Shuster cashed checks. Sometimes, the checks bounced. Often, they never came at all. Still, the paltry income allowed the pair to continue working on their big idea in the background.

The pair wouldn't need to wait long. Unpaid debts with his printing company forced a change at Wheeler-Nicholson's National Periodical Publications. To save his company from bankruptcy, he would take on two new partners, distributor Harry Donenfeld and accountant Jack Liebowitz, who were unique characters in their own right.

Like Siegel and Shuster, Donenfeld and Liebowitz were Jewish immigrants, making a living in the rough-and-tumble world of New York publishing in the Roaring 20s. In those years, "naughty" publications could make bank. Okay, let's dispense with the euphemisms; they were soft-core pornography. However, by the 1930s and the onset of the Great Depression, the moral tenor of the country had changed.[8] Donenfeld and Liebowitz saw the writing on the wall and started looking for a genre change. Wheeler-Nicholson had the perfect answer: the youth audience. It was safe from moral authorities and much more profitable. The trio formed Detective Comics in 1937 (yes, *that* DC), and it wasn't long before Donenfeld and Liebowitz forced the Major out of the business.[9] In the meantime, as you'll recall, Siegel and Shuster continued to refine their Superman concept. In fact, they had assembled (and were pitching to other publishers) a

---

8. Fiorello La Guardia (yeah, *that* La Guardia) used his mayoral bully pulpit to morally clean up New York City in the mod-1930s. (One struggles to imagine a more thankless and fruitless task.) This isn't a book about political figures and their moral crusades—they often serve as more of a motivation for innovators, as in this case. However, if you'd like to know more, try *I Never Did Like Politics: How Fiorello La Guardia Became America's Mayor, and Why He Still Matters*, by Terry Golway.

9. Until the day he died, Wheeler-Nicholson would claim (with some justification) that he discovered Superman. He would often wear a T-shirt emblazoned with the Superman "S" so that he could dramatically rip open his shirt at the appropriate moment. Yeah, he was a weird guy.

series of newspaper strips. Pulp publications may have paid the bills, but getting into the *newspapers* meant true success.

However, when Liebowitz saw the strips, he was impressed. The new bosses at DC reasoned that Superman could be the foundation on which they built a new publishing business. Liebowitz offered Siegel and Shuster a deal to reformat their strips into 13 pages for the inaugural edition of *Action Comics*, set to publish in April 1938. They would be paid $10 per page, or $130, for their work. (That works out to just shy of $3,000 in today's money.) In addition, as was standard practice for publication, the two would also sell the copyrights to their creation. That meant DC could do anything they wanted with the Superman character, even hiring new artists and writers. But for two unknowns in a genre trying to make a name for themselves, the offer was perfectly reasonable. They weren't exactly swimming in options, and money was always tight.

In later years, this transaction would be christened the "original sin" of the comic book industry. The practice of selling copyrights along with a publishing contract would strain the relationship between creators and publishers for decades. We'll come back to that later, but in 1938, there were no guarantees that *Action Comics* would succeed. The Superman idea sounded good, but plenty of ideas sound good. That doesn't mean they'll be commercial successes. No matter. After years of waiting, Siegel and Shuster finally introduced Superman to the world.

. . .

It's tempting to describe Superman sales as *"up, up…and away!"* because that's precisely what happened. Ironically, however, Superman could "leap tall buildings in a single bound," but he couldn't (yet) fly. Still, the comparison is apt. Sales data weren't as easy to track in those days. (There was nothing like the "real-time" transaction data from online platforms today.) The best they could do was watch newsstand owners' *return rates* of unsold issues. Anything that sold over 50 percent of its print run was considered a success. The first issue with Superman sold over *65 percent* of its copies. Subsequent issues would sell 80 percent, 90 percent, and—an unheard of accomplishment for the new medium of "comic books"—sell out.[10]

Let's find out why.

Before we begin, it's important to understand that Siegel and Shuster had the basic concept for Superman in place for the very first issue, but plenty of details would evolve quickly over the first months of published Superman stories. If you read *Action Comics #1* (which you should if you enjoy the Superman mythology), you'll notice some differences in what follows. What we're interested in here are the reasons readers in the Great Depression (and beyond) identify so strongly with Superman, not the precise evolution of his origin story.[11] For more of that story, read or listen to Larry Type's 2012 love letter to the character *Superman: The High-Flying History of America's Most Enduring Hero*. We'll stick with the big ideas here.

As an infant, Kal-El was loaded into a spaceship by his parents to escape their doomed planet. That meant the "last son of Krypton" would be an immigrant in his new home on Earth. That detail is essential. Because he was from a fantasy planet, Superman could be *any* immigrant—or even better, represent all immigrants. Yet, because he landed in the United States, he was an *American*. It made him instantly relatable to vast chunks of the country's youth. In the 1930s, most young people were either first or second-generation Americans. Superman was one of *them*.

Because of the differences between the two planets, Kal-El would be stronger, faster, smarter— basically better at everything—than the humans in his adopted home.[12] It doesn't take much of a leap of the imagination to see that going horribly wrong. (As it turns out, Germany's soon-to-be Führer was actively misinterpreting Nietzsche's *Übermensch*, literally translated as "superman," at

---

10. Donenfeld and Liebowitz even ran a test to ensure it was Superman (and not one of the other comics in the first issue of *Action Comics*) that was the big draw. The results were *super* conclusive.

11. Comic book aficionados, please don't send me nasty emails.

12. Siegel and Shuster felt they needed to explain Superman's amazing strength. They used a natural analog—insects—for example, an ant can carry many times its own weight. The rationalization would evolve, but this was the first one.

precisely that moment. It would *not* end well.) Siegel and Shuster's Superman would need to be different. Kal-El's father was the first to discover Krypton's fate and attempted to warn his planet's scientists, but his *mother* instilled in him the ethical code that would guide her son's behavior on his adopted planet. Those two aspects of power—the head and the heart—were both critical to the moral concept of using power for the right reasons that made Superman a *super* man.

Speaking of the right reasons, Superman was there to help those who needed him from the very beginning. In one particularly poignant scene, Superman rescues a father who is being robbed in his store. It must have seemed like just another heroic act to the boys (and girls, and men, and women) who read that first issue. But to Jerry Siegel, it was who he hoped he could have been for his dad. (It makes you sad to think about it, doesn't it?)

But Superman wouldn't just rely on his brute strength. He would stop abusive husbands, showing them the error of their ways through reason and argument. As an immigrant himself, Superman fought against racism and prejudice of all kinds. In one story, he would use his super intellect to expose the slimy underbelly of the Klu Klux Klan.[13] In both cases, Superman—a fictional character—was able to change the nature of the conversation in the real world, exposing and correcting hidden wrongs. However, to the children of America, abusive homes and rampant racism were very much *not* hidden. Superman was a hero brave enough to take on more than just robbers and evil scientists.

Finally, we need to talk about the elephant in the room: Superman's secret identity and its implications for his personal life. Superman *was* Kal-El. He wouldn't hide from anyone and would never wear a mask. Heck, he wore bright red and blue tights, a flowing red cape, a big "S" across his chest, and briefs outside his pants. Who could miss him?

Unlike other superheroes that would follow (most notably Batman), Superman put on a *disguise* to blend into everyday society. His "Clark Kent" persona was the deception. Filmmaker Quentin Tarantino puts his fascination with this

---

13. The best known version of this storyline was the 1946 radio program titled "Clan of the Fiery Cross." According to its reviewers, "Superman exposed Ku Klux Klan codewords, rituals, and its bigotry—all based on intel collected by activist Stetson Kennedy—before a national audience. The show damaged the group's reputation and led to a steep decline in membership from which the KKK never recovered."

aspect of the Superman character into the mouth of one of his film's characters in this telling monologue:[14]

> Now, a staple of the superhero mythology is, there's the superhero and there's the alter ego. Batman is actually Bruce Wayne, Spider-Man is actually Peter Parker. When that character wakes up in the morning, he's Peter Parker. He has to put on a costume to become Spider-Man. And it is in that characteristic Superman stands alone. Superman didn't become Superman. Superman was born Superman. When Superman wakes up in the morning, he's Superman. His alter ego is Clark Kent. His outfit with the big red "S", that's the blanket he was wrapped in as a baby when the Kents found him. Those are his clothes. What Kent wears—the glasses, the business suit—that's the costume. That's the costume Superman wears to blend in with us. Clark Kent is how Superman views us. And what are the characteristics of Clark Kent? He's weak, he's unsure of himself, he's a coward. Clark Kent is Superman's critique on the whole human race.

That criticism…isn't exactly fair or accurate. Kent's uncertainty and cowardice are more of a performance and less of a critique. It's meant to deflect any suspicion that he is, in fact, Superman and allow him to live a normal life.

As Kent, Superman could hide in private life as a humble reporter. In those days, journalism was more a *trade* than a profession—more mechanic than academic. He wore dorky glasses, dressed in frumpy suits, and had trouble relating to the love of his life. Uncovering the truth and seeking justice was just as much a part of being a journalist as it was for Superman. In short, working professionals also saw themselves.

Speaking of Lois Lane, she was smitten with Superman but thought her colleague Clark Kent was a heel. It was the same duality that many boys faced—they saw themselves one way in their minds, but the rest of the world (primarily young

---

14. This comes from *Kill Bill: Volume 2*, released in 2004.

girls) saw them differently. Not only could people relate to Superman, but they could also relate to Clark.

Over the years, there's been criticism that Superman was just a modern-day Samson or Hercules—a cheap American copy of a biblical or classical hero. But Kal-El was so much more than that. He was the best of everything: strong, smart, caring, moral, and, despite all those assets, still humble. He was the best of what Americans saw in themselves. He was what they hoped they could be. He was precisely the hero we needed in the Great Depression.

...

Being Superman, it was probably inevitable that Siegel and Shuster's creation would break free.

We've already alluded to how that happened. Donenfeld and Liebowitz were shrewd businesspeople. They knew they had a gold mine and weren't about to be told what to do by two "kids." Of course, Superman's writer and illustrator were popular with readers, so DC paid them well. The pair made just under $64,000 in 1942, translating to over $1.2 million dollars in today's money. During the decade spanning 1937 to 1947, Siegel and Shuster would make over $4 million in today's money—all at a time when most people still struggled to make ends meet. Despite the wealth and fame, the creative pair regretted their decision. Everyone knew that Superman was worth much more than even the rich salaries they were making. What's more, Superman was *their* creation. Emotionally, the character was priceless.

The pair would alternately work with and attempt to sue DC multiple times over the years. In each case, they would either lose outright or earn modest settlements. The contract they signed in 1937 was clear. There was no clause in the contract to address what happened with a runaway hit. Remember, most new comics failed. Donenfeld and Liebowitz took the risk, compensating the creative pair more than they were legally required to for many years. All the wrangling would finally end in 1975 when Siegel learned DC was planning a movie adaption. DC finally agreed to a lifetime stipend if the pair would stop trying to sue them.

For his part, Liebowitz remained a force in the comics industry, taking advantage of another upheaval in the 1950s. The new Comics Code Authority banned publications that included scenes of a "horrific, violent, or sexual" nature. What was a rich tapestry of comic options for all ages collapsed by more than half within just a few years. Due to the youth market focus of Liebowitz and Donenfeld's DC comics, they weren't significantly impacted. During the resulting fire sale of other publishing properties, the company went on a buying spree. In a weird return to his "Spicy Detective" roots in the 1920s (that title represents precisely what you think it does), Liebowitz bought Hugh Hefner's *Playboy*.[15]

However, perhaps the most exciting story was Superman's.

Not only was Kal-El's backstory more fully developed (including his parents as well as other citizens of Krypton), but Superman also acquired a whole list of new powers—flight, heat vision, x-ray vision, icy breath, super hearing, invulnerability, as well as the fine muscle control necessary to mimic voices, a seemingly odd power to add to the mix, but hey, what's "super" if not Superman? In the 1978 movie, he could even fly fast enough to reverse time.

However, as Superman acquired powers, writers have strained to develop fresh stories. If Superman was all-powerful, what could possibly challenge him? Future writers would invent "Kryptonite" as a plot device, contact with which would rob the Man of Steel of his powers, as well as become a culture touchstone for all "critical weaknesses" in any context. Somewhat less well-known is Superman's vulnerability to "magic" in its various forms—magical characters in the DC universe have been able to manipulate Superman to various ends.

And finally, a super *hero* requires super *villains*. This is the first time we see the creation of this evil archetype, starting with the Ultra-Humanite, a character inspired by the very first scientist in the "Reign of the Super Man" in 1939, and Lex Luthor, another character inspired by the image of Dunn's terrifying bald head. None of these villains bore an obvious resemblance to the bad guys of the time, which was a smart move.[16] It was one of the first times we had a sense of a fantasy "universe" that could evolve quickly in a way that J.R.R. Tolkien's *Lord of the Rings* and *Hobbit* stories could not. Superman's villains could represent

---

15. Other notable acquisitions from Liebowitz included *Mad Magazine* and a company whose staff would eventually form Marvel.

16. Although Superman did fight "Fascists" and play a role in the war supporting the armed forces.

archetypes, not real people. In the same way Superman could be the best of us, the villain could be the worst. That simple contrast drew a clear line between right and wrong, which Superman has always represented.

Maintaining that vision—set down visually by Shuster and thematically by Siegel—hasn't been easy. Superman has appeared on the radio, in print, in several television series, multiple movies, and countless animated programs. (Some animations are the most highly regarded of all of Superman's comic adaptations.) None of that includes merchandising, which reaches into the billions of dollars and countless Halloween costumes. What kid (boy or girl) hasn't trick or treated, at least once, wearing the "S" and a cape?

Estimates of the value of the Superman brand vary (it's likely in the billions), but perhaps the most telling measure is the public outcry whenever a new incarnation of Superman is portrayed as something less than the very best. In the 2013 film directed by Zach Snyder, Superman's color scheme was muted to portray a grittier, tortured character coming to grips with a nasty world. While reviews of the film were mixed, almost no one liked the color scheme.[17] Superman is bright and bold. When he needs to get away, he retreats to a hidden fortress. When he's with us humans, Superman is a beacon of hope, not a study in grayscale.

Even the "original sin" seems to be in the process of being forgiven. Creators today are leaving the major publishers to strike out on their own. Of course, new technology platforms allow them to do that at a reasonable price, but it's still surprising how many of them do it. When publishers return to creators to negotiate a deal, it's on a more equal footing. Siegel and Shuster self-published their first stories. One thinks they would have approved of the flood of new characters coming onto the scene from around the globe.

Much has changed since the Great Depression, but Superman's message remains the same in every way that matters: Superman represents the best of us. He is what we are in our minds…or at least, what we could be if we tried hard enough. Superman is an ideal made real. It's up to us to live up to him.

---

17. To be fair, Snyder's film helped popularize the lore of the "S" the El family wears. It means "Hope" in Kryptonian. In the early days, Shuster would have agreed with Lois Lane's character in the movie. It's an "S."

18

TRUE GRIT

The Travel Air Type R "Mystery Ship" was the fastest non-military plane you could buy in 1930, and Florence Lowe "Pancho" Barnes would fly nothing less.

The story of this particular aircraft suited her personality perfectly. Its manufacturer, the Travel Air company, was frustrated that the military always had access to the fastest planes. That meant any pilot flying those aircraft would dominate air races, which were just becoming popular in the 1920s. However, instead of allowing military planes to dominate a *civilian* sport, they decided to do something about it. The company's first two prototypes (the R613K and R614K) were built in complete secrecy—hence the name, the "Mystery Ship."

Aircraft geeks will appreciate the advancements on display in this new aircraft, but even the novice would notice a significant departure from the boxy bi-wing planes of the prior generation.[1] This aircraft looked more like a World War II fighter. It featured a rounded, single-wing design and the most powerful engine

---

1. Travel Air's innovations actually forced military planners to redesign *their* airplanes. The company's founders Clyde Cessna, Walter Beech, and Lloyd Stearman remain well-known in aviation circles today. Perhaps not quite as well-known as "Henry Ford," but close.

they could fit in its fuselage without tearing it apart.[2] It looked...cool. There's simply no other way to describe it. The Type R was the very first aircraft designed from the ground up to feel the need...the need for speed![3]

The first "Maverick" to fly the Type R in competition had her eye on one pilot and one airspeed record: Amelia Earhart's 184 miles per hour.

Barnes's focus on Earhart (and her thinly veiled disdain for her competition) might seem a bit surprising to the modern reader. Today, Earhart is hailed as both an aviation hero as well as a feminist trailblazer. Her list of accomplishments and "firsts" spans multiple pages. Let's hit some of the highlights. She set the woman's altitude record at 14,000 feet in 1922. Remember, those were the days before pressurized and...well, *heated* cabins. At that altitude, the outside temperature averages negative 10 degrees Fahrenheit. (Bring a scarf.) A few years later, she'd fly even higher—over 18,000 feet. (Bring two scarves.) Earhart was the first woman to fly solo across the Atlantic Ocean in 1932. That same year, she became the first woman to fly across the United States.

Earhart also one-upped her male counterparts on several occasions. She was the first *person* to fly across the Atlantic Ocean *twice*, the first person to make the Oakland, California, to Honolulu, Hawaii, run, and the first person to fly several routes in Asia. The next logical step was only natural: A first-of-its-kind around-the-world flight. It was on a *second* attempt of that journey that Earhart and navigator Fred Noonan were lost at sea somewhere over the South Pacific.[4]

Beyond her accomplishments in the cockpit, Earhart was the confidant of First Lady Eleanor Roosevelt. She wrote three books. She formed the Ninety-Nines, an advocacy group for female pilots (so named for the 99 initial signatories, of which

---

2. Want to see one? Check out the "Texaco 13" hanging in the Museum of Science and Industry in Chicago.

3. Couldn't resist. This turn of phrase is an omage to all the GenXers who could recite this line from *Top Gun* by heart.

4. There is plenty of speculation about the flight and no shortage of books on the subject. You can read her own diary entries in *Last Flight*, published in 1937. How many of the entries were really hers and how many were embellished by her husband, publisher George Palmer Putnam, is impossible to know. Still, it's a fascinating peek into the mind of one of early aviation's most successful pioneers. The diary entries cover March to July, 1937, with the last entry on July 1, the day before her plane was lost.

Barnes was one), and served as its first president. She met Presidents Coolidge, Hoover, and Roosevelt.

She died an aviation and feminist martyr in 1937.

That wasn't what bothered Barnes.

Barnes respected accomplishments in the air, as we'll see her demonstrate repeatedly. What irritated her was the reception Earhart received on her *first* flight across the Atlantic. She was indeed the "first woman" to fly the route, but she didn't do any *actual* flying in 1928. (In Earhart's words, she was a "sack of potatoes" that pilot Wilmer Stultz needed to carry as baggage.) Still, she returned home to a ticker-tape parade in New York. The press fawned over her. She wasn't exactly beautiful in the movie star beauty of that era, but she projected a particular strength and dignity that catapulted her to celebrity and endeared her to feminists. It probably helped that she reminded people of that other famous aviator, Charles Lindbergh. She even resembled him...a bit.

Earhart got all the publicity and breathless media coverage for simply sitting in a plane. Barnes was a pilot's pilot. She certainly felt a competitive urge to best Earhart's flying achievements (all pilots of that era did), but what drove her was that Earhart was being feted for something she didn't accomplish herself. Barnes would use that motivation to fuel her attempt to break the 184-mile-per-hour barrier.

So, in 1930, Barnes climbed into the fastest plane she could buy. The Type R cost over $13,000, enough to buy *four* average homes, or nearly $250,000 today.

On that flight, Barnes didn't just beat the record. She smashed it.[5] When Barnes landed after setting a new record of 196.19 miles per hour, a reporter asked her how it felt. Her response says more about the person we're going to get to know than probably anything else:

> I feel like a sex addict in a whore house with a pocket full of $100 bills!

---

5. This was a significant accomplishment, but not necessarily surprising. Other men and women had set speed records with this plane.

Buckle up. This is going to be a wild ride.

...

Let's step back and understand the woman born "Florence" who would become "Pancho."

Florence Leontine Lowe was born into a wealthy society family in Pasadena, California, in 1901. Although she attended all of the best schools and dressed up for all the swankiest soirees of turn-of-the-century Southern California, her father recognized—almost immediately—that his little girl would not be like all the others. She was what we used to call (and sometimes still do call) a "Tom Boy." Little Florence loved the outdoors and animals more than she liked dresses and parties, so her father encouraged her love of both. During her youth, she became an outstanding equestrian. (Remember that part; it will become important later.) Her supportive father also took her to an air show in 1911—one of the first of its kind—and the young girl knew that flying would be part of her life; she just didn't realize how (or how much) it would matter.

But all those dreams would need to wait. Pasadena had expectations for a society girl coming of age in the early 1920s.

Florence married because that's what her *mother* wanted for her. It was part of what it meant to live in respectable society. Her first husband (that qualifier should give you a clue as to what was to come) was a minister—a handsome man who was the swoon of all the local women. And he knew it. And so did she. Despite bearing one child with him, it was not a happy marriage. Florence Lowe, now Florence Barnes, bristled at the restrictions and expectations being a society wife would entail, especially a *minister's* wife, and even more especially, one that other women (still) followed around. It wasn't a good match, to say the least.

There is one thing we need to get out of the way before we go too much further. You'll read it if you read *anything* about her. Barnes was not an attractive woman. Her looks were once compared to a "mud fence," and this by someone who *really* liked her. (Future astronaut Buzz Aldrin's wife. More on that connection later.) Before we judge the assessment too harshly, Barnes agreed with them. She didn't want to be a pretty little thing. She wanted to be out in the mud and dirt, looking for adventures and thrills. That she wasn't physically attractive in the "classic" sense (whatever that was or is), didn't dampen her libido in the slightest. Suffice it to say, four husbands give us a clue. Oh, and that response to a reporter's question. *She* was the one with the metaphorical $100 bills.

It should be noted that Barnes could get away with following her passions, at least in the 1920s, because of her family's wealth. If Barnes didn't want to stick around the stifling California society culture, she simply didn't. In 1927, her son Billy went to nannies, and she boarded a ship (in those days, called a "Banana Boat") along the Mexican coast. Little did she know, but this young "man" would spend the next four months having the time of his life evading authorities, learning Spanish, and generally getting into mischief during the Mexican Civil War.

Did you notice the pronoun switch? Well, the Mexican crew didn't. They wouldn't allow a woman on their crew (too dangerous), but that wouldn't stop Barnes. Her unconventional looks were her asset. She dressed up like a man and fooled the entire crew. Stuffing a bandana in her pants, she'd brag later that she had the "best balls" on the boat. During this adventure, Barnes chose the nickname "Pancho," which would become her calling card. More than any other decision, changing her name was probably the most significant symbolic break from her old life. Barnes formally asked her husband for a divorce upon returning from the Mexican coast. He refused. Disappointed but not deterred, she moved on to her next adventure.

The next thrill would bring Barnes back to her childhood fascination with flying. She loved aircraft since that first air show, and flying was only becoming more popular, accessible, and routine since the first Wright Brothers powered flight in 1903. *Women* were even flying these days, and Barnes wanted in on that. However, when she asked for lessons, the instructor wasn't convinced a woman could hack it. (That was an opinion shared by most male pilots of the early days of aviation.) To prove it to her, he strapped her into the back of his two-seat, single-engine plane and proceeded to scare the "pants" off her. He rolled. He dived. He skimmed the treetops. He did everything terrifying move he could think of.

For most people, that would have been it. However, when they landed, Pancho Barnes was laughing. She completed her first solo flight with just six hours of formal instruction. *Six.* She was a natural.

However, that didn't mean squat to the powers that be. They were concerned that allowing women to fly was inherently dangerous to the field. Polite society loved to see women as pilots but blanched at the prospect that one might crash. It would hurt the image of aviation. (And let's be clear: Many men didn't want them in the field.) Most women found it challenging to get a license at all.

Not Barnes. This woman already knew how to fool men into thinking she was one of them. She dressed in male clothes, wrote "Pancho" on the application, and was promptly approved.

Pancho Barnes was, *officially*, a pilot.

. . .

It was a good time to be a pilot. The aviation industry experienced rapid growth in the 1920s.

What most people forget is that flying wasn't necessarily new. No, we're not talking about the first powered flight by the Wright Brothers in 1903 at Kitty Hawk. No, we're not talking about all the others who were close to accomplishing the same thing around the same time.[6] And no, we're not talking about the bi-planes just starting to take to the air over European battlefields in the Great War (sadly, now known as World War I). All those events factored into aviation's rise, but it's important to remember that airplanes weren't necessarily what the average person thought of when they thought of air travel.

Before the 1940s, powered airplanes primarily competed with lighter-than-air options. French brothers Joseph and Étienne Montgolfier invented the hot air balloon in 1793—over *100 years* before the Wright Brothers chose a flat, deserted North Carolina barrier island to conduct their tests. As it turns out, Barnes's father had direct experience with one in the American Civil War. He flew a balloon over Confederate lines on President Lincoln's orders to report on troop movements and formations. (He claimed, probably rightfully, to be the most shot-at person in the Army.) In addition to hot air balloons, which could carry only a few people at a time, German inventor Ferdinand von Zeppelin invented his namesake rigid airship (better known today as blimps) in the late 1890s.

---

6. Historian David McCullough's 2015 biography, *The Wright Brothers*, is a good place to learn more about their story.

Zeppelins could carry a small number of passengers in relative comfort. By 1914, they regularly ferried paid passengers to and from several European destinations as well as conducted scheduled *transatlantic* flights.

In other words, when people thought of commercial aviation in the 1920s, it wasn't obvious they were talking about powered aircraft as we think of them today. The first commercial aircraft flight took place in Florida in 1914, but passengers wouldn't be able to book a regular ticket on a scheduled trip until as late as 1926, and the experience wasn't nearly as reliable or comfortable as an airship.

(Before we continue, an important note about timing. It might be tempting to associate Zeppelins with the *Hindenburg* disaster. While that certainly helped "take the hydrogen out of the blimps" for lighter-than-air travel, the crash didn't occur until 1937. Until then, Zeppelins were considered a luxurious option for the well-off traveler.)

Despite lighter-than-air's head start, the powered aircraft industry saw the potential to overtake airships as the primary mode of air travel. Industry boosters and manufacturers pursued aggressive promotion of their new models along several fronts.

The first is one we've already hinted at: military aircraft. Although biplanes didn't play a pivotal role in the First World War, forward-thinking planners conceived of waves of fighters and bombers operating from land bases and ship-based platforms—the first aircraft carriers. Military spending often triggers commercial investment, which was certainly the case here. Companies like Travel Air (the hint as to its business model is in its name) built on research done in military circles to speed the development of their own models.

It's also difficult to understate the impact of Charles Lindbergh's Atlantic crossing in 1927 and Earhart's "sack of potatoes" flight the following year. That's not to say the general public wasn't interested in aviation before then (recall Barnes's 1911 air show visit as a girl), but interest in flying "pulled up and hit the throttle" in the last few years of the Roaring 20s.

To capitalize on the public excitement, flying competitions proliferated. Further catalyzing attention, the contests were *dangerous*. Pilots routinely crashed for various reasons—bad weather, mechanical failure, or simple inexperience. Today, aircraft are (statistically, per mile traveled) the safest mode of travel. That's because of over 100 years of learning, often from fatal crashes. Accidents were much more common in the early days of aviation; we simply didn't know what we didn't know.

Despite, or perhaps because of the danger, aircraft designers *wanted* female pilots to fly their planes. The reason was simple, albeit a bit sexist. If a *woman* could do it, so could you. The "you" implied, of course, a man. That said, competitions for women always drew crowds, though coverage from journalists of the time was not always flattering. When one reporter mocked the women's competition as a "Powderpuff Derby," the women (including Barnes) adopted the slur and ran with it, the insult pushing them to fly their planes faster and attempt crazier stunts. (Several female pilots died in these competitions; the Grim Reaper wasn't sexist when it came to crash deaths.)

What aircraft manufacturers and competition organizers didn't expect was the draw the contests would have for young girls. When they saw *women* risking their lives and flying planes, they saw—in concrete terms, not just an abstraction—that they could aspire to anything a boy could want when he grew up. In some ways, Earhart and Barnes followed in the wake of Susan B. Anthony and Jane Addams. The right to *imagination* was just as necessary as the right to *vote*.

As it happened, plenty of girls were in the audience in 1930, watching Barnes become the fastest woman alive.

. . .

Air races led to a very different initial career path for Barnes than for Earhart. While Earhart focused on celebrity-style flights—new speeds, new heights, and new distances—Barnes didn't have that same media appeal. Instead, she exploited her California connections and the fast-growing Hollywood movie-making industry.

Planes were the newest thing, and all the big movie producers wanted to feature aerial shots in their movies. The most notable aircraft appearance in a major blockbuster that people remember now is 1933's *King Kong*, but that was not the first film to feature airplanes as a main attraction. The film that started it all was director Howard Hughes's *Hell's Angels*. The plot is, frankly, not that important to our story. It involves a fantasy British-German conflict, bombing London from a Zeppelin, and a love triangle. What's important to us is the number of flying scenes.

Nearly 150 stunt pilots were used, three of whom died during filming (including one mechanic), and all were paid half of what they should have been. However, when Barnes appealed directly to Hughes to increase their pay because of the risk, he balked. Barnes took matters into her own hands. She organized the men (and other than her, they were all men) into the first stunt pilot union, pushing for better wages and working conditions. Given what we know now about Barnes, it should come as little surprise that she won. Also not surprisingly, she refused to allow the pilots to exclude anyone based on gender, but she also insisted the union include stunt pilots from any race or religion. What mattered was what you could do in the air, not what country you were born in or what God, god, or gods you prayed to. In one case, she personally insisted that Jewish pilots be allowed into the union over the objections of some very tough-minded men. This was a *very* big deal at that time. When you read stories about other unions, they were both implicitly and explicitly sexist, racist, and religiously intolerant—often violently so. The stunt pilot union was different because *Barnes* was different. No one had met—or was prepared—for anyone like her. In her spare time, she organized the first women's medical air corps. Nurses in planes could get to where they were needed faster than nurses in cars, especially in the rough, wide-open spaces of the western United States.

However, just when you thought this was all high-minded altruism, that was also not who Barnes was. She had a bone-deep sense of right and wrong but also liked to play as hard as she worked. She *loved* the Hollywood party scene. In her words, the movie sets were great for three reasons. Everyone there could "fly, fight, and"…well, the last word is exactly what you're thinking.

Barnes didn't mention booze as one of her three Fs, but her parties were legendary, fueled by a free-flowing tap of inheritance money from her mother. In addition to the parties, she bankrolled apartment buildings for the pilots and even bought them groceries when they were short of cash. Unsurprisingly, the largely young, fit, attractive daredevil men loved her. She was fully liberated and took every advantage of it.

There's a good argument that she "roared" louder than anyone else in the Roaring 1920s.

But it wouldn't last.

What follows is the story of reinvention and transformation and why Barnes is the true aviation hero of the 1930s.

. . .

Barnes might have been better off than most, but as the early 1930s dragged on, it became clear that she was overspending her means. Eventually, she was forced to sell *everything*, including her beloved Mystery Ship, to scrape together enough money to buy a piece of ranch property in the Mohave desert—basically, a parachute strategy. It wasn't a great situation, but she and her son would have a place to live.

Right. Her son. Did we forget about him and the marriage to the preacher back in Pasadena? Barnes eventually was granted a divorce. So the story goes, she rode a white horse into his church *during a service* to ask him. Oh, and she wasn't wearing any clothes. As in, she was full-on nude. Was that story entirely true? Like many stories about Barnes, that's impossible to know. She understood how the mystique of a story was just as important as the facts of the matter, and she would let this one stand. What makes this unbelievable story believable is that Barnes wasn't shy about running around without clothes. (Several pilots in later years would attest to that.)

So, there she was. On an abandoned dude ranch nestled up against the Muroc Army Air Base (the future Edwards Air Force Base) in the California desert. A single mom. Raising alfalfa and livestock. The good news, as it turned out, was all about location, location, location. It's no mistake Barnes snuggled up to the Army's aircraft test range (there was no "Air Force" branch then). She knew those guys. Ever the opportunist, Barnes would take advantage.

Before we see how, though, we must understand how aviation was still a big deal in the 1930s when everything else was falling apart.

First, the statistics. Between 1929 and 1934, the worst of the psychological crisis of the Great Depression, the number of commercial air passengers increased from just about 6,000 to over 450,000—an increase of more than *75 times*. By 1938 (remember, still well inside the Great Depression), the number of passengers nearly tripled to 1.2 million. Of course, ridership was not evenly distributed among the population. According to the National Air and Space Museum, a round-trip ticket cost about $260 in the 1930s, or about half the cost of a new *car*. For reference, that's nearly $5,000 in today's money—only people who could afford it flew.[7] Because of the high cost, aircraft only carried about seven percent of overall cross-country passengers. In the 1930s, most people still took the train long distance.

Taking a page from the improvements in long-distance railroad creature comforts (themselves competing with cars and busses), air travel got a lot more comfortable, too. People point to the introduction of stewardesses (and yes, "ess" refers to only women), but the real features that made things better were more mechanical.[8] The most obvious was simply adding padding to the seats and armrests. The less obvious was the introduction of pressurized cabins, allowing the new DC-2 and DC-3 models to fly at altitudes of about 20,000 feet. At that height, turbulence significantly decreases. (Ever wonder why your flight is more bumpy on takeoff and landing? Now you know.) And heat. No more scarves needed, unless you wanted to make a fashion statement.

It should come as little surprise that the stocks did well.[9] High finance didn't matter much to Barnes, trying to eke out a living by picking up food waste from the Army base, feeding it to her pigs, and selling the pigs back to the base. But as you might guess, aircraft were such a big deal that the number of pilots (and related staff) made her circular economy endeavor instantly successful.

Speaking of the base, the Army Air Corps was testing a considerable number of different models of planes. Barnes herself flew dozens of models, and test pilots in that era did as well. Today, a test pilot might fly only a few models in their career. In the 1930s, they might fly *thirty* different models. It was a massive challenge

---

7. In the most famous example, FDR flew to Chicago to accept the nomination for President in 1932. It was that convention where he gave his famous "New Deal" speech.

8. Because of the tight fit on planes, women could be no more than five feet tall and no more than 118 pounds. Because of…well, sexism…they couldn't be married. This practice continued on most airlines until the 1960s.

9. Well enough that *King Kong* director Merian C. Cooper didn't have to worry about money when he worked on the first blockbuster monster movie in 1933.

and highly risky. These were the men (and they were all military men) leading the charge on aviation's readiness for what everyone knew would be an upcoming global conflict. Some pilots moonlighted for the movie studios, but either way (real bombs or fake ones), it was dangerous work. There was a very real possibility they might not come home. They all wanted a place to unwind.

Can you guess what Pancho Barnes did next as the 1930s came to a close? Sure, you can.

Barnes used money from selling livestock from her ranch to the Army to rebuild her life around the "Happy Bottom Riding Club." (And yes, that was a play on words. Horse riding. Sure. She had horses. Of course, that's all she meant.) It featured horseback riding, a hotel, and a full restaurant and bar. She also knew what the men (pilots) wanted. *Women.* She would hire young women to work as servers and bartenders. To protect their identities, Barnes gave them all "secret identities." Each of them used the last name Smith. They could choose days of the week or months of the year for their first name. Think "January Smith" or "Wednesday Smith." You get the idea.

Later, people would accuse Barnes of running a brothel in the desert. (She wasn't.[10]) However, she was okay with the rumors because they brought Hollywood celebrities and all manner of aviation industry types to her ranch to see what the fuss was about. Barnes offered pilots and celebrities the most fun they could have with their clothes on. (Or off).

In short, she recreated the kind of life and connection she wanted with aviation, Hollywood, and parties—just with the Army next door.

But what's more important, and something we can only see in retrospect, is what Barnes meant for aircraft testing and war readiness. The test pilots didn't just need a place to blow off steam. They needed a place to relax and discuss their flight strategies with others—including Barnes—who knew what they were going through. Think about it. How did the United States achieve air superiority so quickly in World War II and its aftermath? It wasn't an accident. Many of those

---

10. This would come up during a lawsuit over eminent domain proceedings in the 1950s. Whether pilots didn't want to admit to paying for sex or whether it didn't actually happen is a matter of debate. The court couldn't find any evidence of it. (The one witness who tried wasn't credible.) As Barnes put it, test pilots never needed to "pay for it."

pilots—with names like Chuck Yager (who broke the sound barrier) and Buzz Aldrin (who walked on the moon)—speak fondly in books and documentaries about how important Barnes was.

You can read more about that in Lauren Kessler's fantastic biography, *The Happy Bottom Riding Club: The Life and Times of Pancho Barnes*, or the similarly-named PBS documentary.[11] However, if you've heard of Pancho Barnes before today, it's likely from the 1979 book, *The Right Stuff*, or its 1983 movie adaptation. (In the movie, Barnes is played by Kim Stanley.) The movie follows the selection of seven pilots for the first human mission to space. Although the film didn't do well at the box office, it's one of those films that means more the further we get away from it.

In the movie, we get to hear from Barnes as she describes the selection process:

> Around here, we got two kinds of pilots: the hotdogs who get all the hot planes, and then you got your pudknockers who dream of flying the hot planes. So, what are you two pudknockers gonna have?

Now, there's no evidence Barnes actually said those words, though she did describe pilots as either "prime" who fly the best equipment or newer "pudknockers" who only dream about it. The term pudknockers is still used today to describe a pretentious or unskilled pilot. (Think about that for a second. It's...not flattering.) How do we know Barnes didn't say it like that? She would have used more profanity.

...

Unfortunately, this story doesn't have the happiest of endings.

As Muroc Army Air Base became Edwards Air Force Base, part of the expansion was driven by larger Cold War-era bombers that required longer runways. That meant acquiring land Barnes owned. Using eminent domain powers, the government made Barnes a lowball offer for her property, which she promptly

---

11. The documentary is a good introduction. It's only 90 minutes and available (as of this writing) on Amazon Prime Video for rent or purchase.

refused, kicking off a years-long court battle. (The battle in which the government would try to cast Barnes as a whore and a madam.)

During the proceedings, her hotel and restaurant mysteriously burned down. Yeah.

Mysteriously.

Of course, no one could ever prove wrongdoing, and Barnes eventually did win a significant sum from the government for her property, but by the 1960s, her spirit was broken. The light at the end of this tunnel is a heartwarming story where Barnes was able to repurchase her old plane at auction. When attendees knew whose plane it was and that she was in the audience, the room sat silent so that Barnes would have the only bid. Sadly, that victory was short-lived. In 1975, Barnes succumbed to breast cancer at her home in California.

However, Barnes has not been forgotten. Test pilots from all service branches convene yearly at the Happy Bottom Riding Club site for a barbeque and remembrance. DC Comics has honored her in an issue featuring test pilot Hal Jordan's *Green Lantern*. (Hal is shown visiting the club as a child.) More recently, the 2019 Marvel film *Captain Marvel* featured a fighter pilot bar named "Pancho's Bar" in honor of Barnes.

Barnes and her club had a deep and lasting impact on the aviation industry, and especially the pilots who went on to become astronauts. In their words, her support, encouragement, and camaraderie were essential to their success. In short, in addition to everything else we've discussed, Barnes certainly played a role in human space flight.

But perhaps Barnes's most significant legacy is her unyielding spirit.

She bristled against expectations of her upbringing and her gender. Barnes, more than perhaps anyone else, is the spiritual role model of the Great Depression—a person unwilling to yield in the face of tragedy and heartbreak. Not in a stoic way, either. Barnes approached her challenges with a zest for life and a smile on her face. In fact, she had an ear-to-ear grin in nearly every photo we have of her. No matter what happened, she didn't complain. She didn't march in the streets. She didn't seek media attention. She just *did it*.

19

THE HERO WE DESERVED?

There is no easy way to talk about this.

The stress of the 1930s produced more than its fair share of people who saw an opportunity to channel that frustration into material gain for themselves. But let's not sugarcoat it. Often—*too often*—those people took advantage of latent racism, sexism, homophobia, anti-Semitism, and anti-immigrant feelings to amplify and supercharge their messages. They tapped that well of hate and anger because it worked well—*too well*.

In this chapter, we'll focus on Father Charles Coughlin, the so-called "Radio Priest" whose star rose and fell during the worst years of the Great Depression. However, it's important to remember that he wasn't alone.

Louisiana Governor (and Senator) Huey Pierce Long Jr. used some of the same techniques to rule his state with an iron fist, ostensibly in the name of "justice" for "the ordinary people." His story was cut short in 1935 by an assassin's bullet.[1]

---

1. Historian Alan Brinkley wrote a joint biography of Long and Coughlin in 1982 titled *Voices of Protest: Huey Long, Father Coughlin and the Great Depression*. It's a well-regarded biography, providing the context for each man and how the uniquely took advantage of the same situation to boost their own careers.

Or how about Father Devine—aka Reverend Major Jealous Divine, aka...we don't really know his actual name—who channeled the anger of the black community to many of the same ends? Devine dressed to the nines and thought himself, well, *divine*. Hence, his chosen name.[2] He was quite the character.

Or how about the complex story of social activist (and anarchist) Dorothy Day? She tapped into the same general sentiment to advocate a violent overthrow of oppressive governments and their greedy corporate collaborators. To be fair, her views and tactics evolved. Her Catholic Worker Movement (what she is most known for) focused on peaceful and non-violent civil disobedience, but many struggle with where to place her in this group...or if she deserves to be in it at all.[3] Unlike the others, however, she was on the FBI's sedition watch list for decades. Only recently has her reputation undergone a reevaluation.

All are worth learning about in their own right.

Although scholars are quick to label each of them (to varying degrees) with the loaded term "demagogue," we cannot—and should not—dismiss them so easily. That's because this isn't a book about what historians, experts, and policymakers thought. This is a book about who Americans chose to elevate as their heroes, who they chose to listen to, and more than that, who they chose to send their (scarce) dollars.

On that measure, Father Coughlin stands alone. Although each person we highlighted commanded a significant audience, no one spoke to as many Americans as the Radio Priest. Estimates vary, but his weekly radio broadcasts likely reached as many as 40 *million* people.

That's a lot, even in today's media market. Of a 2024 *adult* population of about 260 million people, Coughlin would have reached a weekly audience of about 15 percent. To put that number into perspective, an average National Football

---

2. Followers addressed letters to him simply "God, Harlem U.S.A." Yep. It got weird. There aren't many biographies on Divine, which is a shame. For more, read *God, Harlem U.S.A.: The Father Divine Story*, by Jill Watts.

3. If you'd like to learn more, read *Dorothy Day: Dissenting Voice of the American Century*, by John Loughery and Blythe Randolph, or on the Catholic Worker Movement website—an organization she founded in the 1930s. The Catholic Church has opened the case for possible canonization as a saint, but as of this writing, that remains unresolved.

League game reaches about half that audience; the Super Bowl reaches about three times as many. No other media broadcast (news or otherwise) comes close.

But that's 2024 numbers. We need to talk *1935* numbers.

That year, the U.S. Census Bureau estimated a total adult population of about 114 million. Using those numbers, let's rerun the math. At his peak, Coughlin reached more than one in three American adults. By comparison, that's about the same audience President Roosevelt reached with his famous "Fireside Chats" many of us learned about in high school.

Scholars endlessly debate and lionize FDR's broadcasts, but they largely write off Coughlin as an aberration who spouted hate on the radio. If they go further (and they usually don't), Coughlin is cast as a cautionary tale of allowing too much "free speech." It's easy to see why. There's good evidence Coughlin plagiarized a speech from Joseph Goebbels in 1938. Yeah, *that* Goebbels. The Nazi propaganda chief.

As you might guess, the story is much more complicated than that. Father Coughlin's messages seemed reasonable—at least in the beginning. And FDR appreciated his support—at least in the beginning. And yes, after Coughlin's messages turned dark, the U.S. government (with help from the Vatican) pulled the plug on his broadcasts.

It might seem tempting to dismiss Coughlin the way scholars have, only dragging him back into the light when they compare him to some new person displaying the same behaviors and strategies. However, forty million people would seem to disagree. It's clear his messages resonated with a significant group of the American public.

We need to understand how Coughlin did it, why it worked, and why it *continues to work* in today's America.

. . .

Coughlin's story begins like many other immigrants around the turn of the century.

Born in 1891, ordained in 1916, and emigrating from Canada to the Detroit, Michigan, area in 1923, Coughlin inherited a parish that was not doing well. It wasn't only that anti-Catholic sentiment was high in the mid-1920s—the Klu

Klux Klan burned a cross on his lawn—it was also that the "National Shrine of the Little Flower" was wilting financially.

An important side note that's relevant to the "popular appeal" angle in this story: Most people think of the KKK as focused on the states of the former Confederacy. That was true for a time. However, as waves of formerly enslaved people migrated north to escape repressive "Jim Crow" laws, the KKK found an audience in urban northern cities as well. Detroit was just one example of many. Additionally, many people also mistakenly associate the KKK only with African Americans and their descendants. While that certainly was (and is) true, the organization has plenty of hate to go around. They have a special place in their dark hearts for Catholics—case in point: the burning cross directed at Father Coughlin. As we'll see later with his messages concerning other religious groups (notably, Jewish people), there is no small amount of irony here.

Back to the story.

Despite an empty collection plate and a scorched lawn, Father Coughlin would not be deterred. Like many innovators facing a fresh challenge, he decided to make a play for a broad audience on a new medium that no priest (or religious leader) had seriously tried before: radio. Yes, many early stations featured religious programming (mostly to fill time), but Coughlin's unique blend of personal appeal and shrewd strategy was unique.[4]

This Canadian priest of Irish stock had one of the smoothest voices on the radio. That wasn't as easy as it is today with sophisticated audio correction software built into today's broadcast equipment. Microphones of that time didn't pick up certain voice tones very well. Transmission systems (still mostly AM until the late 1930s) constrained the sound further. And finally, most home radio speakers were...terrible. There's no other word for it. Coughlin's unique vocal profile was just about perfect for this technology-constrained era in broadcasting.

On October 17, 1926, Coughlin took advantage of his God-given voice with his first on-air message, broadcast on Detroit station WJR. Although his sermon didn't focus explicitly on the church's financial position (he focused on love and

---

4. We cover the early days of radio programming strategy in much more detail in Chapters 8 and 14 of *Booze, Babe, and the Little Black Dress: How Innovators of the Roaring 20s Created the Consumer Revolution*.

forgiveness), Coughlin *did mention* the parish's predicament. The outpouring of support was more than anyone expected or could have hoped—not the least of whom was its preacher.

Coughlin wasn't the only one impressed. WJR inked a deal with the smooth-sounding Irishman and gave him a weekly show, dubbing him the "Radio Priest." Only a few months later, Coughlin leveraged his newfound success to create a financial innovation familiar to anyone who listens to today's televangelists. In January 1927, Coughlin introduced the "Radio League of the Little Flower." For a $1 donation, you could become a member and support the church's mission. In the first year alone, his organization raised more than $500,000. That works out to over $9 *million* in today's money. More critical is the half million people who saw fit to part with a dollar of their money to support Coughlin on the radio. That's some of the best early evidence we have of broad-based consumer support. The first "radiovangelist" didn't have "investors" or "venture capital." He drew his support from everyday people. Remember that as we continue.

Not only did Coughlin manage to pull his parish out of debt, but he also built a new state-of-the-art radio station to serve as his studio for future broadcasts. As the 1920s wound to a close, the Radio Priest was finding success, but still only at the local and regional levels.

Little did he, or anyone else, know what would happen at the end of the 1920s to catapult Coughlin to the national stage.

. . .

Let's be clear: Troubling economic and class issues were always bubbling beneath the surface in the 1920s. However, for most of the decade, the general "roar" of the economy meant that people calling attention to those inequities found little audience among policymakers, mainstream media, or pretty much anyone else. There was so much that was new and exciting—automobiles, electronics, radio, fashion, speakeasies, and real estate, just to name a few—that it crowded out most discussions of those who weren't sharing in the prosperity.

Add to that a quiet global environment, at least from the American perspective. Although President Wilson's "14 Points" didn't make much of an impact in the post-war peace conference in 1919, and the United States Senate failed to ratify membership in the League of Nations (the precursor to the United Nations), that didn't mean the United States didn't come out on top in the great global scramble for power. New York was now the world's undisputed financial capital, displacing London as Europe struggled in the aftermath of a terrible conflict. Where money flows, prosperity tends to follow.

Where were the cultural elites and social justice advocates during the Roaring 20s? Mostly, they were fawning over the new communist experiment in the Soviet Union (Joseph Stalin launched a massive charm offensive for American intellectuals in the 1920s) or escaping to Europe to write, paint, and drink too much. Ernest Hemingway set his groundbreaking novel *The Sun Also Rises* in 1920s France and Spain. That story was more truth than fiction.

The mood began to change at the end of 1929 when the stock market crashed, but it was when things started to get nasty for the average person (and not just the stock market speculator) that all the frivolity of the past decade seemed to evaporate. Playtime was over. This was clearly a *big* problem that demanded *big* solutions for which everyday Americans were willing to entertain *big* ideas. Exiled cultural elites returned, finding an eager audience in the media, with many eventually securing official posts in Roosevelt's so-called "Brain Trust." But the general public wasn't waiting on pins and needles for what the brainiest among them had to say. They cast a wide net for those big ideas. Coughlin was one of those who caught their attention.

We've bandied around the loaded word "demagogue" used to describe Coughlin's approach, but it's time we added another one: populism. That word is (perhaps) just as loaded, but it better explains *why* Coughlin's approach struck a chord with Americans amid an economic crisis.

German historian Jan-Werner Müller attempts to tease out the nuances. He chooses to define populism in ideological terms—it casts "the people" as a morally upright group against the corrupt "elites" who only want to line their own pockets. As we'll see in Coughlin's example, "the people" may be defined however the populist leader chooses to define them—including some groups and excluding others—even if they share many characteristics. For example, "the people" might include people from one ethnic or religious group and not another. In Coughlin's case, he made a distinction between "Good Jews" who were religiously observant and those "Bad Jews" who exerted controlling influence over world affairs through financial means. More broadly, the elites usually encompass the ruling political party (although sometimes an out-of-power party can serve as a scapegoat), large businesses (although usually not small businesses, although the difference between the two is never quite defined), and even foreign powers.

To dispense with the academic language, being a populist requires creating a large group of people of your choosing. The more powerless and frustrated they are (or seem), the better. Next, create an enemy of another group. Ensure this group is somehow "elite" and has some real (or perceived) power. Convince the first that they're being oppressed by the second.

Müller reminds us that although we immediately see the boogeyman we want to see (insert name of person here), populists are just as common on both the right and left wings. They often combine their populist appeals with other political ideologies, such as communism, socialism, capitalism, or consumerism. To complicate matters further, religion can enter the mix. It certainly did with Coughlin, Day, and Devine. Specifically, the Catholic tradition includes a strong social justice component.[5] That makes populist politics tough to nail down. For example, although Coughlin is largely considered a right-wing populist, sociologist Musa al-Gharbi reminds us that the 1920s and 1930s saw a rise in left-wing populism as well—an "awakening" as he terms it. He argues this movement had little to do with the true needs of disadvantaged people but rather an elite desire to gain status and power.[6] Think of it as populism in reverse. In short, the word can cut both ways.

That brings up a sticky issue of motives, doesn't it? Is the populist simply tapping into popular anger for their own benefit? Or must they forgo all personal gain and strive only for the popular good? Is it okay if there is some of both? Where do we draw the line between "populist" and "demagogue?"

---

5. Tom Holland explores this concept more fully in *Dominion: How the Christian Revolution Remade the World*. In it, he argues (in part) that the early Christian church served a social need the Roman authorities were not. In a Roman Empire full of competing faiths, Christian charity helped the religion outcompete its rivals and emerge as the dominant religion by the middle ages.

6. You can read more in al-Gharbi's 2024 cultural study: *We Have Never Been Woke: The Cultural Contradictions of a New Elite*.

It's about time we let Coughlin speak so we can answer for ourselves.

...

Let's start where Coughlin started. As the economic crisis deepened, he felt compelled (or saw the opportunity, depending on your point of view) to speak out about the state of affairs. He coined the then-famous phrase to describe the choice between re-electing Herbert Hoover (and the bankers Coughlin saw as responsible for the crisis) and choosing FDR: "Roosevelt or Ruin."

We could tap plenty of broadcasts from the early years, but it's more instructive to examine the 16 principles that Coughlin believed should guide his "National Union of Social Justice" organization. Mind you, these aren't Catholic doctrine, but they're not *not* rooted in that faith tradition.

We'll talk soon about the persuasion techniques Coughlin used to deliver his messages in the *late* 1930s, but it's important to get a sample of what he was talking about in the early years. Where would *you* draw the line between a populist and a demagogue?

Here are the first three:

1. I believe in the right of liberty and conscience of education, not permitting the state to dictate either my worship or my chosen avocation in life.
2. I believe that every citizen willing to work and capable of working shall receive a just and living annual wage which will enable him to maintain and educate his family according to the standards of American decency.
3. I believe in nationalizing those public necessities which by their very nature are too important to be held in the control of private individuals. By these I mean banking, credit and currency, power, light, oil and natural gas and our God-given natural resources.

The first one is more a reaction to anti-Catholic sentiment than any broader economic idea. We can skip that one for our purposes. But the next two are telling. In the early 1930s, wealth was extremely concentrated in the hands of elites. While their stock portfolios took a hit in the 1929 crash, they weren't wondering where their next meal was coming from. The average person, however, didn't have that luxury. In 1932, one in four were out of work, with the remaining working majority underemployed and *everyone* scared they might be next. It's not difficult to understand how Coughlin's message of wealth redistribution and caring for your neighbor would resonate.

4. I believe in private ownership of all other property.
5. I believe in upholding the right to private property and controlling it for the public good.

And just to be clear, Coughlin's populism and wealth distribution schemes were not communist in nature; they were capitalistic. In other words, private people would own all means of production that were not "essential."

6. I believe in the abolition of the privately owned Federal Reserve Banking system and in the establishment of a Government owned Central Bank.
7. I believe in rescuing from the hands of private owners the right to coin and regulate the value of money, which right must be restored to Congress where it belongs.
8. I believe that one of the chief duties of this Government owned Central Bank is to maintain the cost of living on an even keel and the repayment of dollar debts with equal dollar values.

Coughlin believed (partially rightly and partially wrongly) that the American central bank—created in 1913—was the root of the current crisis. We won't slip into a discussion of the role of the central bank in American finance, but suffice it to say that new central bankers were learning as they went, and it didn't always go well. Coughlin's position on the bank reflected his view of bankers generally, but it wasn't out of the mainstream. Not at all.

9. I believe in the cost of production plus a fair profit for the farmer.

Farm prices and the plight of farmers were major issues in the early 1930s. Significant areas of the country were in an environmental crisis (the so-called "Dust Bowl"), farm prices were collapsing, and people were going hungry. Classical economics would have predicted the opposite of these effects, but everything was topsy-turvey in the Great Depression. It wasn't unusual for policymakers to advocate for the farmer.

10. I believe not only in the right of the laboring man to organize in unions but also in the duty of the Government which that laboring man supports to facilitate and protect these organizations against the vested interests of wealth and of intellect.

Coughlin also supported labor unions and the government's role in ensuring they could operate. In the 1930s, that was certainly *not* the case. Yes, there were unions. But also yes, the government often was called in to quell "unrest," which usually meant they sided with management, not labor.

11. I believe in the recall of all non-productive bonds and thereby in the alleviation of taxation.
12. I believe in the abolition of tax-exempt bonds.
13. I believe in the broadening of the base of taxation founded upon the ownership of wealth and the capacity to pay.
14. I believe in the simplification of government, and the further lifting of crushing taxation from the slender reserves of the laboring class.

To be fair, some of Coughlin's issues with bonds (a type of debt financial instrument) get a little wonky. That's not what's important here. Look at what he's driving at—lower taxes, a broader base, and a *progressive* tax based on the ability to pay.

15. I believe that in the event of war for the defense of our nation and its liberties, there shall be a conscription of wealth as well as a conscription of men.

The United States would indeed do this in the Second World War. As just one example, all automotive plants were converted to military use.

16. I believe in the sanctity of property rights. I believe that the chief concern of government shall be for the poor because, as it is witnessed, the rich have ample means of their own to care for themselves.

Perhaps most interesting is what Coughlin omits, not what he includes. The careful observer will notice these are *not* racial or gender social justice issues, these are *economic* social justice issues. (Albeit with one note of a religious issue up front.) Although race and gender played significant roles in the Great Depression, Coughlin certainly knew what would draw an audience.

Let's ask ourselves: Which of these 16 points sounds "evil" and "dangerously subversive?"

FDR certainly didn't think so. He actively courted Coughlin's support (and audience) when he campaigned for President in 1931 and continued to woo the Radio Priest once he won in 1932. If the new President had any reservations, it was that he couldn't control Coughlin in the same way he could a Cabinet member or politician, not that the two differed in any meaningful way on the substance of their messages.

Coughlin's message also resonated with the rest of the country—especially the vast interior and Midwest. The appeal was understandable. To someone in Des Moines or Tulsa struggling to make ends meet, Coughlin sounds like he is speaking directly to them. Although many of them weren't Catholic, the authority that came with the Roman collar didn't hurt, and Coughlin *always* dressed the part in public.

It all seemed reasonable.

Until it didn't.

A warning: Here's where it will get uncomfortable.

...

FDR's "First 100 Days" are famous.[7] It was a flurry of legislative and executive activity meant to take dramatic action to change course on a rapidly deteriorating economic situation. The cooperative, incremental, hope-it-gets-better approach

---

7. We often now talk about what a new administration hopes to accomplish in the first 100 days, but this was the first time.

favored by his predecessor wasn't working. The new President wouldn't make the same mistakes. This isn't a book about those initiatives and their legacy—Anthony Badger's *FDR: The First 100 Days* is a good place to dig in if you're interested—but they're notable for a reason. The level of optimism was infectious. For most Americans, Coughlin included, the new administration seemed to be taking charge and making things happen.

It wouldn't last.

Scholars debate why FDR's policies didn't work. Some claim the aggressive intervention actually *postponed* recovery. That's a reasonable interpretation, but suffers from hindsight bias. The American political and economic system was *very close* to collapse in 1931. If that happened, joblessness would have been the least of our problems.

Others claim FDR didn't go *far enough* with reforms. They claim a "social welfare state" or revolution was needed—something akin to what happened in Europe after World War II. That demonstrates hindsight bias as well. The Roosevelt Administration didn't *want* people on "the dole." Leaders thought it would poison Americans' sense of self.

Another viable perspective is that the American *consumer* emerged in the 1920s, and with them, a choice-making culture that policymakers needed to consider in their planning. Prohibition *should have* shown that heavy-handed and moralized approaches to public behavior wouldn't work, but again, that's also hindsight bias. It would take scholars another half a century to recognize that had happened. There are *still* academics and policymakers who struggle with the concept of consumer choice.[8]

Bottom line: The Great Depression would prove a tough problem to solve.

However, as Americans turned the corner into the middle of the 1930s, they had grown weary of the never-ending drumbeat of bad news and were losing faith in FDR's ability to solve the problem. The mood had turned. When that hap-

---

8. The prequel to this book, *Booze, Babe, and the Little Black Dress: How Innovators of the Roaring 20s Created the Consumer Revolution*, covers this shift in detail. It's telling that most interviews and reviews of the book note that they had no idea this culture shift had happened when it did. It's like asking a fish to describe water; we've been immersed in consumer culture so long, it's hard to describe anything else.

pens, and struggles turn from immediate crises into chronic conditions, people (naturally) start to look for deeper root causes.

Often, that's useful. To *truly* solve a knotty problem, you can't just treat the symptoms; you need to address the underlying cause. Even today, scholars and economists struggle to pinpoint the cause of the Great Depression. With over a century of hindsight, our best explanation is a mix of factors with complex interactions. Imagine trying to solve it *then*, as people were going hungry. It was not easy, to say the least.

It's also natural, sadly, for a search for complex root causes to metastasize into a search for simple scapegoats.

That certainly happened in Germany. Facing a difficult situation after losing the Great War, that country was ripe for a leader to come to power saying he could solve all their problems, return them to a place in the sun, and blame *someone else*. It was a predictable adaptation of the classic formula. In Adolf Hitler's mind, the root cause was obvious: the Jews.

We won't dive into Hitler's rise to power here, nor his views on race and religion. There are plenty of excellent books on that subject. What gets uncomfortable for Americans (and what's relevant here) is how popular those ideas became in the United States. The gist was that Jews controlled events behind the scenes. No, Roosevelt wasn't a Jew himself, but he had Jews in his cabinet and listened to Jewish bankers. In turn, they dictated policies that worsened the situation while enriching themselves and those around them. To "solve" the "problem" meant expelling this influence from government and society.

One of the many things that made America unique in the 1930s was the number of new celebrities with their own direct access to the public. Before the 1920s, governments could more reliably control the "official" line and interpretation of events. However, with the explosion of mass media, anyone with a platform could have an opinion. One of the most famous examples was aviator Charles Lindbergh. Like Coughlin, his fame allowed him to gather an audience for his political views. And like Coughlin, he wasn't an economist or policymaker. To simplify his early opinion, Hitler might be a bad guy, but he wasn't America's concern; besides, it was better to have the German war machine pointed at the Soviet Union. Why did people listen to Lindbergh? When we strip away the celebrity aura, he was just a guy with an opinion. However, people listen to celebrities, whether or not their opinion carries rational credibility.

Roosevelt was the first President to deal with a crisis of this scale in a new mass media and celebrity environment. His instinct was correct about both Lindbergh and Coughlin. They were impossible to control. FDR curtailed Lindbergh's involvement in the upcoming war effort. He would also eventually censor Coughlin after a nasty speech in 1938 where the Radio Priest explained away the *Kristallnacht* reign of terror directed at Jewish people in Germany as the fault of the Jewish people themselves.[9]

Largely in response to that speech and partially as a justification for the need to censor Coughlin, Alfred McClung Lee and Elizabeth Briant Lee wrote and published *The Fine Art of Propaganda: A Study of Father Coughlin's Speeches* in 1939. The book walks through Coughlin's speeches line by line to diagnose what techniques he was using. The idea was to teach Americans how to recognize this sort of manipulation when they heard it.

Their book is the best way to understand Coughlin's mass appeal and, paradoxically, why this husband-and-wife team missed the forest for the trees in their analysis.

. . .

The Lees dissect Coughlin's speeches using eight "Tricks of the Trade." The short book briefly explains each technique, uses examples from Coughlin's own words, and provides a detailed refutation of each point. The idea is simple: If Americans only *understood* how they were being manipulated, they could resist Coughlin's emotional appeals. It's a nice idea, and it *seems like it should work*, but it doesn't. We'll step through a shorthand version of the author's arguments to see why.

The first of the "tricks" is the easiest to understand: name-calling. The strategy is simple. Give an idea (or person or group) a negative label. Psychologically, it triggers us to associate a negative feeling with the person or group on the receiving end and, *worse*, makes us less likely to respond to rational counterarguments. It's

---

9. The Vatican also didn't appreciate Coughlin's views, but they could control him in a way the American political and media system could not. They gave him the directive to "cease and desist" any political talk and radio broadcasting and confine his duties to those appropriate to a parish priest.

highly effective, which is why it's the first line of attack for playground bullies everywhere.

Coughlin used several examples in his speeches. His favorites included "imported radicals" (immigrants who came to the United States to sow dissent), "communist Jews" (who were supposed to have orchestrated the Soviet revolution and were now attempting to expand from there), and straight from the Bible, "money changers" (a reference to the Biblical story of Jesus expelling banking types from the temple in Jerusalem).

This is the first time the authors deploy their rational counterstrategy. They take pains to describe the distinction between Israelis as an ethnicity and Jews as a religion. They refute the argument that "Jewish bankers" financed the Russian Revolution. And so on, and so on, for multiple pages. It's a reasonable approach, but psychological evidence suggests it doesn't work. In short, humans are rationalizers, not rational. Using name-calling is a first-mover advantage. It colors everything that comes after. It's difficult to overcome an emotional trigger with logic and explanations.[10]

It won't get any easier from here.

Next up is the opposite of name-calling: glittering generalities. Coughlin sprinkles his favorites throughout his speeches, including "Americanism" and "democracy." Obviously, those aren't bad things, but just like the negative associations of name-calling, the positive nature of glittering generalities fools us into *not* questioning what comes after. If something is "American," and America is good, then that thing must be good.[11] Think of this as verbal flag-waving. Every politician does it—*every* one of them.

---

10. This is part of the basis for Cognitive Behavioral Therapy (CBT), in which people are attempting to break a negative thought pattern by dissecting it rationally. It can work, but it's slow, deliberate, and requires the full buy-in of the person using the technique. If the person doesn't want to correct the opinion, or doesn't have the time to devote to the effort, it won't work. In a way, the Lees were attempting to perform a group CBT session. It only worked on people who already wanted it to work.

11. In mathematics, this is called the transitive property. If A equals B, and B equals C, then A must equal C. Who knew you'd ever use that math lesson?

(Play a fun drinking game next political season to see if you can identify name-calling and glittering generalities. Be careful, though. Call a cab or Uber to get home. You'll be hammered inside of ten minutes.)

The Lees name the next technique "transfer," but it would be better called "symbols and images." Again, all politicians (and good speakers) do this. Instead of words, the speaker invokes appearance and concepts. Remember that Coughlin always wore his Catholic garb—a dark shirt with the Roman white collar at a minimum, but usually his full robes and vestments. Those clothes carry authority that even a nice suit simply does not. He is "transferring" the authority from his appearance into what he's saying.

(It's the same reason most people try to look their best at an interview.)

But remember, Coughlin was the "Radio" Priest—operative word: *radio*. No one could see his clothes on the radio. We've already mentioned he had a smooth voice. That's a symbol in and of itself. (Most communication is non-verbal, and the tone of speech is a non-verbal queue.) In addition to his voice, Coughlin would begin and end his broadcasts with religious organ music—the same kind you'd hear at a Catholic mass. That music would conjure images in the listeners' minds in the same way his clothing would if they could see him.

Unfortunately, this is one of the shortest chapters in the book. The reason is that there is not much to refute logically. However, the authors are almost dismissive of the power of symbols and images; they seem to imply that simply acknowledging them is enough. They shouldn't have made this mistake. Publishing icon William Randolph Hearst, (supposedly) speaking a few decades before the Lees wrote their book, remarked, "You furnish the pictures, and I'll furnish the war." In Hearst's day, many Americans (and especially recent immigrants) couldn't read. That's what most people think he meant. It's not. A better way to say it would be the classic: A picture is worth a thousand words. Unsurprisingly, most politicians have their photo taken in front of a flag. More recently, most tech founders want to show you their "garage," even if they never started their company in one. The *image* is more important than the reality.[12]

Testimonials are fourth on the list of tricks. A good testimonial can come from authoritative people *or* documents. In one notable example, Coughlin referenced a document titled "Official White Paper by the British Cabinet (Jew activity)." In his interpretation, a "Jewish" banking firm financed the Bolshevik Revolution in Russia in 1918-1919. The document was purportedly obtained by the American Secret Service, and the "French" guaranteed its accuracy. To add another source of credibility, Coughlin said he "called" Dublin to discuss the document's contents. That last part is pretty silly from a logical perspective—why would the Irish government discuss a British cabinet report with an American priest?—but it was a brilliant use of the testimonials technique. It makes it seem like Coughlin checked the facts himself...the same thing *you would do* in a similar position.

The document in question doesn't actually say what Coughlin says it says, but by this point, we should know that doesn't matter. Most people don't have the time, experience, or contacts to fact-check the specifics. If they believe Coughlin, and they believe his sources, they're likely to believe his interpretation.

Earlier in this chapter, we defined populism as an appeal to the "people" and their interests. That's the next strategy: plain folks. When you employ this strategy, you link your message to something "everybody knows" and that no special or advanced knowledge is required. It's "common sense."

Coughlin routinely portrayed himself as a "simple Catholic priest" who was "persecuted" for telling you "the truth." This is "your presentation" (his broadcasts), and he is honored to be a "guest in *your* home." Like symbols and images, there isn't much to logically refute. That doesn't mean it wasn't (or isn't still) effective. In the 1930s, most educated elites viewed the people who settled in the vast American interior as uneducated and unsophisticated simpletons. They were deserving of pity for the hardships they faced, but they weren't seen as competent

---

12. Benjamin Franklin was a master of this technique. He considered his outfit a "costume" that would confirm to what people wanted to see. His plain, outdoorsy image was what people in Europe imaged America to be like before the Revolutionary War. You can read more about this story in the Prologue to *Marketer in Chief: How Each President Sold the American Idea*.

enough to figure it out on their own. It's easy to see Coughlin's appeal. He didn't talk down to his audience.

Most readers will recognize the more modern version of "card stacking"—technique number seven. Many regular television viewers of a certain age will remember the ubiquitous "whiteboard" presentations, where a breathless commentator would connect multiple facts on a dry-erase board with bold lines, all while using ominous phrases. It's so convincing because it's visual, happens fast, and viewers don't have time to check all the connections.

This was one of Coughlin's favorite techniques. It's also easy to refute with logic, and that's why the Lees devote so much of their book to it. Think of the argument as links in a chain; if one link breaks, the entire argument falls apart. A few examples: Coughlin would often cite a convenient (and largely false) reason for the rise of Naziism as only a response to communism. He would confuse the democratic and communist revolutions in Russia, which to be fair, still confuse modern readers. And he would cite examples of school districts in Cleveland and Bridgeport removing prayer from classrooms—something the communists *had* done. It all sounds ominous. If you follow the breadcrumbs, you might be inclined to conclude that communists were making inroads in the United States and that *they* were the real threat, not Hitler's Germany.

The authors go to great lengths to break the links in that chain, but their explanations never sound as emotionally compelling or simplistically satisfying as Coughlin's broadcasts. It's tempting to claim that if only people were as smart as the authors, they could break the chain as well, but there's a seemingly paradoxical reason why giving Coughlin the benefit of the doubt *is indeed* rational. Instead of using the "links in the chain" metaphor, consider "where there's smoke, there's fire." There's a reason this strategy works; it's hardwired into the human survival instinct. Think of our ancestral home in Africa. Was that rustle in the weeds a lion or the wind? It pays to assume it's a lion and act appropriately. Those who don't tend to get eaten...and removed from the gene pool.

And finally, the authors show us how Coughlin used the "bandwagon" technique. This is simple: Others (ideally, others *like you*) are doing, thinking, or saying it. You should, too. In Coughlin's case, he combined glittering generalities and bandwagon into "Americans should not support European wars." The word for this that many of us learned in high school history was "isolationism," which was a common opinion at the time. It's why Roosevelt couldn't directly support Great Britain even after World War II began and France was overrun.

The authors end with a full takedown of one of Coughlin's most famous speeches. Interjected in line with the text are icons (added by the authors) that denote when any of the tricks have been used. The speech is littered with icons.

It seems satisfying and final. Logic beats Coughlin. And if *you* learn that logic, you can inoculate yourself against the next Coughlin that comes around.

Huh.

So, if this was all it took, why did Roosevelt and the Vatican need to pull Coughlin off the air?

It's because this approach *doesn't* work. It's more of a rationalization for censorship than a logical examination of the effectiveness of Coughlin's speeches. Remember, humans make emotional decisions and justify them later with facts—and only the convenient facts, at that. If you want to beat an emotional argument, you need to counter it with the same. During the war years in the first half of the next decade, the government used (what we now see) as "cheesy" propaganda films to stir up patriotic feelings. We'll cover those in the next book.

But for now, it's important to stay right here for a while. Where it feels uncomfortable. In a time and a place where the Radio Priest had our full attention.

AMERICAN MYTHOLOGY

Before 1900, most people lived their entire lives within a few miles of where they were born. According to the U.S. Census Bureau, six in 10 people *still* do. If we extend the radius to 100 miles (a little more than the distance between New York and Philadelphia), eight in 10 people live within a 90-minute drive of their birthplace.[1]

Laura Ingalls Wilder was not one of those people.

Young Laura Ingalls moved *six times* between her third and thirteenth birthdays. They were the "pioneers" we imagine and idealize from American history—a covered wagon, a scattering of noisy chickens, a pair of sturdy oxen, one strong horse, and a happy determination to make a new life on the vast prairie.

This is the first myth we'll debunk in this chapter, but it won't be the last. Her family's journey was more like a mashup between the 1980s computer game *Oregon Trail* and the 2020s party game *Cards Against Humanity*. Instead of a picturesque Conestoga wagon plodding through tall prairie grass, imagine a

---

1. This is one of those U.S. Census Bureau/Harvard University collaborations that's notable for its obviousness. How many people from your high school still live within a 90-minute drive of where they donned their cap and gown? (Don't count snowbirds.)

horde of locusts the width of Texas. Or a blizzard in June. Or the third crop failure in a row.

In those ten years, the Ingalls' journey would span five Midwestern states, not to mention territories that were not yet states. The family started in the fall of 1869 with the four of them—Laura's sister Mary included—moving from their log cabin in Wisconsin to a territory just north of Oklahoma in what would become Kansas. During this stay, the family welcomed young Carrie. The problem was that "Ma" and "Pa" were squatters on Osage land, and they knew it.

When the buyer of their Wisconsin farm couldn't continue making the promised payments, the Ingalls family took the opportunity to avoid inevitable conflict and head back to Wisconsin in 1871. They wouldn't stay long. By 1873, they were back on the trail, this time to Walnut Grove in central Minnesota. That's where they'd meet the locusts—3.5 *trillion* of them, by the best estimates—a mega-swarm spanning thousands of square miles. They ate everything in sight two years in a row. Despite the hardship, the family welcomed Freddie.

Exhausted from living through what they had only read about in *Exodus*, the family packed up again for a spot just south of the Minnesota border in Iowa. Unfortunately, Freddie didn't make it; he died of an unrecorded disease along the path from Iowa to the family's final stop (at least for Ma and Pa) in De Smet, Dakota Territory. The Ingalls took advantage of land offered through the Homestead Act to secure their new home.[2]

By the way, that's another myth we'll get to in due course. We'll read plenty of how the Ingalls family championed "self-reliance" and "limited government," but remember this decision to take advantage of land the U.S. government had cleared of Indigenous people for new settlers.

To be fair to the Ingalls, it's difficult to imagine *not* taking advantage of that opportunity. The family was fleeing war, famine, pestilence, and death (the literal meaning of the word "apocalypse") for the *chance* at subsistence farming and

---

2. The big idea with the Homestead Act (enacted during the Civil War) was to provide 160 acres of land to anyone who would "improve" on it. However, because most of the people were poor and the law was vaguely worded as to what "improved" meant, unintended consequences kicked in. Most of the land fell into the hands of ranchers, miners, and speculators rather than the salt-of-the-earth farmers it was intended to help. Search for the Homestead Act (1862) in the National Archives online to learn more.

ranching. These weren't easy times, but the Ingalls—like so many other families—persevered through tireless hard work and stoic determination.

These stories would become a series of books many of us read as children or watched on television: *The Little House on the Prairie*. For a generation of young Americans (multiple generations, in fact), the story of the Ingalls family created the mythology surrounding the pioneer era. Although they might have faced challenges, the rough splinters of death and despair had been sanded down to a happy, smiling shine.

That was just what young people needed during the Great Depression. Times were tough now; they saw it all around them and were powerless to do anything about it. They could take heart in Laura's example as a hard-working daughter. Ma's tireless dedication to the home. Pa's endless hard work. Her sister Mary building a life even though she had become blinded by disease.

It was inspiring. It was uplifting. And it wasn't *really* true. It was a sanitized, kids' version of truth.

But the story behind the story is just as full of contradictions and questions.

It's about a collaboration between an estranged mother and daughter born of a desire to tell their stories as well as financial necessity—a partnership only recently discovered. It's about the myth *and the reality* of American self-reliance. It's about a Libertarian backlash against the New Deal and the birth of a new political movement. And it's also about the battles (and odd bedfellows) to educate the next generation.

So, in the end, is *Little House on the Prairie* mythology? History? Reality? Does it matter?

Let's go find out.

. . .

After Laura married Almanzo Wilder in 1885, her life didn't get easier. In fact, she seemed destined for the same challenges her parents faced. Laura gave birth to Rose in 1886 and a son three years later, who died within two weeks (sadly, quite common in that time and place). They moved several times. After a nasty bout of diphtheria left her husband partially paralyzed, Laura Ingalls Wilder took on more of the farmwork—the dangerous, backbreaking work usually reserved for men alone.

As Rose recalled years later, the series of tragedies gave her mother a certain stoic resolve...and probably contributed to her daughter's difficult upbringing. Wilder could be distant, nasty, and short with her daughter—perhaps understandable from an adult's perspective, but nonetheless difficult for a young child to accept.

Despite the challenges, the Wilder family enjoyed a handful of good years and a respectable income. That was especially true in the 1920s. Their stocks were performing well, and despite the fact that most average Americans weren't invested in the equity markets, prairie settlers often were. They were risk-takers by temperament. However, that also meant the Wilders were vulnerable to a major market collapse—precisely the kind that happened in 1929. By the early 1930s, the family was desperate for additional sources of income.

All pioneers were resourceful; the needy and thin-skinned didn't make it that far west. However, not all pioneers happened to have a famous literary daughter in the family.

Rose Wilder Lane was in some ways very much like her mother—tough, resourceful, and fearless—but in almost every other way, not like her at all.

As soon as she was able, she ran as far as she could from her hardscrabble upbringing in the Midwest. She married. She divorced. She would not have any children who would die prematurely like her baby brother had. Lane's articles would appear in all the top magazines of the day, fetching hundreds (sometimes thousands) of dollars each. Remember, this is 1920s money, not today's money. To get a sense of the average rate per article we're talking about, multiply by ten. It's close enough.

Young Rose may have traveled far from home, but her heart and mind remained tethered to the prairie. She wrote stories of people who grew up on farms and went on to achieve greatness—figures like Herbert Hoover, Henry Ford, and Charlie Chaplin. These celebrated biographies gave Lane the literary connections with major New York publishers she would leverage for her mother's work in the years to come.

But before that could happen, Lane would venture even further. During a European trip in the 1920s, she met Helen Dore Boylston, a nurse injured in the First World War who would go on to write her own series of semi-autobiographical stories to wide acclaim. If most people know Boylston, they don't know her by that name. They remember her from the nickname Lane gave her when they met. When Lane asked her name, Boylston replied, "They call me 'trouble.'" That was what Lane would call her: "Troub."

Like Lane, Troub would never have children (and unlike Lane, wouldn't choose to marry either). Not quite the domesticated vision of pre-Depression-era America most of us imagine, is it? That's another myth to challenge and set aside. Many people—most, in fact—married and bore children. But not all. Not by a long shot. You might also be thinking: Lane and Troub were inseparable after they met, traveling the world together and even moving back to Missouri to the Wilder homestead in the early 1930s when things got tough. Were the two in a more-than-friends relationship? That wasn't something "talked about" very often in that era, but it's important to remember that gay, lesbian, bisexual, and queer relationships were not uncommon.

It also says something about Laura and Almanzo Wilder that they didn't simply tolerate Troub; they welcomed her. Almanzo was especially fond of his daughter's companion, and the two bonded over a shared love of horses.

The more challenging relationship was the strained one between a mother and daughter who were perhaps more alike than they cared to admit to each other. This tension, balanced with mutual respect, would define children's literature for a generation.

...

As we said, fortunately for Wilder, her daughter had a literary agent and publishing connections in New York.

Unfortunately, it didn't matter. At first.

Wilder's first manuscript—a biographical retelling of her childhood—was rejected out of hand. It shows the limits of even the most well-connected people. Their rejection was based on the same sound reasoning all publishers use: Who was the intended audience? That part wasn't clear. Memoirs often struggle with this. Unless the subject is a celebrity or the story is superbly compelling, they simply don't sell well. Wilder's story was harrowing but not uncommon. Plenty of pioneer children grew up as she did.

You might be inclined to think that gripping tales of stoic determination in the face of a fresh national catastrophe would be a must-read thriller. But they're not. During economic downturns, people will read uplifting stories about overcoming adversity (sometimes), but they tend to shy away from *depressing* stories in that genre. And Wilder's first manuscript was a bit...*too stoic*. People enjoy escape and distraction when stressed—more *King Kong* and *Snow White*, less locusts and blizzards. Publishers knew what their readers would buy; it was (and is) their business to know. More to the point, just like all businesses during the Great Depression, they couldn't risk a flop. Wilder's biography risked falling flat.

Despite the setback, Lane desperately wanted success for her mother. Part of that drive was supporting the family that was supporting her. Part of that was financial security. Part of that was avoiding poverty and destitution—anyone who has been truly poor (as in, wondering where food will come from) knows this feeling in their bones. However, it was *not* ego. How do we know Lane didn't want the success (at least partly) for herself? Because she kept her collaboration with her mother a secret.

In fact, it's only been in the past few decades that historians have examined primary sources (diaries and letters) closely enough to discover the truth. We'll discuss Caroline Fraser and Christine Woodside's groundbreaking research work soon enough, but for now, it's enough to know that both Wilder and Lane took their secrets to their graves.

Wilder had the stories, but Lane had the gift of words, publishing experience, and connections. It was Lane who asked her mother to recast her childhood not from the perspective of an adult looking back but as a child living through them. In short: Write children's stories.

It speaks to the pair's mutual respect that Wilder did just that, sending Lane a new manuscript for *Little House in the Big Woods*, a story set at the outset of her family's journey in Wisconsin. Lane enhanced the original, carefully edited the depressing parts, and submitted the new version.

It didn't take long to get the word back from Virginia Kirkus at Harper and Brothers.[3] In a reflection years later, Kirkus remembered that the story was so gripping that she rode past her train stop:

> The real magic was in the telling. One felt that one was listening, not reading. All of us were hoping for that miracle book that no Depression could stop.

From a publishing business perspective, kid lit was routinely a strong seller. However, before Wilder, very little was written about the pioneer era for *children*. Why? To understand, we need a brief detour into the state of education during the Great Depression.

. . .

General education has been a dream of America's founders since the country's earliest days. John and Abigail Adams, for example, wrote the right to childhood education into the Massachusetts state constitution, which is itself a model for the United States Constitution.[4]

They and others saw education as more than simply rote memorization or skills training, but as a place to instill morality and citizenship. John Dewey is the biggest proponent of this approach, beginning his writing in the late 1800s. He dubbed it "Progressive Education" after the Progressive movement was just getting started at that time.[5] He was passionate about educating *teachers* because those people have an outsize influence on the actual outcomes of the education process with students—especially young students.

---

3. Virginia Kirkus was a big deal in the publishing world, and frankly, still is. Her namesake company, Kirkus Reviews, still provides independent review services to both traditionally-published and self-published authors. The company has reviewed all my books so far.

4. Read more about that in Chapter 2 of *Marketer in Chief: How Each President Sold the American Idea* or on the Constitution Center's website.

5. Dewey is a fascinating figure, worthy of much more attention han we can give him here. Basically, he was the first American psychologist. For more, read *The Philosophy of John Dewey* in two volumes, edited by John J. McDermott.

However, despite all the high-minded ideals and almost universal agreement throughout American history that "education was critical to democracy," the reality did not match the rhetoric.

To put it mildly, schooling was a challenge.

As late as 1930—much later than you were probably thinking—149,000 of the roughly 238,000 elementary classrooms in the United States were still one-room schoolhouses. That's just shy of two-thirds. As a refresher, that's where one teacher handles all ages of students in one classroom at one time. In many rural areas and small towns (which still made up *most* of the school-aged population at the beginning of the Great Depression), that arrangement made sense. A schoolhouse averaged 22 students enrolled and only 15 in class on any given day.[6]

To Dewey's point, teacher education (and pay) were sorely lacking. A typical teacher outside of a major city was a local farmer's daughter with *a little* extra training.[7] She taught an average of 152 days each year, as opposed to today's 180-day standard instructional year, and could expect to earn $874 for her efforts. In today's money, that's $15,500. So, it was not a compelling, lucrative career. For the students, a typical day included memorizing provided texts and waiting for the teacher to come around and listen to their responses. Need to use the bathroom? The "well-equipped" schoolhouses featured an outhouse. Most featured a hole behind a tree. Forget about forced-air heating or air conditioning; these buildings were lucky to have a leak-proof *roof*.

Historian Andrew Gulliford summed it up this way:

> Rural schools were frequently overcrowded, materials were hard to obtain, and repairs and improvements were subject to the financial whims of parsimonious school boards hesitant even to replace dog-eared textbooks.

---

6. Education quality varied *much more* than it does today...and today's educational quality varies quite a bit from region to region.

7. Most, but not all. My great-grandfather was one of these teachers. I've got the grainy pictures to prove it—John Paul (JP) with a rag-tag group of a dozen or so kids of varying ages surrounding him. He went on to run a successful insurance brokerage in Southeast Minnesota.

The better word for "parsimonious" and "hesitant" is *cheap*. But why was that? Didn't everyone agree that education was critical? Sure, but not for the reasons you might be thinking—the high-minded ideals stuff. Oh, no.

The prevailing idea of education was an extreme version of meritocracy. The purpose was to separate the very few intelligent people from the teeming mass of idiots. What about those students who had the simple misfortune of being born into a rural area with an untrained teacher and a hole in the backyard for a toilet? The logic was brutal. If those students were brilliant and tough enough, they would find a way to succeed despite those disadvantages. It...wasn't exactly a nurturing environment.

That's not to say there weren't good teachers or that everyone thought this way—especially parents; more on that shortly—but it spoke to a difference in how most people saw the much-more-limited role of government before the Great Depression.

Given what we just discussed, it might be surprising that the *business* community was the strongest advocate for compulsory childhood education up to this point. It shouldn't be. They were externalizing the cost of job training. Since the Industrial Revolution took hold in the United States in the 1880s, factories and offices needed workers with basic reading, writing, and arithmetic skills. Their efforts were most pronounced in urban and suburban schools. Education provided not only future job training but also daytime childcare. Why was that important? It's one more myth we need to address. At least one in four women worked outside the home during the Great Depression—a significant increase over the 1920s—because they needed to work to help the family make ends meet.

Speaking of the Great Depression, as you might expect, the economic downturn *really* hurt schools. Budgets, such as they were, got cut. Teachers went unpaid. For their part, businesses were simply trying to survive. A long-term investment in workforce development was a luxury they could no longer afford to support with taxes and donations.

As you might also guess, education was a focus of the Progressive members of Roosevelt's new administration. As you might *not* guess, the focus wasn't on teacher training or educational standards. That's myth number...five? Six? It's difficult to keep count.

Hundreds (thousands) of school buildings from that era remain. Construction was a primary focus of "back to work" efforts embedded in the New Deal, and schools were no exception. But these weren't one-room schoolhouses. These were large, multi-grade buildings. How was that possible with so few students? One word: consolidation. The Great Depression saw a major consolidation from small, independent schools into *unified* school districts. The reason was simple: efficiency. Educating children became more standardized. Many people believe the business community (that wanted schools to train *workers*) encouraged this consolidation, but the Progressive administration pushed it through. Their goals were different (they wanted schools to train secular morality and citizenship), but the effect was the same: the industrialization of schooling in America. Whether the objective of factory education is to produce *workers* or *citizens* is a battle that continues to rage to this day.

On the positive side of the ledger, consolidation helped reduce per-student costs, equalized tax burdens, broadened the curriculum, (eventually) improved teacher preparation and performance (but not right away), increased instructional time in the year, boosted attendance, and dramatically improved the facilities most students used.

(We say "most" because this is the era of "separate but equal" in education from a racial lens. They were certainly separate. They were *not* equal.)

However, not everyone was on board with consolidation. Students, especially in rural areas, needed transportation. Busses cost money. Many communities lost their school because they were too small, and in the process, lost a center of their community. Taxes were better equalized, yes, but they went up at a time most could ill afford to pay. Yes, students had access to better facilities, materials, and curriculum, but each student received far less attention. And finally, with less classroom supervision and many more students came an increase in both physical and psychological bullying.

There are no easy answers *today*, and there certainly weren't in the 1930s. However, from the mid-1930s, education changed radically in the United States.

Still, you might have noticed that we only casually mentioned an essential stakeholder in this debate: the teacher. Unfortunately, New Deal programs largely *failed* to include increased teacher training and higher educational standards.

Part of the reason came from the Roosevelt Administration's strangely anti-elite view of teaching. They felt teachers needed very little additional formal training. Anyone could be a teacher, and restricting access to the profession was a sign of "professional" educators blocking access to new entrants to maintain their status.

Ultimately, we built plenty of new schools modeled on the factory ideal. We consolidated schools into districts. We added a lot of (poorly trained) teachers. We got efficiency. We didn't really get *effectiveness*.

Parents were not blind to what was happening—the pros or the cons. (Today, about 10 percent of all students attend religious schools, and another three to four percent are educated at home.) In the Great Depression, polling showed the importance of education *falling* in the broader list of concerns, but that doesn't mean parents simply gave up.

We're finally ready to circle back to the *publishers'* insight regarding children's books. They knew they'd sell. That's because parents were taking education into their own hands and buying their own books that instilled the lessons and skills *they* wanted their children to learn.

It's about time we truly understand what Wilder and Lane were trying to say in their books about a little girl on the prairie.

...

As it should be obvious by now, not everyone agreed with FDR's approach.

It was more than just political opposition, though there was plenty of that. This was different. This was grassroots opposition. Many people, especially in the country's vast interior, didn't appreciate the Federal government involving itself in what prairie settlers considered their business.

Of course, the Ingallses, Wilders, and Lanes understood the magnitude of the problem. They were also quick to take advantage of the Homestead Act, rural electrification programs, telephone service, and better roads. What bothered them were the rules, regulations, and restrictions—not to mention higher taxes—that came alongside all those benefits.

However, explaining people's frustration as accepting benefits without accompanying costs is too simplistic. It was a problem with the *mindset* these programs instilled. Something about the character of America was changing, and Wilder and Lane didn't like it. It's not difficult to imagine why. Remember where we started—a harrowing ten-year span of Laura's life when disease, starvation, and death were constant companions. When there was a problem on the prairie, people were used to handling it themselves. You might be able to call on your neighbor for help, but even the state government was many days away by foot or by horse. No one was coming to help. That bred a certain self-sufficient mindset that bristled at what Wilder called "too much whining" about economic issues in the cities. Yes, a bread line might be humiliating, but at the end of the line, at least there was bread.[8]

Both Wilder and Lane were what we would today call political *libertarians*. Reconsidering the *Little House* stories with that in mind, it's easy to understand the underlying message both women inserted into their children's stories. Rely on yourself, your family, and your local community. When times get tough, you persevere with grit, gumption, determination, and a cheerful attitude. All other times, you did your thing. Others did theirs. Live and let live.

These stories resonated *profoundly* with parents of the Great Depression who wanted to instill those values in their children at a difficult time. Was it the *real* story of Laura's upbringing? No. Was it the sanitized, kid-safe version? Yes. But isn't that what parents *often* share with their children?

How profoundly did those stories resonate? Wilder published five books during the Great Depression and three more during the war years that followed: *Little House in the Big Woods* (1932), *Farmer Boy* (1933), *Little House on the Prairie* (1935), *On the Banks of Plum Creek* (1937), *By the Shores of Silver Lake* (1939), *The Long Winter* (1940), *Little Town on the Prairie* (1941), and *These Happy Golden Years* (1943). They roughly parallel the major events in Laura's childhood, becoming the best-selling children's series of that era. Since then, the series (and a handful of additional books) have sold over 60 *million* copies, putting them in the top tier of children's books of all time.[9]

---

8. Harold Gray's Little Orphan Annie comic strip took a similar tack in the comics. He railed against FDR and government intervention in business. However, he never had the moral authority granted by Wilder's prairie upbringing. There aren't any solid biographies of Gray, which is a shame. The best places to look for more are collections of the original comic strips or his archived papers at Purdue University.

9. The top-seller (and it's not even close) is the *Harry Potter* series with over 600 million books sold.

But the influence is much deeper than that. Fans of the series go on pilgrimages to see the sites and homesteads. (State and local governments are keen to help you if you're interested. De Smet, South Dakota, isn't expecting many other tourists.) The influence crosses generations as well. The *Little House on the Prairie* television series ran for nine seasons (1974 to 1982), was nominated for 17 prime-time Emmys, and won four. It averaged more than 15 million viewers each season. As a reference point, *All in the Family* and *M*A*S*H* drew 20 million and 18 million viewers, respectively. The *Little House* was a big deal.

Wilder passed away in 1957 at 90 years old, which, if you count backward, means she *started* writing the series at 65. Her daughter Rose would never reveal her involvement in the series, satisfied that her mother's legacy—and the messages in the books—would live on. Lane would go on to help found the Libertarian Party in the United States in the 1950s and 1960s. Although the party often doesn't factor into the "top of the ticket" in most places, the ideas and ideals mother and daughter taught children through the *Little House* series are surprisingly pervasive, especially in the Midwest.

The rest of the pair's legacy is decidedly mixed. In *Prairie Fires: The American Dreams of Laura Ingalls Wilder*, Pulitzer Prize-winning author Caroline Fraser details the differences between Wilder's real life and the stories she chose to tell and uses diaries and letters to piece together her daughter's involvement. It's a must-read for fans of the series. However, Fraser wasn't the first. Two years earlier, in 2016, Christine Woodside reached the same conclusions in *Libertarians on the Prairie: Laura Ingalls Wilder, Rose Wilder Lane, and the Making of the Little House Books*. She explores more of the politics and philosophy embedded in the pages of each book. It's a must-read for those who want to better understand the mindset of middle America.

A more recent reconsideration comes from Wilder's portrayal of Native Americans in her books, with some groups (notably the American Library Association) removing her name from its children's book award. That's a bit ironic, given the Libertarian approach to racism in general—their perspective is that race is irrelevant; only the individual and their actions matter.

Despite the controversy, for nearly 100 years, parents have voted with their wallets with one of the most consequential decisions they can make: What values do they want to pass along to their children? Sixty million books seem to give us a clear answer.

Yes, Wilder's stories are as much fiction as fact. Perhaps a better word than *myth* is *parable*—an instructional story. During the worst of times, parents wanted to raise children with determination, perseverance, and, above all, hope.

ART IMITATES LIFE

F red Astaire wasn't amused. Neither was his dance partner, Ginger Rogers.

On the set of the upcoming Hollywood movie *Top Hat*, a film that would cement the duo as silver-screen icons, Rogers had an idea. If you're a fan of Golden Age cinema, you already know the scene we're talking about. For everyone else, let's set the stage.

The script called for an elegant ballroom dance, with Astaire wearing his soon-to-be trademark top hat, cane, and tailcoat. Rogers didn't just want to wear a lovely dress; she wanted to make a statement. She had an instinct for that sort of thing, but this particular fashion choice had…problems.

Rogers approached the costume designers to create a gown featuring hundreds of authentic ostrich feathers. As you might guess, being the largest bird comes with some of the largest feathers.[1] That makes the task a bit easier than covering the same amount of a dress with parrot feathers. Sure, they might be more colorful, but you'd need ten times as many. Even so, the dress required about

---

1. Though not the *longest* feathers. That honor belongs to the Crested Argus Pheasant sporting feathers reaching up to 5.7 feet in length.

$1,000 worth of feathers—about $23,000 in today's money—for one dress in one scene. That's expensive *today*. During the Great Depression, it was a significant investment. Despite the cost, Rogers knew the dress needed to be bold.

The first dress from costuming was indeed spectacular…until the pair started to dance.

Have you ever seen a chicken coop after a coyote gets in there? Astaire clearly had, because that's how he described the avian carnage on the dance floor after only a few steps. Feathers. Were. Everywhere.

Astaire was the ultimate perfectionist, and wardrobe malfunctions drove him berserk. (He hated wearing tails for precisely that reason. Unlike a flowing dress, he couldn't predict how they would move while he danced.) As the pair rehearsed, Astaire kept getting dislodged feathers flying in his face before they'd settle onto the dance floor.

To be fair, this was a dangerous situation for both of them. Random feathers covering the dance floor—which would move at the slightest whiff of air—created slick spots that could have caused a nasty fall. Neither Astaire nor Rogers could afford a rolled ankle or broken wrist.

In a characteristic rage, Astaire demanded that Rogers choose a different dress. (He had it written into his contract that he approved all costumes.) Rogers was heartbroken. The dress *was* stunning. More than that, it was *her idea*. She *knew* it would steal the show. She was comfortable going toe-to-toe with Astaire to argue her point, but this was too much. She started to cry. That's all it took for Rogers' mother (who often accompanied her on set) to rise to her daughter's defense. She laid into Astaire with a fury that only a mother whose little girl was crying could manage.

It was tense, to say the least, but Rogers would not relent. She *knew* this was right. We'll get to Astaire's talent for choreography, pacing, comedy, and singing later. We'll also describe how Astaire was, in fact, the better dancer. *Peerless* is the word most commonly used. Justifiably. (Some of you reading are furious at that assessment, but even Rogers admitted as much.) However, *Rogers* was the better actress. She better understood how the dress would appear on screen and the message it would send to the audience. She knew they would eat it up.

After a period of "negotiations," all parties agreed to allow the costume department to correct the problem.

In a solution that one must assume involved a shocking amount of glue and thousands of individual feathers stitched into the fabric, the dress finally held itself together.

The result, to Rogers' credit, was *iconic*. It's the scene everyone points to as perhaps the best dance pairing of all time, anywhere, on any screen. The dress makes Rogers appear to be floating along, guided by Astaire's gentlest of leading motions. It's stunning to watch.[2]

(Despite the costume department's best efforts, if you look closely enough, you can see a handful of feathers lose their grip, but the scene went off without a hitch.)

Astaire and Rogers were different heroes for Americans during the Great Depression. Yes, they represented an escape to a world of luxury, music, and dance when many people struggled to get enough to eat. But their relationship—both on screen and off—can tell us much more about the broader relationship between men and women during the 1930s. Economic and cultural pressures combined to force a rethinking and realignment of gender roles in a way no one had envisioned before.

This is a story of a partnership that created something more than the sum of its parts, even if both parties in the relationship didn't quite want to admit it.

We're not done seeing feathers fly.

Let's get started.

. . .

For those of you still smarting from the assessment (from dance professionals, it should be noted) that Astaire was the better dancer, there's likely a quip—attributed to Rogers years later, though she denied it—that she "could do anything Fred Astaire could do, only backward and in high heels."

Like most catchy sayings, this one has the benefit of conjuring not only a striking visual, but a deep feeling as well. Although Rogers probably never said

---

2. You can watch only that scene on YouTube if you don't want to buy or rent the full movie.

it, she channeled the frustration of many women who felt their accomplishments didn't hold the same weight as their male partners.

We'll get to that soon, but it's important to understand a bit more about the two people at the center of this conflict.

Using "high heels" to criticize Astaire was an odd choice, especially given his upbringing. Born Frederick Austerlitz, the younger of two siblings, he wasn't the "talented" one. That gift of fate belonged to his older *sister*, Adele Marie. "Dellie" was three years older and several inches taller than her brother for most of their formative years.

Creating a new family name for themselves that sounded vaguely like the then-famous "Astors," the Astaire family looked to their talented children as their ticket out of a hum-drum ordinary life in Omaha, Nebraska.[3] Well, talented *child*. And it wasn't their youngest boy. Dellie had a natural gift, which was evident from an early age. Fred was talented, but not to the same inherent degree. He always had to work harder than his sister to get the same result. Perhaps due to their upbringing and difference in natural ability, Adele would never quite feel the urge to work as hard to hone her talent, and Fred could never shake an inferiority complex that would drive his perfectionism.

Put simply, Fred was figuratively and literally in his sister's shadow. As dance partners, Fred was both younger and shorter, so he often played the *female* role. In other words, Fred Astaire *also* could do everything his sister could do, but backward and in high heels.

(Can we put that entire debate about shoes and direction to bed? It's a bit silly. Rogers wore heels, but not very high ones. In fact, they didn't have much more height than Astaire's tap shoes. Also, when you watch the two dance, *both* partners move in all directions. Okay, back to the story.)

---

3. To be fair, the Austerlitz surname wasn't their choice either. Many Jewish families in central Europe were forced to adopt family names that said something about them, their wealth, or their trades. Two obvious ones are "Goldstein" and "Rosenberg," as well as Loureiro (laurel tree) and Pereira (pear tree) further east on the Iberian peninsula. Many converted to Christianity, as was the case with the Austerlitz family. That name was common and denoted the family did not have any specific characteristic to anchor a name. One wonders what name they *might have chosen* had they known what Fred and Adele would become.

Adele and Fred cut their teeth on the Vaudeville circuit—traveling almost continuously and making a decent living—throughout their childhood.[4] As they matured, the pair made the leap to Broadway in New York and the West End in London. Not only did that improve their finances, it also exposed them to high society and top-tier entertainment industry connections. It's when Fred acquired a penchant for British tailoring, and Adele found herself a British nobleman to marry.

It was also about this time when Fred's tireless work started to pay off; he was eclipsing his sister's natural talent. It wasn't just his dancing skill, though that was considerable. He learned ballet (which he didn't like), ballroom (which suited his love of fine clothes), tap (which he clearly did), and swing (in which he had no equal). He also learned to play the piano (quite well, in fact), developed his singing voice, developed groundbreaking, complex choreography for his dance routines, and honed his comedic timing. Fred Astaire was a Renaissance-man performer in the mold of what people today might think of in the late Prince Rogers Nelson. (Who, by the way, deeply respected Astaire for precisely that reason.)

Despite that, it wasn't all upside for Astaire. Putting it diplomatically, he didn't have "leading man" looks. Astaire had an egg-shaped head, a weak chin, big eyes, bigger ears, and prematurely thinning hair. He might have weighed 130 pounds soaking wet, and we can only believe his 5-foot, 9-inch purported height if we include tap heels. (Other performers claim he was two inches shorter.)

He made up for those deficiencies by leaning into them. His looks gave him the license to use them for comedic effect—his huge, expressive eyes and forehead, especially. His ah-shucks personality gave him a sort of boy-next-door sex appeal that was hard to put your finger on but that audiences adored. And despite the oft-repeated (and not quite true) evaluation from a Hollywood talent scout, Astaire—"Can't act. Can't sing. Slightly bald. Can dance a little."—that man could dance your breath away. His movements were so fluid, even an *outstanding* dancer like Ginger Rogers (and his sister Adele, for that matter) looked a bit stiff and robotic next to him.

---

4. That was a sore point with regulators. It was about this time when child labor laws come into effect, especially with children under 14. Adele and Fred often needed to skirt these rules (or turn down gigs) until they came of age.

Bottom line: Astaire was ready to be on his own. He felt like he *deserved* to be on his own. And because he was still stung by losing his original dance partner (when Adele married, she left the performing arts), he didn't want to be "hitched" to another performer.

However, Astaire didn't realize that the audience *really* wanted a *pair*.

We've already met her, but let's get to know Rogers better, shall we?

. . .

Born Virginia Katherine McMath, Ginger Rogers was more than just an interesting stage name.

Many people think her first name was a nickname. They are correct, but for the wrong reason. It's not about strawberry blond hair or freckles, but instead, because a young cousin couldn't say "Virginia" and shortened it to Ginger.

The choice of "Rogers" isn't what most people think it is, either. Rogers was her *stepfather's* surname.

Her parents, Lela Emogene Owens, a newspaper reporter, scriptwriter, and movie producer, and William Eddins McMath, an electrical engineer, only had one child who survived. (An older sibling died in the hospital. Sadly, it was pretty common in the days before antibiotics.) McMath was a devout Christian Scientist. After Owens left him, he tried to reconnect with his family...by kidnapping his only daughter. Twice.

A divorce (naturally) followed.

Owens remarried John Logan Rogers, and although Ginger was never formally adopted, she took her stepfather's family name. Like the Astaires, the Rogers family didn't live on the coasts, near the cultural centers. They lived in Texas, which meant (in those days) that she'd need to move if she wanted any level of commercial success in the entertainment industry. And again, like the Astaires, Ginger's mother drove her early career. She routinely traveled to Hollywood and Broadway to pitch her daughter to screenwriters and directors. It's striking how similar their upbringings really were.

Want more?

Rogers' career mirrors the path the Astaires took from Vaudeville to Broadway as well. However, instead of crossing the pond to build a stage career in London, Rogers headed west to Hollywood to begin her film career. Like Fred's sister

Adele, Ginger had the looks and the talent. Unlike Adele, she was much more willing to work at it. (Though, it should be said that *no one* could keep up with Fred's rehearsal schedule. It made Ginger's feet bleed.) Although she never achieved Astaire's level of skill at dancing, she had a stronger command of the stage and could act in a wider variety of roles.

It's not as if supportive (pushy?) parents were (or are) new to Vaudeville, Broadway, or Hollywood. However, it helps us understand that Fred and Ginger understood each other. Both hailed from flyover country, and both were encouraged to develop their talents from childhood. In Ginger's case, she wanted to escape her home situation. In Fred's case, he wanted to escape his sister's shadow.

Their first chance to work together was on the set of the 1933 film *Flying Down to Rio*.

. . .

Astaire and Rogers received fourth and fifth billing on *Rio*, but they're the pair people remembered. Their dance numbers made up for a weak overall storyline. It was one of those surprising times when the backup characters stole the show.

It was the first time audiences saw what Rogers could do. She "made people feel like dancing with Fred Astaire was the most wonderful thing in the world." Her expressions and presence complemented his dance skills. Rogers could show the audience what *they* would feel if they were dancing alongside Astaire.

Why was that so important? Consider this. Imagine you're watching one of those talent shows with famous entertainment judges. (Thinking of one? Good.) When the *judges* are impressed, so are you. They're signaling to you consciously through their expressions and unconsciously through their inherent expert authority.

But Rogers was more than a backup dancer for Astaire. She was a true partner. He played off her expressions, often with comedic timing and his own aw-shucks expressions, making everyone in the audience imagine what it would be like to dance with *Rogers*.

Audiences couldn't help themselves. It was only a matter of time before executives at film company RKO did the obvious: give them the lead in a dance-centered musical.

From 1933 to 1939, Astaire and Rogers appeared together in nine musicals, all produced by RKO: *Flying Down to Rio* (1933), *The Gay Divorcee* (1934), *Roberta* (1935), *Top Hat* (1935), *Follow the Fleet* (1936), *Swing Time* (1936), *Shall We Dance* (1937), *Carefree* (1938), and *The Story of Vernon and Irene Castle* (1939).[5]

We won't be able to do the films justice in print, nor is that why we're here. This isn't a film critique. And it's a good thing it isn't. The plots...weren't that strong. They were *musicals*, not dramas, but that said, these films did much to reinvigorate the genre during the 1930s. If you enjoy a good musical (live-action or animated), you have this decade in RKO history to thank for it.

The on-screen chemistry between Rogers and Astaire made these films work, especially *Top Hat* and *Swing Time*. More than that, the pair insisted on a superb quality of dance musical filmmaking. Specifically, they avoided cut shots—that's when the best pieces of a dance routine are spliced together in the editing room. It's a good way to hide the fact a dancer can't quite master a series of steps in one take. Astaire and Rogers insisted the camera show their whole bodies and the entire sequence. This style not only showed off how good they were but also captivated the audience's attention in a way an edited scene could not. Additionally, Astaire insisted that music and dance were integral to the plot—there wasn't a dance just to have a dance or a song just to have a song. These were musicals, and they should act like it.

Conflict always bubbled beneath the surface—see previous discussion about feathers—but as long as the pair's movies did well at the box office, they could contain that tension. It's like a sports team with an underlying conflict between its players. So long as the team wins games, conflict gets swept up in positive emotions. Sometimes, that conflict is even celebrated as part of the *cause* of success; it keeps team members on their toes.

But when they start losing...

---

5. The second film, *The Gay Divorcee*, does not imply homosexuality. The word "gay" refers to "happy," which was (surprisingly) just as "problematic" for film studios attempting to follow the self-censorship regimen outlined in the so-called Hays Code. Showing divorced people as "happy" was frowned on. Divorce happened, but people weren't supposed to be happy about it, and the Code stipulated only married people were to be portrayed as satisfied and content.

By the end of the 1930s, the shine started to wear off. Although Rogers and Astaire raised the stakes (search for the dance scene on roller skates to see an example), audiences grew bored. That boredom showed up in box office numbers, and the lack of performance brought conflict back to the surface.

For her part, Rogers wanted to expand her acting range; she didn't want to be typecast as *either* a dancer who could only do musicals *or* Astaire's partner. For his part, Astaire always resented having a "locked-in" partner and wanted to show he could succeed on his own.

Both were correct in their own ways, but neither fully recognized that what they could accomplish together was more than they could manage alone.

That tension mirrored the broader changes in gender dynamics driven by the Great Depression. Stable relationships with some underlying stress could survive "good times" and even minor shocks, but not as tense months ground on into years.

Let's turn our attention to the broader conflict.

...

In our discussions about the Great Depression to this point, we've usually focused on economic conditions and how those factors impacted all aspects of culture—the products we bought, the entertainment we enjoyed, and the heroes we chose.[6] However, we haven't talked much about one of the most obvious impacts—the relationships closest to home—between married men and women.

Let's start in the easiest place: employment—specifically, how having (or not having) a stable job impacted household finances. As many as 25 percent of all men were out of work at the height of the Great Depression, but that figure doesn't address two aspects you wouldn't immediately consider. The first was job insecurity. Even if you weren't unemployed now, you *could be* very soon. Many people would find a job only to have that job last only a few weeks. You may not be unemployed today, but that didn't mean you wouldn't be tomorrow.

Second, just because you had a job didn't mean the job was full-time. Many job seekers would take what they could get. That included day labor or part-time

---

6. We haven't talked much about *malnutrition*, but we will in the next book in this series focusing on the war years. A startling number of young men appearing before draft boards we unfit for service.

work. Also, remember that jobs didn't pay as well, either. We've discussed how prices (for example, to Astaire and Rogers' movies) fell during the Great Depression, making it challenging to compare box office returns to today's numbers (or even numbers from a decade before in the Roaring 20s). But wages *also* fell during the 1930s. Although things you may buy might be cheaper, taking home less money doesn't feel good.

At this point, when we say "job seeker," we usually mean *male* workers and applicants. However, many women found jobs during the Great Depression to supplement family incomes. Over the decade, the number of employed women jumped from 10.5 to 13 million—an increase of nearly 25 percent.

As you might not guess, it was *easier* for women to find work. That's because so-called "women's work," such as clerical positions, telephone operators, and seamstresses, were more insulated from economic conditions. That didn't mean it was *well-paid* work. Women earned less than men, in many cases, by law and statute, not simply custom or misogyny. Many businesses found that it was cheaper to hire women and took advantage. That was partly the reason for the (seemingly baffling) response from the *female* Secretary of Labor in the Roosevelt Administration, who advocated for policies that stipulated that when the male household member found work, businesses *must* let go of the woman they had hired. They didn't want businesses, through cost control measures, to prolong male unemployment.

Perhaps the larger reason women could find work was psychological. *Men wouldn't do it*. Even when offered "women's work" positions, men would rather remain unemployed.[7] That may seem startling given the level of the economic crisis, but we're talking about humans. Humans are not rational creatures. We *rationalize*.

These economic issues unearthed and amplified existing conflicts in the gender power dynamic, surfacing them in surprising ways.

---

7. It's even more striking that man would take jobs formerly held by African American and immigrant men, but not women. It's easy to say that sexism was stronger than racism, but a simpler explanation would hold that it was more personal: husbands and wives lived together. Men of different races did not.

Researchers weren't blind to these dynamics as they were happening. Sociologist Mirra Komarovsky noted in her 1940 book, *The Unemployed Man and His Family*, that husbands and wives would often stop having sex after the man lost his job. Researcher Eli Ginsburg found a similar pattern, writing that some women would refuse to engage in sex with their husbands because he was no longer "supporting her" and didn't "deserve it."

Both perspectives treat sex as somehow transactional. It seems more reasonable to explain the change in sexual habits between married couples as a mix of shame and depression on the part of the husband not being able to fulfill his "provider" duties, economic stress dampening sex drive for both parties, and poor timing from both people working whatever job they could get—often with conflicting schedules. We have plenty of evidence (simply read the diaries of couples during that era) that men and women enjoyed sex and wanted more of it.

Speaking of marriage, new unions fell during the 1930s, reaching a low point of 7.9 per 1,000 people in 1932, down from 10.1 per 1,000 people in 1929. Given the state of the panic that developed after the stock market crash, many couples weren't feeling blissful. However, marriage rates recovered within two years and would hold steady for the rest of the decade. That said, birth rates *did not* recover. That had been happening since the 1920s (and the broad introduction of effective birth control measures—condoms and diaphragms) but accelerated during the Great Depression. Again, this isn't surprising. Children are expensive. Ask anyone who has them. Many parents chose to limit their family size for economic reasons. The birth rate fell from 181 per 10,000 women in 1921 to 152 by 1928 and to 126 in 1935 before flattening out.

(Speaking of the *opposite* of marriage, divorces increased, though many couples would not go through the formal process. It's not simply because of the social taboo—although it was partly that—but because the couple couldn't afford it. It's estimated that as many as 1.5 million couples lived apart in a sort of "poor man's divorce." It's one of those things that makes census and statistical data challenging to read.)

The government, as we've seen, delivered a mixed response. Secretary of Labor Frances Perkins (the first woman to hold the role, it should be noted) wasn't against *female* employment, just *married* female employment. She, like most other officials, believed that labor market health depended on *male* employment.[8] It wouldn't be until decades later that retrospective analysis shows the market grew in absolute terms as women entered it. In other words, from an economic perspective, female employment helped. The social impacts are another matter, as we've also seen. Whether we judge those changes as *good* or *bad* isn't as important as understanding the nature of the *change* itself.

This change didn't simply impact married couples, but those approaching typical marriage age as well. (For men in 1935, age 27, and women, age 24.) Although very few men *or* women attended college before the 1950s, they also changed.

Those who could afford it often entered college because it meant avoiding the job market. That was true for both men and women. Complicating matters, college women weren't keen to get married to men without job prospects, so this was the beginning of the era that saw women attend college and attain better degrees in more competitive fields, including scientific and business degrees. (This would aid the upcoming war effort and space race in unanticipated ways, but no one knew that then.) This certainly didn't mean that men and women were treated equally on campus, but it did mark an inflection point that continues today, where over half of all undergraduates are women.

One surprising example of this newfound power was women's college athletics. In a history of the University of Washington, the daily student newspaper reported on a new trend. They noticed the increased popularity of women's sports and decided to find a way to capitalize on it.

> In November of 1932, the "Innovations Column" began to run an advertisement for new, more comfortable sports clothing for "the coed who loves to feel dainty and feminine even while she's dressed for sport." The appearance of sports clothing advertising targeted toward women demonstrates not only increased demand

---

8. Though not all. First Lady Eleanor Roosevelt wrote *It's Up to the Women* in 1933. In it, she advocated for a more expansive role for women in society and in the household. She was certainly a trailblazing feminist, but it seems more that women were well on their way to adopting a new role well ahead of the article's publication.

for sports-related products among women and women's increasing interest in sports but also how rapidly women's participation in sports could change daily culture and social expectations on campus.

Considering all these factors, it's unsurprising that people wanted to escape to the fantasy world Rogers and Astaire created—a world with elegant dances, romantic courtships, and happily ever afters. In many ways, what we remember from our grandparents' (or great-grandparents') generation is a similar story of perseverance and happiness. But just like the story of the duck on the surface of the lake—appearing calm but paddling like crazy—most couples during the Great Depression were trying to make the best of it.

What they're telling us through their experience is the lesson Astaire and Rogers learned as well: The whole is greater than the sum of its parts...but it took patience, understanding, and faith. Gender roles needed a rethink. It wouldn't work for everyone, but most couples found a way.

...

That went for Astaire and Rogers, too. Even today, when you say one name, the other immediately springs to mind. The pair meant more to their audience than either of them individually. Both would come to realize that in the decades that would follow.

For her part, Rogers got her wish to expand into new roles. She won the Academy Award in 1941 for her part in *Kitty Foyle*, appropriately subtitled "The Natural History of a Woman." Rogers stuck with film company RKO, and both of them benefitted from the arrangement. Building on this drama's success, she played the wisecracking flapper lead in 1942's *Roxie Hart*, set at the end of Prohibition. That film would serve as the template for the 1975 musical *Chicago*.

She played a prostitute's daughter in one RKO film (a drama), married three different men in a comedy, and pretended to be a woman pretending to be a 12-year-old girl in another. (Lela Rogers, Ginger's real-life mother, also stars in this film as her mother.)

Success followed Rogers after she left RKO as well. Successful films included *Tender Comrade* (1943), *Lady in the Dark* (1944), and *Week-End at the Waldorf*

(1945). During the war years, Ginger Rogers was the highest-paid Hollywood actor, man or woman. She even reunited for one more film with Astaire in 1949, which was a strong success for both of them.

Although many analysts claim Rogers' career peaked by the end of the 1940s, she went on to a blockbuster stage career at the West End in London in the 1960s, raking in the Pounds and becoming the highest-paid actor in the United Kingdom as well.

Rogers remained on good terms with Astaire throughout her life, passing away in 1995 at age 83.

Astaire also found success, though being the perfectionist he was, he struggled to come to grips with it, "retiring" on at least two occasions. He starred with multiple dance partners—Rita Hayworth being the most famous second to Rogers—and co-starred in roles with icons like Bing Crosby. (Can you still hum the melody to *Puttin' On The Ritz*? If you can't, ask your parents.) After retiring and unretiring, Astaire expanded his range into non-dancing dramas and comedies. He even started skateboarding in his 70s. If there were any septuagenarian who could shred like Tony Hawk, Astaire would be that guy.

Despite a spectacular career that would be the envy of nearly any Hollywood actor, the irony is striking. A man with such a natural sense of physical rhythm could never find that sense of pace in his own life. Part of that insecurity could have come from the loss of his wife from breast cancer, to whom he was deeply devoted. Unlike Rogers, who married five times and bounced back each time, Astaire lost his wife Phyllis in 1954. He would remarry, but not until very late in life. He was a deeply personal man strongly attached to his female partners—his sister, his best dance partner, and his wife—all of whom he lost.

Astaire died in 1987 at age 88.

In all this discussion of difficulty, stress, and conflict, it's easy to overlook the *positive* change from the upheaval in gender dynamics of the 1930s. This crucible would create the so-called "Greatest Generation," who would pull the United States (and its allies) through the Second World War and build a seemingly unstoppable commercial powerhouse. Yes, that stress broke some people. It led to abuse and abandonment. But for many—perhaps most—it helped change what a marriage meant. It was not a contract to be kept for whatever reason but a partnership that would endure and grow through mutual understanding and to the benefit of both. Through thick and thin. In sickness and in health. For richer or poorer.

Sure, sometimes the feathers fly, but the Great Depression taught us the benefits of finding a great dance partner.

CONCLUSION
THE GREAT OPPORTUNITY

M ost of us weren't alive during the Great Depression.

My grandparents, and probably yours if they're of that vintage, have passed away. When that happens, we're likely to remember—*and misremember*—their past by comparing it to something more recent. In this case, I'm referring to the so-called "Great Recession."[1]

In the United States, the recession (as defined by economists) officially lasted from December 2007 to June 2009. However, like all economic downturns, the impacts began before the official start and persisted long after the official end.

Here are a few examples: Gross Domestic Product (GDP) fell 4.3 percent and didn't recover until 2011. Household net worth fell further—17.3 percent—and didn't recover until 2012. Employment dropped 6.2 percent (translating to 8.6 million people who lost their jobs) and didn't recover until 2014. At its peak in October 2009, the U.S. unemployment rate reached 10.0 percent and would not recover until 2016.

---

1. Interesting that growth rates were positive for huge chunks of the globe—much of South America, Africa, India, China, and Australia. The Great Recession was an American, European, and Russian phenomenon. There is some doubt about GDP figures in *some* of those countries, and how they dropped from higher highs, but it should be noted that the Great Recession was not the same everywhere. In that way, it is very similar to the Great Depression.

Both the Great Depression and the Great Recession reshaped the political landscape. In 1932, Republican Herbert Hoover lost to Democrat Franklin Roosevelt, ushering in the "New Deal." In 2008, Republican John McCain lost to Democrat Barack Obama, ushering in the first African American president.

Although both economic struggles were unique to their time, the Great Depression and the Great Recession *quite literally* hit home for everyday Americans. One of FDR's signature programs was the Federal Housing Administration (FHA)—an agency tasked with underwriting fixed-rate, 30-year loans that allowed millions of people to own their own homes. Before then, homebuyers faced mortgages with adjustable rates and massive balloon payments. It's ironic, isn't it, that in 2008, about 10 million people lost their homes as adjustable-rate mortgages spiked and balloon payments came due.

In an echo of bullfrog farms in the 1930s, millions of people turned to gardening. The financial system seemed on the verge of collapse, and you couldn't eat money...no matter how much of it you had. The Great Depression and the Great Recession might have been distinct from an economic perspective, but they sure felt the same to people living through them. Quite frankly, people were terrified.

Like the Great Depression, the *psychological* impact of the Great Recession was just as profound—perhaps more so.

Our literature mirrors those emotions. In the 1930s, we immortalized the human cost of the Great Depression in John Steinbeck's *The Grapes of Wrath*. Although this fictional narrative painted an incomplete picture, the emotional impact carried far further than the facts—most of which people would not know, not care about, or care to forget.

In the Great Recession, our historical reckoning was a bit different. Our best example is the true story of the (very few) people who saw the housing bubble getting ready to pop. Through various means, they took advantage of the situation to become rich when the market finally collapsed. *The Big Short: Inside the Doomsday Machine* by Michael Lewis retells those stories and, through them, explains how the American housing and financial markets failed to protect the average person while enriching grifters and opportunists.

The book made a splash in 2010, but it wasn't until five years later, when the film adaptation hit theaters, that the message sunk home. The movie features a who's who of Hollywood A-listers—Brad Pitt, Ryan Gosling, Steve Carell, and Christian Bale—but it was the interjected explanations that translated complex economics into everyday language that truly solidified the cultural impact.

Here's a taste (pun intended) from celebrity foodie Anthony Bourdain explaining the inner workings of a so-called "Collateralized Debt Obligation," or CDO, using an analogy everyone would understand:

> OK, I'm a chef on a Sunday afternoon, setting the menu at a big restaurant. I ordered my fish on Friday, which is the mortgage bond that Michael Burry shorted. But some of the fresh fish doesn't sell. I don't know why. Maybe it just came out halibut has the intelligence of a dolphin. So, what am I going to do? Throw all this unsold fish, which is the BBB level of the bond, in the garbage, and take the loss? No way. Being the crafty and morally onerous chef that I am, whatever crappy levels of the bond I don't sell, I throw into a seafood stew. See, it's not old fish. It's a whole new thing! And the best part is, they're eating 3-day-old halibut. *That* is a CDO.

No, the movie version wasn't fictional, but clever filmmaking gave this dry subject the emotional punch it needed. The film had everything—the heroes (the few people who saw the situation and profited from it), the villains (the leaders either too stupid to see the same thing or, *more to the point,* the systemic problems that led to the crisis), and the victims (everyone who owned a home or worked a regular job).

The heroes in this story seemed to have learned the lesson from this book: with great challenge comes great opportunity. *But wait.* Is this just a story of a handful of socially awkward guys who saw what no one else saw and found a way to make themselves rich? Is this just a story of a broken system bound to reassemble itself and replay the same scenes? Is the average person just a foil—a victim, a non-player character—in this drama?

No.

We're not.

Let's have another (brief) look at how the Great Recession, like its tougher forebearer, catalyzed innovation.

...

The "shorters" weren't the only ones to see an opportunity in all the housing market chaos.

Plenty of people were trying to find ways to earn a little extra money to help cover mortgage payments and maintenance. And just like mini-golf courses during the Great Depression, clever entrepreneurs would find a way to make use of underused properties. Brian Chesky, Joe Gebbia, and Nathan Blecharczyk were struggling to pay rent when they noticed that all the hotels in the San Diego area were booked for a conference. They decided to rent out their living room for the weekend.

That was the first Airbnb.

However, innovation didn't end with the housing market. Consider this list of companies: Uber, Groupon, Venmo, WhatsApp, Square, Dropbox, Glassdoor, Fitbit, Slack, Smashburger, and Warby Parker all got their start in the worst of (recent) times.

Innovation also continued at major research universities and think tanks. Scientists at Northwestern University, Illinois, proved that CRISPR gene editing technology could act on DNA, not just the simpler RNA, paving the way for new therapies. 4G wireless technology dramatically improved smartphone connectivity, making apps like Uber feasible for daily use. Other notable breakthroughs include cement that eats smog, camera pills you swallow, and wind turbines that float at high altitudes to catch the never-ending wind of the jet stream.

However, perhaps the best example of the unification of product, entertainment, and hero was the introduction of the iPhone in 2007. It's easy to forget that Steve Jobs announced the iPhone at the height of the Great Recession. Between January (when the iPhone was announced) and June (when you could get one), things clearly had gone from bad to worse...and would get *even worse* in the months to come. Regardless, tens of thousands of people waited in lines outside Apple stores to buy one.

Yes, part of the reason was the product itself, but that couldn't explain it. Other "smartphones" were (technically) better. Yes, part of the reason was the entertainment value. The iPod music and media player was already a hit, and this new Phone combined those into one device, but an iPod was a *lot* cheaper. And yes, Steve Jobs had reinvigorated a slumbering, floundering tech giant on his triumphant return a decade before in 1997.

However, none of those aspects alone explains the iPhone's success. Combining those three factors—the ones we learned in this book—helps us understand what the smartphone means to us today.

But was innovation in the Great Recession just another story of well-funded and well-connected people convincing us to buy things we (probably) could live without?

No.

It's much more than that.

...

It all comes down to how you define "ingenuity" from the average person.

Robert W. Fairlie and his colleagues at the University of California, Santa Cruz, found that the Great Recession caused the most significant spike in entrepreneurship in decades. (Bluntly, since the last major recession in the late 1970s and early 1980s.) Entrepreneurship rates were highest in areas where job losses were the worst. That makes sense, doesn't it? More people out of work makes the pool of people exploring their options larger. These are everyday businesses you've probably never heard of—handyman services, Airbnb cleaners, pop-up retail, ghost kitchens, craft sales on Etsy, farmer's markets, and everything else under the sun.

They didn't make the cover of *Fortune*. That doesn't mean they weren't important.

However, you may read *other studies* that show innovation, R&D spending, and new "startups" actually slowed down. Again, it's all in how you define terms.

Let's talk about big companies first. Are we talking about "research" or "development?" They are not the same thing. Research is what you think it is: A goal-centric process of open-ended discovery. Think of a research lab or startup "garage." It's messy, chaotic, and fluid. You never quite know what you're going to get. By contrast, *Development* is bringing the best of those ideas to market. It's still difficult, but it is a different challenge. You've got a great idea; now, you need to convince customers to buy it. During recessions, big companies often cut *both* R and D. It's short-sighted, but it happens. Those companies that invest during downturns tend to come out better, but it's hard to justify when you're just trying to survive until the next quarter.

Also, be careful when you read about "startups" and "small business"; those aren't what you think. Usually, startups refer to companies that hire employees and receive significant outside funding. Small business usually refers to businesses employing fewer than 500 people. New businesses founded by everyday people do *not* often meet those criteria—at least, not at first. How many of the companies we discussed in this book would have qualified under that? Very few.

We're focused on how *everyday* people made the best of the worst of times, not established companies. Yes, we can learn something from big companies and funded startups, but we're really paying attention to the creativity happening beneath the surface.

In both the Great Depression and the Great Recession, many Americans re-learned the lesson our grandparents have been trying to reteach us: You may not be able to control what happens, but you can control what it means to you, and that gives you the power to do something about it. Or, perhaps more elegantly said: When the going gets tough, the tough get going.

There aren't many of our grandparents around to remind us, but we have our collective memories. I still occasionally roll spare change and take it to the bank. No, it doesn't make any (financial) sense, but it helps remind me that every penny counts.

That said, we still have a few of those mentors with us.

I'm thinking specifically of Naomi Whitehead, who is 115 years old as of this writing. Born in 1910, she was a young woman during the Great Depression, so she certainly needed to find a way to make it work. It seems fitting to give our grandparents the last word. Mine would have agreed with her, and yours probably would, too.

When a reporter asked the secret to her longevity and success, she replied with the characteristic directness of her generation:

Work hard.

ACKNOWLEDGMENTS

There are dozens of people I need to thank—early readers, coaches (thank you, Stef, Kurt, Raj, Michael, and Tabitha), and the best dance partner I could hope for (thanks, dear). I couldn't have done it without you. However, there are four people who I can't thank...at least in person.

As you might be able to guess by now, my grandparents inspired this book. Vivian and John feature prominently in the introduction, so you've already gotten a chance to get to know them a bit. Maybe they remind you of your grandparents? I hope so. They continue to guide my career. But like most of you, I have two sets of grandparents, and they deserve no less appreciation. José and Zoila emigrated from Cuba in the 1960s, leaving behind everything they had (and I mean everything) for the *chance* to make it in the United States. In one way, their Miami home shared nothing in common with Vivian and John's slice of small-town Americana. However, in every way that mattered, they were the same. For all they had endured, it would have been understandable for them to retreat to bitterness and anger. But they didn't. They worked hard, of course, but they had a joy for life that's hard to describe in words. As this generation of people passes away, have we forgotten how to make the best of a bad situation? I hope not. I want to thank them for reminding us that it can be done. It *should* be done. And God willing, it will be done.

KEY PEOPLE

CHAPTER 1

Richard Gurley Drew (June 22, 1899 – December 14, 1980)

Drew was the inventor most singularly responsible for the creation of the first masking and clear cellphone tapes during his career at Minnesota Mining and Manufacturing Company (3M) in St. Paul, Minnesota, during the 1920s and 1930s. His name appears as the primary inventor or co-inventor on dozens of products, including adhesive sheets, dispensers, stenciling, and process improvements.

William Lester McKnight (November 11, 1887 – March 4, 1978)

A businessperson, executive, and philanthropist, McKnight spent his entire professional career with Minnesota Mining and Manufacturing Company (3M) in St. Paul, Minnesota. Starting as an assistant bookkeeper in 1907, his ideas helped put the company on sound financial footing, eventually elevating him to the helm of the company in 1929. He served in that role for the next 20 years, overseeing 3M's massive expansion during the Great Depression and war years. His guiding management philosophy may be summed up as: "Take good people and leave them alone."

CHAPTER 2

Leopold Saxe Godowsky Jr. (May 27, 1900 – February 18, 1983)

Along with Leopold Mannes, Godowsky was the first to create a commercially viable color photographic film. The invention is widely credited with kicking off the color photography industry in the United States and cementing the primacy of the Eastman Kodak Company as the world's premier innovator and marketer of photographic technology. Godowsky was also a trained classical musician, playing the violin and piano.

Leopold Damrosch Mannes (December 26, 1899 – August 11, 1964)

Along with Leopold Godowsky, Mannes was the first to create a commercially viable color photographic film. Like Godowsky, he was also an accomplished classical musician. While Godowsky continued inventing new products for Kodak, Mannes returned to his classical music career after co-inventing Kodachrome color film.

George Eastman (July 12, 1854 – March 14, 1932)

Eastman was an American inventor and businessperson best known for his namesake company, Eastman Kodak. The name "Kodak" is a complete fabrication. Eastman was reputed to have enjoyed the sound of the letter "K" and wanted to begin and end his company name with strong consonants. The word also had the benefit of being short (five letters) and simple enough to avoid any mispronunciation. Kodak was responsible for inventing and marketing the first affordable camera system for everyday use – the Brownie – as well as dozens of other innovations throughout its long history. Eastman committed suicide in 1932 after a debilitating illness left him in constant pain.

CHAPTER 3

Albert Broel, L.L.B., M.D. (aka Albert Plater, aka Dr. Albert Broel – Plater, aka Count Broel-Plater, 1889-1966)

Although he used the LLB and MD designations throughout his adult life, Broel was (to the best of our evidence) neither a licensed lawyer nor a licensed medical doctor. A Russian/Polish immigrant after World War I (and possibly royalty, though that was disputed), Broel established himself as an entrepreneur in several ventures, including a by-mail matchmaking service, bullfrog breeder, bullfrog merchant, bullfrog leg cannery operator, bullfrog products distributor, and all-around bullfrog educator and promoter. His daughter, Bonnie Broel, is a fashion designer and museum curator in New Orleans, Louisiana, USA.

CHAPTER 4

Clifford E. Clinton (August 3, 1900 – November 20, 1969)

A Los Angeles restauranteur and political activist, Clinton was most well-known during the 1930s as the proprietor of Clifton's Restaurants ("Pacific Seas" Clifton's Cafeteria and the Brookdale Cafeteria) and for successfully mounting a campaign to recall LA mayor Frank Shaw in 1936. His "penny restaurants" were unique in that they engaged his consumers in multiple ways rather than simply providing food relief. For example, he invited their feedback on the quality and selection of the food, assisted them with personal problems, and offered free (or low-cost) leisure and entertainment activities.

CHAPTER 5

Madeleine Vionnet (June 22, 1876 – March 2, 1975)

Vionnet was a leading French fashion designer, most famous for the "bias cut" innovation, which allowed garments to flow more seamlessly over curves in the human body. Her fashions became iconic during the 1930s as female movie stars wore her dresses on the big screen. She championed paid holidays and maternity leave, daycare, and healthcare for her workers, as well as copyright laws for her industry. She retired in 1940 at the outbreak of World War II. A private person, she never attained the prominence of Coco Chanel in the fashion world, although they were contemporaries.

CHAPTER 6

Bernard Rosecrans Hubbard (November 24, 1888 – May 28, 1962)

Jesuit (Catholic) priest and professor of Geology at the University of California at Santa Clara, Hubbard popularized the Alaskan wilderness through a series of books, articles, and lectures throughout the United States beginning in the Great Depression. Nicknamed "The Glacier Priest," he was a highly sought-after lecturer who commanded some of the highest speaking fees in the world. That income allowed him to fund 31 expeditions. Hubbard's legacy may be seen in other nature popularizers in the following decades. He's less well-known for his positive influence on "pet culture" in America, primarily through his fondness for his sled dog team and regular companion, Katmai.

CHAPTER 7

Gerhard Johannes Paul Domagk (October 30, 1895 – April 24, 1964)

Domagk was a German medical scientist and researcher who first discovered the antibiotic properties of sulfa compounds through work with IG Farben's chemical dyes. He went on to be awarded the Nobel Prize in 1939 but was forced to decline the award by Germany's Nazi government. (Domagk spent a week in jail after personally petitioning German Chancellor Adolf Hitler to allow him to accept the award.) He developed additional antibiotics and cancer treatments after World War II.

CHAPTER 8

William Griffith Wilson (November 26, 1895 – January 24, 1971)

More commonly known as "Bill W," Wilson co-founded Alcoholics Anonymous in 1935 along with Dr. Robert Smith, better known as "Dr. Bob." The program developed as an outgrowth of the religious Oxford Group, but shed its evangelical Christian foundation to become a worldwide, secular, and strictly non-political organization. He was the primary author of the so-called "Big Book" of Alcoholics Anonymous, still in print today. Today, the organization has over 120,000 registered groups and nearly two million members worldwide.

Dr. Robert Holbrook Smith (August 8, 1879 – November 16, 1950)

Smith co-founded Alcoholics Anonymous in 1935 along with Bill Wilson. He struggled with alcohol as early as his college days, forcing him to stay in medical school for two extra semesters. Despite a thriving medical practice, Smith continued to abuse alcohol despite efforts from his wife and colleagues. Because Prohibition allowed licensed doctors access to alcohol, Smith continued to drink heavily throughout the 1920s and early 1930s until he met Wilson in 1935. Their meeting on May 12, 1935, is considered the symbolic founding of AA.

CHAPTER 9

Elizabeth J. Magie Phillips (May 9, 1866 – March 2, 1948)

More commonly known as Lizzie Magie, she was a writer, feminist, advocate for Georgian economics (single tax), and game designer. In 1904, she created and patented *The Landlord's Game*, which inspired *Monopoly*. (It should be noted that she received her patent before women could vote in federal elections in the United States.) She renewed her patent with revisions in 1924. She was compensated for her patents by Parker Brothers, and the company published her games, but they never attained the success of *Monopoly*. She continued teaching economics until she died in 1948.

Charles Brace Darrow (August 10, 1889 – August 28, 1967)

A heater salesperson in the Philadelphia area, Darrow and his wife discovered people playing early versions of *The Landlord's Game* and *Monopoly* during the Great Depression. He refined the rules, improved the artwork, and marketed the game himself before eventually selling the rights to the game (along with a commission on every game sold) to Parker Brothers. Darrow received a patent for the game, although it's debatable if the U.S. Patent Office should have issued it. Historians recognize Darrow's role as *one of the people* who created the game, but certainly not the sole inventor.

Ralph Anspach (March 15, 1926 – March 2022)

A professor at San Francisco State University, Anspach, is most famous for creating the board game *Anti-Monopoly*, which was created in response to the popular board game *Monopoly*. In short, he wanted to show players that monopolies were *not* desirable economic outcomes. The resulting trademark lawsuits with

Parker Brothers uncovered Magie's original patents for *The Landlord's Game*. His continued research was the basis for several articles and books.

CHAPTER 10

Merian Caldwell Cooper (October 24, 1893 – April 21, 1973)

Most famous for his work on the original *King Kong* film in the 1930s, Cooper was an early nature documentarian along with partners Ernest Schoedsack and Ruth Rose. Before his movie career, Cooper was a pilot in the United States and Polish armed forces. He was shot down over Germany in the First World War and was rescued (and rehabilitated) by German surgeons. He also served as a Colonel in the Second World War in the U.S. Pacific Theater.

Ernest Beaumont Schoedsack (June 8, 1893 – December 23, 1979)

Nicknamed "Shorty," the 6'5" Schoedsack was an early nature documentary filmmaker in the 1920s as well as a pilot and world traveler. With Merian Cooper and Ruth Rose (whom he married), Schoedsack helped bring *King Kong* to the big screen, focusing on the realism of the natural environment and interactions with native people, whom he knew from firsthand experience.

Ruth Rose (January 16, 1896 – June 8, 1978)

Uncharacteristically for a woman in the 1920s, Rose served as the official historian on a New York Zoological Society expedition to the Galapagos Islands. Her field experience, organizational skills, and writing talent were indispensable to the partnership with Merian Cooper and Ernest Schoedsack (who she married) to bring *King Kong* (and several other nature documentaries) to the big screen throughout the late 1920s and 1930s.

CHAPTER 11

Edwin S. Lowe (1910 in Poland, unclear records – February 23, 1986)

Lowe was a salesperson, toy designer, and real estate developer best known for renaming and popularizing the game Bingo. After its initial success, he created the E. S. Lowe Company to manufacture Bingo supplies and market the game. He also purchased the rights to Yahtzee, bringing the game from private yacht clubs to the mass market. Milton Bradley bought his company in 1973 for $26 million (about $185 million today).

CHAPTER 12

John Garnet Carter (February 9, 1883 – July 21, 1954)

Considered one of the "fathers" of miniature golf, Carter was a real estate investor and developer looking for new ways to draw people to underused property during the late 1920s and Great Depression. He patented the name "Tom Thumb Golf" and opened the first course near his hotel in Lookout Mountain, Georgia, in 1927. His success spawned thousands of imitators nationwide, with developers opening courses on all types of abandoned lots. Carter took advantage of this growth by manufacturing and marketing mini-golf obstacles and supplies.

William Averell Harriman (November 15, 1891 – July 26, 1986)

Harriman is best known for his role as Secretary of Commerce under President Harry Truman and the 48th Governor of New York. However, he also served as Chairman of the Union Pacific Railroad during some of its most challenging years in the Great Depression. Harriman spearheaded the creation of the Sun Valley ski resort in Idaho, which was designed as a railroad destination to boost revenue. Its success led to an explosion of other ski resorts and resort towns in the Western United States.

CHAPTER 13

LeRoy Robert Ripley (February 22, 1890 – May 27, 1949)

Ripley was a cartoonist, entrepreneur, and media personality best known for creating the *Ripley's Believe It or Not!* cartoon panel focusing on odd facts from around the world. Ripley supplemented desk research from Norbert Pearlroth with his own tireless travels to seldom-visited locations to add color commentary and interest for his readers. Unafraid of controversy, he understood how provocation could draw readers in and keep them engaged.

Norbert Pearlroth (May 7, 1893 – April 14, 1983)

A former bank teller born in (what is today) southern Poland, Pearlroth was the primary researcher for the *Ripley's Believe It or Not!* cartoon panel from 1923 until 1975, all from a desk in the New York Library. He worked six days a week, answering thousands of letters (often from people who didn't believe him) and finding new factoids for Ripley to include in the strip. His career survived Ripley's death in 1949, and he continued to conduct research for the strip until he retired in 1975.

CHAPTER 14

Walter Elias Disney (December 5, 1901 – December 15, 1966)

Better known by the shortened name Walt Disney, he was an artist, animator, film producer, and entrepreneur. Disney pioneered animation in the 1920s and 1930s, creating the first commercially successful full-length animated film, *Snow White*. He would go on to personally supervise several more animated and live-action films before he died in 1966. Disney also created the first modern theme park in Anaheim, California. He was a shy, self-deprecating person but driven to realize ambitious creative visions. Disney was the first American entrepreneur to fully acknowledge the marketing power of children.

CHAPTER 15

George Orson Welles (May 6, 1915 – October 10, 1985)

Generally recognized as one of America's greatest filmmakers, Welles specialized in a non-linear storytelling approach. He found his first success (and public controversy) with a live radio adaptation of H.G. Wells's science fiction novel, *The War of the Worlds*. His acting and narrating career spans multiple media, including stage, radio, television, and film. His first film, *Citizen Kane*, is often cited as the "greatest film ever made." Welles's deep, foreboding voice and larger-than-life physical presence made him in demand on both sides of the camera or microphone.

CHAPTER 16

Eliot Ness (April 19, 1903 – May 16, 1957)

Leader of the so-called "Untouchables," Ness led a small group of incorruptible Prohibition offers against the mob in Chicago. Although their efforts did not directly lead to Al Capone's conviction, the group's relentless harassment and break-up of criminal activities severely weakened the mob in Chicago. His biography, *The Untouchables*, spurred portrayals of Ness and his group in television and movies.

August Vollmer (March 7, 1876 – November 4, 1955)

Known as the "father of modern policing," Vollmer was an ex-military officer who brought those ideas into (at that time) a highly unprofessional law enforcement service. He served as the first police chief of Berkeley, California. Vollmer's ideas included college degrees, hiring African American and female police officers, bicycle, motorcycle, and automobile patrols (in addition to walking the streets), centralized information sharing, and the use and application of new technologies—fingerprinting, ballistics, forensic accounting, and crime maps.

George E. Q. Johnson (July 11, 1874 – September 19, 1949)

Most famous for securing a conviction for Al Capone for tax evasion (and not mob violence), Johnson was a United States Attorney in Chicago, Illinois. Although the technical nature of the case was weak, the jury was keen to convict Capone. Johnson went on to secure convictions for other high-profile mobsters. President Hoover appointed him to be a United States district judge of the Northern District of Illinois in 1932, but his nomination was never confirmed, and he served only a short time.

Alphonse Gabriel Capone (January 17, 1899 – January 25, 1947)

Al Capone, nicknamed "Scarface" after a knife fight, was one of the most notorious gangsters in the Prohibition era. Based in Chicago, Capone waged a ruthless campaign to eliminate his rivals. He's famous for his ostentatious style, elegant dress, and positive relationship with the media. Where other mob bosses preferred to remain behind the scenes, Capone helped craft a romanticized image of gangsters who simply "gave the people what they wanted." He was finally convicted of income tax evasion and spent the last 11 years of his life in prison.

CHAPTER 17

Jerome "Jerry" Siegel (October 17, 1914 – January 28, 1996)

Born to Jewish Lithuanian immigrants who changed their name from Segalovich to Siegel when they arrived in the United States, Siegel co-created Superman with Joe Shuster. The character underwent several early iterations before DC began publishing the comic in 1938. In the coming decades, Siegel would continue to write for DC (both for Superman and other series) but had no control over his creations. Although a typical arrangement at the time (and for years after), this loss of control spurred reforms in the relationships between publishers and artists.

Joseph Shuster (July 10, 1914 – July 30, 1992)

Shuster is most famous for co-creating the Superman character with Jerry Siegel. As the initial illustrator, he is responsible for the iconic "look" of Superman, including his hands-on-hip pose, dual identity (with Clark Kent), letter "S" on his chest, red and blue color scheme, cape, tights, and outerpants. Shuster was the primary advocate (along with Siegel) for his rights to Superman royalties over the following decades. Although largely unsuccessful, he did win a large settlement in the 1970s during the run-up to the first major live-action movie starring Christopher Reeve.

CHAPTER 18

Florence Lowe "Pancho" Barnes (July 22, 1901 – March 30, 1975)

Barnes was a pioneering aviator and one of the first female stunt pilots. She was a member of the Ninety-Nines, a group of female pilots that included Amelia Earhart, and formed the first stunt pilots union (including men and women). After the Great Depression forced Barnes to sell her plane, she began a new career as the founder of the Happy Bottom Riding Club, a desert resort that catered to pilots at the nearby Air Force base.

Amelia Mary Earhart (July 24, 1897 – January 5, 1939 (declared))

Earhart is perhaps the most famous early female aviator, holding several "firsts" in aviation—whether male or female. She was the first woman to make a non-stop crossing of the Atlantic by airplane, the first *person* to fly across the Atlantic Ocean *twice*, the first person to make the Oakland, California, to Honolulu, Hawaii run, and the first person to fly several routes in Asia. Earhart and navigator Fred Noonan were lost at sea somewhere over the South Pacific and declared dead on January 5, 1939.

CHAPTER 19

Charles Edward Coughlin (October 25, 1891 – October 27, 1979)

Father Coughlin, a Catholic priest based in the Detroit, Michigan, area, was among the first to use the radio to spread his political message. He also used his National Shrine of the Little Flower organization to raise funds from listeners, an echo of a tactic used in political and evangelical broadcast fundraising in future decades. At his peak in the mid-1930s, Coughlin reached an estimated 30-40 million people—about as many as President Roosevelt's "Fireside Chats." His messages eventually ran afoul of both the Roosevelt Administration and the Catholic Church, which banned him from broadcasting in 1938.

Dorothy May Day (November 8, 1897 – November 29, 1980)

Probably the best-known of the Catholic radical movement, Day was a journalist, social activist, and anarchist. She founded the pacifist Catholic Workers Movement, which advocates for the poor and working class through civil disobedience. The Catholic Church considers her a "Servant of God," a preliminary step to canonization as a saint.

Father Divine (1876 – September 10, 1965)

Details of Devine's life are obscured. He is best known by his self-given name, Reverend Major Jealous Divine, but also went by "The Messenger" and other aliases throughout his life. He was a leader in the black faith community during the Great Depression, founding several faith communes for followers. He was a staunch capitalist who lived comfortably but appreciated the communist approach to equality and civil rights. His endorsement was sought after by political leaders trying to win votes from his followers. Divine was able to parlay that influence into anti-lynching legislation, though laws were slow to pass in state legislatures.

CHAPTER 20

Laura Elizabeth Ingalls Wilder (February 7, 1867 – February 10, 1957)

Wilder wrote the *Little House on the Prairie* series of children's books based mainly on her life growing up in the central American Midwest. The book series proved extremely popular through the 1930s and 1940s, generating secure income for the Wilder family in their later years. (She was 65 when she began writing.) A television series loosely based on the books aired from 1974 to 1983. Although it wasn't public knowledge until after both their deaths, Wilder received significant writing help from her daughter, Rose Wilder Lane, who was herself an accomplished author.

Rose Wilder Lane (December 5, 1886 – October 30, 1968)

A successful writer, author, and journalist, Lane assisted her mother, Laura Elizabeth Ingalls Wilder, in writing the *Little House on the Prairie* children's books and connected her with publishing industry contacts. Like her mother, Lane was a staunch libertarian and bristled at what she believed to be an overbearing government involvement in citizens' day-to-day lives during the 1930s. The Little

House books are infused with messages of self-reliance and independence. Lane helped to found the modern Libertarian Party in the 1970s.

CHAPTER 22

Fred Astaire (born Frederick Austerlitz, May 10, 1899 – June 22, 1987)

Astaire was a dancer, choreographer, signer, presenter, actor, and musician whose career spanned over three-quarters of a century. His older sister, Adele, was his original dance partner. The two made a name for themselves on the Vaudeville circuit before graduating to Broadway in New York and the West End in London. After Adele married, Astaire began his own Hollywood career, most famously partnering with Ginger Rogers in a series of films in the 1930s.

Ginger Rogers (born Virginia Katherine McMath, July 16, 1911 – April 25, 1995)

Rogers was a dancer, actor, and signer originally best-known for her on-screen partnership with Fred Astaire, but who went on to her own successful acting career. The pair helped reinvigorate and reinvent musicals in the 1930s. After they split, Rogers landed several high-profile dramatic roles. In the 1940s, she was Hollywood's most in-demand (and highest-paid) actor. In a second act of her career in London, she was the highest-paid actor in the West End in the late 1960s and early 1970s.

FURTHER READING

CHAPTER 1

3M Archive. Minnesota Historical Society, St. Paul.

Huck, Virginia. *Brand of the Tartan: The 3M Story*. New York: Appleton-Century-Crofts, Inc., 1955.

Richard G. Drew Papers, 1921–1987. Manuscript Collection, Minnesota Historical Society, St. Paul.

Minnesota Mining and Manufacturing Company (1977). *Our Story So Far: Notes from the First 75 Years of 3M Company*. 3M Corporate Publishing.

CHAPTER 2

Collins, D. (1990). *The story of Kodak*. H.N. Abrams.

Gordon, T. S. (2020). *The mass production of memory: Travel and personal archiving in the age of the Kodak*. University of Massachusetts Press.

Harvey, L. (2013). *Retromania: The Funkiest Cameras of Photography's Golden Age*. Focal Press.

Leopold Godowsky Jr. Collection at the George Eastman Museum.

CHAPTER 3

Broel, B. (2007). *House of Broel: The Inside Story*. House of Broel Foundation, LLC.

Broel, A. (1954). *Frog Raising for Pleasure and Profit*. Marlboro House.

Commercial Possibilities and Limitations in Frog Raising (US Dept. of the Interior, 1956) - Fishery Leaflet 436.

Danovich, T., & Krebbel, M. (2024). *Under The Henfluence: Inside the World of Backyard Chickens and the People Who Love Them*. Surrey Books, an imprint of Agate Publishing.

Dodd, C. K. Jr. and M. R. Jennings (2021). *How to Raise a Bullfrog—The Literature on Frog Farming in North America*. Bibliotheca Herpetologica 15(8):77-100.

CHAPTER 4

Clifford E. Clinton Papers (Collection 2018). UCLA Library Special Collections, Charles E. Young Research Library.

Grimes, W. (2010). *Appetite City: A Culinary History of New York*. North Point Press.

Ziegelman, J., & Coe, A. (2016). *A Square Meal: A Culinary History of the Great Depression*. Harper.

CHAPTER 5

Brandes, K. (2009). "Feed Sack Fashion in Rural America: A Reflection of Culture." *The Online Journal of Rural Research and Policy* 4.1: 1-23.

Kirke, B. (2012). *Madeleine Vionnet*. Chronicle Books.

McCray, L.K. (2019). *Feed Sacks: The Colourful History of a Frugal Fabric*. Uppercase.

Nixon, G. (2010). *Feedsack Secrets: Fashion from Hard Times*. Kansas City Star Books.

CHAPTER 6

Beyond the Moon Crater Myth. A New History of the Aniakchak Landscape. A Historic Resource Study for Aniakchak National Monument and Preserve. National Park Service.

Grier, K. (2010). *Pets in America: A History.* University of North Carolina Press.

Hubbard, B. (1932). *Mush! You Malemutes.* The America Press.

Smith, D. *An Enduring Veterinary Legacy: Interviews with Pioneering Veterinarians (2007-2010).* Cornell University Library.

CHAPTER 7

Hager, T. (2006). *The Demon Under the Microscope: From Battlefield Hospitals to Nazi Labs, One Doctor's Heroic Search for the World's First Miracle Drug.* Harmony.

Lesch, J. (2006). *The First Miracle Drugs: How the Sulfa Drugs Transformed Medicine.* Oxford University Press.

CHAPTER 8

Bill W. (1939). *Alcoholics Anonymous: The Story of How More Than One Hundred Men Have Recovered from Alcoholism.* Alcoholics Anonymous World Services.

Edwards, G. (2002). *Alcohol: The World's Favorite Drug.* Thomas Dunne Books.

Kurtz, E. (1991). *Not-God: A History of Alcoholics Anonymous.* Hazelden Pittman.

Mitchel, D. (2002). *Silkworth: The Little Doctor Who Loved Drunks.* Hazelden.

Peele, S. (1999). *The Diseasing Of America: How We Allowed Recovery Zealots and the Treatment Industry to Convince Us We Are Out of Control.* Jossey-Bass.

CHAPTER 9

Thomas Forsyth maintains an excellent online resource on the history of *The Landlord's Game* and *Monopoly*. You can find it at https://landlords-game.com/ or https://landlordsgame.info/ (The former is the newer version, but the latter contains more detail.)

Adams, C. (1979). "Monopoly: From Berks to Boardwalk." Historical Review of Berks County. Volume XLIV, Number 1 Winter, 1978-1979

Anspach, R. (1998). *The Billion Dollar Monopoly Swindle: During a David and Goliath Battle, Anti-monopoly Uncovers the Secret History of Monopoly.* United States: R. Anspach.

Ketcham, C. (2012). "Monopoly Is Theft: The Antimonopolist History of the World's Most Popular Board Game." Harper's Magazine.

Magie, L. (1902). "The Landlord's Game." Single Tax Review.

Pilon, M. (2015). *The Monopolists: Obsession, Fury, and the Scandal Behind the World's Favorite Board Game.* Bloomsbury USA.

Stone, T. L. (2018). *Pass Go and Collect $200: The Real Story of How Monopoly Was Invented.* Henry Holt and Company (BYR).

CHAPTER 10

Cinema: The New Pictures: Mar. 13, 1933. (1933, March 13). TIME, *21*(11).

Goldner, O., & Turner, G. E. (1975). *The Making of King Kong: The Story Behind a Film Classic.* A.S. Barnes.

King Kong (1933), 1931-1980, MSS 2008 Series 5 File 5. Merian C. Cooper papers, MSS 2008. L. Tom Perry Special Collections.

CHAPTER 11

Bingo calls: Complete List of Bingo Nicknames 1-90: Mecca Bingo Blog. Mecca Blog. (2022, May 13).

Obituary Staff. (1986, February 25). *EDWIN S. LOWE, 75; TOY MANUFACTURER POPULARIZED BINGO.* New York Times, p. 31.

Simonds, M. (1997b). *The New Games Treasury: More Than 500 Indoor and Outdoor Favorites With Strategies, Rules and Traditions.* Houghton Mifflin Company.

The History Of Bingo And The Evolution Of The Game. Bingo.org. (2024, August 19).

CHAPTER 12

Curren, J. (1940) *Chair for Aerial Tranways.* US Patent No. 2244650A. (Several other patents in this portfolio.)

Hollis, T. (2015). *The Minibook of Minigolf.* Seaside Publishing.

Huss, P. (2020). *Hemingway's Sun Valley Local Stories Behind His Code, Characters And Crisis.* The History Press.

Lund, M. *The 1930s: The Unexpected Blossoming of Alpine Skiing.* International Skiing History Association. (2024, August 1).

Lundin, J. W. (2020). *Skiing Sun Valley: A History From Union Pacific To The Holdings.* Arcadia Publishing Inc.

Kohlstedt, K. *Peewee Urbanism: Why Miniature Golf Grew Big During the Great Depression.* 99% Invisible. (August 1, 2024).

Union Pacific Railroad (2019). *Surprising Railroad Inventions: The Ski Lift. How the Railroad Revolutionized Skiing.*

CHAPTER 13

Note: Reprints of original strips are available in annual collections wherever books are sold. Search for "Ripley's Believe It Or Not!"

Gaiter, D. (1983, April 15). *Norbert Pearlroth, 89, Researcher For 52 Years For 'Believe It Or Not'.* New York Times, Section D, p. 18.

Martell, M. (2024, June 18). *Before 'Believe It Or Not!' Fame, Robert Ripley Was Just An Awkward Kid in Santa Rosa. Santa Rosa Honored Native Son Robert Ripley With A Museum Over 50 Years Ago.* The Press Democrat.

Ripley's Entertainment. *The Strange But True History Of Robert Ripley. Dubbed The Modern-Day Marco Polo And Once Voted The Most Popular Man In America, Robert Ripley's Legacy Is 100 Years Old!* (August 1, 2024)

Thompson, N. (2013). *A Curious Man: The Strange and Brilliant Life of Robert "Believe It or Not!" Ripley.* Crown Archetype.

CHAPTER 14

Gabler, N. (2006). *Walt Disney: The Triumph of the American Imagination.* Vintage.

Matthes, E. H. (2021). *Drawing the Line: What to Do with the Work of Immoral Artists from Museums to the Movies.* Oxford University Press.

Jacob and Wilhelm Grimm, *Sneewittchen, Kinder- und Hausmärchen, (Children's and Household Tales -- Grimms' Fairy Tales),* final edition (Berlin, 1857), no. 53.

Internet Movie Database (IMDB). *Snow White and the Seven Dwarfs (1937).* (August 1, 2024).

Thomas, B. (2017). *Walt Disney: An American Original.* Disney Editions Publishing.

Walt Disney Corporation. *Snow White and the Seven Dwarfs (1937).* (August 1, 2024).

CHAPTER 15

Schwartz, A.B. (2015). *Broadcast Hysteria: Orson Welles's War of the Worlds and the Art of Fake News.* Hill and Wang.

Welles, O. (1938). *"The War of the Worlds"* original script as performed by Orson Welles & the Mercury Theatre on the Air and broadcast on the Columbia Broadcasting System on Sunday, October 30, 1938 from 8:00 to 9:00 P. M.

Wells, H.G. (1898). *The War of the Worlds.* William Heinemann (UK) and Harper & Bros (US).

CHAPTER 16

Collins, M.A. and Schwartz, A.B. (2019). Scarface and the Untouchable: Al Capone, Eliot Ness, and the Battle for Chicago. William Morrow.

Latzer, B. (2022). *The Roots of Violent Crime in America: From the Gilded Age through the Great Depression.* LSU Press.

Ness, E. (1957). *The Untouchables.* Julian Messner.

CHAPTER 17

Daniels, Les (1998). *Superman: The Complete History*. Titan Books.

Gordon, Ian (2017). *Superman: The Persistence of an American Icon*. Rutgers University Press.

Ricca, Brad (2014). *Super Boys: The Amazing Adventures of Jerry Siegel and Joe Shuster – the Creators of Superman*. St. Martin's Griffin.

Scivally, Bruce (2007). *Superman on Film, Television, Radio and Broadway*. McFarland.

Siegel, J. (Unknown). *Creation of a Superhero*. Unpublished Notes.

Tye, Larry (2012). *Superman: The High-Flying History of America's Most Enduring Hero*. Random House.

CHAPTER 18

Earhart, A. (1937) *Last Flight*. Harcourt, Brace and Company.

Kessler, L. (2000). *The Happy Bottom Riding Club: The Life and Times of Pancho Barnes*. Random House.

Oliver, M. (2001, Jan 19). *Eugene McKendry; Ran 'The Right Stuff' Club'*. Los Angeles Times.

Pope, A. (Director). (2009, June 6). *The Legend of Pancho Barnes and the Happy Bottom Riding Club* [Film]. Nick Spark Productions LLC.

CHAPTER 19

Brinkley, A. (2011). *Voices of Protest: Huey Long, Father Coughlin, & the Great Depression*. Vintage.

Charles River Editors (2016). *Father Charles Coughlin: The Life of the Controversial Catholic Priest Who Revolutionized Radio*. Charles River Editors.

Day, D. (1952). *The Long Loneliness: The Autobiography of the Legendary Catholic Social Activist*. HarperCollins.

Lee, A.M. & Lee, E.B. (1939). *The Fine Art of Propaganda: A Study of Father Coughlin's Speeches.* Institute for Propaganda Analysis. New York: Harcourt, Brace and Co.

Watts, J. (1992). *God, Harlem U.S.A.: The Father Divine Story.* University of California Press.

CHAPTER 20

The first eight "Little House" books in the series by Laura Ingalls Wilder:

Little House in the Big Woods (1932)

Farmer Boy (1933)

Little House on the Prairie (1935)

On the Banks of Plum Creek (1937)

By the Shores of Silver Lake (1939)

The Long Winter (1940)

Little Town on the Prairie (1941)

These Happy Golden Years (1943)

Dewey, J. and Boydston, J (editor). *The Early Works, 1882–1898* (5 volumes), *The Middle Works, 1899–1924* (15 volumes), *The Later Works* (17 volumes). Southern Illinois University Press.

Fraser, C. (2018). *Prairie Fires: The American Dreams of Laura Ingalls Wilder.* Picador.

Goetz, Kathryn. "Wilder, Laura Ingalls (1867–1957)." MNopedia, Minnesota Historical Society.

Woodside, C. (2016). *Libertarians on the Prairie: Laura Ingalls Wilder, Rose Wilder Lane, and the Making of the Little House Books.* Arcade.

CHAPTER 21

Search for "Fred Astaire and Ginger Rogers" on YouTube.

Astaire, F. (1959). *Steps in Time: An Autobiography.* University of Michigan.

Astaire, F. and Thomas, B. (1987). *The Man, The Dancer: The Life of Fred Astaire.* St Martins Press.

Hyam, H. (2007). *Fred and Ginger.* New Generation Publishing.

Levinson, P. (2009). *Puttin' On the Ritz: Fred Astaire and the Fine Art of Panache, A Biography.* Macmillan.

Rogers, G. (2008). *Ginger: My Story.* It Books.

Introduction and Conclusion

Allen, F. (1940). *Since Yesterday: The 1930s in America, September 3, 1929–September 3, 1939.* Harper & Brothers

Brands, H. W. (2009). *Traitor to His Class: The Privileged Life and Radical Presidency of Franklin Delano Roosevelt.* United States: Knopf Doubleday Publishing Group.

Brokaw, T. (2004). *The Greatest Generation.* Random House.

Egan, T. (2005). *The Worst Hard Time: The Untold Story of Those Who Survived the Great American Dust Bowl.* Houghton Mifflin

Favreau, M. (2018). *Crash: The Great Depression and the Fall and Rise of America.* United States: Little, Brown Books for Young Readers.

Kindleberger, C. P. (1986). *The World in Depression, 1929-1939.* United Kingdom: University of California Press.

Shlaes, A. (2007). *The Forgotten Man: A New History of the Great Depression.* Harper.

Smith, J. E. (2008). *FDR.* United States: Random House Publishing Group.

ABOUT THE AUTHOR

My arrival in marketing started early. I was born into a family of artists, immigrants, and entrepreneurs. Frankly, it's lucky I didn't end up as a circus performer. I'm sure I would have fallen off the tightrope by now. My father was an advertising creative director. One grandfather manufactured the first disposable coffee filters in pre-Castro Cuba. Another grandfather invented the bazooka. A great-grandfather invented Neapolitan ice cream. I was destined to invent the first disposable soft-serve grenade launcher, but the ice cream just kept melting!

I took bizarre ideas like those to the University of Wisconsin, the University of Minnesota, and the MIT Sloan School of Management. It should surprise no one that they are all embarrassed to have let me in.

I've launched hundreds of new products over a career that's spanned more than 25 years—as an entrepreneur, product designer, advertising strategist, and executive—everything from medical devices, to virtual healthcare, to non-dairy consumer cheese, to next-generation alternatives to the dreaded "cone of shame" for pets, to sex aides for cows (really!).

Like all periods of stress and turmoil, the Great Depression was a source of tremendous ingenuity and innovation. After reading this book, I think you'll agree.

ALSO BY JASON VOIOVICH

Booze, Babe, and the Little Black Dress: How Innovators of the Roaring 20s Created the Consumer Revolution
Available in paperback, ebook, and audiobook.

Marketer in Chief: How Each President Sold the American Idea
Available in paperback, ebook, and audiobook.

Connect with Jason:
Website: repeathistory.com
LinkedIn: https://www.linkedin.com/in/jasonvoiovich/

Made in United States
Orlando, FL
05 August 2025